Professional SQL Server High Availability and Disaster Recovery

Implement tried-and-true high availability and disaster recovery solutions with SQL Server

Ahmad Osama

Professional SQL Server High Availability and Disaster Recovery

Author: Ahmad Osama

Reviewer: Mohit Gupta

Managing Editor: Taabish Khan

Acquisitions Editor: Aditya Date

Production Editor: Nitesh Thakur

Editorial Board: David Barnes, Ewan Buckingham, Shivangi Chatterji, Simon Cox, Manasa Kumar, Alex Mazonowicz, Douglas Paterson, Dominic Pereira, Shiny Poojary, Saman Siddiqui, Erol Staveley, Ankita Thakur, and Mohita Vyas.

First Published: January 2019

Production Reference: 1300119

ISBN: 978-1-78980-259-7

Published by Packt Publishing Ltd.

Livery Place, 35 Livery Street

Birmingham B3 2PB, UK

Table of Contents

Configuring and Managing Log Shipping   469

Preface

About

This section briefly introduces the author, the coverage of this book, the technical skills you'll need to get started, and the hardware and software required to complete all of the included activities and exercises.

About the Book

Professional SQL Server High Availability and Disaster Recovery explains the high availability and disaster recovery technologies available in SQL Server: replication, AlwaysOn, and log shipping. You'll learn what they are, how to monitor them, and how to troubleshoot any related problems. You will be introduced to the availability groups of AlwaysOn and learn how to configure them to extend your database mirroring. Through this book, you will be able to explore the technical implementations of high availability and disaster recovery technologies that you can use when you create a highly available infrastructure, including hybrid topologies.

By the end of the book, you'll be equipped with all that you need to know to develop robust and high performance infrastructures.

About the Authors

Ahmad Osama works for Pitney Bowes Pvt Ltd as a database engineer and is a Microsoft Data Platform MVP. In his day to day job at Pitney Bowes, he works on developing and maintaining high performance on-premises and cloud SQL Server OLTP environments, building CI/CD environments for databases and automation. Other than his day to day work, he regularly speaks at user group events and webinars conducted by the Dataplatformlabs community.

Objectives

- Understand how to choose high availability and disaster recovery topologies for your environment
- Design high availability and disaster recovery for SQL Server
- Configure replication, AlwaysOn, and log shipping in a production environment
- Use best practices to apply and troubleshoot replication, log shipping, and AlwaysOn
- Use T-SQL to configure replication, AlwaysOn, and log shipping
- Use transactional replication to migrate from an on-premises SQL Server to Azure SQL database

Audience

This book is for you if you're a database administrator or database developer who wants to improve the performance of your production environment. Prior experience of working with SQL Server will help you get the most out of this book.

Approach

Professional SQL Server High Availability and Disaster Recovery is a fast-paced, practical, hands-on book aimed at experienced administrators. As you progress, you'll find helpful tips and tricks, and useful self-assessment material, exercises, and activities to help benchmark your progress and reinforce what you've learned.

Hardware Requirements

For an optimal student experience, we recommend the following hardware configuration:

- Processor: 1.8 GHz or higher Pentium 4 (or equivalent)

- Memory: 8 GB RAM

- Hard disk: 200 GB free space

- Internet connection

Software Requirements

You'll also need the following software installed in advance:

- Windows 8 or above

- The latest version of Google Chrome

- An Azure subscription

- SQL Server Management Studio 17.2 or above

- PowerShell 5.1

- SQL Server 2014 SP2 or above installed as named instance Server\SQL2014

- SQL Server 2016 SP2 installed as named instance Server\SQL2016

Conventions

Code words in text, database table names, folder names, filenames, file extensions, pathnames, dummy URLs, user input, and Twitter handles are shown as follows: "As discussed earlier, there is an option to compress snapshot files in the .cab format."

A block of code is set as follows:

```
REM -- Change the variable values as per your environment

SET Publisher=WIN2012R2\SQL2016

SET PublisherDB=WideWorldImporters
```

New terms and important words are shown in bold. Words that you see on the screen, for example, in menus or dialog boxes, appear in the text like this: "In the **View Synchronization Status** window, select **Start** to start the distributor agent."

Installation

You will need an Azure account for a few exercises in this book. If you don't have one, create a free account here: https://azure.microsoft.com/en-in/free/.

The latest version of SQL Server Management Studio can be downloaded from https://docs.microsoft.com/en-us/sql/ssms/download-sql-server-management-studio-ssms?view=sql-server-2017. Installation instructions are also available on the same web page.

Installing the Code Bundle

Download the code bundle for the book from the GitHub repository and copy it to the C:\Code folder.

Additional Resources

The code bundle for this book is also hosted on GitHub at https://github.com/TrainingByPackt/Professional-SQL-Server-High-Availability-and-Disaster-Recovery.

We also have other code bundles from our rich catalog of books and videos available at https://github.com/PacktPublishing/. Check them out!

Getting Started with SQL Server HA and DR

Learning Objectives

By the end of this lesson, you will be able to:

- Describe high availability and disaster recovery
- Explain the different HA and DR concepts and terminology
- Describe the different HA and DR solutions available in SQL Server
- Describe replication concepts and terminology
- Describe the different types of replication
- Configure and troubleshoot snapshot replication

This lesson will discuss the common concepts related to high availability and disaster recovery. We will then see how to configure snapshot replication.

Introduction

Business continuity is of utmost importance in today's world. An application downtime that's even as low as a few minutes may result in potential revenue loss for companies such as Amazon and Flipkart. Downtime not only results in direct revenue loss as transactions are dropped as and when downtime happens, it also contributes to a bad user experience.

Often, application downtime because of programming or functional issues doesn't affect the entire application and can be fixed by the developers quickly. However, downtime caused by infrastructure or system failure affects the entire application and can't be controlled functionally (by the developers).

This is where **high availability** (**HA**) and **disaster recovery** (**DR**) are required. In this lesson, you'll learn about high availability and disaster recovery concepts and terminology, and the different solutions that are available in Microsoft SQL Server to achieve HA and DR.

The type of HA and DR solution implemented by a business depends majorly on the **service level agreement** (**SLA**). The SLA defines the **recovery point objective** (**RPO**) and **recovery time objective** (**RTO**), which will be discussed in detail later in this lesson.

What is High Availability and Disaster Recovery?

High Availability

High availability refers to providing an agreed level of system or application availability by minimizing the downtime caused by infrastructure or hardware failure.

When the hardware fails, there's not much you can do other than switch the application to a different computer so as to make sure that the hardware failure doesn't cause application downtime.

Disaster Recovery

Business continuity and disaster recovery, though used interchangeably, are different concepts.

Disaster recovery refers to re-establishing the application or system connectivity or availability on an alternate site, commonly known as a DR site, after an outage in the primary site. The outage can be caused by a site-wide (data center) wide infrastructure outage or a natural disaster.

Business continuity is a strategy that ensures that a business is up and running with minimal or zero downtime or service outage. For example, as a part of business continuity, an organization may plan to decouple an application into small individual standalone applications and deploy each small application across multiple regions. Let's say that a financial application is deployed on region one and the sales application is deployed on region two. Therefore, if a disaster hits region one, the finance application will go down, and the company will follow the disaster recovery plan to recover the financial application. However, the sales application in region two will be up and running.

High availability and disaster recovery are not only required during hardware failures; you also need them in the following scenarios:

- **System upgrades**: Critical system upgrades such as software, hardware, network, or storage require the system to be rebooted and may even cause application downtime after being upgraded because of configuration changes. If there is an HA setup present, this can be done with zero downtime.

- **Human errors**: As it's rightly said, to *err is human*. We can't avoid human errors; however, we can have a system in place to recover from human errors. An error in deployment or an application configuration or bad code can cause an application to fail. An example of this is the GitLab outage on January 31, 2017, which was caused by the accidental removal of customer data from the primary database server, resulting in an overall downtime of 18 hours.

> **Note**
>
> You can read more about the GitLab outage post-mortem here: https://about. gitlab.com/2017/02/10/postmortem-of-database-outage-of-january-31/.

- **Security breaches**: Cyber-attacks are a lot more common these days and can result in downtime while you find and fix the issue. Moving the application to a secondary database server may help reduce the downtime while you fix the security issue in most cases.

Let's look at an example of how high availability and disaster recovery work to provide business continuity in the case of outages.

Consider the following diagram:

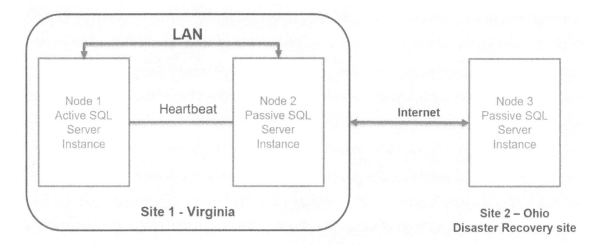

Figure 1.1: A simple HA and DR example

The preceding diagram shows a common HA and DR implementation with the following configuration:

- The primary and secondary servers (SQL Server instance) are in Virginia. This is for high availability (having an available backup system).

- The primary and secondary servers are in the same data center and are connected over LAN.

- A DR server (a third SQL Server instance) is in Ohio, which is far away from Virginia. The third SQL Server instance is used as a DR site.

- The DR site is connected over the internet to the primary site. This is mostly a private network for added security.

- The primary SQL Server (node 1) is active and is currently serving user transactions.

- The secondary and DR servers are inactive or passive and are not serving user transactions.

Let's say there is a motherboard failure on node 1 and it crashes. This causes node 2 to be active automatically and it starts serving user transactions. This is shown in the following diagram:

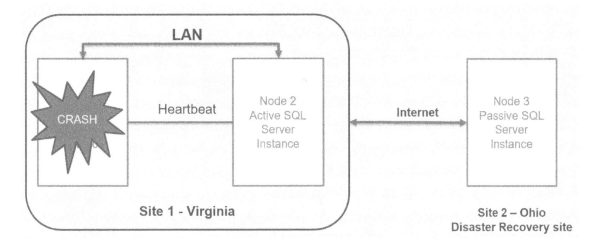

Figure 1.2: A simple HA and DR example – Node 1 crashes

This is an example of high availability where the system automatically switches to the secondary node within the same data center or a different data center in the same region (Virginia here).

The system can fall back to the primary node once it's fixed and up and running.

> **Note**
>
> A data center is a facility that's typically owned by a third-party organization, allowing customers to rent or lease out infrastructure. A node here refers to a standalone physical computer. A disaster recovery site is a data center in a different geographical region than that of the primary site.

Now, let's say that while the primary server, node 1, was being recovered, there was a region-wide failure that caused the secondary server, node 2, to go down. At this point, the region is down; therefore, the system will fail over to the DR server, node 3, and it'll start serving user transactions, as shown in the following diagram:

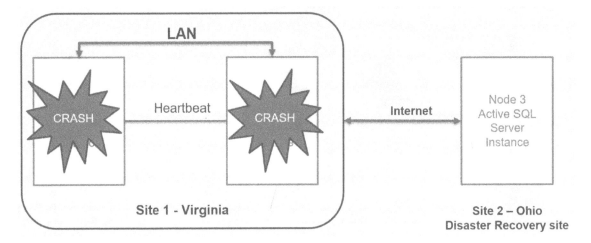

Figure 1.3: A simple HA and DR example – Nodes 1 and 2 crash

This is an example of disaster recovery. Once the primary and secondary servers are up and running, the system can fall back to the primary server.

> **Note**
>
> Organizations periodically perform DR drills (mock DR) to make sure that the DR solution is working fine and to estimate downtime that may happen in the case of an actual DR scenario.

HA and DR Terminologies

The following terms are important in the world of HA and DR so that you can correctly choose the best possible HA and DR solutions and for the better understanding of HA and DR concepts.

Availability

Availability or uptime is defined as the percentage that a system or an application should be available for in a given year. Availability is expressed as *Number of Nines*.

For example, a 90%, *one nine*, availability means that a system can tolerate a downtime of 36.5 hours in a year, and a 99.999%, *five nines*, availability means that a system can tolerate a downtime of 5.26 minutes per year.

The following table, taken from https://en.wikipedia.org/wiki/High_availability#"Nines", describes the availability percentages and the downtime for each percentage:

> **Note**
>
> This link also talks about how this is calculated. You can look at it, but a discussion on calculation is out of the scope of this book.

Availability %	Downtime per year	Downtime per month	Downtime per week	Downtime per day
90% ("one nine")	36.5 days	72 hours	16.8 hours	2.4 hours
95% ("one and a half nines")	18.25 days	36 hours	8.4 hours	1.2 hours
97%	10.96 days	21.6 hours	5.04 hours	43.2 minutes
98%	7.30 days	14.4 hours	3.36 hours	28.8 minutes
99% ("two nines")	3.65 days	7.20 hours	1.68 hours	14.4 minutes
99.5% ("two and a half nines")	1.83 days	3.60 hours	50.4 minutes	7.2 minutes
99.8%	17.52 hours	86.23 minutes	20.16 minutes	2.88 minutes
99.9% ("three nines")	8.76 hours	43.8 minutes	10.1 minutes	1.44 minutes
99.95% ("three and a half nines")	4.38 hours	21.56 minutes	5.04 minutes	43.2 seconds
99.99% ("four nines")	52.56 minutes	4.38 minutes	1.01 minutes	8.64 seconds
99.995% ("four and a half nines")	26.28 minutes	2.16 minutes	30.24 seconds	4.32 seconds
99.999% ("five nines")	5.26 minutes	25.9 seconds	6.05 seconds	864.3 milliseconds
99.9999% ("six nines")	31.5 seconds	2.59 seconds	604.8 milliseconds	86.4 milliseconds
99.99999% ("seven nines")	3.15 seconds	262.97 milliseconds	60.48 milliseconds	8.64 milliseconds
99.999999% ("eight nines")	315.569 milliseconds	26.297 milliseconds	6.048 milliseconds	0.864 milliseconds
99.9999999% ("nine nines")	31.5569 milliseconds	2.6297 milliseconds	0.6048 milliseconds	0.0864 milliseconds

Figure 1.4: Availability table

In the preceding table, you can see that as the *Number of Nines* increases, the downtime decreases. The business decides the availability, the *Number of Nines*, required for the system. This plays a vital role in selecting the type of HA and DR solution required for any given system. The higher the *Number of Nines*, the more rigorous or robust the required solution.

Recovery Time Objective

Recovery time objective, or RTO, is essentially the downtime a business can tolerate without any substantial loss. For example, an RTO of one hour means that an application shouldn't be down for more than one hour. A downtime of more than an hour would result in critical financial, reputation, or data loss.

The choice of HA and DR solution depends on the RTO. If an application has a four-hour RTO, you can recover the database using backups (if backups are being done every two hours or so), and you may not need any HA and DR solution. However, if the RTO is 15 minutes, then backups won't work, and an HA and DR solution will be needed.

Recovery Point Objective

Recovery point objective, or RPO, defines how much data loss a business can tolerate during an outage. For example, an RPO of two hours would mean a data loss of two hours won't cost anything to the business; however, if it goes beyond that, it would have significant financial or reputation impacts.

Essentially, this is the time difference between the last transaction committed before downtime and the first transaction committed after recovery.

The choice of HA and DR solution also depends on the RPO. If an application has 24 hours of RPO, daily full backups are good enough; however, for a business with four hours of RPO, daily full backups are not enough.

To differentiate between RTO and RPO, let's consider a scenario. A company has an RTO of one hour and an RPO of four hours. There's no HA and DR solution, and backups are being done every 12 hours.

In the case of an outage, the company was able to restore the database from the last full backup in one hour, which is within the given RTO of one hour; however, they suffered a data loss as the backups are being done every 12 hours and the RPO is of four hours.

SQL Server HA and DR Solutions

The following are the most commonly used HA and DR solutions available in Microsoft SQL Server.

Windows Server Failover Cluster Installation

Commonly known as **FCI**, this requires SQL Server to be installed as a cluster service on top of the Windows failover cluster.

The SQL Server service is managed by a Windows cluster resource. The example we took to explain HA and DR earlier in this lesson was largely based on this.

This book covers creating a Windows Server Failover Cluster; however, it doesn't cover troubleshooting a failover cluster.

Log Shipping

Log shipping is one of the oldest SQL Server solutions, and is mostly used for DR and SQL Server migration. It takes transaction log backups from the primary server and restores them on one or more secondary servers. It is implemented using SQL Agent jobs.

Log shipping is covered in more detail later in this book.

AlwaysOn Availability Groups

Introduced in SQL Server 2012, **AlwaysOn AG** is one of the newest and most impressive HA and DR features in SQL Server. When launched, it worked on top of Windows Server Failover Cluster; however, this restriction has been removed in Windows Server 2016 and SQL Server 2016.

AlwaysOn Availability Groups allows you to manually or automatically fail over one or more databases to a secondary instance if the primary instance is unavailable. This book talks about AlwaysOn in detail in a later lesson.

Replication

Replication is one of the oldest SQL Server features that replicates data from one database (commonly known as a publisher) to one or more databases (known as subscribers) in the same or different SQL Server instances.

Replication is commonly used for load balancing read and write workloads. The writes are done on the publisher and reads are done on the subscriber. However, as it replicates data, it is also used as an HA and DR solution.

Hybrid Scenarios

The solutions described here can be used together as well. Using one feature doesn't restrict you from using others. Consider a scenario where a company has a transactional database and logging database. The transactional database is of more importance and has stringent RTO and RPO compared to the logging database. A company can choose AlwaysOn for the transactional database and log shipping/replication for the logging database.

> **Note**
>
> There are other solutions such as database mirroring and third-party solutions. Database mirroring is deprecated and will be removed in future SQL Server versions. This book only talks about SQL Server features and not any third-party HA and DR solutions.

In this section, you have learned about high availability and disaster recovery concepts and terminology.

The next section talks about replication and how it can be used as an HA and DR solution.

Replication is one of the oldest features in SQL Server. It allows you to sync or replicate data from one or more databases on the same or different SQL Server instances. In this section, we will cover replication concepts and terminology. We will also talk about the different types of replications available in SQL Server. We will then cover snapshot replication in detail.

Introduction to SQL Server Replication

Replication is a SQL Server feature that synchronizes data from a database (known as a publisher) to one or more databases (known as subscribers) on the same or different SQL Server instances.

Consider the following diagram:

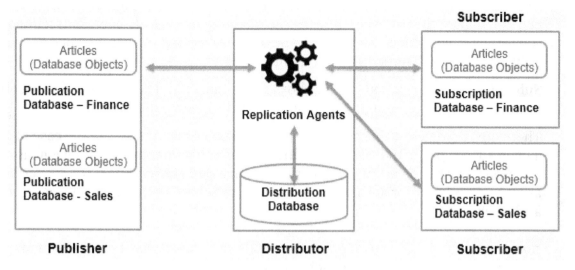

Figure 1.5: Replication example

The preceding diagram depicts a typical implementation of replication. A replication has a number of components that work together to synchronize data between databases.

Let's look at these components in detail:

- **Publisher**: A publisher is a database that facilitates the data for replication.

- **Publication**: A publication is a set of objects and data to replicate. A publisher (database) can have one or more publications. For example, a database has two schemas, `finance` and `sales`. There's one publication that has objects and data for the `finance` schema and another publication that has objects and data for the `sales` schema.

- **Articles**: Articles are the database objects that are to be replicated such as tables and stored procedures. A publication can include one or more selected database objects and data.

- **Distributor**: A distributor is a database (distribution database) that stores the data to be replicated from one or more publishers. The distribution database can be on the same instance as the publisher (which happens in most cases) or can be on a different SQL Server instance. Created as part of the replication database, it also stores the replication metadata such as publisher and subscriber details.

  A better understanding of distribution databases is crucial in troubleshooting replication.

- **Subscriber**: A subscriber is a database that subscribes to one or more publications from the one or more publishers in order to get the replicated data. A subscriber can also update the publisher data in case of merge or peer-to-peer transactional replication. A subscriber database can be on the same SQL Server instance as the publisher or on a different SQL Server instance.

- **Subscription**: Subscription is the opposite of publication. The subscriber connects to the publisher by creating a subscription for the given publication.

  There are two types of subscriptions, push and pull subscriptions. In the case of a **push subscription**, the distributor updates the subscriber as and when data is received (distribution agent is at distributor). In a **pull subscription**, the subscriber asks the distributor for any new data changes, as scheduled (distribution agent is at the subscriber).

If we now look at the preceding diagram, the publisher database has two publications, one for **finance** and one for the **sales** schema. The replication agent gets the changes from the publisher and inserts them into the distribution database.

The distribution agent then applies the changes to the relevant subscribers. There are two subscribers: one has a subscription to the **finance** publication and another subscribes to the **sales** publication.

Replication Agents

Replication agents are the standalone executables that are responsible for replicating the data from a publisher to a subscriber. In this section, we will cover replication agents in brief, and we will look at them in detail later in this book.

Snapshot Agent

The snapshot agent creates the selected articles and copies all of the data from the publisher to the subscriber whenever executed. An important thing to note here is that the subsequent execution of the agent doesn't copy the differential data; rather, each run clears out the existing schema and data at the subscriber and copies the schema and data from the publisher.

The snapshot agent is run at the distributor and is used via snapshot replication. It is also used in transactional and merge replication to initialize the subscriber with the initial data.

Log Reader Agent

The log reader agent scans the transaction log for the transactions marked for replication and inserts them into the distribution database. It is used only in transactional replication and provides continuous replication from the publisher to the subscriber.

Each publication has its own log reader agent; that is, if there are two different databases with transactional replication, there will be two log reader agents, one for each database.

The log reader agent runs at the distributor.

Distribution Agent

As the name suggests, the distribution agent distributes (applies) the data that's inserted into the distribution database by the log reader agent to the subscribers.

The distribution agent runs at the subscriber if it's a pull subscription and at the distributor if it's a push subscription.

> **Note**
>
> There's also a queue reader agent that's used in bidirectional transactional replication. Bidirectional transactional replication is now obsolete.

Merge Agent

Used in merge replication, the merge agent applies the initial snapshot to the subscriber (generated by the snapshot agent) and then replicates the changes from the publisher to the subscriber and from the subscriber to the publisher as and when they occur, or when the subscriber is online and available for replication.

There is one merge agent for one merge subscription.

Types of Replication

SQL Server has snapshot, transactional, and merge replication. Each replication type is best suited for one or more sets of scenarios. This section discusses different types of replication and scenarios in which they should be used.

Transactional Replication

Transactional replication, as the name suggests, replicates the transactions as and when they are committed at the publisher to the subscribers.

It's one of the most commonly used replications to load balance read-write workloads. The writes are done at the publisher and the reads (or reporting) are done at the subscriber, thereby eliminating read-write blocking. Moreover, the subscriber database can be better indexed to speed up the reads and the publisher database can be optimized for **Data Manipulation Language (DML)** operations.

The log reader and distribution agent carry out the transactional replication, as stated earlier. The agents are implemented as SQL agent jobs, that is, there's a SQL agent job for a log reader agent and a SQL agent job for the distribution agent.

There are two other transactional replications that allow changes to flow from subscriber to publisher: transactional replication with updatable subscription (bidirectional transactional replication) and peer-to-peer transactional replication.

Transaction replication is discussed in detail in *Lesson 2, Transactional Replication.*

Merge Replication

Merge replication, as the name suggests, replicates changes from publishers to subscribers and from subscribers to publishers. This sometimes results in conflict in cases where the same row is updated with different values from the publisher and subscriber.

Merge replication has a built-in mechanism to detect and resolve conflicts; however, in some cases, it may get difficult to troubleshoot conflicts. This makes it the most complex replication type available in SQL Server.

Merge replication uses the merge agent to initialize subscribers and merge changes. Unlike transaction replication, where the snapshot agent is used to initialize subscribers, in merge replication, the snapshot agent only creates the snapshot. The merge agent applies that snapshot and starts replicating the changes thereafter.

Merge replication isn't covered in this book as it's not used as an HA and DR solution anymore.

Snapshot Replication

Snapshot replication generates a snapshot of the articles to be replicated and applies it to the subscriber. The snapshot replication can be run on demand or as per schedule. It's the simplest form of replication and is also used to initialize transactional and merge replication.

Consider the following diagram:

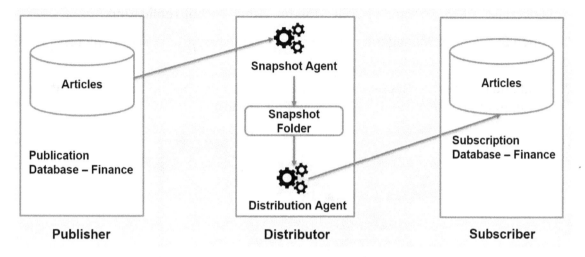

Figure 1.6: Snapshot replication example

The preceding diagram demonstrates how snapshot replication works. The **finance** database is replicated from publisher to subscriber. Here's how it works:

1. A publication for the **finance** database is created at the publisher.

2. The snapshot agent creates the snapshot (**.sch** files for object schema and **.bcp** files for data). The snapshot files are kept at a shared folder that's accessible by the publisher and the distributor.

3. A subscription for the **finance** publication is created at the subscriber.

4. The distribution agent applies the snapshot at the subscriber's **finance** database.

Configuring Snapshot Replication Using SQL Server Management Studio

Throughout this book, we will be using SQL Server Management Studio. You should already be familiar with this. Installation instructions are available in the preface, and all exercises can be completed on the free tier.

Configuring snapshot replication is a two-step process: the first step is to create the publication and the second step is to create the subscription. We will first create the publication.

Exercise 1: Creating a Publication

In this exercise, we will create a publication for our snapshot replication:

1. Open SQL Server Management Studio and connect to the Object Explorer (press F8 to open and connect to Object Explorer).

2. Find and expand the **Replication** node and right-click on the **Local Publication** node. In the context menu, select **New Publication**:

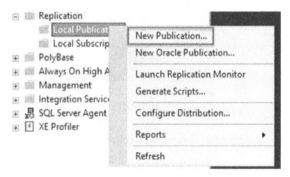

Figure 1.7: Select New Publication

3. In the **New Publication Wizard** introduction page, click **Next** to continue:

Figure 1.8: The New Publication Wizard window

4. The **New Publication Wizard | Distributor** page defines where the distribution database will be created. The first option specifies that the publisher server will act as the distribution server and will host the distribution database and distributor jobs.

    The second option allows you to add a new server to act as the distribution server.

    Leave the first option checked and click **Next** to continue:

Figure 1.9: The Distributor window

5. In the **New Publication Wizard | Snapshot Folder** window, specify the location where snapshots (schema: **.sch** files and data) are stored. This needs to be a network path, and both the distributor and the subscriber should have access to this path.

    Create a new folder in any location on your computer and share it with everyone by modifying the sharing settings of the new folder that's been created.

Copy the shared path in the **Snapshot folder** box, as shown in the following screenshot. Click **Next** to continue:

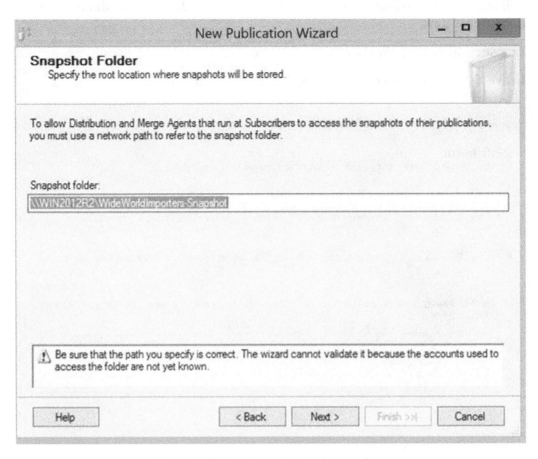

Figure 1.10: The Snapshot Folder window

6. In the **New Publication Wizard | Publication Database** window, choose the database you wish to publish or replicate. Click **Next** to continue:

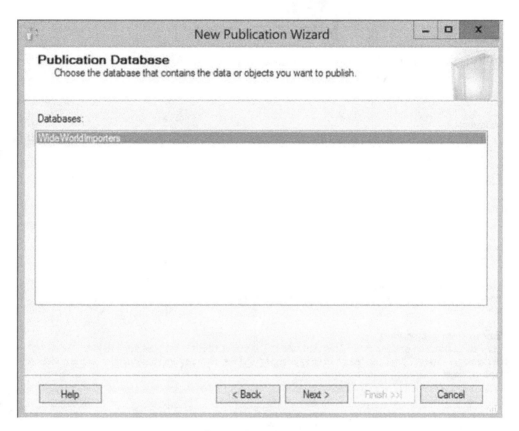

Figure 1.11: The Publication Database window

7. In the **New Publication Wizard | Publication Type** window, select **Snapshot publication** and click **Next** to continue:

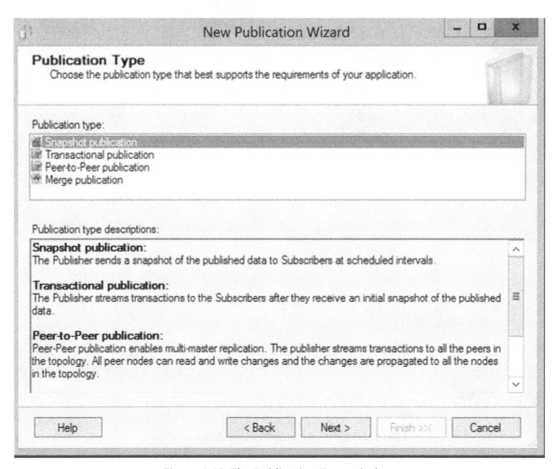

Figure 1.12: The Publication Type window

8. In the **New Publication Wizard | Articles** window, select the database objects to be replicated.

Expand **Tables** and select the required tables, as shown in the following screenshot:

Figure 1.13: The Articles window

Do not select any other objects for now.

Select the `BuyingGroups` table and then click **Article Properties**. Then, select **Set properties of Highlighted Table Article**.

The **Article Properties** window lists multiple article properties that you may have to change as and when required. For example, you can change the table name and owner at the subscriber database or you can copy the non-clustered `Columnstore` index from the publisher to the subscriber. This property is disabled by default:

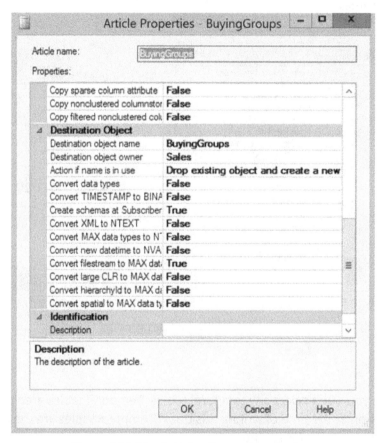

Figure 1.14: The Articles Properties window

9. The **New Publication Wizard | Filter Table Rows** window allows you to filter out data to be replicated to the subscriber:

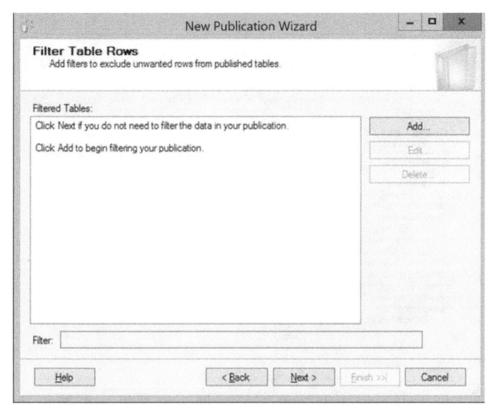

Figure 1.15: The Filter Table Rows window

In the **Filter Table Rows** window, click on the **Add** button to add filters. In the **Add Filter** window, add the filter, as shown in the following screenshot:

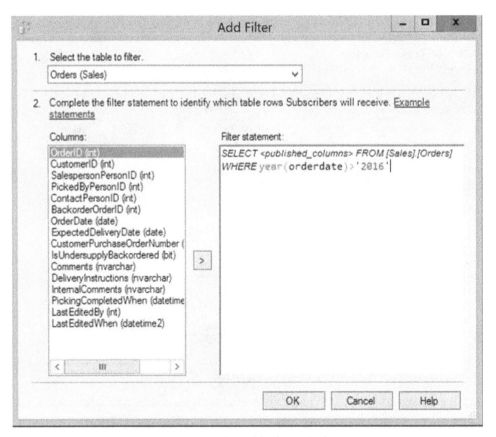

Figure 1.16: The Add Filter window

The shown filter will filter out any order with an order year of less than 2016 and will replicate all orders made after the year 2016.

Click **OK** to go back to the **Filter Table Rows** window:

Figure 1.17: The Filter Table Rows window

Observe that the filter has been added.

You can't add filters by joining one or more tables. The filter only works on a single table. It is therefore advised that you add the filter to other tables as well. Otherwise, all tables other than the **Orders** table will have data for all the years. This example, however, applies the filter on the **Orders** table only.

Click **Next** to continue.

10. In the **New Publication Wizard | Snapshot Agent** window, check the **Create a snapshot immediately and keep the snapshot available to initialize subscriptions** option.

This will generate the snapshot in the snapshot folder that's specified:

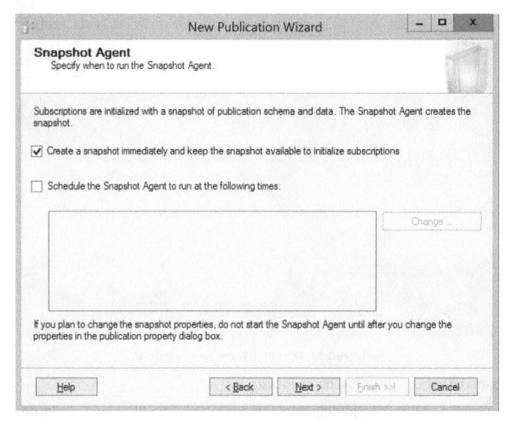

Figure 1.18: The Snapshot Agent window

Click **Next** to continue.

> **Note**
>
> It is recommended that you schedule the snapshot agent during off business hours so as to avoid performance degradation that occurs as a result of snapshot generation.

11. In the **New Publication Wizard | Agent Security** window, specify the service account under which the snapshot agent process will run and how it connects to the publisher:

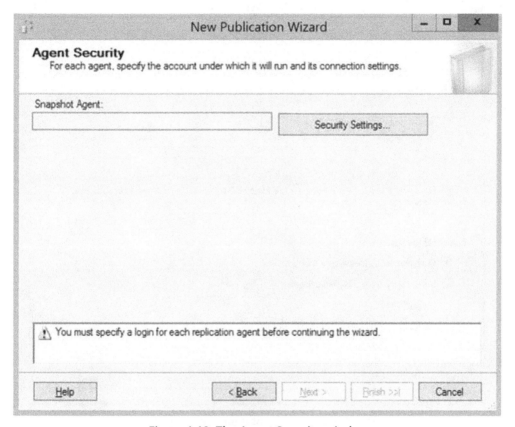

Figure 1.19: The Agent Security window

Click on **Security Settings** to continue.

In the **Snapshot Agent Security** window, choose options, as shown in the following screenshot:

Figure 1.20: The Snapshot Agent Security window

> **Note**
>
> Running the snapshot agent process under a SQL agent service account isn't a good practice on production environments as a SQL agent service account has more privileges than required by the snapshot agent. However, we are only using it for demonstrative purposes.

The minimum permissions required by the Windows account under which the snapshot agent process runs are **db_owner** rights on the distribution database, **db_owner** rights on the publisher database, and read, write, and modify rights on the shared snapshot folder.

Click **OK** to continue. You'll be redirected to the **Agent Security** window. In this window, click **Next** to continue:

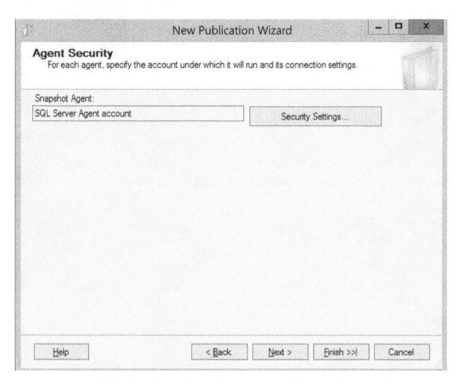

Figure 1.21: The Agent Security window with account selected

12. In the **Wizard Actions** window, select **Create the publication**, and then click **Next** to continue:

Figure 1.22: The Agent Security window with account selected

13. In the **Complete the Wizard** window, provide the publication name, as shown in the following screenshot, and then click on **Finish** to complete the wizard and create the publication:

Figure 1.23: The Complete the Wizard window

The wizard creates the publication, adds the selected articles, and creates and starts the snapshot agent job:

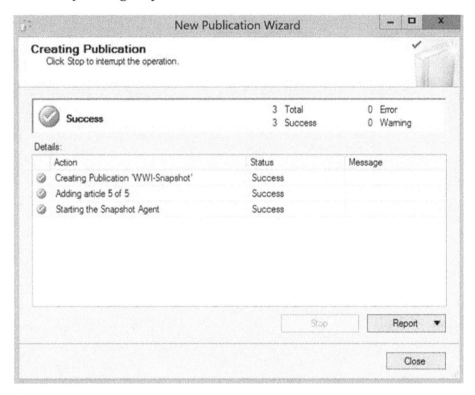

Figure 1.24: The Creating Publication window

14. After the publication is created, click on **Close** to exit the wizard.

Now, let's look at the objects or components that are created as part of creating the publication.

Exercise 2: Exploring the Distribution Database

In *step 4* of the previous exercise, we specified that the publisher will act as its own distributor. This results in the creation of a distribution database and snapshot agent job on the publisher itself. We can also use a different instance for distribution, however, let's keep it simple for this demonstration.

In SQL Server Management Studio, connect to the Object Explorer, expand **Databases**, and then expand **System Database**. Observe that a new system database distribution has been added as a result of the previous exercise:

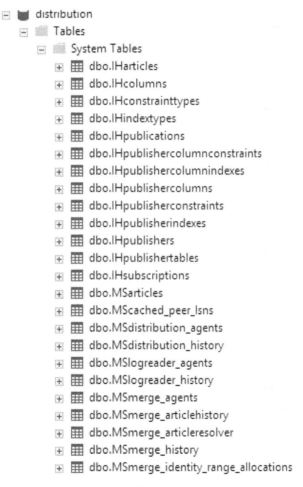

Figure 1.25: System tables

The **distribution** database has system tables that keep track of replication metadata. Let's explore the metadata tables that are related to snapshot replication.

Open a new query window in SSMS and execute the following queries one by one:

1. To get publication information, run this query:

```
SELECT [publisher_id]
      ,[publisher_db]
      ,[publication]
      ,[publication_id]
      ,[publication_type]
      ,[thirdparty_flag]
      ,[independent_agent]
      ,[immediate_sync]
      ,[allow_push]
      ,[allow_pull]
      ,[allow_anonymous]
      ,[description]
      ,[vendor_name]
      ,[retention]
      ,[sync_method]
      ,[allow_subscription_copy]
      ,[thirdparty_options]
      ,[allow_queued_tran]
      ,[options]
      ,[retention_period_unit]
      ,[allow_initialize_from_backup]
      ,[min_autonosync_lsn]
  FROM [distribution].[dbo].[MSpublications]
```

You should see the following output:

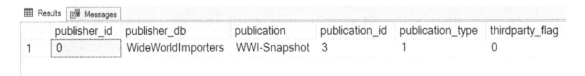

	publisher_id	publisher_db	publication	publication_id	publication_type	thirdparty_flag
1	0	WideWorldImporters	WWI-Snapshot	3	1	0

Figure 1.26: Publication information

You can get the publication details from Object Explorer as well:

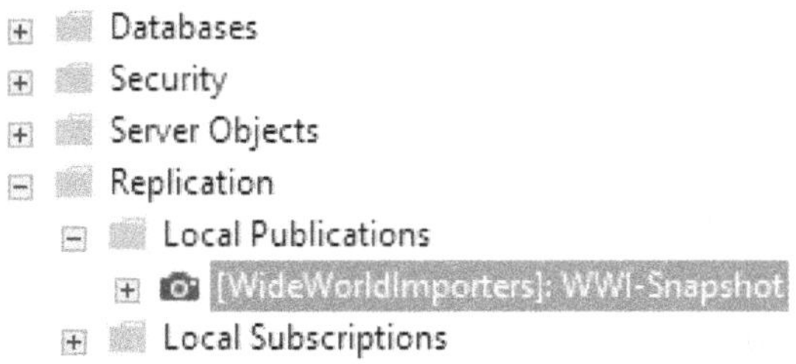

Figure 1.27: Publication details from the Object Explorer

2. To get the article information, run this query:

```
SELECT [publisher_id]
      ,[publisher_db]
      ,[publication_id]
      ,[article]
      ,[article_id]
      ,[destination_object]
      ,[source_owner]
      ,[source_object]
      ,[description]
      ,[destination_owner]
  FROM [distribution].[dbo].[MSarticles]
```

You should get the following output:

	publisher_id	publisher_db	publication_id	article	article_id	destination_object	source_owner	source_object
1	0	WideWorldImporters	3	CustomerTransactions	1	CustomerTransactions	Sales	CustomerTransactions
2	0	WideWorldImporters	3	InvoiceLines	2	InvoiceLines	Sales	InvoiceLines
3	0	WideWorldImporters	3	Invoices	3	Invoices	Sales	Invoices
4	0	WideWorldImporters	3	OrderLines	4	OrderLines	Sales	OrderLines
5	0	WideWorldImporters	3	Orders	5	Orders	Sales	Orders

Figure 1.28: Article information

3. To get the snapshot agent information, run this query:

```
SELECT [id]
      ,[name]
      ,[publisher_id]
      ,[publisher_db]
      ,[publication]
      ,[publication_type]
      ,[local_job]
      ,[job_id]
      ,[profile_id]
      ,[dynamic_filter_login]
      ,[dynamic_filter_hostname]
      ,[publisher_security_mode]
      ,[publisher_login]
      ,[publisher_password]
      ,[job_step_uid]
  FROM [distribution].[dbo].[MSsnapshot_agents]
```

You should get the following output:

Figure 1.29: Snapshot agent information

> **Note**
>
> The preceding output is also useful in identifying which snapshot agent job belongs to which publication when there are multiple snapshot agent jobs configured on a SQL Server instance.

4. To get the snapshot agent's execution history, run this query:

```
SELECT [agent_id]
      ,[runstatus]
      ,[start_time]
      ,[time]
      ,[duration]
      ,[comments]
      ,[delivered_transactions]
      ,[delivered_commands]
      ,[delivery_rate]
      ,[error_id]
      ,[timestamp]
  FROM [distribution].[dbo].[MSsnapshot_history]
```

You should get the following output:

Figure 1.30: Snapshot agent execution history

You can also get the snapshot agent and its history from the Object Explorer under the **SQL Server Agent** node:

Figure 1.31: Snapshot agent history from the object explorer

Right-click on the snapshot agent job and select **View History** from the context menu.

Database Snapshot

Navigate to the snapshot folder (**WideWorldImporters-Snapshot**) that was provided in *step 5* of the previous exercise. This contains the snapshot files for the articles that were selected for replication.

Observe that this folder acts as a base and has a subfolder named **WIN2012R2$SQL2016_ WIDEWORLDIMPORTERS_WWI-SNAPSHOT**. The subfolder is named by concatenating the SQL Server instance name and the publication name to the base snapshot folder. This is done to separate out snapshots for different publications; the base snapshot folder can therefore have snapshots from multiple publications.

Every time a snapshot agent is run, a new folder is created inside **WIN2012R2$SQL2016_ WIDEWORLDIMPORTERS_WWI-SNAPSHOT**. This is named by the timestamp when the snapshot agent ran and contains the schema and data files. This is shown in the following screenshot:

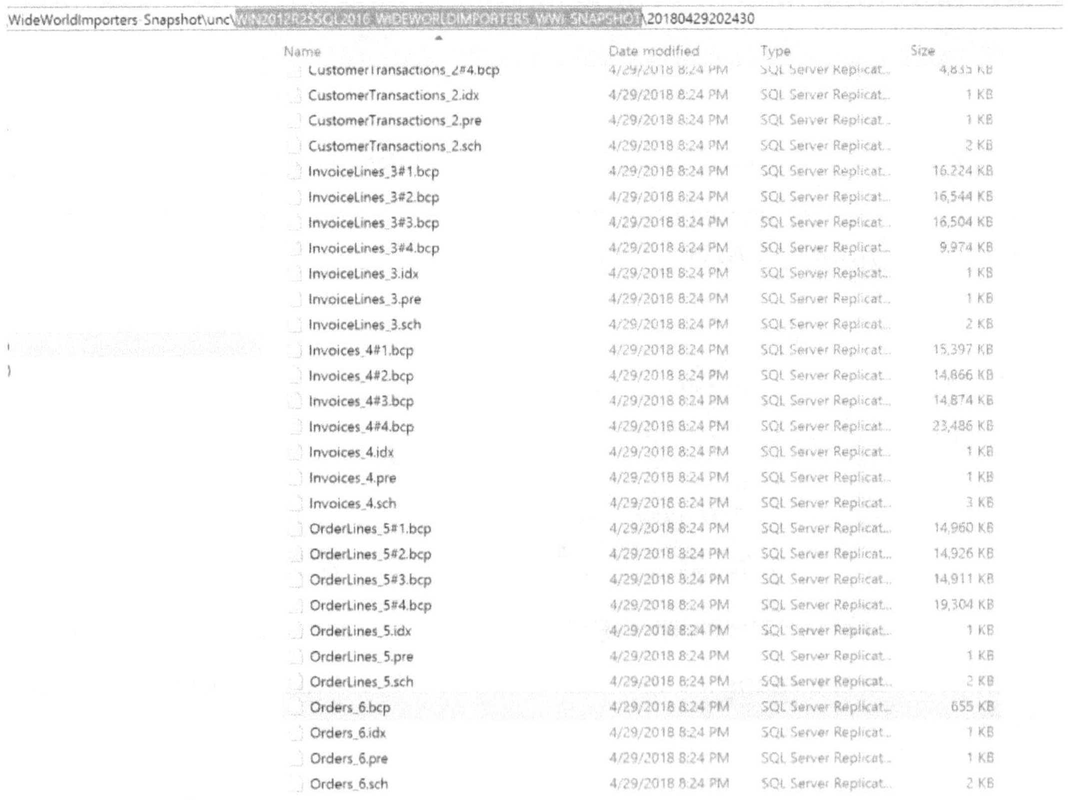

Figure 1.32: Snapshot folder

Observe that the snapshot folder has .**sch**, .**idx**, .**pre**, and .**bcp** files. Let's see what these files are used for.

.pre Files

The .**pre** files are the pre-snapshot scripts that drop the object at the subscriber if it exists. This is because every time a snapshot runs, it initializes the tables from scratch. Therefore, the objects are first dropped at the subscriber. Let's look at an example:

```
SET QUOTED_IDENTIFIER ON

go

if object_id('sys.sp_MSrestoresavedforeignkeys') < 0 exec sys.
sp_MSdropfkreferencingarticle @destination_object_name =
N'CustomerTransactions', @destination_owner_name = N'Sales'

go

drop Table [Sales].[CustomerTransactions]

go
```

The preceding query is from the **customertransactions.pre** file. It first drops foreign keys, if any, for the **CustomerTransactions** table and then drops the **CustomerTransactions** table.

> **Note**
>
> Another way to do this is to set the **Action if name is in use** option in the **Article Properties** window to the value **Drop existing object and create a new one**.

.sch Files

The .**sch** files contain the creation script for the articles to be replicated. Let's look at an example:

```
drop Table [Sales].[CustomerTransactions]

go

SET ANSI_PADDING ON

go

SET ANSI_NULLS ON

GO

SET QUOTED_IDENTIFIER ON
```

```
GO
CREATE TABLE [Sales].[CustomerTransactions](
   [CustomerTransactionID] [int] NOT NULL,
   [CustomerID] [int] NOT NULL,
   [TransactionTypeID] [int] NOT NULL,
   [InvoiceID] [int] NULL,
   [PaymentMethodID] [int] NULL,
   [TransactionDate] [date] NOT NULL,
   [AmountExcludingTax] [decimal](18, 2) NOT NULL,
   [TaxAmount] [decimal](18, 2) NOT NULL,
   [TransactionAmount] [decimal](18, 2) NOT NULL,
   [OutstandingBalance] [decimal](18, 2) NOT NULL,
   [FinalizationDate] [date] NULL,
   [IsFinalized]  AS (case when [FinalizationDate] IS NULL then
CONVERT([bit],(0)) else CONVERT([bit],(1)) end) PERSISTED,
   [LastEditedBy] [int] NOT NULL,
   [LastEditedWhen] [datetime2](7) NOT NULL
)
GO
```

This query is from the **customertransactions.sch** file.

.idx Files

The .**idx** files contain the indexes and constraints on the tables to be created at the subscriber. Let's look at an example:

```
CREATE CLUSTERED INDEX [CX_Sales_CustomerTransactions] ON [Sales].
[CustomerTransactions]([TransactionDate])

go

ALTER TABLE [Sales].[CustomerTransactions] ADD CONSTRAINT [PK_Sales_
CustomerTransactions] PRIMARY KEY NONCLUSTERED ([CustomerTransactionID])

Go
```

This query is from the **customertransactions.idx** file.

.bcp Files

The **.bcp** files contain the table data to be inserted into the tables at the subscriber. There can be multiple **.bcp** files, depending on the table size.

Snapshot Agent Job

The snapshot agent job is a SQL Server agent job that executes **snapshot.exe** to generate the snapshot (these are the files we discussed earlier: **.sch**, **.pre**, **.idx**, and **.bcp**).

The snapshot agent job is created as part of creating the snapshot publication. You can locate the job in Object Explorer under the **SQL Server Agent | Jobs** node:

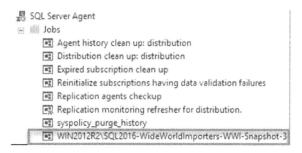

Figure 1.33: Snapshot agent job location

Double-click on the job to open it.

> **Note**
>
> The job name may be different in your case.

In the **Job Properties** window, click on **Steps** on the left-hand side in the **Select a page** pane:

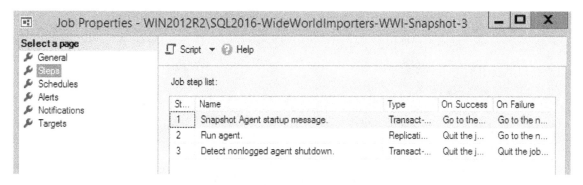

Figure 1.34: The Job Properties window

This job has three steps.

- Step 1 - **Snapshot Agent startup message**: This inserts the **Starting Agent** message in the `Msnapshot_history` table in the `distribution` database:

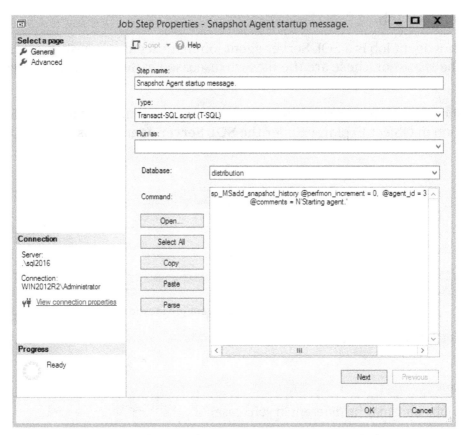

Figure 1.35: The Snapshot Agent startup message window

It uses the system-stored **sp_MSadd_snapshot_history** procedure to insert a row in the **Msnapshot_history** table, indicating the start of the snapshot agent.

- Step 2 - **Run agent**: This runs the **snapshot.exe** command with the required parameters to generate the snapshot:

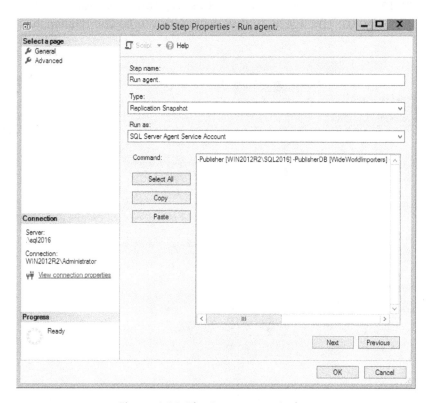

Figure 1.36: The Run agent window

Observe that the **Type** parameter shows **Replication Snapshot** (this points to **snapshot.exe**). The **Command** text is the list of parameters that are passed to the **snapshot.exe** process. Similar to the previous step, where the **Starting Agent** status is written to the **MSsnapshot_history** table, **snapshot.exe** also logs the progress to the **MSsnapshot_history** table.

- Step 3 - **Detect nonlogged agent shutdown**: This step uses the systems-stored **sp_MSdetect_nonlogged_shutdown** procedure to check if the agent is shut down without logging any message to the **MSsnapshot_history** table. It then checks and logs a relevant message for the agent that was shut down to the **MSsnapshot_history** table:

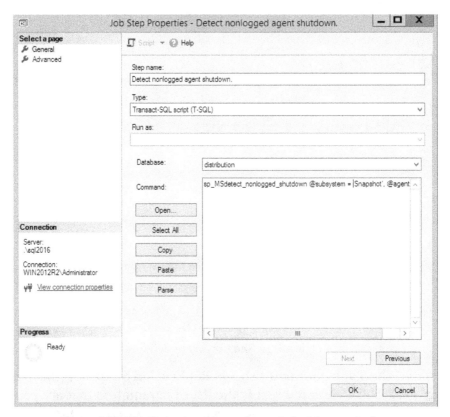

Figure 1.37: The Detect nonlogged agent shutdown window

This completes the objects and components that were created as part of creating a publication.

We'll now look into the **snapshot.exe** process in detail.

Replication Snapshot (snapshot.exe)

The **snapshot.exe** process is installed with SQL Server (if you choose to install replication when installing SQL Server) and is stored in the **C:\Program Files\Microsoft SQL Server\130\COM** folder (for SQL Server 2016 installation).

The **snapshot.exe** process accepts quite a few parameters that are used to generate snapshots and to tune snapshot generation.

> **Note**
>
> This book covers the most important parameters, and not all parameters. For a complete list of parameters, go to https://docs.microsoft.com/en-us/sql/relational-databases/replication/agents/replication-snapshot-agent?view=sql-server-2017.

The **snapshot.exe** process can be run independently from the command line by passing the relevant parameters.

Execute the following commands in a command-line window to run **snapshot.exe** with the default parameters, as specified in *step 2* of the snapshot agent job that we discussed previously:

```
REM -- Change the variable values as per your environment

SET Publisher=WIN2012R2\SQL2016

SET PublisherDB=WideWorldImporters

SET Publication=WWI-Snapshot

"C:\Program Files\Microsoft SQL Server\130\COM\SNAPSHOT.EXE" -Publisher
%Publisher% -PublisherDB %PublisherDB% -Distributor %Publisher% -Publication
%Publication% -DistributorSecurityMode 1
```

> **Note**
>
> You can also copy the code from the **C:\Code\Lesson01\snapshot.txt** file.

You will have to change the **Publisher** variable with the SQL Server instance you created in the snapshot publication. You may have to change the **PublisherDB** and **Publication** parameters if you chose a different database and publication name when creating the snapshot publication in *Exercise 1: Creating a Publication*.

Once it runs successfully, it generates the following output:

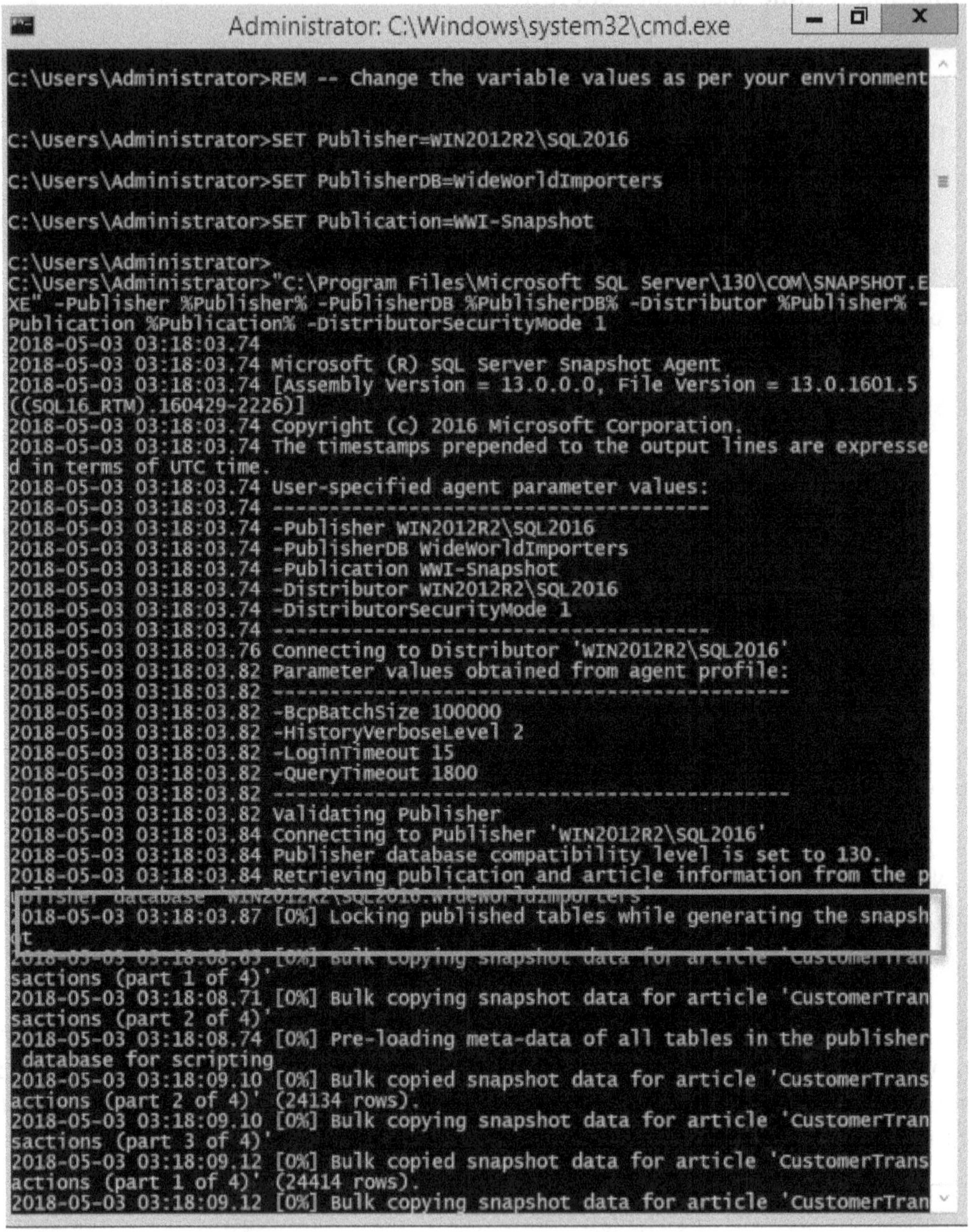

Figure 1.38: Running snapshot.exe

The snapshot agent also logs the progress status in the **distribution.dbo.MSsnapshot_history** table. You can query the table to verify these steps.

An important thing to note here is that the snapshot agent locks the published tables (schema lock and exclusive locks) while generating the snapshot. This is to make sure that no changes are made to the schema when a snapshot is being generated. Any changes to the schema during snapshot generation will leave the snapshot in an inconsistent state and it will error out when applying the snapshot to the subscriber.

For example, when the snapshot agent generated a **.sch** file, a table had two columns; however, when it exports the data for that table, another transaction modifies the table by adding one more column to it. Therefore, the table creation script, **.sch**, has two columns and **.bcp**, which is the data file, has three columns. This will error out when applied to the subscriber.

This also means that for large databases, generating snapshots may result in blocking issues.

To review the locks being applied during snapshot generation, run the **snapshot.exe** process, as described earlier. Then, quickly switch to SQL Server Management Studio and execute the following query to get lock details:

```
select
    resource_type,
    db_name(resource_database_id) As resource_database_name,
    resource_description,
    request_mode,
    request_type,
    request_status,
    request_session_id
from sys.dm_tran_locks
```

You should get an output similar to what is shown in the following screenshot:

	resource_type	resource_database_name	resource_de...	request_mode	request_type	request_status	request_session_id
16	OBJECT	WideWorldImporters		Sch-S	LOCK	GRANT	64
17	OBJECT	WideWorldImporters		IX	LOCK	GRANT	63
18	HOBT	WideWorldImporters		S	LOCK	GRANT	63
19	RID	WideWorldImporters	3:7480:3	X	LOCK	GRANT	63
20	OBJECT	WideWorldImporters		S	LOCK	GRANT	63
21	APPLICATION	WideWorldImporters	16384:[WIN2...	X	LOCK	GRANT	63
22	OBJECT	WideWorldImporters		S	LOCK	GRANT	63
23	PAGE	WideWorldImporters	3:7480	IX	LOCK	GRANT	63
24	RID	WideWorldImporters	3:7480:0	X	LOCK	GRANT	63
25	RID	WideWorldImporters	3:7480:4	X	LOCK	GRANT	63
26	OBJECT	WideWorldImporters		S	LOCK	GRANT	63
27	OBJECT	WideWorldImporters		Sch-S	LOCK	GRANT	66
28	OBJECT	WideWorldImporters		Sch-S	LOCK	GRANT	64

Figure 1.39: Reviewing the applied locks

Observe that the **IX**, **X**, and **Sch-S** locks are applied on the `WideWorldImporters` database during snapshot generation.

> **Note**
>
> The relevant **snapshot.exe** switches/parameters will be discussed in the *Optimizing Snapshot Replication* section.

Modifying an Existing Publication

This section explores existing publication properties and how to modify an existing publication so that you can add or remove articles, change agent security settings, and more.

To view publication properties, connect to Object Explorer, expand **Replication**, and then expand **Local Publications**.

Right-click on the snapshot (**WWI-Snapshot**) and select **Properties** from the context menu:

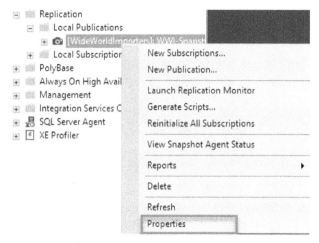

Figure 1.40: Selecting Properties from the context menu

This opens the **Publication Properties** window:

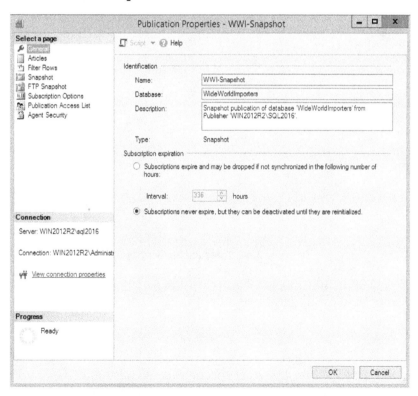

Figure 1.41: The Publication Properties | General window

The **Publication Properties** window has different options on the left-hand side (**Select a page**) pane to modify or change publication properties. We'll now look at these options in detail.

Articles

The **Articles** page allows you to add or remove an article to or from the publication. Once you add or remove one, you'll have to generate a snapshot for the changes to take effect:

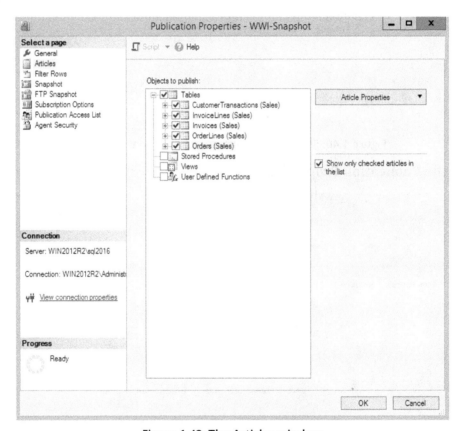

Figure 1.42: The Articles window

Adding or removing an article is very simple. Uncheck the **Show only checked articles in the list** option to display all database objects.

> **Note**
>
> When adding a new article, the article properties can be changed if required using the **Article Properties** dropdown, as shown earlier. The article properties can, however, be changed later if required.

Then, select or remove the objects as required and click on **OK** to apply the changes.

Filter Rows

The **Filter Rows** page allows you to add or remove row filters to the tables. This is similar to *step 9* of *Exercise 1: Creating a Publication*:

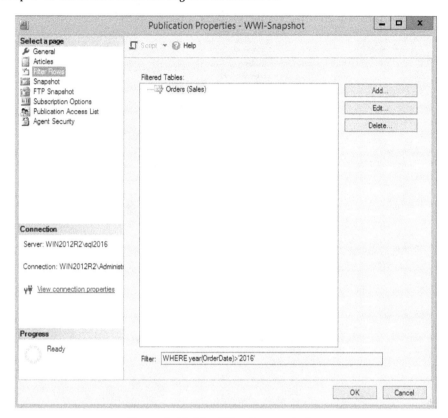

Figure 1.43: The Filter Rows window

Snapshot

The **Snapshot** page allows you to do the following:

- Modify the snapshot format to **Native SQL Server** or **Character**.

- Modify the location of the snapshot folder.

- Compress the snapshot files in the snapshot folder. This saves storage for large publications. When compression is specified, a single cabinet (compressed) file is generated. However, if an article file size exceeds 2 GB, cab compression can't be used.

- Run additional scripts before and after applying the snapshot at the subscriber:

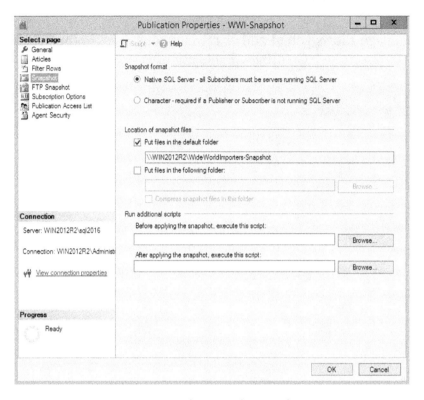

Figure 1.44: The Snapshot window

FTP Snapshot

The **FTP Snapshot** page allows subscribers to download snapshots using FTP. You'll have to specify the FTP folder as the snapshot folder:

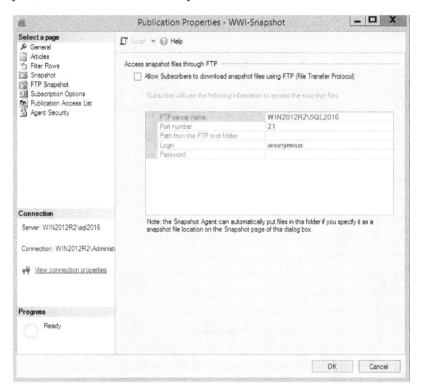

Figure 1.45: The FTP Snapshot window

You'll have to set up the FTP by specifying the connection details so that the snapshot agent can then push and pull snapshot files to and from the specified FTP folder.

Subscription Options

The **Subscription Options** page lets you control subscriber-level settings:

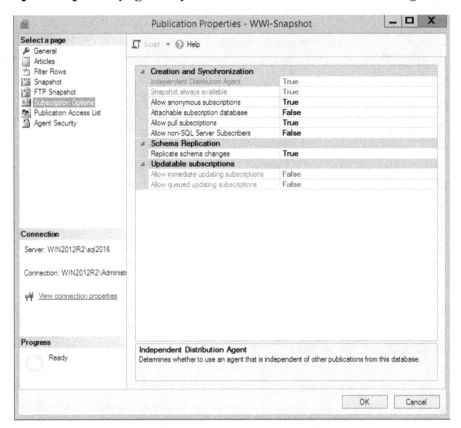

Figure 1.46: The Subscription Options window

The important settings for snapshot replication are as follows:

- **Allow pull subscriptions**: This determines whether or not to allow pull subscriptions. The default value is **True**. Pull subscription is the only option available when an FTP snapshot is used.

- **Allow non-SQL Server Subscribers**: This determines whether or not to allow non-SQL Server, that is, Oracle, MySQL, and so on, subscribers. The default value is **False**.

- **Replication schema changes**: This determines whether or not to replicate schema changes to the published articles. The default value is **True**.

Publication Access List

The **Publication Access List (PAL)** page is a list of logins that have permission to create and synchronize subscriptions. Any login that has access to the publication database (`WideWorldImporter`) and is defined in both the publisher and distributor can be added to PAL:

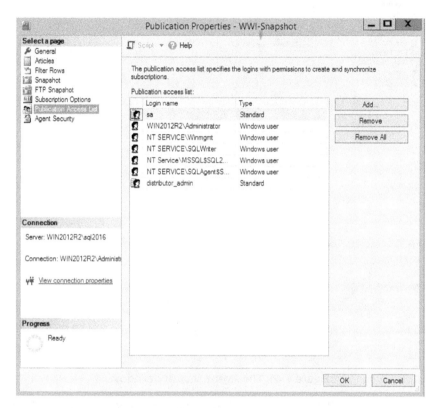

Figure 1.47: The Publication Access List window

> **Note**
>
> Do not remove the **distributor_admin** login as it's used by replication.

Agent Security

In the **Agent Security** page, you can modify the agent security settings, as defined in *step 11* of *Exercise 1: Creating a Publication*:

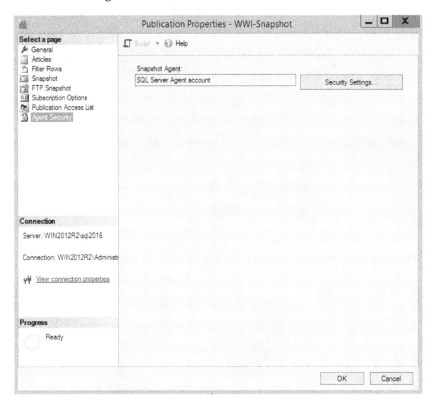

Figure 1.48: The Agent Security window

To change or modify security settings, click on the **Security Settings** button and change as required.

Exercise 3: Creating a Subscription

In this exercise, we'll create the subscription at the subscriber end. A subscriber is usually a separate SQL Server instance.

To create a new subscription for the publication, follow these steps:

1. Connect to Object Explorer in SSMS. Expand **Replication | Local Publications**.

2. Right-click on the **[WideWorldImporters]: WWI-Snapshot** publication and select
New Subscriptions:

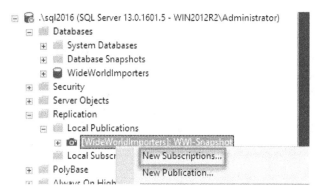

Figure 1.49: The New Subscriptions option in the Object Explorer

3. This will open the **New Subscription Wizard**. Click **Next** to continue:

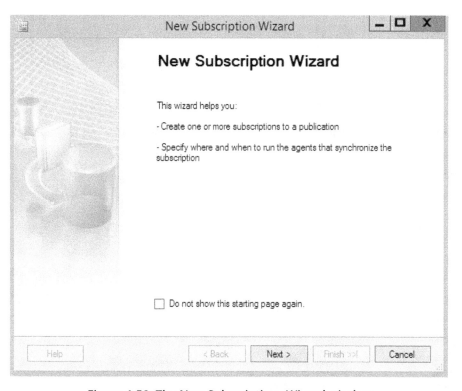

Figure 1.50: The New Subscriptions Wizard window

4. In the **Publication** window, under the **Publisher** dropdown, select the publisher server and then the publication:

Figure 1.51: The Publication window

Click on **Next** to continue.

5. In the **Distribution Agent Location** window, select **pull subscriptions**:

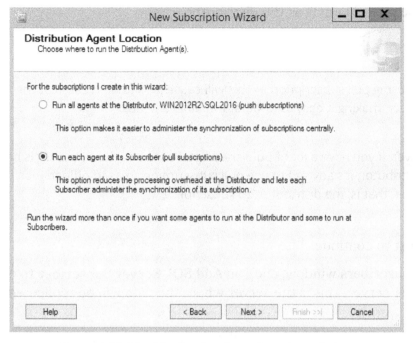

Figure 1.52: The Distribution Agent Location window

Pull subscriptions will create the distribution job at the subscriber server. This option reduces overhead at the distributor, and this becomes more important when the publisher acts as the distributor.

> **Note**
>
> We are using pull subscription as this will cause jobs to be created at the subscriber, making it easy to understand different jobs.
>
> Moreover, if you have a lot of published databases and the publisher is being used as a distributor, it's advised to use pull subscription so as to offload jobs from the publisher, that is, the distributor, to subscribers.

Click **Next** to continue.

6. In the **Subscribers** window, click on **Add SQL Server Subscriber** to connect to the subscriber server. This is the server where the data will be replicated:

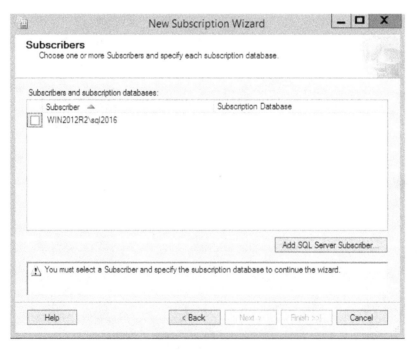

Figure 1.53: The Subscribers window

In the **Connect to Server** window, enter the subscriber server name and credentials. Click on **Connect** to continue:

Figure 1.54: The Connect to Server window

You'll be taken back to the **Subscribers** window:

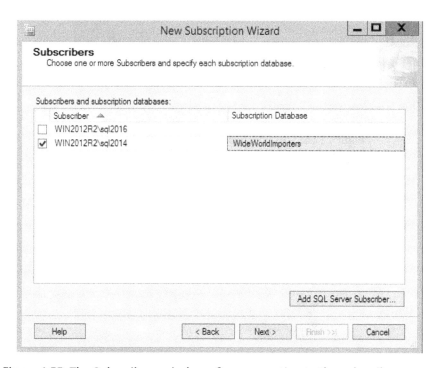

Figure 1.55: The Subscribers window after connecting to the subscriber server

Under **Subscription Database**, select **WideWorldImporters**. Although you can replicate data to a different database name, it's advised that you use the same database name.

If the database doesn't exist at the subscriber, create one.

Click **Next** to continue.

7.   In the **Distribution Agent Security** window, you can specify the distribution agent process account and how the distribution agent connects to the distributor and the subscriber. Select the button with three dots:

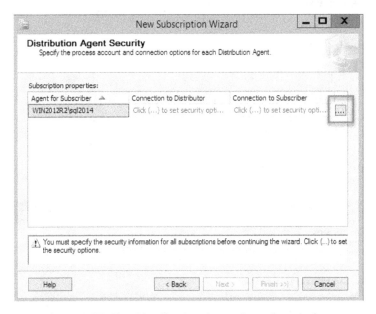

Figure 1.56: The Distribution Agent Security window

This opens the following window:

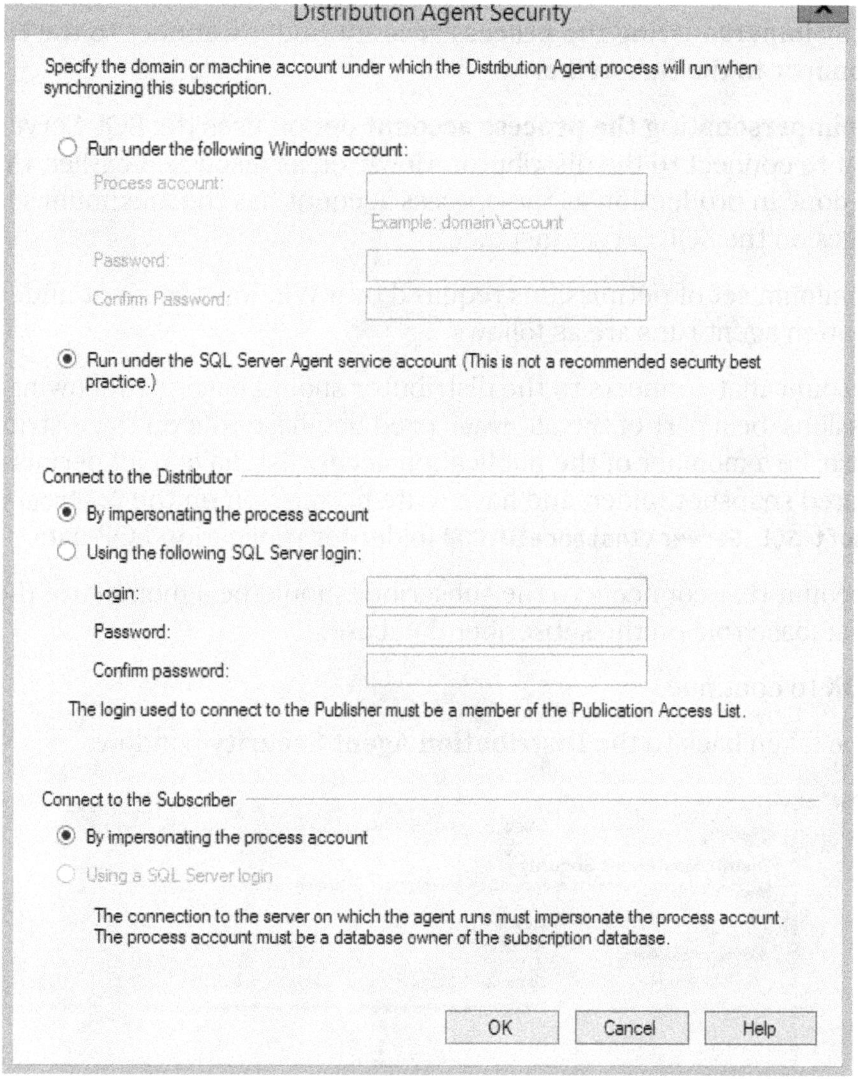

Distribution Agent Security

Specify the domain or machine account under which the Distribution Agent process will run when synchronizing this subscription.

○ Run under the following Windows account:

Process account:

Example: domain\account

Password:

Confirm Password:

⦿ Run under the SQL Server Agent service account (This is not a recommended security best practice.)

Connect to the Distributor

⦿ By impersonating the process account

○ Using the following SQL Server login:

Login:

Password:

Confirm password:

The login used to connect to the Publisher must be a member of the Publication Access List.

Connect to the Subscriber

⦿ By impersonating the process account

○ Using a SQL Server login

The connection to the server on which the agent runs must impersonate the process account. The process account must be a database owner of the subscription database.

| OK | Cancel | Help |

Figure 1.57: The Distribution Agent Security properties window

Select **Run under the SQL Server Agent service account** as the distribution agent process account.

Select **By impersonating the process account** under **Connect to the Distributor** and **Connect to the Subscriber**.

The **By impersonating the process account** option uses the SQL Server service account to connect to the distributor. However, as discussed earlier, this should not be done in production as the process account has the maximum set of privileges on the SQL Server instance.

The minimum set of permissions required by a Windows account under which the distribution agent runs are as follows.

The account that connects to the distributor should have the following permissions: be a part of the **db_owner** fixed database role on the distribution database, be a member of the publication access list, have read permission on the shared snapshot folder, and have write permission on the `C:\Program Files\ Microsoft SQL Server\InstanceID\COM` folder for replication LOB data.

The account that connects to the subscriber should be a member of the **db_owner** fixed database role on the subscriber database.

Click **OK** to continue.

You'll be taken back to the **Distribution Agent Security** window:

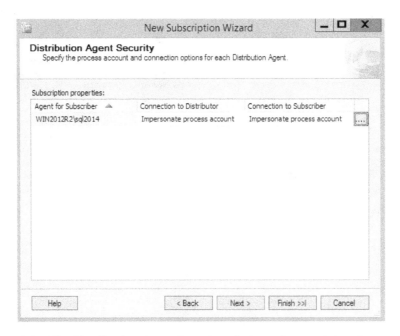

Figure 1.58: The Distribution Agent Security window after applying the settings

Click **Next** to continue.

8. In the **Synchronization Schedule** window, select **Run on demand only** under **Agent Schedule**.

The synchronization schedule specifies the schedule at which the distribution agent will run to replicate the changes:

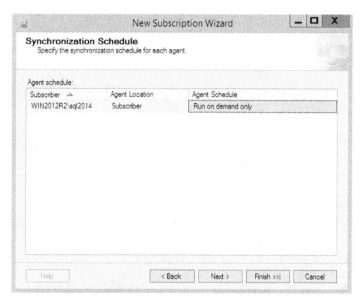

Figure 1.59: The Synchronization Schedule window

Click **Next** to continue.

9. In the **Initialize Subscriptions** window, check the **Initialize** box and then select **At first synchronization** under the **Initialize When** option:

Figure 1.60: The Initialize Subscriptions window

The initialize process applies the snapshot to the subscriber to bring it in sync with the publisher. If the **Initialize** checkbox is left unchecked, the subscription isn't initialized. If it's checked, then there are two options available: **Immediately** and **At first synchronization**. The **Immediately** option will start the initialization as soon as the wizard is complete, and the **At first synchronization** option will start the initialization when the distribution agent runs for the first time.

10. In the **Wizard Actions** window, check the **Create the subscription(s)** option and click on **Next** to continue:

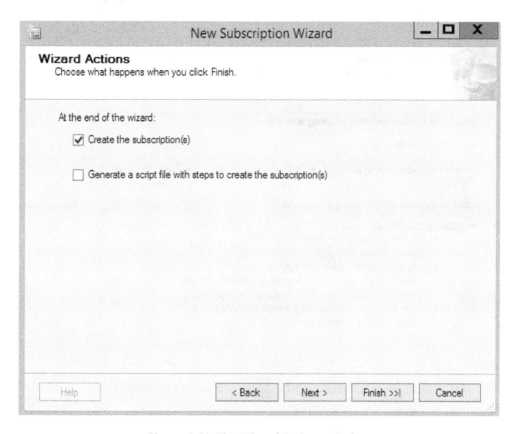

Figure 1.61: The Wizard Actions window

11. In the **Complete the Wizard** window, review the subscription settings and click on **Finish** to create the subscription:

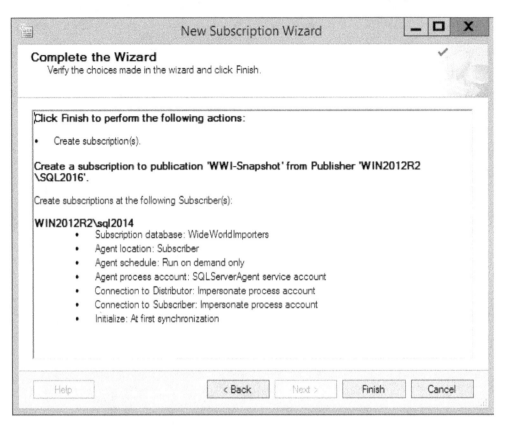

Figure 1.62: The Complete the Wizard window

This ends the wizard. The wizard creates the subscription and the distributor agent job. At this point, the snapshot is not yet applied to the subscriber as we chose to run the distribution agent on demand.

Now, let's look at the objects that were created as part of creating the subscription.

Exercise 4: Exploring the Distribution Database (Metadata)

Let's look at the changes that are made to the distribution tables after creating the subscription.

Open SSMS and connect to the **distribution** database on the **publisher** server. You can execute the following queries to find out how the subscription details are stored:

1. Subscriber information is stored in the **distribution.dbo.subscriber_info** table. Execute the following query to return the subscriber details:

```
SELECT [publisher]
      ,[subscriber]
      ,[type]
      ,[login]
      ,[description]
      ,[security_mode]
FROM [distribution].[dbo].[MSsubscriber_info]
```

You should get a similar output to the following:

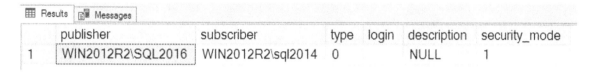

	publisher	subscriber	type	login	description	security_mode
1	WIN2012R2\SQL2016	WIN2012R2\sql2014	0		NULL	1

Figure 1.63: Subscriber information

The publisher and subscriber will be different in your case.

> **Note**
>
> The **MSsubscriber_info** table will be deprecated in a future version of SQL Server.

2. Execute the following query to get all of the information about the articles being replicated:

```
SELECT [publisher_database_id]
      ,[publisher_id]
      ,[publisher_db]
      ,[publication_id]
      ,[article_id]
      ,[subscriber_id]
      ,[subscriber_db]
      ,[subscription_type]
      ,[sync_type]
      ,[status]
      ,[subscription_seqno]
      ,[snapshot_seqno_flag]
      ,[independent_agent]
      ,[subscription_time]
      ,[loopback_detection]
      ,[agent_id]
      ,[update_mode]
      ,[publisher_seqno]
      ,[ss_cplt_seqno]
      ,[nosync_type]
  FROM [distribution].[dbo].[MSsubscriptions]
```

You should get a similar output to the following:

	publisher_database_id	publisher_id	publisher_db	publication_id	article_id	subscriber_id	subscriber_db	subscription_type	sync_type	status	subscription
9	3	0	WideWorldImporters	3	4	-2	virtual	0	1	2	0x0000028
10	3	0	WideWorldImporters	3	5	-2	virtual	0	1	2	0x0000028
11	3	0	WideWorldImporters	3	1	2	WideWorldI...	1	1	0	0x0000028
12	3	0	WideWorldImporters	3	2	2	WideWorldI...	1	1	0	0x0000028
13	3	0	WideWorldImporters	3	3	2	WideWorldI...	1	1	0	0x0000028
14	3	0	WideWorldImporters	3	4	2	WideWorldI...	1	1	0	0x0000028
15	3	0	WideWorldImporters	3	5	2	WideWorldI...	1	1	0	0x0000028

Figure 1.64: Replicated articles

3. Execute the following query to get the distribution run history:

```
SELECT [agent_id]
        ,[runstatus]
        ,[start_time]
        ,[time]
        ,[duration]
        ,[comments]
        ,[xact_seqno]
        ,[current_delivery_rate]
        ,[current_delivery_latency]
        ,[delivered_transactions]
        ,[delivered_commands]
        ,[average_commands]
        ,[delivery_rate]
        ,[delivery_latency]
        ,[total_delivered_commands]
        ,[error_id]
        ,[updateable_row]
        ,[timestamp]
    FROM [distribution].[dbo].[MSdistribution_history]
```

You should get a similar output to the following:

	agent_id	runstatus	start_time	time	duration	comments	xact_seqno
1	5	0	2018-04-29 20:24:26.610	2018-04-29 20:24:26.610	0	Distribution agent for subscription added.	0x00000000000000000000000000000000
2	6	0	2018-04-29 20:24:26.623	2018-04-29 20:24:26.623	0	Distribution agent for subscription added.	0x00000000000000000000000000000000
3	7	0	2018-05-04 13:05:43.243	2018-05-04 13:05:43.243	0	Distribution agent for subscription added.	0x00000000000000000000000000000000

Figure 1.65: Distribution run history

Observe that the duration is 0 as the agent hasn't run until now.

Distribution Agent Job

The distribution agent job that was created at the subscriber (pull subscription) runs the **distribution.exe** process to apply the snapshot that was created by the snapshot agent on the subscriber database.

To view the job, you can open SSMS and connect to the **subscriber** server using Object Explorer. Then, you can expand the **SQL Server Agent** node.

You should see a job similar to what is shown in the following screenshot:

```
⊟ 🖧 SQL Server Agent
  ⊟ ▨ Jobs
       🖳 collection_set_5_collection
       🖳 collection_set_5_upload
       🖳 collection_set_6_collection
       🖳 collection_set_6_upload
       📧 mdw_purge_data_[MDW]
       📧 mdw_purge_data_[MDW_New]
       📧 syspolicy_purge_history
       📧 sysutility_get_cache_tables_data_into_aggregate_tables_daily
       📧 sysutility_get_cache_tables_data_into_aggregate_tables_hourly
       📧 sysutility_get_views_data_into_cache_tables
       📧 WIN2012R2\SQL2016-WideWorldImporters-WWI-Snapshot-WIN2012R2\SQL2014-WideWorldImporters-6EF5B5F1-A6C0-4DFA-BAE2-23BAF9F5FB29
  🐵 Job Activity Monitor
```

Figure 1.66: The distribution agent job

Note

The job name includes the publisher server, published database, and the publication name. This helps in identifying the publication the job is for. The job name also includes the subscriber server and database, as well as the job ID. This helps in identifying the publisher and subscriber when the job is on the distributor server and multiple replications have been configured.

You can double-click on the job to open its **Job Properties** window:

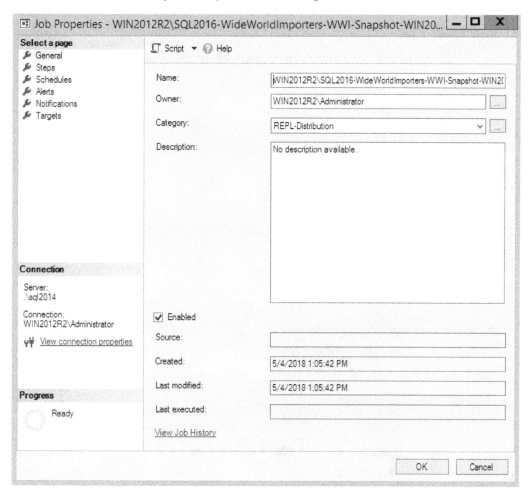

Figure 1.67: The Job Properties window

The **Job Properties** window lists out the general information about the job. You can select the **Steps** page from the **Select a page** pane on the left-hand side of the **Job Properties** window:

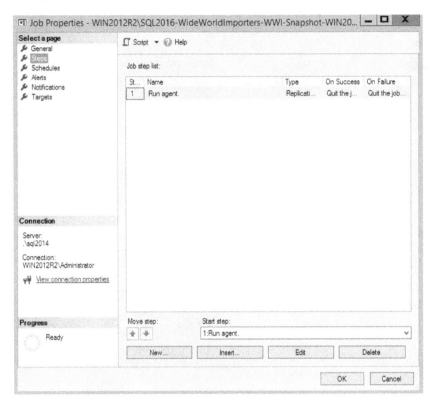

Figure 1.68: The Steps page

This job has only one step. You can double-click on the step name or select **Edit** at the bottom of the window to check the step details:

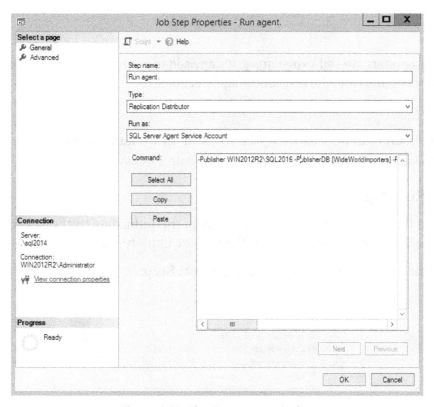

Figure 1.69: The Run agent window

Observe that the **Run agent** step calls the `distributor.exe` executable with a set of parameters.

> **Note**
>
> The parameters are self-explanatory. It's advised to go through the parameters and understand what the distributor agent is doing.

The job wasn't run until now as we opted for **Run on Demand** when configuring the subscription. Close the **Job Properties** window.

Exercise 5: Running the Job

Now, let's run the job and replicate the data from the publisher to the subscriber. To run the job manually, navigate to the job on the Object Explorer, as mentioned earlier:

1. Right-click on the job and select **Start Job at Step**:

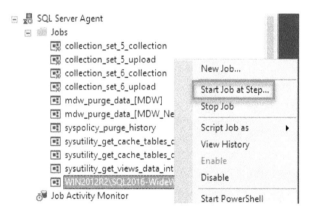

Figure 1.70: The Start Job at Step option

Once the job is successful, you'll get a **Success** message on the **Start Jobs** window, as shown in the following screenshot:

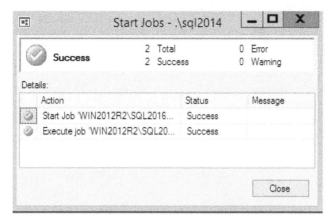

Figure 1.71: The Start Jobs window

Click **Close** to close the **Start Jobs** window.

2. Right-click on the job under the **SQL Server Agent | Jobs** node and select **View History** from the context menu:

Figure 1.72: The View History option

This opens the job's history:

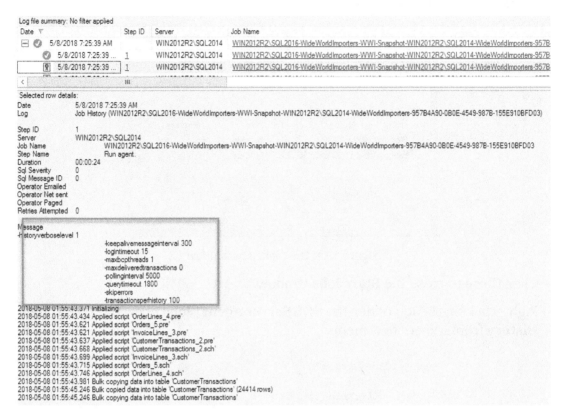

Figure 1.73: The View History window

Observe that the agent has completed successfully. An important thing to observe is the values for the `distribution.exe` parameters (highlighted in red). We'll discuss these later in this lesson.

The job history is also a good place to start troubleshooting snapshot replication. Errors, if any, show up in the job history, and we can then fix these issues based on the errors.

Note

You can also start/stop snapshot view history by right-clicking on **Replication | Local Publications | Publication name** (on publisher server) and selecting **View Snapshot Agent Status**.

Similarly, to start/stop the distribution agent and to view history, right-click on **Replication | Local Subscription | Subscription Name** and then select **View Synchronization Status** from the context menu.

---

3. In the Object Explorer, navigate to the **Databases** node and expand the **WideWorldImporters** database on the **subscriber** server.

    Observe that it now has the replicated tables:

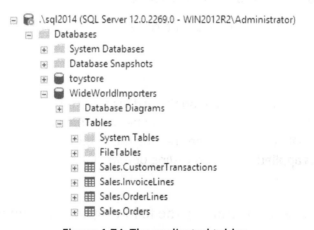

Figure 1.74: The replicated tables

Note

You can query the **MSdistribution_history** table to review the distribution run status.

Exercise 6: Distribution Agent Process (distrib.exe)

distrib.exe is the executable that does the actual work of replicating the data from the publisher to the subscriber:

> **Note**
>
> This section discusses the parameters that are relevant for snapshot replication. For a complete list of parameters, refer to https://docs.microsoft.com/en-us/sql/relational-databases/replication/agents/replication-distribution-agent?view=sql-server-2017.

1. First, let's run the distribution agent from the command line (similar to how we ran **snapshot.exe**) and get familiar with the common parameters. As we have already applied the snapshot, let's modify the **orders** table and generate a new snapshot.

   Execute the following query to update the **orders** table on the **publisher** database:

   ```
   UPDATE [Sales].Orders SET ExpectedDeliveryDate = '2017-12-10' WHERE
       Customerid = 935 and Year(OrderDate)>2016
   ```

   The preceding query will update four rows.

   > **Note**
   >
   > If you perform a count operation on the **orders** table on the publisher and subscriber, the count won't match. Remember that we applied the **year(orderdate)>2016** filter when creating the publication. This also explains why the year filter is applied on the preceding update query.

2. Generate the snapshot by running the following on the command line:

   ```
   REM -- Change the variable values as per your environment
   SET Publisher=WIN2012R2\SQL2016
   SET PublisherDB=WideWorldImporters
   SET Publication=WWI-Snapshot
   ```

```
"C:\Program Files\Microsoft SQL Server\130\COM\SNAPSHOT.EXE" -Publisher
%Publisher% -PublisherDB %PublisherDB% -Distributor %Publisher%
-Publication %Publication% -DistributorSecurityMode 1
```

> **Note**
>
> You can also copy the code from the **C:\Code\Lesson01\snapshot.txt** file.

You should get an output similar to the following screenshot:

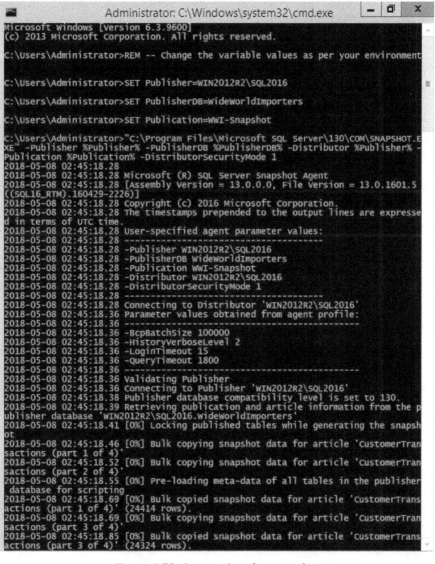

Figure 1.75: Generating the snapshot

You can also verify the new snapshot generation by looking into the snapshot folder for the snapshot files dated to the date you ran the command. Moreover, you can query the **MSsnapshot_history** table in the **distribution** database for the run status.

3. We have a fresh snapshot now. Run **distrib.exe** to apply the snapshot to the **subscriber** database:

    ```
    "C:\Program Files\Microsoft SQL Server\130\COM\DISTRIB.EXE" -Publisher
    WIN2012R2\SQL2016 -PublisherDB [WideWorldImporters] -Publication
    [WWI-Snapshot] -Distributor [WIN2012R2\SQL2016] -SubscriptionType 1
    -Subscriber [WIN2012R2\SQL2014] -SubscriberSecurityMode 1 -SubscriberDB
    [WideWorldImporters]
    ```

    Note

    You can also copy the code from the **C:\Code\Lesson01\distributor.txt** file.

    You'll have to replace the publisher and subscriber SQL Server instance name in this command. If you are replicating a database other than **WideWorldImporters** and have a different publication name, replace those parameters as well.

You should get a similar output to what's shown in the following screenshot:

Figure 1.76: Applying the snapshot

The distribution agent runs and applies the snapshot on the subscriber. Note that the replication agent runs under the security context of the administrator. This is because the command-line console is open as an administrator.

> **Note**
>
> If you run the distributor agent again, you'll get a message saying that there are no replicated transactions available. This is because a snapshot can only be applied once.

4. Now, query the **orders** table at the **subscriber** database to verify the changes made at the **publisher** database:

```
SELECT ExpectedDeliveryDate FROM WideWorldImporters.Sales.Orders
WHERE Customerid = 935 and YEAR(OrderDate)>2016
```

You should get the following output.

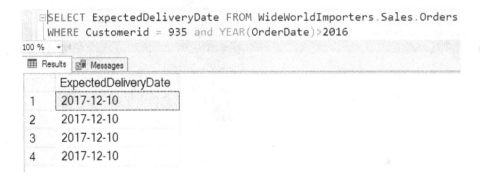

Figure 1.77: Querying the Orders table

The changes are therefore replicated.

Optimizing Snapshot Replication

In this section, we'll discuss optimizing snapshot replication by following best practices and tuning the snapshot and distributor agent parameters.

Snapshot Replication Best Practices

Let's look at a few of the best practices you should consider when working with snapshot replication.

Minimizing Logging at Subscriber

Snapshot replication uses **bcp** to bulk insert data from the publisher to the subscriber database. It's therefore advised to switch to a bulk-logged or simple recovery model to minimize logging and optimize bulk insert performance.

> **Note**
>
> To find out more about recovery models, refer to https://docs.microsoft.com/en-us/sql/relational-databases/backup-restore/recovery-models-sql-server?view=sql-server-2017.

Minimizing Locking

As we discussed earlier, snapshot generation applies exclusive locks on tables until the snapshot is generated. This stops any other applications from accessing the tables, resulting in blocking. You can look at the following options to minimize blocking:

- Change the isolation level to read-committed snapshot to avoid read-write blocking. You'll have to research and find out how the read-committed snapshot will not affect any other application or functionality of your environment.

- Another way to avoid read-write blocking is to selectively use the NoLock query hint. This is not a good practice; however, it's being used in many applications to fix read-write blocking.

- Schedule snapshot generation at off-peak hours when there is less workload on the server.

Replicating Only Required Articles

Understand the business requirements and replicate only what is required. Replicating all articles in a large database will take time and resources for snapshot generation.

Using Pull Subscription

Consider using pull subscription. In pull subscription, the distribution agent is on the subscriber and not on the distributor. This reduces workload on the distributor. Moreover, if the publisher is acting as its own distributor, its workload is reduced.

Compressing the Snapshot Folder

As discussed earlier, there is an option to compress snapshot files in the `.cab` format. This reduces the size of the snapshot files and speeds up network transfer. However, it takes time to compress the files by the snapshot agent and decompress by the distribution agent.

Modifying Agent Parameters

The following table discusses snapshot and distribution agent parameters that can be modified so as to optimize snapshot replication:

Parameter	Agent	Description
OutputVerboseLevel	Snapshot and Distribution	Set to 0 so as to print only error messages.
HistoryVerboseLevel	Snapshot and Distribution	Set to 1. Previous history messages are updated with the new status. No new row inserted for a new status message.
MaxBcpThreads	Snapshot and Distribution	Number of bcp operations that are performed in parallel. The default is 1—consider increasing it to 2. You can further test it with a higher number to find out the number you get the optimal speed.
UseInprocLoader	Distribution	When specified, the distribution agent uses the bulk insert command when applying the commands to the subscriber. This is deprecated as it's not compatible with the XML data type. However, it can be used if you don't have a XML data type in any of the replicated tables.

Figure 1.78: The Agent Parameters table

Activity 1: Troubleshooting Snapshot Replication

In this activity, we'll troubleshoot snapshot replication.

You have been asked to set up snapshot replication for the **WideWorldImporters** database. The **subscriber** database will be used to run daily reports. You configured the replication so that the initial snapshot is applied successfully. You schedule it to occur daily at 12:00 AM, as directed by the business. However, the next day you are informed that the data isn't synced.

In this activity, you'll find and fix the issue.

Setup Steps

To simulate the error, follow these steps:

1. Use the existing snapshot replication that was configured in this lesson. You do not need to configure it again. If you didn't configure it, then follow the previous exercises to configure the snapshot replication.

2. Open a PowerShell console and run the following PowerShell script on the **subscriber** database:

   ```
   C:\Code\Lesson01\1_Activity1B.ps1 -SubscriberServer .\sql2014
   -SubscriberDB WideWorldImporters -SQLUserName sa -SQLUserPassword sql@2014
   ```

   Modify the parameters as per your environment before running the script.

Generating a New Snapshot

Follow these steps to generate a new snapshot:

1. Open SQL Server Management Studio and connect to the **publisher** server in the Object Explorer.

2. Expand **Replication | Local Publication**. Right-click on the **[WideWorldImporters]:WWI-Snapshot** publication and select **View Snapshot Agent Status** from the context menu:

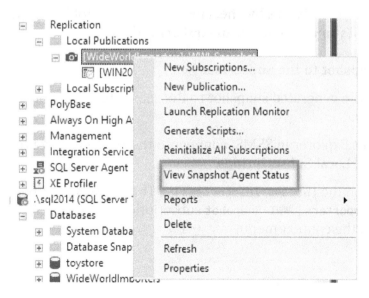

Figure 1.79: The View Snapshot Agent Status option

3. In the **View Snapshot Agent Status** window, select **Start** to generate a new snapshot. This is another way to generate the snapshot:

Figure 1.80: The View Snapshot Agent Status window

Once the snapshot is generated, you'll get a success message, as shown in the preceding screenshot.

You can further verify this by checking the snapshot folder or querying the `MSsnapshot_history` table in the `distribution` database.

Applying the Snapshot to the Subscriber

You'll now apply the generated snapshot to the subscriber. To apply the snapshot, follow these steps:

1. In the Object Explorer in SSMS, connect to the **subscriber** server. Expand **Replication | Local Subscriptions**.

2. Right-click on the `[WideWorldImporters]` - `[WIN2012R2\SQL2016]`. `[WideWorldImporters]:WWI-Snapshot` subscription and select **View Synchronization Status** from the context menu.

This is another way to run the distributor agent:

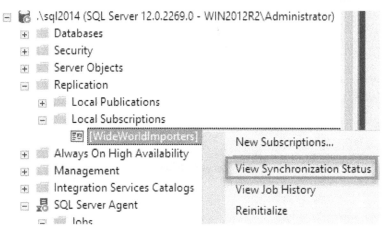

Figure 1.81: The View Synchronization Status option

3. In the **View Synchronization Status** window, select **Start** to start the distributor agent. The agent will error out and the snapshot won't be applied to the subscriber:

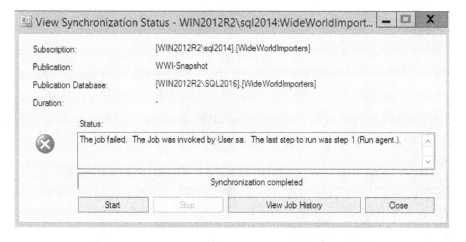

Figure 1.82: The View Synchronization Status window

4. To find out what the error is, click on **View Job History** in the **View Synchronization Status** window.

This will open the SQL Server agent job history for the distributor job. You should see the following error in the agent history:

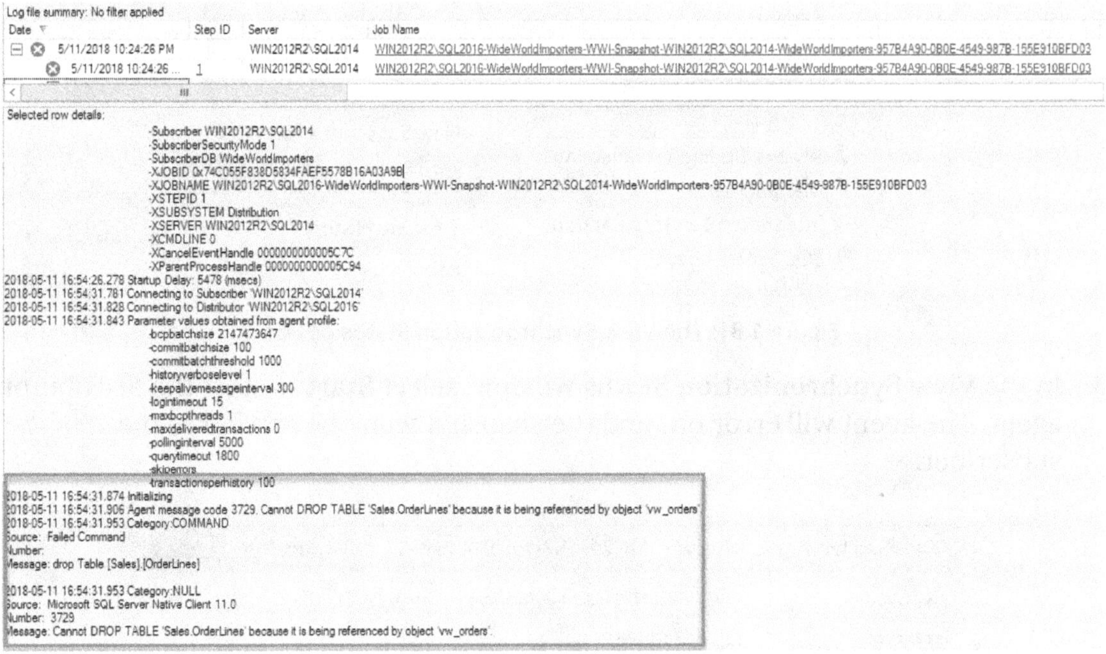

Figure 1.83: The job history

The distribution agent fails to drop the `Sales.Orders` and `Sales.Orderlines` tables because they are referenced by a view, `vw_orders`.

An easy solution to this problem is to drop the view at the `subscriber` database. However, the business tells you that the view can't be dropped as it's being used by the daily report.

Another solution to this problem is to modify the publication properties to include pre- and post-snapshot scripts so that you can delete and create the view, respectively.

> **Note**
>
> If you wish to apply the current snapshot, you will have to drop the view on the subscriber, apply the snapshot, and then create the view.

> The solution for this activity can be found on page 438.

Summary

In this lesson, we have learned about high availability and disaster recovery concepts, as well as the terminology and the different solutions available in SQL Server to achieve HA and DR. We have discussed the importance of RTO and RPO and the role they play in selecting an HA and DR strategy or solution.

We have also learned about replication concepts and terminology, and different types of replications that are available in SQL Server. We looked at how to configure and troubleshoot snapshot replication.

In the next lesson, we'll learn about transactional replication.

Transactional Replication

Learning Objectives

By the end of this lesson, you will be able to:

- Configure and troubleshoot transactional replication
- Configure Azure SQL Database as a subscriber
- Configure and troubleshoot peer-to-peer transactional replication

This lesson will teach us how to configure transactional replication and P2P transactional replication. We will also see how to troubleshoot, monitor, and optimize the same.

Introduction

In the previous lesson, we were introduced to replication and its types. We also took a deep dive into how to configure snapshot replication. In this lesson, we will continue our tour of replication and look at transactional replication and peer-to-peer transactional replication.

This lesson teaches you how to configure, troubleshoot, monitor, and optimize transactional replication. Transactional replication is the most common type of replication used to synchronize data between two databases. It is often used to load-balance read and write operations and is also a cost-effective solution for high availability.

Understanding Transactional Replication

In this section, we'll look at how transactional replication works. The following diagram describes how transactional replication works:

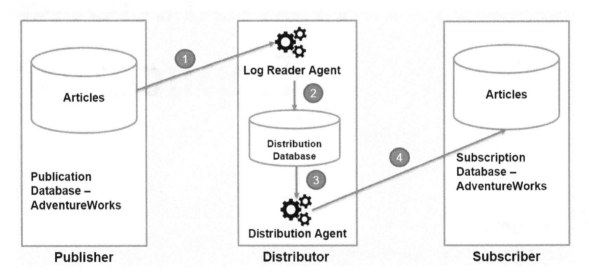

Figure 2.1: Transactional replication example

This diagram shows the `AdventureWorks` database being replicated using transactional replication. Once transactional replication is configured, the snapshot agent, log reader agent, and distribution agent are created as part of the replication. The agents then work together, as described here, to replicate the transactions.

The snapshot agent is used once to initialize the subscriber database schema with that of the publisher. This isn't shown in the diagram, however, it's the first thing that happens when the transactional replication starts.

The subscriber database can be initialized using the publisher database backup, which is covered later in this lesson.

Once initialized, the transactions are replicated as follows:

- **Steps 1 and 2**: The log reader agent continuously scans for committed transactions in the publisher database transaction log and inserts the transactions to be replicated into the distribution database.

  The log reader agent is at the distributor or at the publisher if the publisher acts as its own distributor.

- **Steps 3 and 4**: The distribution agent reads the transactions from the distribution database and applies them to the subscriber. The distribution agent is at the distributor if it's a push subscription and at the subscriber if it's a pull subscription.

Configuring Transactional Replication

We'll now look at how to configure or set up transactional replication between two databases using T-SQL.

Exercise 7: Creating the Publication

The first step in configuring replication is to create the publication. Follow these steps to create a publication for transactional replication:

1. Navigate to **C:\Code\Lesson02\Transactional** and open **1_CreatePublication.sql** in SQL Server Management Studio.

2. In SSMS, from the top menu, select **Query** and then select **SQLCMD**. This changes the mode of the **1_CreatePublication.sql** query to SQLCMD from SQL.

3. Modify the parameters in the script (shown in the following screenshot) as per your environment:

```
1_CreatePublication...Administrator (51))  ⊅ ✕
        :setvar Publisher "WIN2012R2\SQL2016"
        :setvar Subscriber "WIN2012R2\SQL2014"
        :setvar Distributor "WIN2012R2\SQL2016"
        :setvar DatabaseName "AdventureWorks"
        :setvar PublicationName "AdventureWorks-Tran_Pub"
```

Figure 2.2: Parameters in creating a publication

The preceding screenshot shows the parameters being used in the script. The parameters are self-explanatory. The publisher and distributor are the same, as the publisher acts as its own distributor.

4. To run the script and create the publication, change the parameters as specified earlier and press F5 or click on **Execute** in the top menu.

You should get the following output:

```
Messages
Connecting to WIN2012R2\SQL2016...
The replication option 'publish' of database 'AdventureWorks' has already been set to true.
Job 'WIN2012R2\SQL2016-AdventureWorks-17' started successfully.
Starting Snapshot Agent WIN2012R2\SQL2016-AdventureWorks-AdventureWorks-Tran_Pub-17....
Job 'WIN2012R2\SQL2016-AdventureWorks-AdventureWorks-Tran_Pub-17' started successfully.
Disconnecting connection from WIN2012R2\SQL2016...
```

Figure 2.3: Output of creating the publication

This creates three objects: the publication named **AdventureWorks-Trans_Pub**, the log reader agent job named **WIN2012R2\SQL2016-AdventureWorks-17**, and the snapshot agent job named **WIN2012R2\SQL2016-AdventureWorks-AdventureWorks-Tran_Pub-17**.

This completes this exercise.

Now, we'll dissect different parts of the script and understand what different procedures in the script do. You are, however, supposed to run the script immediately after modifying the parameters to create the publication.

The following command connects to the publisher server and changes the database context to the publisher database, that is, **AdventureWorks**:

```
-- connect to the publisher and set replication options
:CONNECT $(Publisher)
USE "$(DatabaseName)"
```

> **Note**
>
> You can also copy the code from the **Code\Lesson02\Transactional\1_CreatePublication.sql** file.

The following command enables the **AdventureWorks** database for publication:

```
-- Enable database for publication
EXEC sp_replicationdboption
```

```
@dbname = "$(DatabaseName)",

@optname = N'publish',

@value = N'true'
```

> **Note**
>
> You can also copy the code from the **Code\Lesson02\Transactional\1_CreatePublication.sql** file.

The **sp_replicationdboption** procedure is a system procedure that enables or disables the publication, as specified by the **@optname** parameter.

The **publish** option specifies that the database can be used for transactional and snapshot publication.

> **Note**
>
> For details on the procedure and other options, go to https://docs.microsoft.com/en-us/sql/relational-databases/system-stored-procedures/sp-replicationdboption-transact-sql?view=sql-server-2017.

The following command creates the log reader agent job:

```
-- Create the log reader agent
-- If this isn't specified, log reader agent is implicitly created
-- by the sp_addpublication procedure
EXEC sp_addlogreader_agent
  @job_login = NULL,
  @job_password = NULL,
  @publisher_security_mode = 1;
GO
```

> **Note**
>
> You can also copy the code from the **Code\Lesson02\Transactional\1_CreatePublication.sql** file.

The **sp_addlogreader_agent** procedure creates the SQL Server agent job that runs the log reader agent. The **@job_login** and **@job_password** parameters are the Windows username and password under which the log reader agent process runs. When **NULL**, the log reader process runs under the security context of the SQL Server agent service account.

@publisher_security_mode specifies the security mode used by the log reader agent to connect to the publisher. **1** is for Windows authentication and **0** for SQL Server authentication.

In this case, the log reader agent connects to the publisher by impersonating the SQL Server agent service account.

> **Note**
>
> For details on the procedure and other options, go to https://docs.microsoft.com/en-us/sql/relational-databases/system-stored-procedures/sp-addlogreader-agent-transact-sql?view=sql-server-2017.

The following command creates the publication:

```
-- Create publication
EXEC sp_addpublication
  @publication = "$(PublicationName)",
  @description =
N'Transactional publication of database ''AdventureWorks'' from Publisher
''WIN2012R2\SQL2016''.'
,
@sync_method = N'concurrent',
@retention = 0,
@allow_push = N'true',
@allow_pull = N'true',
@snapshot_in_defaultfolder = N'true',
@repl_freq = N'continuous',
@status = N'active',
@independent_agent = N'true',
```

```
@immediate_sync = N'true',

@replicate_ddl = 1
```

> **Note**
>
> You can also copy the code from the **Code\Lesson02\Transactional\1_ CreatePublication.sql** file.

The **sp_addpublication** procedure creates a new publication for the transactional replication. The procedure has a lot of parameters; however, a description of the important parameters is provided here:

- **@publication**: The name of the publication to be created.

- **@description**: The optional description of the publication.

- **@sync_method**: This is the synchronization mode for the snapshot agent when generating the snapshot. A value of **concurrent** means that when producing .**bcp** files, the shared lock isn't taken on tables. This option is only available for transactional replication.

- **@retention**: This is the retention period of the subscriber. If the subscriber isn't active for the specified retention period, it's expired and should be reinitialized to activate again. A value of **0** specifies that the subscription never expires.

- **@allow_push**: This specifies whether or not a push subscription can be created for the publication.

- **@allow_pull**: This specifies whether or not a pull subscription can be created for the publication.

- **@snapshot_in_defaultfolder**: This specifies whether or not the snapshot files are stored in the default folder. If not, then the snapshot files are stored at the location specified by the **@alt_snapshot_folder** parameter.

- **@repl_freq**: This defines the type of replication frequency, either **continuous** or **scheduled**. A value of **continuous** specifies that the log reader agent runs continuously and transmits the logs as and when captured; **scheduled** specifies that the logs are provided as per the given schedule.

- **@status**: This defines whether or not the publication data is available to the subscriber immediately. A value of **active** means that the publication data is available to subscribers immediately as they subscribe and a value of **inactive** means that the data isn't available when the publication is created.

- **@independent_agent**: This specifies if the publication uses a standalone distribution agent or a shared distribution agent. A value of **false** specifies the shared distribution agent.

- **@immediate_sync**: This specifies whether or not the snapshot is generated each time the snapshot agent runs. A value of **true** means that the snapshot is generated each time the snapshot agent is started. New subscriptions that are created after the snapshot agent runs receive the latest snapshot generated or the last snapshot generated by the snapshot agent.

- **@replicate_ddl**: This specifies whether or not the schema changes are replicated. A value of **1** means that the schema changes are replicated.

> **Note**
>
> For details on the procedure and other options, go to https://docs.microsoft.com/en-us/sql/relational-databases/system-stored-procedures/sp-addpublication-transact-sql?view=sql-server-2017.

The following command adds the snapshot agent for the publication:

```
-- Create the snapshot agent
EXEC sp_addpublication_snapshot
  @publication = "$(PublicationName)",
  @frequency_type = 1,
  @frequency_interval = 1,
  @frequency_relative_interval = 1,
  @frequency_recurrence_factor = 0,
  @frequency_subday = 8,
  @frequency_subday_interval = 1,
  @active_start_time_of_day = 0,
  @active_end_time_of_day = 235959,
  @active_start_date = 0,
  @active_end_date = 0,
  @job_login = NULL,
```

```
@job_password = NULL,
@publisher_security_mode = 1
```

> **Note**
>
> You can also copy the code from the **Code\Lesson02\Transactional\1_CreatePublication.sql** file.

The **sp_addpublication_snapshot** procedure creates the snapshot agent job that is used to initialize the transactional replication. The important parameters for this procedure are as follows:

- **@publication**: The name of the publication the snapshot agent is created for.

- **@frequency_type**: The frequency with which the snapshot is executed. The value **1** specifies that the snapshot agent is only run once.

- **@job_login** and **@job_password**: These are the Windows username and password under which the snapshot agent process runs. When **NULL**, the snapshot agent process runs under the security context of the SQL Server agent service account.

- **@publisher_security_mode**: This specifies the security mode used by the snapshot agent to connect to the publisher; **1** is for Windows authentication and **0** is for SQL Server authentication.

In this case, the snapshot agent connects to the publisher by impersonating the SQL Server agent service account.

> **Note**
>
> For details on the procedure and other options, go to https://docs.microsoft.com/en-us/sql/relational-databases/system-stored-procedures/sp-addpublication-snapshot-transact-sql?view=sql-server-2017.

The following command adds an article to the publication:

```
EXEC sp_addarticle
    @publication = "$(PublicationName)",
    @article = N'Address',
    @source_owner = N'Person',
```

```
@source_object = N'Address',
@type = N'logbased',
@description = NULL,
@creation_script = NULL,
@pre_creation_cmd = N'drop',
@schema_option = 0x000000000803509F,
@identityrangemanagementoption = N'manual',
@destination_table = N'Address',
@destination_owner = N'Person',
@vertical_partition = N'false',
@ins_cmd = N'CALL sp_MSins_PersonAddress',
@del_cmd = N'CALL sp_MSdel_PersonAddress',
@upd_cmd = N'SCALL sp_MSupd_PersonAddress'
```

> **Note**
>
> You can also copy the code from the **Code\Lesson02\Transactional\1_
> CreatePublication.sql** file.

The **sp_addarticle** procedure adds a table called **Address** to the publication. One procedure call adds a single article. The script here shows only one article addition for the sake of explanation and brevity. The script, however, has multiple **sp_addarticle** calls to add other articles to the publication.

> **Note**
>
> Transactional replication requires a table to have a primary key constraint if it is to be replicated.

The following are the important parameters:

- **@publication**: This is the name of the publication.

- **@article**: This is the name of the article.

- **@source_owner**: This is the schema the article belongs to at the publisher database.

- **@source_object**: This is the name of the article at the publisher database.

- **@type**: This is the article type. There are multiple article types available. The default is **logbased**.

- **@description**: This is an optional description of the article.

- **@creation_script**: This is the full path of the optional article creation script.

- **@pre_creation_cmd**: This specifies the action to be taken if the article already exists at the subscriber when applying the initial snapshot. The default action is to drop the article at the subscriber.

- **@schema_option**: This is a bitmask that defines what schema generation options are applicable to the article.

- **@identityrangemanagementoption**: This specifies how identity columns are being handled in replication. A value of **manual** specifies that the identity column is marked as *Not for Replication* and is therefore not replicated to the subscriber.

- **@destination_table** and **@destination_owner**: This is the article schema and the article name at the subscriber database.

- **@vertical_partition**: This specifies whether or not to filter out columns from the table article. A value of **false** specifies that no column filtering is applied and that all columns are replicated. A value of **true** excludes all columns except the primary key. The columns to be replicated are then specified by the procedure **sp_articlecolumn**.

- **@ins_cmd**: This specifies the command to be used when replicating inserts. The default is to call the **sp_MSins_tablename** procedure. A custom stored procedure can also be used to replicate inserts.

- **@del_cmd**: This specifies the command to be used when replicating deletes. The default is to call the **sp_MSdel_tablename** procedure. A custom stored procedure can also be used to replicate deletes.

- **@upd_cmd**: This specifies the command to be used when replicating updates. The default is to call the **sp_MSupd_tablename** procedure. A custom stored procedure can also be used to replicate updates.

The **sp_Msins_tablename**, **sp_Msdel_tablename**, and **sp_Msupd_tablename** procedures are created for each table being replicated, as part of the replication setup, automatically. The procedures can also be modified if required.

> **Note**
>
> For details on the procedure and other options, go to https://docs.microsoft.com/en-us/sql/relational-databases/system-stored-procedures/sp-addarticle-transact-sql?view=sql-server-2017.
>
>
> Check the **@schemaoptions**, **@pre_creation_cmd**, and **@type** parameter values.

The following command starts the snapshot agent so as to generate the snapshot. The snapshot is applied to the subscribers to initialize the subscriber database:

```
DECLARE @jobname NVARCHAR(200)

SELECT @jobname=name FROM [distribution].[dbo].[MSsnapshot_agents]

WHERE [publication]='$(PublicationName)' AND [publisher_db]='$(DatabaseName)'


Print 'Starting Snapshot Agent ' + @jobname + '....'

-- Start the snapshot agent to generate the snapshot

-- The snapshot is picked up and applied to the subscriber by the
distribution agent

EXECUTE msdb.dbo.sp_start_job @job_name=@jobname
```

> **Note**
>
> You can also copy the code from the **Code\Lesson02\Transactional\1_CreatePublication.sql** file.

This command gets the name of the snapshot agent job that was created earlier in the script from the **MSsnapshot_agents** table in the distribution database. It then starts the job by calling the **sp_start_job** system-stored procedure in the **msdb** database.

> **Note**
>
> You can verify the status of the snapshot agent job so as to make sure that the job ran successfully and that the database snapshot was created at the provided snapshot share folder.

This completes the create publication script explanation.

You can now verify the following:

- The jobs, by going to the **SQL Server Agent | Jobs** node in SSMS.

- The publication, by going to the **Replication | Local Publication** node.

- The snapshot generated in the default snapshot agent folder. To find the snapshot folder, right-click the **Replication** node and select **Distributor Properties**.

  The job name will be different in your case. The number at the end of the job name is incremented every time a new distribution job is created.

The next step is to create the subscription for the newly created transactional publication.

Exercise 8: Creating the Subscription

In this exercise, we'll create a subscription for the transactional publication that we created earlier. To create a subscription, connect to a different SQL Server instance.

Follow these steps to create a subscription for transactional replication:

1. Navigate to **C:\Code\Lesson02\Transactional** and open **2_CreateSubscription.sql** in SQL Server Management Studio.

2. In SSMS, from the top menu, select **Query** and then select **SQLCMD**. This changes the mode of the **2_CreateSubscription.sql** query to SQLCMD from SQL.

3. Modify the parameters in the script, as per your environment:

2_CreateSubscriptio...Administrator (51)) ⊕ ✕

```
-----------------BEGIN: Script to be run at Publisher 'WIN2012R
:setvar Publisher "WIN2012R2\SQL2016"
:setvar Subscriber "WIN2012R2\SQL2014"
:setvar Distributor "WIN2012R2\SQL2016"
:setvar DatabaseName "AdventureWorks"
:setvar PublicationName "AdventureWorks-Tran_Pub"
```

Figure 2.4: Parameters in creating the subscription

The **Publisher**, **Distributor**, **DatabaseName**, and **PublicationName** parameters should be the ones that were used in *Exercise 1: Creating a Publication*.

You will need to replace the **Subscriber** value with your subscriber's SQL Server instance name.

4. Before you run the script, make sure that you are in SQLCMD mode and the **AdventureWorks** database exists at the subscriber instance. Run the script by pressing F5 or clicking on **Execute** in the top menu.

You should get the following output after successful execution of the script:

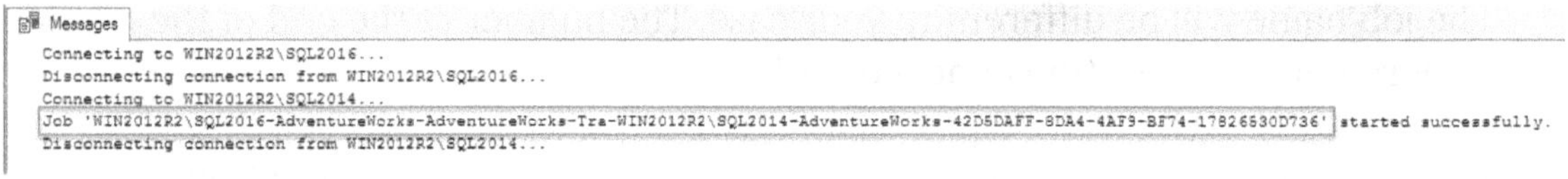

```
Messages
Connecting to WIN2012R2\SQL2016...
Disconnecting connection from WIN2012R2\SQL2016...
Connecting to WIN2012R2\SQL2014...
Job 'WIN2012R2\SQL2016-AdventureWorks-AdventureWorks-Tra-WIN2012R2\SQL2014-AdventureWorks-42D5DAFF-8DA4-4AF9-BF74-17826630D736' started successfully.
Disconnecting connection from WIN2012R2\SQL2014...
```

Figure 2.5: Output of creating the subscription

The script creates the subscription and the distribution pull agent. At this point, you have successfully configured transactional replication.

This completes this exercise.

Now, we'll dissect different parts of the script and understand what the different procedures in the script do. You are, however, supposed to run the script at once after modifying the parameters to create the subscription.

The following command connects to the publisher and adds the subscriber at the publisher:

```
-- Connect to the publisher
:CONNECT $(Publisher)


USE $(DatabaseName)


-- Add subscription at publisher
EXEC sp_addsubscription
  @publication = "$(PublicationName)",
  @subscriber = "$(Subscriber)",
  @destination_db = $(DatabaseName),
  @sync_type = N'Automatic',
  @subscription_type = N'pull',
  @update_mode = N'read only'
```

> **Note**
>
> You can also copy the code from the **Code\Lesson02\Transactional\2_ CreateSubscription.sql** file.

The **sp_addsubscription** procedure adds the subscription at the publisher server. This tells the publisher that the given subscriber has subscribed for a particular publication and sets the subscription properties.

The following are the important parameters and their descriptions:

- **@sync_type**: This specifies the synchronization type. The default is **Automatic**, which means that the schema and data for the articles is first applied to the subscriber database.

- **@subscription_type**: This is the type of subscription: push or pull.

- **@update_mode**: This specifies whether or not the changes at the subscriber are applied to the publisher. A value of **read only** specifies that changes at the subscriber are not applied to the publisher.

> **Note**
>
> For details on the procedure and other options, go to https://docs.microsoft.com/en-us/sql/relational-databases/system-stored-procedures/sp-addsubscription-transact-sql?view=sql-server-2017.
>
> Check the other values that are available for the **@sync_type** and **@update_mode** parameters. Replication also supports memory-optimized tables. The **@memory_optimized** parameter, when set to **1**, indicates that the subscription contains memory-optimized tables. You can read more about memory-optimized tables here: https://docs.microsoft.com/en-us/sql/relational-databases/in-memory-oltp/in-memory-oltp-in-memory-optimization?view=sql-server-2017.

The following query connects to the subscriber and creates the subscription:

```
:CONNECT $(Subscriber)


USE $(DatabaseName)


-- Create subscription at the subscriber
EXEC sp_addpullsubscription
   @publisher = "$(Publisher)",
   @publication = "$(PublicationName)",
   @publisher_db = $(DatabaseName),
   @independent_agent = N'True',
   @subscription_type = N'pull',
   @description = N'',
```

```
@update_mode = N'read only',
@immediate_sync = 1
```

> **Note**
>
> You can also copy the code from the **Code\Lesson02\Transactional\2_ CreateSubscription.sql** file.

The **sp_addpullsubscription** procedure creates a new subscription for the given publication. The important parameters and their descriptions are given here:

- **@independent_agent**: This is the property of the publisher and should have the same value as given when creating the publication. Check the explanation in *Exercise 1: Creating a Publication.*

- **@immediate_sync**: This too is the property of the publisher and should have the same value as given when creating the publication. Check the explanation in *Exercise 1: Creating a Publication.*

The following query creates the distribution agent at the subscriber:

```
EXEC sp_addpullsubscription_agent
    @publisher = "$(Publisher)",
    @publisher_db = $(DatabaseName),
    @publication = "$(PublicationName)",
    @distributor = "$(Distributor)",
    @distributor_security_mode = 1,
    @distributor_login = N'',
    @distributor_password = NULL,
    @frequency_type = 64,
    @frequency_interval = 0,
    @frequency_relative_interval = 0,
    @frequency_recurrence_factor = 0,
    @frequency_subday = 0,
    @frequency_subday_interval = 0,
    @active_start_time_of_day = 0,
    @active_end_time_of_day = 235959,
```

```
@active_start_date = 20180515,

@active_end_date = 99991231,

@job_login = NULL,

@job_password = NULL,

@publication_type = 0
```

The **sp_addpullsubscription_agent** procedure creates a SQL Server agent job that runs the distribution agent at the subscriber instance. An explanation of the important parameters is given here:

- **@distributor_security_mode**: This specifies the security method to use when connecting to the distributor. **1** means Windows authentication and **0** refers to SQL Server authentication. If you set it to **0**, you need to specify the values for the **@distributor_login** and **@distributor_password** parameters.

- **@publication_type**: This specifies the type of replication: **0** is transactional, **1** is snapshot, and **2** is merge replication.

All other parameters with **frequency** as the prefix define the schedule of the distribution agent. The **@frequency_type** parameter defines the schedule's frequency, for example, daily, weekly, or monthly. A value of **64** means that the agent runs continuously.

> **Note**
>
> For details on the procedure and other options, go to https://docs.microsoft.com/en-us/sql/relational-databases/system-stored-procedures/sp-addpullsubscription-agent-transact-sql?view=sql-server-2017.

This completes the script.

If you now look under the **Replication | Local Publications** node, you will see the new publication. Expand the publication and you will see all of the subscribers to that publication.

At the publisher:

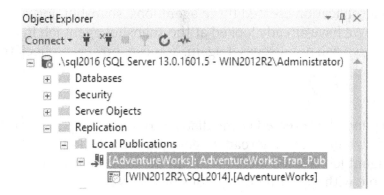

Figure 2.6: The new publication at the publisher

At the subscriber:

Figure 2.7: The new subscription at the subscriber

Another quick way to verify replication is to navigate to the subscriber database and verify whether the articles have been created. If they have, then the snapshot agent ran successfully and has initialized the subscriber database.

To verify the continuous sync, make a transaction at the publisher database by deleting/updating/inserting a row in the replicated article. Check for the changes at the subscriber. If the changes are replicated, the log reader agent and distribution agent are working properly.

Another way is to look at the different transactional replication agents' job history.

Transactional Replication Agents

The transactional replication created three agent jobs: snapshot, log reader, and distributor agent. We have already looked at the snapshot agent job in the previous lesson. Therefore, we will not discuss it again. You can, however, check the agent job properties.

Log Reader Agent

The log reader agent job is created at the distributor or at the publisher if the publisher acts as its own distributor. The log reader agent job runs the log reader process. The log reader agent job is just a medium to run the log reader executable and calls the **logread.exe** file with the parameter values provided by us when configuring the replication.

It's advised to use the SQL Server agent job to run the log reader executable. However, it can be run through a different application as well. For example, **logread.exe** can be run from the command prompt or scheduled in Windows scheduler.

The log reader process (**logread.exe**) is an executable that reads the transaction logs of each database that is configured for transactional replication and inserts the transactions marked for replication into the distribution database.

First, let's explore the log reader agent job. You can connect to the publisher server in the Object Explorer and then go to **SQL Server Agent | Jobs**. Under the jobs, look out for the job with the following naming convention: **[Publisher Server]-[Published database]-[Log Reader Agent ID]**.

The log reader agent ID is from the **MSlogreader_agents** table in the distribution database (at publisher).

You can also get the name from the **PublicationName** parameter in *Exercise 1: Creating a Publication*:

```
🗎 Messages
    Connecting to WIN2012R2\SQL2016...
    The replication option 'publish' of database 'AdventureWorks' has already been set to true.
    Job 'WIN2012R2\SQL2016-AdventureWorks-17' started successfully.
    Starting Snapshot Agent WIN2012R2\SQL2016-AdventureWorks-AdventureWorks-Tran_Pub-17....
    Job 'WIN2012R2\SQL2016-AdventureWorks-AdventureWorks-Tran_Pub-17' started successfully.
    Disconnecting connection from WIN2012R2\SQL2016...
```

Figure 2.8: Our publication job name

The job name will differ on your system:

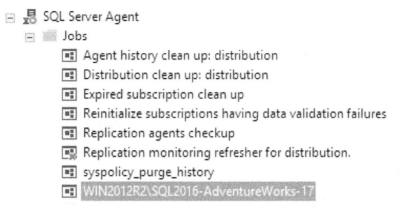

Figure 2.9: Selecting the job

You can double-click on the job to open its properties. In the **Job Properties** window, you can select the **Steps** page from the left-hand pane:

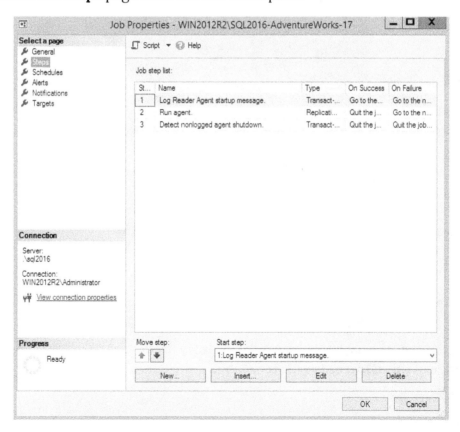

Figure 2.10: The Job Properties window

There are three steps in the job. These are similar to the steps in the snapshot agent job:

- **Step 1 – Log Reader Agent startup message**: You can double-click on step **1** to open its properties:

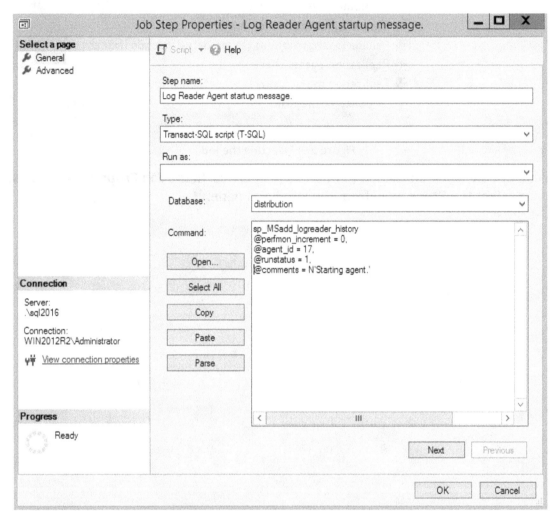

Figure 2.11: The Job Properties window – Step 1

This step runs the **sp_MSadd_logreader_history** procedure to log the startup message in the **MSlogreader_history** table in the distribution database.

- **Step 2 - Run agent**: In the **Job Step Properties** window, you can click on **Next** to navigate to the properties of step **2**:

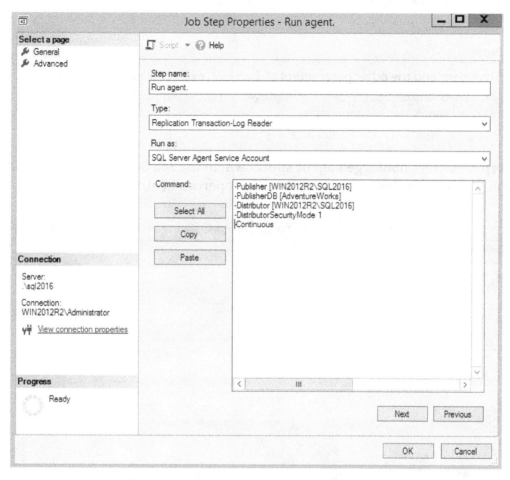

Figure 2.12: The Job Properties window – Step 2

This step calls the **logread.exe** executable (type: **Replication Transaction-Log Reader**) with the parameters specified under the **Command** section. Observe that the parameter values are the same as the ones we provided when configuring the replication.

Note

Know that **logread.exe** can be run separately from the command line by giving the same parameters as given in the log reader agent job. This is similar to running the snapshot agent from the command prompt as we did in *Lesson 1, Getting Started with SQL Server HA and DR*.

`logread.exe` accepts a lot more parameters than what's specified in the job. However, for all the parameters that aren't specified, the default value is considered. The important parameters are covered later in this book.

> **Note**
>
> To understand the other parameters of `logread.exe`, refer to https://docs. microsoft.com/en-us/sql/relational-databases/replication/agents/replication-log-reader-agent?view=sql-server-2017.

- **Step 3 - Detect nonlogged agent shutdown**: In the **Job Step Properties** window, you can click on **Next** to navigate to the properties of step **3**:

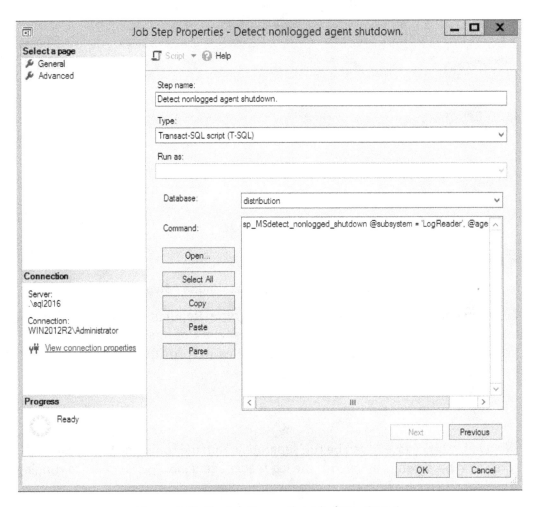

Figure 2.13: The Job Properties window – Step 3

This step uses the system-stored procedure **sp_MSdetect_nonlogged_shutdown** to check if the agent is shut down without logging any message to the **MSlogreader_ history** table. It then checks and logs a relevant message for the agent being shut down to the **MSlogreader_history** table.

Distributor Agent

The distributor agent applies the transactions from the distribution database to the subscriber. The distributor agent job runs the **distrib.exe** executable process with the parameter values we provided when configuring the replication.

Let's look at the distributor agent job. You can connect to the subscriber server in the Object Explorer and then go to **SQL Server Agent** | **Jobs**. Under the jobs, look out for the job with the following naming convention: **[Publisher Server]- [Published database]-[PublicationName]-[Subscriber Server]-[Subscriber Database]- [UniqueIdentifier]**.

The distribution agent details are stored in the **MSdistributor_agents** table in the distribution database (at the publisher).

You can also get the name from *Exercise 2: Creating a Subscription:*

```
Messages
  Connecting to WIN2012R2\SQL2016...
  Disconnecting connection from WIN2012R2\SQL2016...
  Connecting to WIN2012R2\SQL2014...
  Job 'WIN2012R2\SQL2016-AdventureWorks-AdventureWorks-Tra-WIN2012R2\SQL2014-AdventureWorks-42D5DAFF-8DA4-4AF9-BF74-17826580D796' started successfully.
  Disconnecting connection from WIN2012R2\SQL2014...
```

Figure 2.14: Our subscription job name

The job name will differ on your system:

Figure 2.15: Selecting the job

You can double-click on the job to open its properties. In the **Job Properties** window, you can select the **Steps** page from the left-hand pane:

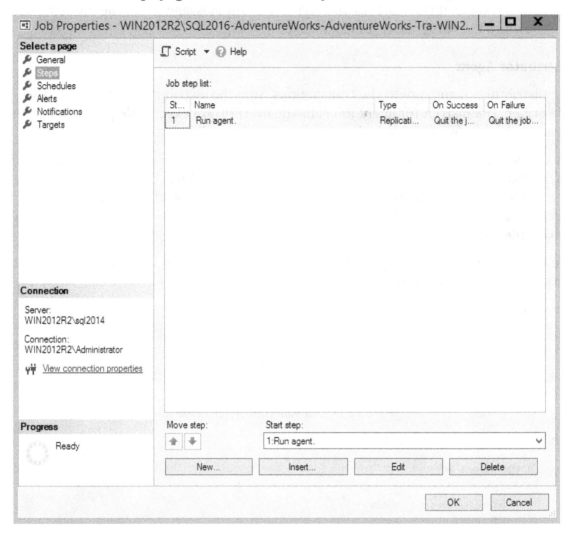

Figure 2.16: The Job Properties window

Double-clicking on the **Run agent** step opens its properties:

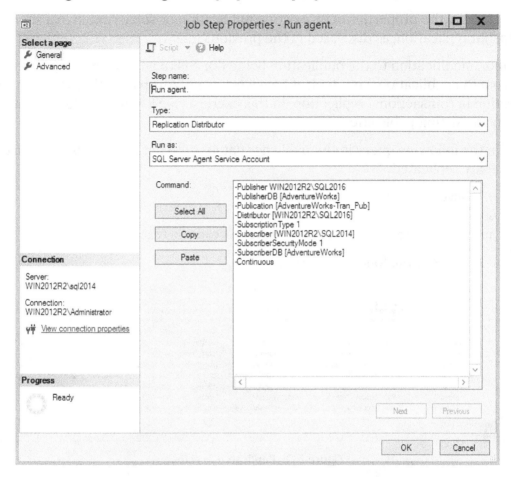

Figure 2.17: The Job Properties window – Step 1

Observe that this step calls the **distrib.exe** executable (type: **Replication Distributor**) with the parameter values, as specified under the **Command** textbox. The parameter values are the same as provided when configuring the replication.

distrib.exe accepts a lot more parameters than shown here. For all the other parameters that are relevant and have not been defined explicitly, the default value is considered. The important parameters are covered later in this lesson.

> **Note**
>
> To understand the other parameters of **distrib.exe**, refer to https://docs. microsoft.com/en-us/sql/relational-databases/replication/agents/replication-distribution-agent?view=sql-server-2017.

Exercise 9: Modifying the Existing Publication

You can modify the properties of an existing publication or subscription in a similar way to snapshot replication, as discussed in the previous lesson.

A common modification to the publication being done is to add or remove an article to or from the publication. Let's look at how we can add/drop an article to/from the publication in transactional replication. In this exercise, we'll learn to add/drop articles to/from an existing publication:

1. Run the following query in the publisher database to get the details of the articles that are replicated:

   ```
   USE AdventureWorks
   GO
   sp_helparticle @publication = 'AdventureWorks-Tran_Pub'
   ```

   You should get the following output:

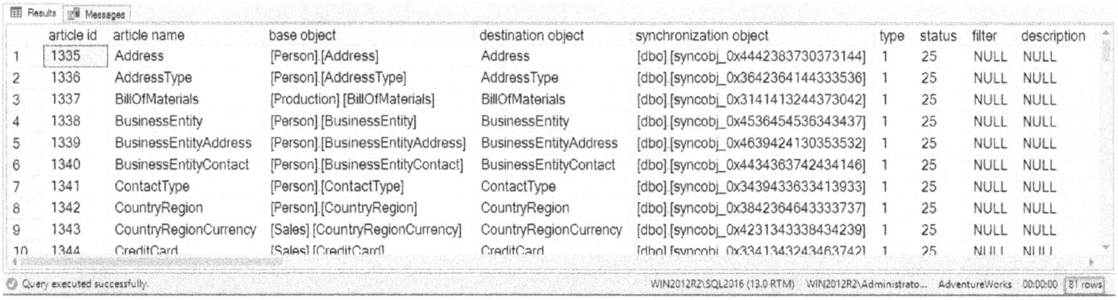

	article id	article name	base object	destination object	synchronization object	type	status	filter	description
1	1335	Address	[Person].[Address]	Address	[dbo].[syncobj_0x4442383730373144]	1	25	NULL	NULL
2	1336	AddressType	[Person].[AddressType]	AddressType	[dbo].[syncobj_0x3642364144333536]	1	25	NULL	NULL
3	1337	BillOfMaterials	[Production].[BillOfMaterials]	BillOfMaterials	[dbo].[syncobj_0x3141413244373042]	1	25	NULL	NULL
4	1338	BusinessEntity	[Person].[BusinessEntity]	BusinessEntity	[dbo].[syncobj_0x4536454536343437]	1	25	NULL	NULL
5	1339	BusinessEntityAddress	[Person].[BusinessEntityAddress]	BusinessEntityAddress	[dbo].[syncobj_0x4639424130353532]	1	25	NULL	NULL
6	1340	BusinessEntityContact	[Person].[BusinessEntityContact]	BusinessEntityContact	[dbo].[syncobj_0x4434363742434146]	1	25	NULL	NULL
7	1341	ContactType	[Person].[ContactType]	ContactType	[dbo].[syncobj_0x3439433633413933]	1	25	NULL	NULL
8	1342	CountryRegion	[Person].[CountryRegion]	CountryRegion	[dbo].[syncobj_0x3842364643333737]	1	25	NULL	NULL
9	1343	CountryRegionCurrency	[Sales].[CountryRegionCurrency]	CountryRegionCurrency	[dbo].[syncobj_0x4231343338434239]	1	25	NULL	NULL
10	1344	CreditCard	[Sales].[CreditCard]	CreditCard	[dbo].[syncobj_0x3341343243463742]	1	25	NULL	NULL

Query executed successfully. | WIN2012R2\SQL2016 (13.0 RTM) | WIN2012R2\Administrato… | AdventureWorks | 00:00:00 | 81 rows

Figure 2.18: Replicated articles

There is a total of 81 replicated articles in the publication.

In this exercise, we'll drop the **ErrorLog** article from the publication. Make sure that the table exists in the publication by checking the preceding output.

2. To drop the **ErrorLog** table from the publication, we first have to drop it from the subscription. Connect to the publisher database and execute the following script to drop the **ErrorLog** table from the subscription:

   ```
   USE AdventureWorks
   GO
   sp_dropsubscription
    @publication = 'AdventureWorks-Tran_Pub',
    @article = 'ErrorLog',
    @subscriber = 'WIN2012R2\SQL2014',
    @destination_db = 'AdventureWorks';
   ```

The **sp_dropsubscription** procedure removes the subscription for a particular article or publication. You should modify the value of the **@subscriber** parameter as per your environment.

3. The next step is to drop the article from the publication. Execute the following query to drop the article from the publication:

    ```
    EXEC sp_droparticle
        @publication = 'AdventureWorks-Tran_Pub',
        @article = 'ErrorLog',
        @force_invalidate_snapshot = 1;
    ```

    The **sp_droparticle** procedure removes the articles from the publication. If you don't set the **@force_invalidate_snapshot** parameter to **1**, you will get the following error:

    ```
    Msg 20607, Level 16, State 1, Procedure sp_MSreinit_article, Line 101
    [Batch Start Line 11] Cannot make the change because a snapshot is already
    generated. Set @force_invalidate_snapshot to 1 to force the change and
    invalidate the existing snapshot.
    ```

    This is because we already generated the snapshot when configuring transactional replication. If we don't invalidate the existing snapshot, the same snapshot will be applied to any new subscribers. It is therefore recommended to generate the snapshot after removing an article from the publication.

    Removing an article from the publication doesn't drop it from the publisher or the subscriber database. This will only stop replicating the schema and the data changes from the publisher to the subscriber.

4. To confirm this, execute the following query on the publisher database:

    ```
    sp_helparticle
    @publication = 'AdventureWorks-Tran_Pub',
    @article = 'ErrorLog';
    ```

    You should get the following output:

```
Messages
Msg 20027, Level 11, State 1, Procedure sp_MSrepl_helparticle, Line 164 [Batch Start Line 0]
The article 'ErrorLog' does not exist.
```

Figure 2.19: Confirmation of removing an article

If you provide an article that exists in the publication, the query will list its properties.

> **Note**
>
> Make sure that you check referential integrity before removing the article. For example, if you remove a parent table from the replication, then you may end up breaking the replication when a new row is added to the parent table and a new row is added to the child table that refers to the new row.

> When this change is replicated to the subscriber, it will break because the parent table isn't replicated, and it won't have that new row that was added to the publisher database.

5. Now, let's add an article to an existing publication.

   Execute the following query at the publisher database to verify the **immediate_sync** and **allow_anonymous** property values for the publication:

   ```
   USE AdventureWorks
   GO
   sp_helppublication
      @publication = 'AdventureWorks-Tran_Pub'
   ```

   You should get the following output:

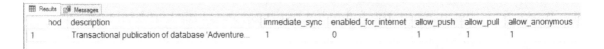

Figure 2.20: Output of adding an article

The **immediate_sync** and **allow_anonymous** values are set to **1**, as configured earlier in *Exercise 1: Creating a Publication*.

The value for these properties should be set to **0 (false)** so as not to generate the snapshot for all the articles when adding a new article. The value of **false** or **0** will result in the generation of the snapshot for the new article only.

6. Execute the following query to disable the **immediate_sync** and **allow_anonymous** properties:

```
USE AdventureWorks
GO
EXEC sp_changepublication
@publication = 'AdventureWorks-Tran_Pub',
@property = N'allow_anonymous',
@value = 'false'
GO
EXEC sp_changepublication
@publication = 'AdventureWorks-Tran_Pub',
@property = N'immediate_sync',
@value = 'false'
GO
```

The **sp_changepublication** procedure sets the value of the mentioned properties to **false**. This can also be done from the GUI from the publication properties. You can verify if the property values have been correctly set by running the query in step 1 again.

You should get the following output:

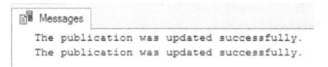

Figure 2.21: Output of disabling the immediate_sync and allow_anonymous properties

7. Execute the following query to add the **ErrorLog** article to the publication:

```
USE AdventureWorks
GO
EXEC sp_addarticle
        @publication = 'AdventureWorks-Tran_Pub',
        @article = 'ErrorLog',
        @source_object = 'ErrorLog',
        @force_invalidate_snapshot=1
GO
```

The **sp_addarticle** procedure adds the new article to the publication. This is the same as adding the articles to the publication when creating the publication. The difference is the **@force_invalidate_snapshot** parameter. This parameter has to be set to **1** so as to force the change and invalidate the existing snapshot. The new snapshot has to be generated - this includes the new article.

8. Execute the following command to refresh the subscription so as to include the new article that was added in the previous step:

```
USE AdventureWorks
GO
EXEC sp_refreshsubscriptions 'AdventureWorks-Tran_Pub'
GO
```

The stored procedure **sp_refreshsubscriptions** adds subscriptions for the newly added articles in the publication for all subscriptions. This procedure is only valid for pull subscriptions.

For push subscriptions, the following query needs to be run to include the new article to the subscription on the publisher database:

```
EXEC sp_addsubscription
@publication = 'AdventureWorks-Tran_Pub',
@subscriber = 'Neptune\SQL2014',
@destination_db = 'AdventureWorks',
@reserved='Internal'
```

9. The next step is to run the snapshot and generate the snapshot for the new article. Execute the following query to run the snapshot agent. You can also use the GUI to run the snapshot agent, as explained in *Lesson 1, Getting Started with SQL Server HA and DR*:

```
USE AdventureWorks
GO
DECLARE @jobname NVARCHAR(200)
SELECT @jobname=name FROM [distribution].[dbo].[MSsnapshot_agents]
WHERE [publication]='AdventureWorks-Tran_Pub' AND [publisher_
db]='AdventureWorks'
Print 'Starting Snapshot Agent ' + @jobname + '....'
-- Start the snapshot agent to generate the snapshot
EXECUTE msdb.dbo.sp_start_job @job_name=@jobname
```

To view the snapshot agent history, locate the snapshot agent job under the **SQL Server Agent | Jobs** node. Right-click on the job and then select **View History**:

Figure 2.22: The snapshot agent history

Observe that the snapshot is generated only for one article.

10. Execute the following query to set the **immediate_sync** and **allow_anonymous** properties' values back to **true**:

```
USE AdventureWorks
GO
EXEC sp_changepublication
@publication = 'AdventureWorks-Tran_Pub',
@property = N'immediate_sync',
@value = 'true'
GO
EXEC sp_changepublication
@publication = 'AdventureWorks-Tran_Pub',
@property = N'allow_anonymous',
@value = 'true'
GO
```

Stopping Transactional Replication

Stopping or pausing transactional replication can be done by either stopping the log reader agent or the distribution agent. When the log reader agent is stopped, the transaction log is not scanned for transactions and transactions aren't inserted into the distribution database. This will cause the transaction log to grow, even if you have scheduled regular log backups. This is because the log backups don't remove the transactions from the transaction log that are marked for replication.

As the log reader agent isn't running, transactions that are marked for replication aren't scanned and the transaction log grows. It is therefore not recommended to stop the log reader agent.

Moreover, stopping the log reader agent stops the transactions from being replicated to all subscribers for the particular publication.

When the distributor agent is stopped, the transactions from the distribution database aren't applied to the subscribers. This results in the distribution database growing in size. However, this doesn't affect the publisher database, unlike stopping the log reader agent, as explained earlier.

Moreover, for pull subscriptions, stopping the distribution agent for a particular subscriber only stops the replication for that subscriber and not all subscribers for the particular publication.

Stopping the Log Reader Agent

The log reader agent can be either stopped by stopping the log reader agent job or by stopping the synchronization (from SSMS), which eventually stops the log reader agent job.

You can execute the following query on the publisher server to stop the log reader agent job:

```
DECLARE @Publisher_db nvarchar(100) =  N'AdventureWorks'

DECLARE @jobname NVARCHAR(200)

SELECT @jobname=name FROM [distribution].[dbo].[MSlogreader_agents]

WHERE [publisher_db]=@Publisher_db


Print 'Stopping Log Reader Agent ' + @jobname + '....'


EXECUTE msdb.dbo.sp_stop_job @job_name=@jobname

/* Execute below query to start the job */

EXECUTE msdb.dbo.sp_start_job @job_name=@jobname
```

The preceding snippet queries the `MSlogreader_agents` table to get the name of the log reader agent job. It then stops the job by calling the `sp_stop_job` stored procedure.

> **Note**
>
> You can verify that the job has been stopped by checking the job's status in **Job Activity Monitor** under the **SQL Server Agent** node in SQL Server Management Studio.

Another way to stop the log reader agent is by stopping the log reader agent synchronization from SSMS:

1. You can connect to the publisher server in the Object Explorer and then go to **Replication Node | Local Publications**.

2. You can then right-click on the publication and select the **View Log Reader Agent Status** option from the context menu:

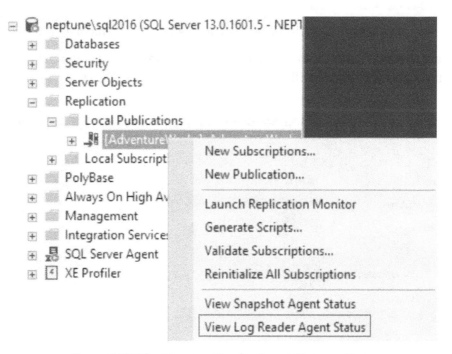

Figure 2.23: The View Log Reader Agent Status option

3. If you ran the previous query to stop the log reader agent, then the log reader agent status will be as shown here:

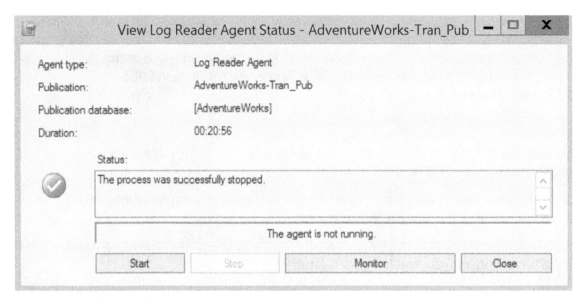

Figure 2.24: The View Log Reader Agent Status window

To start the log reader agent, you can click on **Start**. This will start the log reader agent job and the status will change, as shown here:

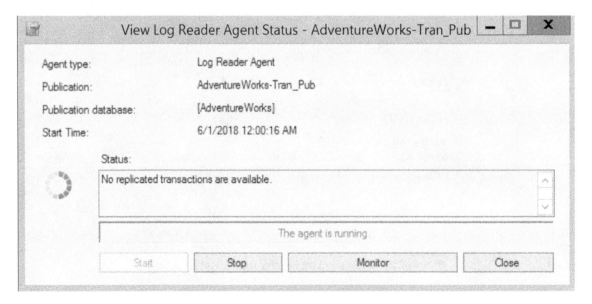

Figure 2.25: Starting the log reader agent

Stopping the Distribution Agent

Similar to the log reader agent, to stop the distribution agent, you can connect to the subscriber server and execute the following query:

```
USE AdventureWorks

GO

sp_stoppullsubscription_agent
    @publisher='Neptune\SQL2016',
    @publisher_db='AdventureWorks',
    @publication='AdventureWorks-Tran_Pub'
```

The stored procedure **sp_stoppullsubscription_agent** finds and stops the distribution agent job.

You should get the following output:

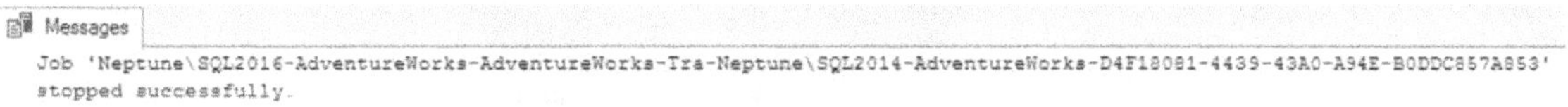

```
Messages
Job 'Neptune\SQL2016-AdventureWorks-AdventureWorks-Tra-Neptune\SQL2014-AdventureWorks-D4F18081-4439-43A0-A94E-B0DDC857A853'
stopped successfully.
```

Figure 2.26: Output of stopping the distribution agent

To start the distribution agent, execute the following query:

```
USE AdventureWorks

GO

sp_startpullsubscription_agent
    @publisher='Neptune\SQL2016',
    @publisher_db='AdventureWorks',
    @publication='AdventureWorks-Tran_Pub'
```

The stored procedure **sp_startpullsubscription_agent** finds and starts the distribution job on the subscriber.

Another way to stop the distribution agent is to stop the synchronization from SSMS:

1. You can connect to the subscriber server in the Object Explorer and then expand **Replication | Local Subscription**. You can then right-click on **View Synchronization Status** from the context menu:

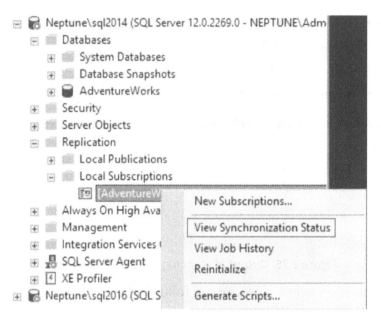

Figure 2.27: The View Synchronization Status option

2. You can start and stop the distribution agent from the **View Synchronization Status** window:

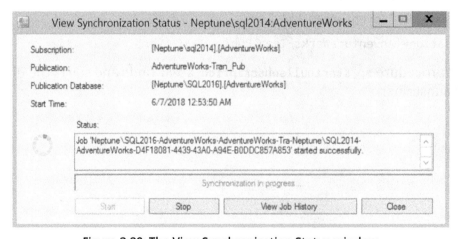

Figure 2.28: The View Synchronization Status window

Exercise 10: Removing Transactional Replication

Removing transactional replication consists of the following steps:

1. Removing the subscription for the publication to be deleted

2. Removing the publication

3. Disabling the database for publication (optional)

4. Removing replication metadata from the subscriber (optional)

Let's remove the replication that was configured in this lesson by following the aforementioned steps:

1. Execute the following query on the publisher database to remove the subscription:

```
DECLARE @publication AS sysname;
DECLARE @subscriber AS sysname;
SET @publication = N'AdventureWorks-Tran_Pub';
SET @subscriber = 'Neptune\SQL2014';

USE [AdventureWorks]

EXEC sp_dropsubscription
  @publication = @publication,
  @article = N'all',
  @subscriber = @subscriber;
GO
```

You should get the following output:

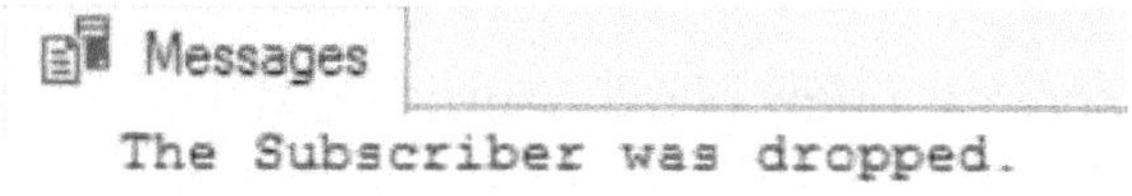

Figure 2.29: Output of removing the subscription

2. Execute the following query on the publication database to remove or drop the publication:

```
DECLARE @Database AS sysname;
DECLARE @Publication AS sysname;
SET @Database = N'AdventureWorks';
SET @Publication = N'AdventureWorks-Tran_Pub';

-- Remove Publication
```

```
USE [AdventureWorks]

EXEC sp_droppublication
  @publication = @publication;
```

This query removes the publication for the **AdventureWorks** database that was created earlier. You may verify this by going to **SSMS** | **Object Explorer** | **Replication** | **Local Publication**.

Azure SQL Database as a Subscriber in Transaction Replication

An Azure SQL database is a database-as-a-service offering from Microsoft Azure. An Azure SQL database can be configured as a subscriber to an on-premises SQL Server publisher. This is one of best methods to use for migrating an on-premises database to an Azure SQL database. Moreover, the Azure SQL database subscriber can also be used as a backup or to offload reads from the publisher.

Exercise 11: Configuring and Verifying Azure SQL Database as a Subscriber for an On-Premises Transactional Replication

To configure Azure SQL database as a subscriber for an on-premises transactional replication, follow these steps:

> **Note**
>
> Open a new PowerShell console (running as administrator) and execute the **Install-Module AzureRm** command to install the **AzureRm** PowerShell module. The **AzureRm** module is a prerequisite for this exercise.

1. The first step is to create a new blank Azure SQL database. Open a new PowerShell console window and execute the following command:

    ```
    Login-AzureRmAccount
    ```

In the login dialog box, provide your Microsoft Azure email address and password. This ensures that the commands that are run after this step are against the Microsoft Azure account you provided:

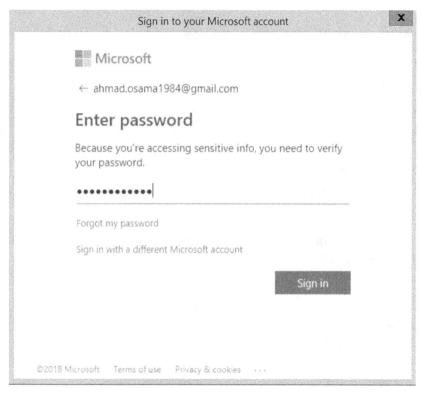

Figure 2.30: The login dialog box

2. Execute the following PowerShell command to create a new Azure resource group:

   ```
   New-AzureRmResourceGroup -Name myrg -Location "East US"
   ```

3. Execute the following PowerShell command to create a new Azure SQL Server:

   ```
   $creds = New-Object -TypeName System.Management.Automation.PSCredential
   -ArgumentList "sqladmin", $(ConvertTo-SecureString -String "Packt@pub1234"
   -AsPlainText -Force)
   New-AzureRmSqlServer -ServerName packtsqlserver
   -SqlAdministratorCredentials $creds -Location "East US" -ResourceGroupName
   myrg
   ```

You'll have to use a different server name for the **-ServerName** parameter.

This command will create a new Azure SQL Server named **packtsqlserver**. The SQL admin user is **sqladmin** with a password of **Packt@pub1234**.

4. Execute the following query to create a new blank Azure SQL Database, **AdventureWorks**, in **packtsqlserver**, which we created just now:

```
New-AzureRmSqlDatabase -DatabaseName AdventureWorks -Edition basic
-ResourceGroupName myrg -ServerName packtsqlserver
```

You'll have to use a different database name for the **-DatabaseName** parameter.

5. Execute the following command to add the firewall rule so as to connect to the Azure SQL database:

```
$mypublicip = (Invoke-RestMethod http://ipinfo.io/json).ip
New-AzureRmSqlServerFirewallRule -FirewallRuleName Home -StartIpAddress
$mypublicip -EndIpAddress $mypublicip -ServerName packtsqlserver
-ResourceGroupName myrg
```

This command adds the public IP of the client machine to the **packtsqlserver** firewall rule.

6. Now, let's configure the transaction publication for the **AdventureWorks** database. To do this, open SSMS, connect to the SQL2016 SQL Server instance, and execute the following query:

```
-- Enabling the replication database
use master
exec sp_replicationdboption
  @dbname = N'AdventureWorks',
  @optname = N'publish',
  @value = N'true'
GO

-- Adding the transactional publication
use [AdventureWorks]
exec sp_addpublication
  @publication = N'Pub-AdventureWorks',
  @description = N'Transactional publication of database
''AdventureWorks'' from Publisher ''NEPTUNE\SQL2016''.',
  @sync_method = N'concurrent',
  @retention = 0,
  @allow_push = N'true',
  @allow_pull = N'true',
  @allow_anonymous = N'true',
  @snapshot_in_defaultfolder = N'true',
  @repl_freq = N'continuous',
  @status = N'active',
```

```
    @independent_agent = N'true',
    @immediate_sync = N'true',
    @replicate_ddl = 1

GO

exec sp_addpublication_snapshot
    @publication = N'Pub-AdventureWorks',
    @frequency_type = 1,
    @frequency_interval = 1,
    @frequency_relative_interval = 1,
    @frequency_recurrence_factor = 0,
    @frequency_subday = 8,
    @frequency_subday_interval = 1,
    @active_start_time_of_day = 0,
    @active_end_time_of_day = 235959,
    @active_start_date = 0,
    @active_end_date = 0,
    @job_login = null,
    @job_password = null,
    @publisher_security_mode = 1

use [AdventureWorks]
GO
exec sp_addarticle
    @publication = N'Pub-AdventureWorks',
    @article = N'Address',
    @source_owner = N'Person',
    @source_object = N'Address',
    @type = N'logbased',
    @description = null,
    @creation_script = null,
    @pre_creation_cmd = N'drop',
    @schema_option = 0x000000000803509F,
    @identityrangemanagementoption = N'manual',
    @destination_table = N'Address',
    @destination_owner = N'Person',
    @vertical_partition = N'false',
    @ins_cmd = N'CALL sp_MSins_PersonAddress',
    @del_cmd = N'CALL sp_MSdel_PersonAddress',
    @upd_cmd = N'SCALL sp_MSupd_PersonAddress'
GO
```

This query creates a transactional publication called **Pub-AdventureWorks** for the **AdventureWorks** database and adds the **Address** table as a published article.

> **Note**
>
> Only one table has been published for the sake of this demo. However, more articles can be added and are supported.

7. Execute the following query to add the Azure SQL database **AdventureWorks** as a subscriber to the **Pub-AdventureWorks** publication (change the server name and database name in this script with the names you provided in *step 4*):

```
use [AdventureWorks]
GO
exec sp_addsubscription
   @publication = N'Pub-AdventureWorks',
   @subscriber = N'packtsqlserver.database.windows.net',
   @destination_db = N'Adventureworks',
   @subscription_type = N'Push',
   @sync_type = N'automatic',
   @article = N'all',
   @update_mode = N'read only',
   @subscriber_type = 0
GO
exec sp_addpushsubscription_agent
   @publication = N'Pub-AdventureWorks',
   @subscriber = N'packtsqlserver.database.windows.net',
   @subscriber_db = N'Adventureworks',
   @job_login = null,
   @job_password = null,
   @subscriber_security_mode = 0,
   @subscriber_login = N'sqladmin',
   @subscriber_password = 'Packt@pub1234'
GO
```

Observe the **@subscriber** parameter. The subscriber server is **packtsqlserver. database.windows.net**. Observe the parameters **@subscriber_login** and **@ subscriber_password**. The distributor agent connects to the subscriber using the Azure SQL Server admin user.

We now have transactional replication between an on-premises database and Azure SQL database.

Let's start the snapshot agent and verify the replication.

8. To start the snapshot agent, connect to the Object Explorer of the SQL2016 SQL Server instance. Expand **Replication** | **Local Publications** and right-click on the [AdventureWorks]:Pub-AdventureWorks publication. Select **View Snapshot Agent Status** from the context menu:

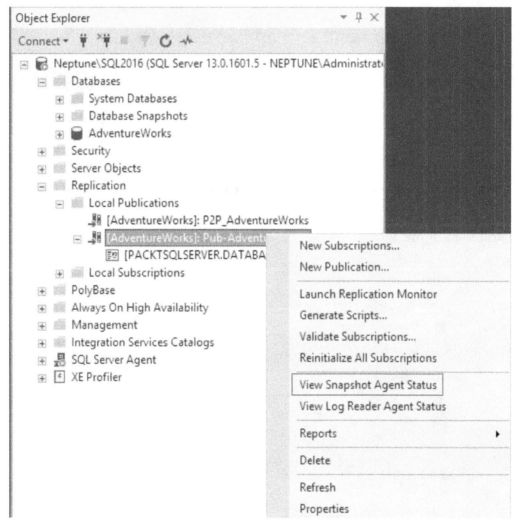

Figure 2.31: The View Snapshot Agent Status option

In the **View Snapshot Agent Status** dialog box, click on the **Start** button to start the snapshot agent:

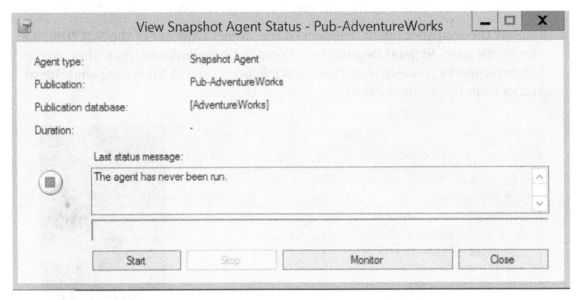

Figure 2.32: The View Snapshot Agent Status window

9. To verify the replication, in the Object Explorer menu, click on **Connect** and select **Database Engine**:

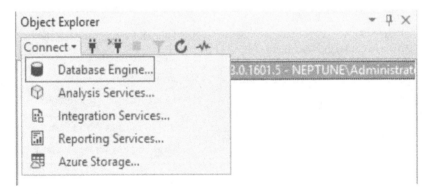

Figure 2.33: The Database Engine option

10. In the **Connect to Server** dialog box, enter **Server name** as `packtsqlserver.database.windows.net`. Provide the Azure SQL Server administrator username and password, as given in *step 3*:

Figure 2.34: The Database Engine option

11. In the Object Explorer, expand **packtsqlserver.database.windows.net** | **Databases** | **AdventureWorks** | **Table**. Observe that the database contains the `Address` table.

> **Note**
>
> You can also verify the replication using the replication monitor.

12. To drop the replication, execute the following query at the SQL2016 SQL instance:

```
USE [AdventureWorks]
GO
EXEC sp_dropsubscription
  @publication = 'Pub-AdventureWorks',
  @article = N'all',
  @subscriber = 'packtsqlserver.database.windows.net';
GO
EXEC sp_droppublication @publication = 'Pub-AdventureWorks';
```

You may get the following error when running this script. Ignore the error as the replication is dropped:

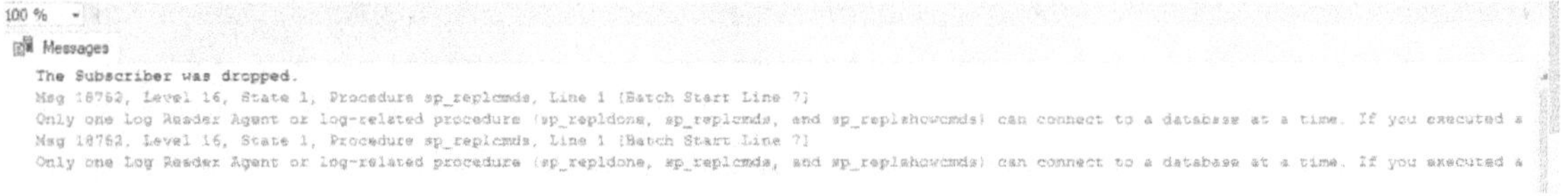

Figure 2.35: Output of dropping the replication

This completes this exercise.

The following PowerShell command can be used to drop the resource group, Azure SQL Server, and Azure SQL database:

```
Remove-AzureRmResourceGroup -Name myrg -Force
```

Understanding Peer-To-Peer Transactional Replication

Peer-to-peer replication, also referred to as master-master replication, is built upon transactional replication in which changes at the subscriber are also replicated to the publisher.

A peer-to-peer topology consists of two or more databases where a change in each node (database) gets replicated at every other node (database) in the topology. Peer-to-peer replication therefore provides a scalable high availability solution.

A typical peer-to-peer transactional replication topology is shown in the following diagram:

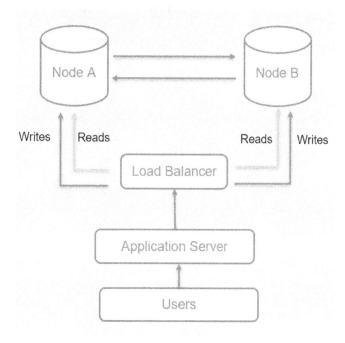

Figure 2.36: P2P replication example

Node A and **Node B** are in a peer-to-peer replication. Any changes made at **Node A** are replicated to **Node B** and any changes made at **Node B** are replicated to **Node A**.

This topology has the following benefits:

- Reads are load-balanced between two nodes, thereby optimizing the read performance.

- Writes are load-balanced between two nodes. For example, let's say there is a customer table that stores customer information. Customer information can be distributed between the two nodes based on location (or any other logic). Each node will have all customer data as the information is replicated. Similarly, updates can also be load-balanced.

- It provides high availability in case a node goes down because of a hardware or application failure. The load balancer automatically redirects the users to the active (working) node. As the nodes are part of replication, each node has all the data.

With all the benefits that we've mentioned, peer-to-peer replication may result in a conflict when the same row is updated/inserted/deleted at multiple nodes at the same time. Conflict detection and resolution is discussed later in this book.

Configuring Peer-To-Peer Transactional Replication

In this section, we'll configure peer-to-peer transactional replication. The topology is as follows:

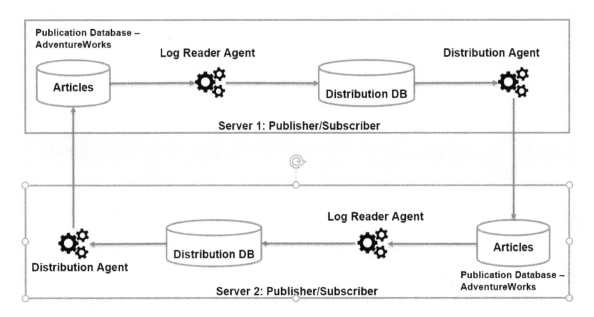

Figure 2.37: P2P Replication example

The preceding diagram illustrates peer-to-peer topology with two nodes with a push subscription:

- There isn't any additional replication agent involved.

- Each server acts as a publisher and subscriber.

- The log reader agent picks up the transactions from **AdventureWorks** and inserts them into the distribution database. The push subscription agent (distribution agent) pushes the transactions to the Server 2 **AdventureWorks** database.

Configuring P2P replication consists of the following steps:

1. Creating the publication and adding articles to the publication on Server 1.

2. Creating the subscription and then pushing the subscription agent (distribution agent) on Server 1.

3. Taking the backup of the **AdventureWorks** database on Server 1. Unlike standard transactional replication, P2P transactional replication is initialized using backup.

4. Restoring the **AdventureWorks** database from Server 1 on Server 2.

5. Creating the publication and adding articles to the publication on Server 2.

6. Creating the subscription and pushing the subscription agent on Server 2.

Exercise 12: Creating the Publication, Adding Articles, Adding the Subscription, and Pushing the Subscription Agent to the Publication on Server 1

In this exercise, we will perform the first two steps of configuring peer-to-peer replication, as explained in the previous section:

1. Navigate to **C:\Code\Lesson02\Peer-to-Peer** and open **1_ConfigureReplication_Node1.sql** in SQL Server Management Studio.

   > **Note**
   >
   > If the distribution is not enabled on the SQL Server instance, then first run the **0_EnableDistribution_Publisher.sql** script to enable the distribution.

2. In SSMS, from the top menu, select **Query**, and then select **SQLCMD**. This changes the mode of the **1_ConfigureReplicationNode1.sql** query to SQLCMD from SQL.

3. Modify the following parameters in the script as per your environment:

```
1_ConfigureReplicat...Administrator (54))*  ⊨ ×
    -- Node 1: Neptune\SQL2014
    :setvar Publisher "Neptune\SQL2014"
    -- Node 2: Neptune\SQL2016
    :setvar Subscriber "Neptune\SQL2016"
    :setvar DatabaseName "AdventureWorks"
    :setvar PublicationName "P2P_AdventureWorks"
```

Figure 2.38: Parameters for creating the publication

This code defines the parameters being used in the script. The parameters are self-explanatory. The publisher and distributor are the same as the publisher acts as its own distributor.

4. To run the script, change the parameters as specified earlier and press F5 or click on **Execute** in the top menu.

You should get the following output.

```
Messages
Connecting to Neptune\SQL2014...
The replication option 'publish' of database 'AdventureWorks' has already been set to true.
Job 'NEPTUNE\SQL2014-AdventureWorks-8' started successfully.
Warning: The logreader agent job has been implicitly created and will run under the SQL Server Agent Service Account.
Job 'Neptune\SQL2014-AdventureWorks-P2P_AdventureWorks-NEPTUNE\SQL2016-23' started successfully.
Warning: The distribution agent job has been implicitly created and will run under the SQL Server Agent Service Account.
Job 'Neptune\SQL2014-AdventureWorks-P2P_AdventureWorks-NEPTUNE\SQL2016-23' started successfully.
Disconnecting connection from Neptune\SQL2014...
```

Figure 2.39: Output of creating the publication

Observe that the log reader and distributor agent job have been successfully created.

Now, we'll dissect different parts of the script and understand what the different procedures in the script do. You are, however, supposed to run the script immediately after modifying the parameters to create the publication.

The following command connects to the publisher server and enables the **AdventureWorks** database for publication using the **sp_replicationdboption** system stored procedure:

```
:CONNECT $(Publisher)


-- Enabling the replication database
USE master


EXEC sp_replicationdboption
  @dbname = "$(DatabaseName)",
  @optname = N'publish',
  @value = N'true'
GO
```

> **Note**
>
> You can also copy the code from the **C:\Code\Lesson02\Peer-to-Peer\1_ConfigureReplication_Node1.sql** file.

The following command creates the publication for the **AdventureWorks** database:

```
-- Adding the transactional publication
USE $(DatabaseName)


EXEC sp_addpublication
@publication ="$(PublicationName)",
@description = N'Peer-to-Peer publication of database ''AdventureWorks''
from Publisher ''NEPTUNE\SQL2016''.' ,
@sync_method = N'native',
@allow_push = N'true',
@allow_pull = N'true',
@allow_anonymous = N'false',
@repl_freq = N'continuous',
@status = N'active',
@independent_agent = N'true',
```

```
@immediate_sync = N'true',
@allow_queued_tran = N'false',
@allow_dts = N'false',
@replicate_ddl = 1,
@allow_initialize_from_backup = N'true',
@enabled_for_p2p = N'true',
@p2p_conflictdetection = N'true',
@p2p_continue_onconflict=N'true',
@p2p_originator_id = 1
```

> **Note**
>
> You can also copy the code from the **C:\Code\Lesson02\Peer-to-Peer\1_ ConfigureReplication_Node1.sql** file.

The **sp_addpublication** procedure creates the publication for the **AdventureWorks** database. Most of the parameters are similar to those of the script that we used to create the publication for transactional replication in *Exercise 7: Creating the Publication*. You will, however, notice the following additional parameters:

- **@enabled_for_p2p**: As the name suggests, this enables the publication for P2P replication.

- **@allow_initialize_from_backup**: This enables the subscription to be initialized from the database backup.

- **@p2p_conflictdetection**: This enables the distribution to detect conflicts as and when they occur. The replication monitor can be used to send email alerts when conflicts are detected. This is covered later in this lesson.

- **@p2p_continue_onconflict**: When this option is enabled, the conflict rows are ignored (not replicated) and other transactions are replicated. When **false**, the replication stops whenever a conflict is detected. P2P replication may get conflicts, therefore, it's better to enable this and fix the conflict later.

- **@p2p_originator_id**: This is the ID that's assigned to the node participating in a P2P topology. This is useful when resolving conflicts to identify the node from which the transactions originate.

> **Note**
>
> If you get the following error when running the script, try using a different ID value for the **@p2p_originator_id** parameter. The following error means that the given ID is already being used by a SQL Server instance in the P2P topology:
>
> Msg 22806, Level 16, State 1, Procedure sp_MSrepl_addpublication, Line 1364 [Batch Start Line 19]
>
> The originator ID '1' is not valid. You must specify a non-zero ID that has never been used in the topology.

The following query adds two articles to the publication:

```
-- Adding the transactional articles
EXEC sp_addarticle
  @publication = "$(PublicationName)",
  @article = N'SalesOrderDetail',
  @source_owner = N'Sales',
  @source_object = N'SalesOrderDetail',
  @destination_table = N'SalesOrderDetail',
  @destination_owner = N'Sales',
  @ins_cmd = N'CALL [sp_MSins_SalesSalesOrderDetail01166611037]',
  @del_cmd = N'CALL [sp_MSdel_SalesSalesOrderDetail01166611037]',
  @upd_cmd = N'SCALL [sp_MSupd_SalesSalesOrderDetail01166611037]'

GO
```

```
EXEC sp_addarticle
  @publication = "$(PublicationName)",
  @article = N'SalesOrderHeader',
  @source_owner = N'Sales',
  @source_object = N'SalesOrderHeader',
  @destination_table = N'SalesOrderHeader',
  @destination_owner = N'Sales',
  @ins_cmd = N'CALL [sp_MSins_SalesSalesOrderHeader0611538077]',
  @del_cmd = N'CALL [sp_MSdel_SalesSalesOrderHeader0611538077]',
  @upd_cmd = N'SCALL [sp_MSupd_SalesSalesOrderHeader0611538077]'
```

> **Note**
>
> You can also copy the code from the **C:\Code\Lesson02\Peer-to-Peer\1_ ConfigureReplication_Node1.sql** file.

The articles are added using the **sp_addarticle** procedure, which is similar to how the articles were added in the standard transactional replication.

The following queries add the subscription and the push subscription agent on Server 1:

```
EXEC sp_addsubscription
  @publication = "$(PublicationName)",
  @subscriber = "$(Subscriber)",
  @destination_db = "$(DatabaseName)",
  @subscription_type = N'Push',
  @sync_type = N'replication support only',
  @article = N'all',
  @update_mode = N'read only',
  @subscriber_type = 0


GO
EXEC sp_addpushsubscription_agent
  @publication ="$(PublicationName)",
  @subscriber = "$(Subscriber)",
```

```
@subscriber_db = "$(DatabaseName)",

@job_login = NULL,

@job_password = NULL,

@subscriber_security_mode = 1,

@frequency_type = 64,

@frequency_interval = 1,

@frequency_relative_interval = 1,

@frequency_recurrence_factor = 0,

@frequency_subday = 4,

@frequency_subday_interval = 5,

@active_start_time_of_day = 0,

@active_end_time_of_day = 235959,

@active_start_date = 0,

@active_end_date = 0
```

> **Note**
>
> You can also copy the code from the **C:\Code\Lesson02\Peer-to-Peer\1_ ConfigureReplication_Node1.sql** file.

The **sp_addsubscription** procedure adds the subscription for Node 2 at Node 1. The parameters are the same as they were for the standard transactional replication, except for the following parameter values:

- **@subscription_type**: This specifies whether the type of subscription is push and not pull. The standard transactional replication configured earlier in this lesson used pull subscription. It's not mandatory or a limitation to use push subscription for P2P replication. It's done to make it easier to understand the concepts.

- **@sync_type**: The sync type **replication support only** creates the object that's required for replication and does not create the database objects and sync the data. This is because in P2P replication, the subscriber already has the database with the required objects.

  A key point to note here is that there should not be any change in the publication database after the publication is created. If there is, then use the sync type as **Initialize from backup**. Take the database backup and provide the backup file path in the **@backupdevicename** parameter.

The **sp_addpushsubscription_agent** procedure adds the distributor agent at the publisher. This is the same as what we saw for the standard transactional replication. The difference is that the distribution agent job in the case of P2P is created at the publisher (push subscription), whereas in standard transactional replication, it's created at the subscriber node (pull subscription).

This completes the first two steps for configuring peer-to-peer transactional replication, as mentioned in the previous section.

Exercise 13: Taking the Backup of the Publication Database on Server 1

In this exercise, we will perform the third step of configuring peer-to-peer transactional replication:

1. Navigate to **C:\Code\Lesson02\Peer-to-Peer** and open **2_BackupAdventureWorks_Publisher.sql** in SQL Server Management Studio:

   ```
   -- Backup AdventureWorks on the Publication Server
   BACKUP DATABASE AdventureWorks TO DISK=
   'C:\Code\Lesson02\Backup\AdventureWorks_Publisher.bak' WITH compression,
   init,stats= 10
   ```

   > **Note**
   >
   > You can also copy the code from the **C:\Code\Lesson02\Peer-to-Peer\2_BackupAdventureWorks_Publisher.sql** file.

2. Execute this query at Server/Node 1. This query takes the full backup of the **AdventureWorks** database at Server/Node 1. If there is a change in the database after the full backup, it takes the transaction log backup and specifies the backup in the add subscription procedure when creating the subscription, as explained earlier.

This completes the third step in configuring peer-to-peer transactional replication, as mentioned in the previous section.

Exercise 14: Restoring the Database on the Subscriber Server

In this exercise, we will perform the fourth step in configuring peer-to-peer transactional replication:

1. Navigate to **C:\Code\Lesson02\Peer-to-Peer** and open **3_RestoreAdventureWorks_ Subscriber.sql** in SQL Server Management Studio:

   ```
   -- Restore AdventureWorks on Subscriber
   USE [master]
   GO
   RESTORE DATABASE [AdventureWorks] FROM DISK =
   N'C:\Code\Lesson02\Backup\AdventureWorks_Publisher.bak' WITH FILE = 1,
   MOVE N'AdventureWorks2014_Data' TO N'E:\AdventureWorks\AdventureWorks2016_
   subs_Data.mdf',
   MOVE N'AdventureWorks2014_Log' TO N'E:\AdventureWorks\AdventureWorks2016_
   subs_Log.ldf',
   stats = 10
   ```

   > **Note**
   >
   > You can also copy the code from the **C:\Code\Lesson02\Peer-to-Peer\3_ RestoreAdventureWorks_Subscriber.sql** file.

2. Execute this command at Server/Node 2. This command restores the **AdventureWorks** database from the backup taken in the previous step. You may have to modify the physical path of the files, depending on your environment.

This completes the fourth step in configuring peer-to-peer transactional replication, as mentioned in the previous section.

Exercise 15: Creating the Publication, Adding Articles, Adding the Subscription, and Pushing the Subscription Agent to the Publication on Server 2

In this exercise, we will perform the fifth and sixth steps of configuring peer-to-peer replication, as explained in the previous section:

1. Navigate to **C:\Code\Lesson02\Peer-to-Peer** and open **4_ConfigureReplication_Node2.sql** in SQL Server Management Studio.

2. In SSMS, from the top menu, select **Query** and then select **SQLCMD**. This changes the mode of the **4_ConfigureReplication_Node2.sql** query to SQLCMD from SQL.

3. Modify the following parameters in the script as per your environment:

4_ConfigureReplicat...Administrator (55))   ⇌ ✕   3_RestoreAdventure...Administrat

```
:setvar Publisher "Neptune\SQL2014"
:setvar Subscriber "Neptune\SQL2016"
:setvar DatabaseName "AdventureWorks"
:setvar PublicationName "P2P_AdventureWorks"
```

Figure 2.40: Parameters for creating the subscription

Observe that the parameter values are similar to the ones that were used to create the publication on Server 1. The publisher and distributor are the same as the publisher acts as its own distributor.

4. To run the script, change the parameters, as specified earlier, and press F5 or click **Execute** in the top menu.

You should get the following output:

Messages

```
Connecting to Neptune\SQL2016...
Job 'NEPTUNE\SQL2016-AdventureWorks-4' started successfully.
Warning: The logreader agent job has been implicitly created and will run under the SQL Server Agent Service Account.
Job 'Neptune\SQL2016-AdventureWorks-P2P_AdventureWorks-NEPTUNE\SQL2014-12' started successfully.
Warning: The distribution agent job has been implicitly created and will run under the SQL Server Agent Service Account.
Job 'Neptune\SQL2016-AdventureWorks-P2P_AdventureWorks-NEPTUNE\SQL2014-12' started successfully.
Disconnecting connection from Neptune\SQL2016...
```

Figure 2.41: Output of creating the subscription

Observe that the log reader and distribution agent jobs have been created.

This completes this exercise.

Now, we'll dissect different parts of the script and understand what the different procedures in the script do. You are, however, supposed to run the script immediately after modifying the parameters to create the publication.

The script is similar to the one used for creating the publication at Server 1. Any changes, however, are explained.

The following command connects to the subscriber server and enables the **AdventureWorks** database for publication using the **sp_replicationdboption** system stored procedure:

```
:CONNECT $(Subscriber)
-- Enabling the replication database
USE master

EXEC sp_replicationdboption
  @dbname = N'AdventureWorks',
  @optname = N'publish',
  @value = N'true'
GO
```

> **Note**
>
> You can also copy the code from the **C:\Code\Lesson02\Peer-to-Peer\4_ ConfigureReplication_Node2.sql** file.

The following command creates the publication for the **AdventureWorks** database at Server 2:

```
USE $(DatabaseName)


EXEC sp_addpublication

@publication = "$(PublicationName)",

@description = N'Peer-to-Peer publication of database ''AdventureWorks''
from Publisher ''NEPTUNE\SQL2014''.' ,

@sync_method = N'native',

@allow_push = N'true',

@allow_pull = N'true',

@allow_anonymous = N'false',

@repl_freq = N'continuous',
```

```
@status = N'active',

@independent_agent = N'true',

@immediate_sync = N'true',

@replicate_ddl = 1,

@allow_initialize_from_backup = N'true',

@enabled_for_p2p = N'true',

@p2p_conflictdetection = N'true',

@p2p_continue_onconflict=N'true',

@p2p_originator_id = 2
```

> **Note**
>
> You can also copy the code from the **C:\Code\Lesson02\Peer-to-Peer\4_ ConfigureReplication_Node2.sql** file.

The parameters and parameter values are the same as specified in the first step (creating the publication at Server 1), except for the description and **@p2p_originator_ id**. The **@p2p_originator_id** parameter is set to **2**, that is, Server 2 has the ID of 2 to uniquely identify it in the topology.

The following query adds two articles to the publication:

```
-- Adding the transactional articles


EXEC sp_addarticle
  @publication = "$(PublicationName)",

  @article = N'SalesOrderDetail',

  @source_owner = N'Sales',

  @source_object = N'SalesOrderDetail',

  @identityrangemanagementoption = N'manual',

  @destination_table = N'SalesOrderDetail',

  @status = 24,

  @ins_cmd = N'CALL [sp_MSins_SalesSalesOrderDetail01166611037473422351]',

  @del_cmd = N'CALL [sp_MSdel_SalesSalesOrderDetail01166611037473422351]',

  @upd_cmd = N'SCALL [sp_MSupd_SalesSalesOrderDetail01166611037473422351]'
```

```
GO

EXEC sp_addarticle
  @publication = "$(PublicationName)",
  @article = N'SalesOrderHeader',
  @source_owner = N'Sales',
  @source_object = N'SalesOrderHeader',
  @destination_table = N'SalesOrderHeader',
  @destination_owner = N'Sales',
  @ins_cmd = N'CALL [sp_MSins_SalesSalesOrderHeader06115380772026372895]',
  @del_cmd = N'CALL [sp_MSdel_SalesSalesOrderHeader06115380772026372895]',
  @upd_cmd = N'SCALL [sp_MSupd_SalesSalesOrderHeader06115380772026372895]'

GO
```

> **Note**
>
> You can also copy the code from the **C:\Code\Lesson02\Peer-to-Peer\4_ ConfigureReplication_Node2.sql** file.

These queries are the same as specified at the first step (creating the publication at Server 1). Make sure you add the same articles and that the data for the tables is in sync. If not, then sync the data. This, however, doesn't stop you from configuring the replication. We'll cover the issues caused by inconsistent data in the next lesson.

The following queries add the subscription and the push subscription agent on Server 2:

```
EXEC sp_addsubscription
  @publication = "$(PublicationName)",
  @subscriber = "$(Publisher)",
  @destination_db = "$(DatabaseName)",
  @subscription_type = N'Push',
  @sync_type = N'replication support only',
  @article = N'all',
  @update_mode = N'read only',
```

```
@subscriber_type = 0


EXEC sp_addpushsubscription_agent
  @publication = "$(PublicationName)",
  @subscriber = "$(Publisher)",
  @subscriber_db = "$(DatabaseName)",
  @job_login = NULL,
  @job_password = NULL,
  @subscriber_security_mode = 1,
  @frequency_type = 64,
  @frequency_interval = 1,
  @frequency_relative_interval = 1,
  @frequency_recurrence_factor = 0,
  @frequency_subday = 4,
  @frequency_subday_interval = 5,
  @active_start_time_of_day = 0,
  @active_end_time_of_day = 235959,
  @active_start_date = 0,
  @active_end_date = 0
```

> **Note**
>
> You can also copy the code from the **C:\Code\Lesson02\Peer-to-Peer\4_ ConfigureReplication_Node2.sql** file.

These queries are the same, except for the **@subscriber** parameter value, which is set to **$(publisher)** instead of **$(subscriber)** in the first step (creating the publication at Server 1). This is because Server 1 is subscribing to Server 2, therefore the subscriber here is Server 1 and not Server 2.

This completes the fifth and sixth steps in configuring peer-to-peer transactional replication, as mentioned in the previous section.

At this point, you have successfully configured peer-to-peer transactional replication.

Exercise 16: Verifying the Replication

You can verify replication by completing one of the following actions:

- Checking the log reader and distribution agent status or the history.

- Using tracer tokens in the replication monitor. This is explained in the next lesson.

- Performing a DML operation and verifying if it's replicated.

1. We'll use the third option and perform an update on one of the replicated articles. To do this, navigate to **C:\Code\Lesson02\Peer-To-Peer** and open the **5_ VerifyReplication.sql** file.

   Change the query mode to **SQLCMD**:

```
-- Node 1: Neptune\SQL2014
:setvar Publisher "Neptune\SQL2014"
-- Node 2: Neptune\SQL2016
:setvar Subscriber "Neptune\SQL2016"
:setvar DatabaseName "AdventureWorks"


-- Update a record at Node 1: Publisher
:CONNECT $(Publisher)
USE $(DatabaseName)


PRINT 'Set OrderQty=11 at the publisher'

GO


UPDATE Sales.SalesOrderDetail SET OrderQty=11 WHERE SalesOrderDetailID=1

GO


SELECT @@ServerName As ServerName,OrderQty FROM Sales.SalesOrderDetail
WHERE SalesOrderDetailID=1

GO



-- Give 5 seconds to replicate the transaction to the subscriber Node 2
WAITFOR DELAY '00:00:10'


:CONNECT $(Subscriber)
```

```
USE $(DatabaseName)

GO

PRINT 'Get OrderQty at the publisher'

SELECT @@ServerName As ServerName,OrderQty FROM Sales.SalesOrderDetail
WHERE SalesOrderDetailID=1

GO
```

> **Note**
>
> You can also copy the code from the **C:\Code\Lesson02\Peer-To-Peer\5_
> VerifyReplication.sql** file.

This query sets **OrderQty** to **11** for **SalesOrderDetaildID** 1 at Node 1, the publisher. It then waits for 10 seconds for the change to be replicated. It then connects to Node 2, the subscriber, and checks if the **OrderQty** value is the same as that of the publisher for the **SalesOrderDetailId** 1.

You should get the following output:

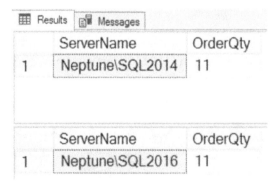

Figure 2.42: Output of verifying change from Node 1 to Node 2

2. The preceding output confirms that the change was replicated from Node 1 to Node 2. To verify that the changes are being replicated from Node 2 to Node 1, update the value at Node 2 and check the value at Node 1.

You can also refer to the **5.1_VerifyReplication.sql** file, which has been placed at **C:\Code\Lesson02\Peer-To-Peer**:

```
-- Node 1: Neptune\SQL2014
:setvar Publisher "Neptune\SQL2014"
-- Node 2: Neptune\SQL2016
:setvar Subscriber "Neptune\SQL2016"
:setvar DatabaseName "AdventureWorks"

-- Update a record at Node 1: Publisher
:CONNECT $(Subscriber)

USE $(DatabaseName)

PRINT 'Set OrderQty=11 at the publisher'

GO

UPDATE Sales.SalesOrderDetail SET OrderQty=110 WHERE SalesOrderDetailID=1

GO

SELECT @@ServerName As ServerName,OrderQty FROM Sales.SalesOrderDetail
WHERE SalesOrderDetailID=1

GO

-- Give 5 seconds to replicate the transaction to the subscriber Node 2
WAITFOR DELAY '00:00:10'


:CONNECT $(Publisher)
```

```
USE $(DatabaseName)

GO

PRINT 'Get OrderQty at the publisher'

SELECT @@ServerName As ServerName,OrderQty FROM Sales.SalesOrderDetail
WHERE SalesOrderDetailID=1

GO
```

> **Note**
>
> You can also copy the code from the **C:\Code\Lesson02\Peer-To-Peer\5.1_**
> **VerifyReplication.sql** file.

This query is the same as the one we explained earlier; however, it now sets the **OrderQty** to **110** for **SalesOrderDetailID** 1 at Node 2 and verifies that the change is replicated at Node 1.

You should get the following output:

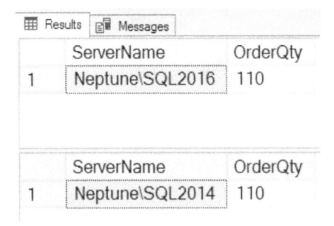

Figure 2.43: Output of verifying change from Node 2 to Node 1

The preceding output confirms that the change was replicated.

Modifying an Existing Publication

The following steps show how the publication properties can be changed, as discussed for the standard transactional replication. We'll now look at how to remove and add an article in a P2P replication.

Exercise 17: Removing an Article

The process of removing an article can be broken down into four main sections:

1. Stopping the distribution agent at each node

2. Dropping the article at each node

3. Verifying that the article has been dropped at each node

4. Starting the distribution agent at each node

Step 1 - Stopping the Distribution Agent at Each Node

Stopping a distribution agent can be easily done by stopping the distribution agent job or by stopping the agent from the **View Synchronization** window.

Stopping the distribution agents at each node will stop the transactions from being applied to the published database. To stop a distribution agent, follow these steps:

1. In SSMS, open Object Explorer and connect to Node 1 (**Neptune\SQL2014**).

2. Expand **Replication | Local Subscriptions**. Right-click on the publication and select **View Synchronization Status** from the context menu:

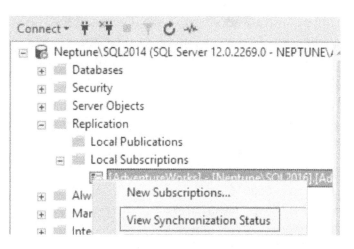

Figure 2.44: The View Synchronization Status option

3. In the **View Synchronization** window, click on **Stop** to stop the distribution agent:

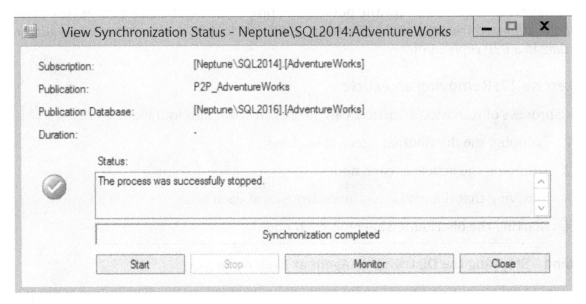

Figure 2.45: The View Synchronization Status window

4. Connect to Node 2 (**Neptune\SQL2016**) and follow the steps from 1 to 3 to stop the distribution agent at Node 2.

   Do not close the **View Synchronization** window. We will need to start the agents once the article has been dropped.

Step 2 - Dropping the Article at Each Node

5. An article is dropped in the same way as we discussed for the standard transactional replication. However, in P2P replication, an article should be dropped from all nodes. P2P replication requires the schema to be in sync at all nodes; if not, the replication terminates with the *schema not in sync* error.

   Navigate to **C:\Code\Lesson02\Peer-To-Peer** and open **6_DropArticle.sql** in SSMS. From the **Query** menu, change the query mode to **SQLCMD**:

```
-- Node 1: Neptune\SQL2014
:setvar Publisher "Neptune\SQL2014"
-- Node 2: Neptune\SQL2016
:setvar Subscriber "Neptune\SQL2016"
:setvar DatabaseName "AdventureWorks"
:setvar PublicationName "P2P_AdventureWorks"
:setvar Article "SalesOrderDetail"

-- Drop the article from Node 1
```

```
:CONNECT $(Publisher)
USE $(DatabaseName)
GO
sp_dropsubscription
 @publication = "$(PublicationName)",
 @article = "$(Article)",
 @subscriber = "$(Subscriber)",
 @destination_db = "$(DatabaseName)";
GO
EXEC sp_droparticle
 @publication = "$(PublicationName)",
 @article = "$(Article)"
GO
WAITFOR DELAY '00:00:5'
GO
-- Drop the article from Node 2
:CONNECT $(Subscriber)
USE $(DatabaseName)
GO
sp_dropsubscription
 @publication = "$(PublicationName)",
 @article = "$(Article)",
 @subscriber = "$(Publisher)",
 @destination_db = "$(DatabaseName)";
GO
EXEC sp_droparticle
 @publication = "$(PublicationName)",
 @article = "$(Article)"
```

Note

You can also copy the code from the **C:\Code\Lesson02\Peer-To-Peer\6_DropArticle.sql** file.

This query uses the **sp_dropsubscription** and **sp_droparticle** procedures to drop an article from the publication from Node 1 and Node 2. This is the same as we did in standard replication.

The query first connects to Node 1 (publisher) and drops the article. It then connects to Node 2 and drops the article from Node 2.

> **Note**
>
> The SQLCMD mode allows you to connect to multiple servers in a single SQL file and therefore removes the need for opening multiple query windows in SSMS. It is therefore used to simplify explanation.

Step 3 - Verifying That the Article is Dropped at Each Node

6. Navigate to `C:\Code\Lesson02\Peer-To-Peer\` and open `7_GetArticles.sql` in SSMS. From the **Query** menu, change the query mode to **SQLCMD**:

```
-- Node 1: Neptune\SQL2014
:setvar Publisher "Neptune\SQL2014"
-- Node 2: Neptune\SQL2016
:setvar Subscriber "Neptune\SQL2016"
:setvar DatabaseName "AdventureWorks"
:setvar PublicationName "P2P_AdventureWorks"

:CONNECT $(Publisher)

USE $(DatabaseName)
go
sp_helparticle @publication = "$(PublicationName)"

GO

:CONNECT $(Subscriber)

USE $(DatabaseName)
GO
sp_helparticle @publication = "$(PublicationName)"
```

> **Note**
>
> You can also copy the code from the `C:\Code\Lesson02\Peer-To-Peer\7_GetArticles.sql` file.

This query connects to the publisher and subscriber and executes the **sp_helparticle** procedure to get all the replicated articles under the **P2P_AdventureWorks** publication. This is similar to what we used in the standard transactional replication earlier in this book.

You should get the following output:

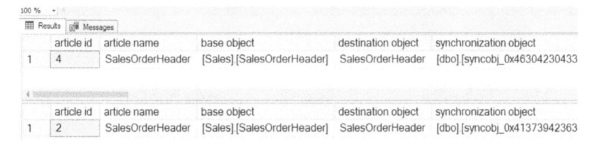

Figure 2.46: The replicated articles

The output doesn't have the **SalesOrderDetail** table and is therefore successfully dropped from the publication.

Step 4 - Starting the Distribution Agent at Each Node

7. To start the distribution agent, navigate to the **View Synchronization Status** window at Node 1 and Node 2 (opened at Step 1) and click on **Start**.

Node 1:

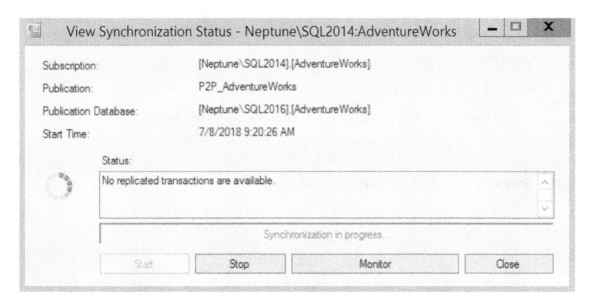

Figure 2.47: The View Synchronization Status window at Node 1

Node 2:

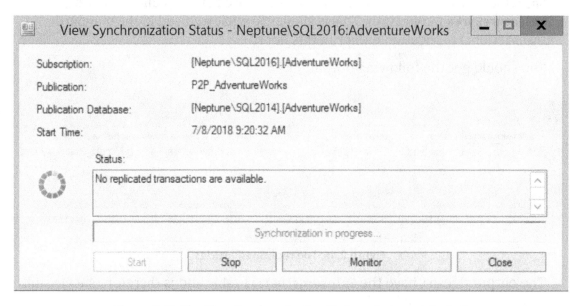

Figure 2.48: The View Synchronization Status window at Node 2

Exercise 18: Adding an Article

The process of adding a new article to a P2P replication is similar to standard transactional replication; however, we need to add the article at each node and make sure that the data in the table is in sync before adding the article.

Adding an article from an existing P2P publication can be broken down into four main sections:

1. Stopping the distribution agent at each node

2. Adding the article at each node

3. Verifying that the article is dropped at each node

4. Starting the distribution agent at each node

Step 1 - Stopping the Distribution Agent at Each Node

1. This step is the same as explained in the *Removing an Article* section. Follow the same steps to stop the distribution agent at each node.

Step 2 - Adding an Article

2. The process of adding an article is the same as that in standard transactional replication; however, the articles should be added at each node.

    Navigate to **C:\Code\Lesson02\Peer-To-Peer** and open **8_AddArticle.sql** in SSMS. From the **Query** menu, change the query mode to **SQLCMD**:

    ```
    -- Node 1: Neptune\SQL2014
    :setvar Publisher "Neptune\SQL2014"
    -- Node 2: Neptune\SQL2016
    :setvar Subscriber "Neptune\SQL2016"
    :setvar DatabaseName "AdventureWorks"
    :setvar PublicationName "P2P_AdventureWorks"
    :setvar Article "SalesOrderDetail"
    :setvar ArticleOwner "Sales"

    -- Add the article from Node 1
    :CONNECT $(Publisher)

    USE $(DatabaseName)

    GO

    EXEC sp_addarticle
      @publication = "$(PublicationName)",
      @article = "$(Article)",
      @source_owner = "$(ArticleOwner)",
      @source_object = "$(Article)",
      @destination_table = "$(Article)",
      @destination_owner = "$(ArticleOwner)"

    GO

    EXEC sp_addsubscription
      @publication = "$(PublicationName)",
      @subscriber = "$(Subscriber)",
      @destination_db = "$(DatabaseName)",
      @reserved='Internal'

    GO

    WAITFOR DELAY '00:00:5'
    ```

```
GO

-- Add the article from Node 2

:CONNECT $(Subscriber)

USE $(DatabaseName)

GO

EXEC sp_addarticle
  @publication = "$(PublicationName)",
  @article = "$(Article)",
  @source_owner = "$(ArticleOwner)",
  @source_object = "$(Article)",
  @destination_table = "$(Article)",
  @destination_owner = "$(ArticleOwner)"

GO

EXEC sp_addsubscription
  @publication = "$(PublicationName)",
  @subscriber = "$(Publisher)",
  @destination_db = "$(DatabaseName)",
  @reserved='Internal'
```

Note

You can also copy the code from the **C:\Code\Lesson02\Peer-To-Peer\8_
AddArticle.sql** file.

This query adds a new article using the **sp_addarticle** and **sp_addsubscription**
procedures, as explained in *Exercise 9*: *Modifying the Existing Publication* for
standard transactional replication.

This query, however, first connects to Node 1 and adds the article and then
connects to Node 2 and adds the article.

Step 3 - Verifying That the Article is Dropped at Each Node

3. To verify that the article has been added to the publication, execute the `C:\Code\Lesson02\Peer-To-Peer\7_GetArticles.sql` script, as explained in **Step 3** of the *Removing an Article* section.

    You should get the following output:

Figure 2.49: Verifying the article has been added

The preceding output clearly shows that the article has been successfully added to the publication at each node.

Step 4 - Starting the Distribution Agent at Each Node

4. Start the distribution agent, as explained in **Step 4** of the *Removing an Article* section.

Activity 2: Configuring Transactional Replication

In this activity, you are required to configure transactional replication for the **AdventureWorks** database. The publication will have the following articles: **Sales.SalesOrderDetail** and **Sales.SalesOrderHeader**.

The steps are as follows:

1. Remove the existing publications, if any, on the **AdventureWorks** database using the steps defined in the *Removing Transactional Replication* section.

2. Drop and create a blank subscription database.

3. Create a publication as **Pub-AdventureWorks** on the SQL2016 instance.

4. Add the articles **Sales.SalesOrderDetail** and **Sales.SalesOrderHeader** to the publication that you created.

5. Create a subscription for the publication that you created on the SQL2014 instance.

6. Verify the replication by deleting a row at the **AdventureWorks** publisher database from the **Sales.SalesOrderHeader** table. The same row should be deleted from the subscriber for the replication to work.

> **Note**
>
> The solution for this activity can be found on page 440.

Summary

In this lesson, we have learned how to configure transactional replication and peer-to-peer transactional replication.

We learned how the different agents, that is, snapshot agent, log reader agent, and distributor agent, work together to replicate the data from the publisher database to the subscriber database.

We then saw how to modify the properties of an existing publication and subscription and how to add and remove articles to/from an existing publication.

In the next lesson, we'll learn how to monitor and troubleshoot transactional replication.

3

Monitoring Transactional Replication

Learning Objectives

By the end of this lesson, you will be able to:

- Set up the replication monitor
- Monitor and troubleshoot transactional replication
- Monitor and troubleshoot peer-to-peer transactional replication

This lesson will show us how to monitor and manage transactional replication. We will also look at how to troubleshoot issues in transactional replication.

Introduction

In the previous lesson, we learned that transactional replication can be used to maintain one or more secondary copies of a database. The secondary database can be used for HA or DR purposes or to offload the reads from the primary database.

In this lesson, we will learn how to monitor transactional replication using the replication monitor. The replication monitor provides real-time replication status (data flow) between the publisher, the distributor, and the subscriber. We'll use the replication monitor and other troubleshooting techniques to fix a few of the common real-world transactional replication problems.

The Replication Monitor

The replication monitor is a GUI that's used to monitor replication agent status and replication performance. It's not specific to transactional replication and can be used to monitor any of the available replication types.

In addition to monitoring capabilities, it allows you to start/stop replication agents, configure alerts, and check agent profiles.

> **Note**
>
> You should set up transactional replication if this was removed in the previous lesson.

This lesson first talks about standard replication issues and then P2P replication issues. Most of the issues that are discussed are common, other than the conflicts specific to P2P replication.

When reconfiguring transaction replication, drop P2P replication, and drop **AdventureWorks** at the two instances. Restore the **AdventureWorks2016** database as **AdventureWorks** on the SQL Server 2016 instance. Create a blank **AdventureWorks** database on the SQL Server 2014 instance. Follow the steps in *Lesson 2, Transactional Replication*, to configure it.

Exercise 19: Setting Up the Replication Monitor

The replication monitor can be used to monitor one or more replication environments, as long as you are able to connect to the instances.

To set up the replication monitor, follow these steps:

1. Open **SSMS | Object Explorer** and connect to a publisher or a subscriber server. In Object Explorer, right-click on the **Replication** node and select **Launch Replication Monitor** from the context menu:

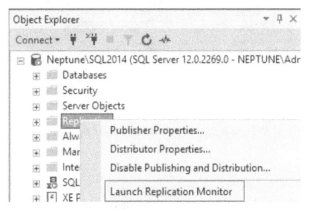

Figure 3.1: The Launch Replication Monitor option

The replication monitor looks as shown in the following screenshot:

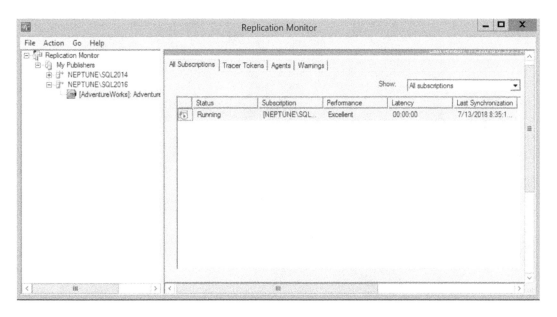

Figure 3.2: The replication monitor

The left-hand pane displays a list of instances grouped by publishers. You can change the grouping to that of distributers if you wish to by right-clicking on **My Publishers** and selecting **Switch to distributor view**.

2. If you don't see the publisher node already added in the replication monitor or the ability to add a new publisher, right-click on the **Replication Monitor | My Publishers** node and select **Add Publisher**:

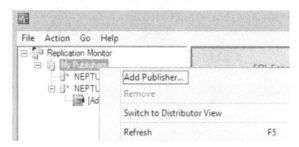

Figure 3.3: The Add Publisher option

> **Note**
>
> The publisher that is to be added should be reachable from the system that hosts the replication monitor.

3. In the **Add Publisher** window, click on the **Add** button and select **Add SQL Server Publisher** from the drop-down menu:

Figure 3.4: The Add Publisher window

> **Note**
>
> The publisher might already be added to the replication monitor. Therefore, in order to add a publisher, drop it from the replication monitor.

You can also add an Oracle publisher or specify a distributor and all publishers associated with it.

4. In the **Connect to Server** window, provide the publisher server name and authentication and click on **Connect**:

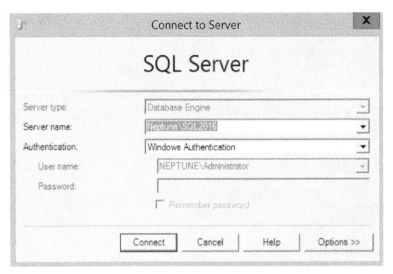

Figure 3.5: The Connect to Server window

The publisher will be displayed in the **Add Publisher** window, as shown here:

Figure 3.6: The Add Publisher window with the publisher added

5. The replication monitor does an auto refresh to get the replication agent status based on the **Refresh rate** value. The default refresh rate is 10 seconds. Leave the **Refresh rate** value as default.

6. We can also group the publishers together. Let's create a new group called **Development** and add the publisher to the **Development** group.

   In the **Add Publisher** window, under the **Publisher group** section, select **New Group**. Type in the group name and click on **OK** to continue:

Figure 3.7: The New Group window

We have added a publisher and a group. The **Add Publisher** window looks as shown here:

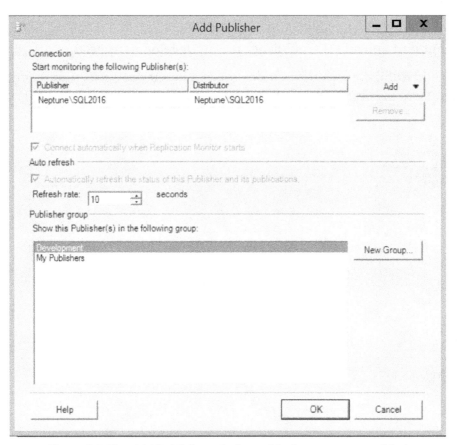

Figure 3.8: The Add Publisher window with the new group added

7. Click **OK** to complete the operation and close the **Add Publisher** window.

Monitoring Replication with the Replication Monitor

Once publishers have been added to the replication monitor, it monitors the publishers for errors and latency. The data is refreshed automatically every 10 seconds. The refresh rate can be changed when adding the publisher, as shown in the last step of the previous exercise.

In the replication monitor, you can click on the server name on the left-hand pane under the **Development** group. The right-hand window shows the status of all the publications for the selected publisher under the **Publications** tab:

Figure 3.9: The Publications tab

The **Subscription Watch List** tab lists out all the subscriptions for the publications on the selected server:

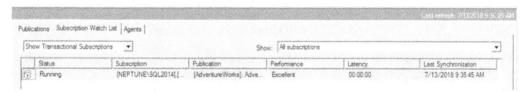

Figure 3.10: The Subscription Watch List tab

It allows you to select from different subscription types:

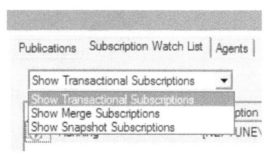

Figure 3.11: The dropdown for subscription types

This gives an overview of subscription performance and latency.

The **Agents** tab lists all the available agents and their performance:

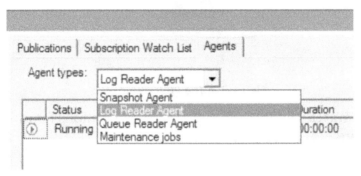

Figure 3.12: The Agents tab

You can select different agents from the **Agent types** dropdown:

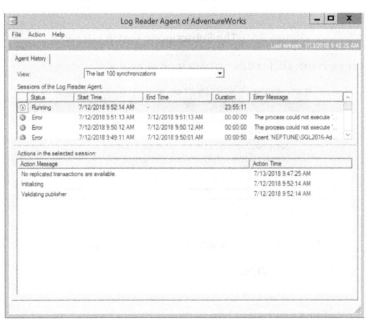

Figure 3.13: The Agent types dropdown

You can double-click on the grid to open the agent history:

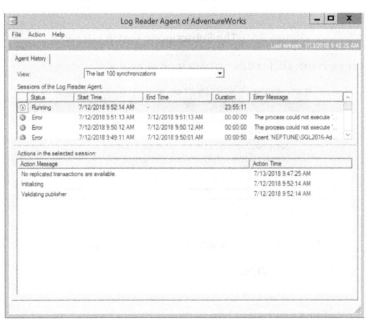

Figure 3.14: The agent history window

The **Agent History** window displays agent run history with errors, if any. If there's an error, it also gives details about the error. It allows you to get the agent history grouped by different views, as shown here:

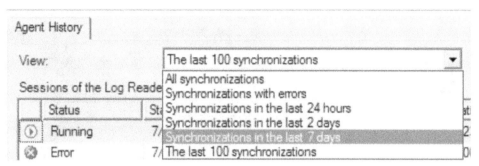

Figure 3.15: The grouping dropdown in the agent history window

You can view the agent history in the last 24 hours, two days, or seven days, or view only the last 100 or all synchronizations.

You can also stop/start or change the job and agent profile from the **Action** menu:

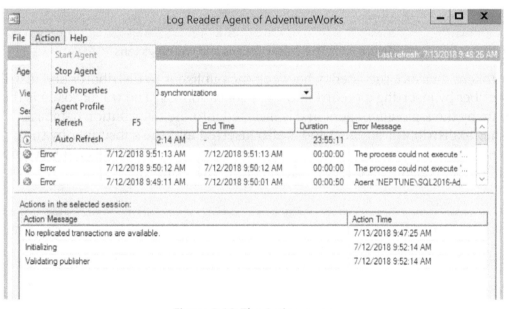

Figure 3.16: The Action menu

In the main replication monitor, on the left-hand pane, you can expand **Development |
Publisher** and then select the publication name. This gives you two additional features,
tracer tokens and warnings, other than the monitoring agents for performance and
latency:

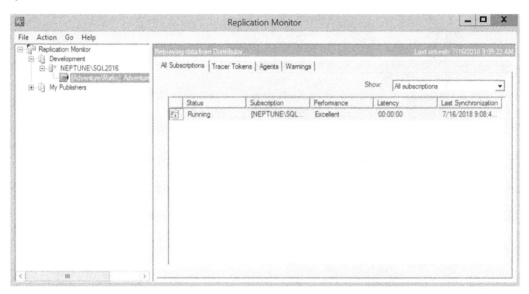

Figure 3.17: The Tracer Tokens and Warnings tabs

Tracer tokens measure the latency between the publisher to distributor and distributor
to subscriber by inserting a record into the publication log. The tracer token is then
picked up by the log reader agent and is inserted into the distribution database
(publisher to distributor latency) and is also inserted into the subscriber by the
distribution agent (distribution to subscriber latency). The tracer token information is
saved in the **MStracer_tokens** and **MStracer_history** tables.

In the replication monitor, going to the **Tracer Tokens** tab and clicking on **Insert Tracer** will show the total latency, which is the time it takes to replicate a single transaction from the publisher to the subscriber:

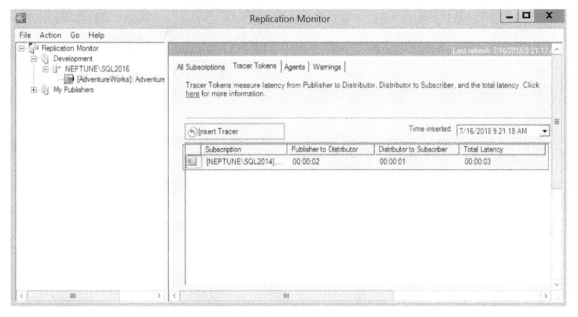

Figure 3.18: Inserting a tracer

Exercise 20: Configuring Replication Alerts

In this exercise, we will add an email alert for our configured replication:

1. In the replication monitor, navigate to the **Warnings** tab.

    Observe that the two warnings related to subscription expiration and latency threshold are already enabled. However, even if the threshold is reached, there won't be any alert being sent as the **Alert** column is unchecked. To enable alerts, select the **Configure Alerts** button in the lower-left corner of the window:

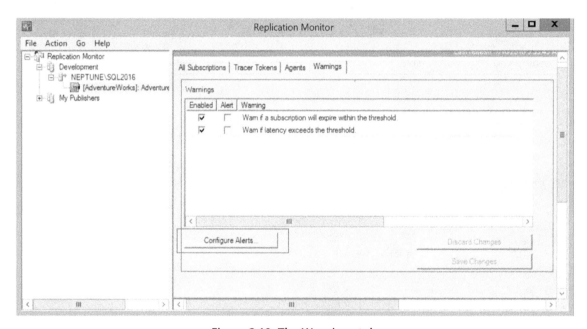

Figure 3.19: The Warnings tab

These warnings are also shown in the replication agent history.

2. In the **Configure Replication Alerts** dialog box, double-click on the alert you want to configure:

Figure 3.20: The Configure Replication Alerts window

3. In the **alert properties** window, in the **General** tab, check the **Enable** checkbox, if not already checked, besides the alert name, and select the database as **AdventureWorks**:

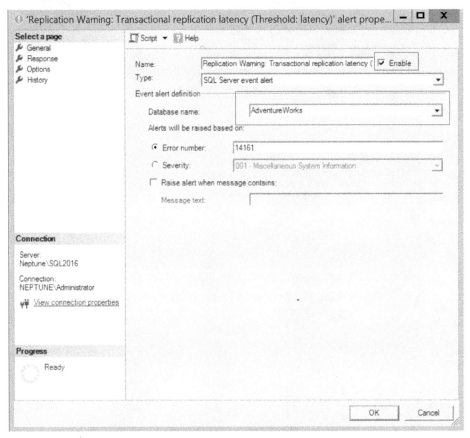

Figure 3.21: The alert properties window

4. In the **Response** tab, check **Notify operators** and check the **E-mail** option for the **Alerts** operator in the operators list. Click **OK** to close the window and configure the alert:

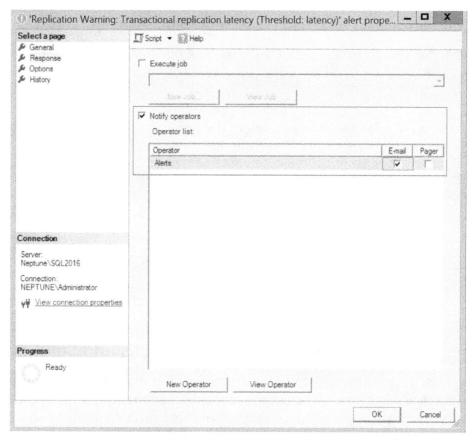

Figure 3.22: The alert properties window with the alert added

> **Note**
>
> The **Alerts** operator should have been created as part of the lab setup. If it doesn't exist, use the `C:\Code\Lesson03\1_CreateOperator.sql` script to create a new operator.

Once an alert has been configured, it sends out an email whenever a threshold is reached.

Activity 3: Configuring an Agent Failure Error

You have configured transactional replication for the `AdventureWorks` database. You want to get email notifications whenever there is a replication agent failure. To do this, you have decided to configure a **Replication: agent failure** alert. The aim of this activity is to configure an agent failure error in an existing transaction replication.

A prerequisite for this activity is that a transactional publication should exist to create this alert.

The steps for this activity are as follows:

1. Open the replication monitor and select the publication you wish to set the alert for. Select the **Warnings** tab in the right-hand pane.

2. In the **Warnings** tab, click on the **Configure Alerts** button. Configure the **Replication: agent failure** replication alert, following the steps in *Exercise 20: Configuring Replication Alerts*.

> **Note**
>
> The solution for this activity can be found on page 441.

Real-World Transactional Replication Problems and Solutions

This section discusses some of the common real-world transactional replication problems that may occur in a transactional replication configuration. There are no specific patterns for these problems. Almost all of these problems can be solved without having to reconfigure the replication.

Transactional replication doesn't require that much management once configured. However, you'd have to look at issues that may occur from time to time. In this section, we'll look at some of those issues.

We can group these issues under the following categories:

- Configuration issues
- Data issues
- Performance issues

> **Note**
>
> This categorization is done for understanding, and is not the standard categorization from Microsoft. This lesson doesn't cover all issues. It covers common issues and explains the solutions to them in a way so that you can fix other issues.

Configuration Issues

As the name suggests, these are issues that may occur if transactional replication isn't configured properly. Let's look at some of these configuration issues.

Exercise 21: Problem 1 – Unable to Connect to Distributor

In this problem, the process cannot connect to the distributor *distributor instance name*.

Setup

To reproduce this problem, follow these steps:

> **Note**
>
> To reproduce the error, we'll set up transactional replication. Any existing publication and subscription should be removed before running the following scripts.

1. Navigate to `C:\Code\Lesson02\Transactional` and open `3_RemoveReplication.sql` in a new query window. Change the query mode to **SQLCMD**. Modify the publisher, the subscriber, and the distributor server name. Modify the `PublicationName` if required. Execute the query to drop the existing replication.

2. Connect to the SQL2014 instance and execute the following command to drop and recreate a blank **AdventureWorks** database:

```
USE master
GO
DROP DATABASE AdventureWorks
GO
CREATE DATABASE AdventureWorks
GO
sp_changedbowner 'sa'
```

3. Navigate to **C:\Code\Lesson03\Problem01** and open **1_CreatePublication.sql**. Change the query mode to **SQLCMD** and modify the following parameters, as instructed earlier:

```
:setvar Publisher "Neptune\SQL2016"
:setvar Subscriber "Neptune\SQL2014"
:setvar Distributor "Neptune\SQL2016"
:setvar DatabaseName "AdventureWorks"
:setvar PublicationName "AdventureWorks-Tran_Pub"
```

After modifying the parameters, execute the query to create the **AdventureWorks-Tran_Pub** publication and the log reader agent job.

4. Navigate to **C:\Code\Lesson03\Problem01** and open **2_CreateSubscription.sql**. Change the query mode to **SQLCMD** and modify the following parameters, as instructed earlier:

```
:setvar Publisher "Neptune\SQL2016"
:setvar Subscriber "Neptune\SQL2014"
:setvar Distributor "Neptune\SQL2016"
:setvar DatabaseName "AdventureWorks"
:setvar PublicationName "AdventureWorks-Tran_Pub"
:setvar DistLogin "repluser"
:setvar DistPwd "repl@user"
```

After modifying the parameters, execute the query to create a pull subscription for the **AdventureWorks-Tran_Pub** publication that was created in *step 3*.

> **Note**
>
> In the **2_CreateSubscription.sql** script, observe that the distribution agent connects using SQL authentication and not Windows authentication, unlike the previous replication configurations.

At this point, you have a transactional replication set up for the **AdventureWorks** database.

Troubleshooting

Now, let's verify whether the replication is configured successfully and is up and running or dead:

1. We can start by verifying the status in the replication monitor. Launch the replication monitor and check the subscription and the snapshot, as well as the log reader agent's status.

2. **Subscription status**: Go to the **Subscription Watch List** tab and observe that the subscription is in the uninitialized state. This may indicate a problem with any of the three agents: snapshot, log reader, or distribution agent:

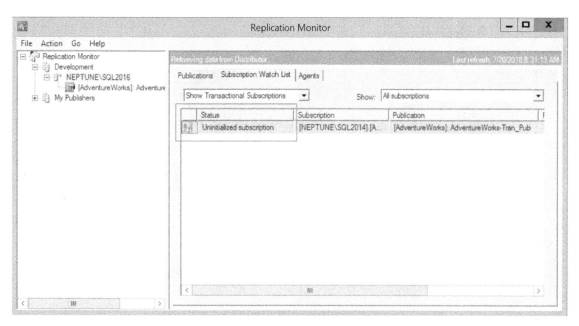

Figure 3.23: The replication monitor showing the error

3. **Snapshot and log reader agent status**: Go to the **Agents** tab and observe that the snapshot agent ran successfully and generated the snapshot. Moreover, the log reader agent should also be running:

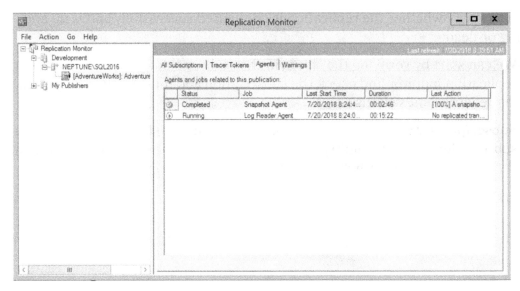

Figure 3.24: The replication monitor showing the snapshot agent ran successfully

4. **Distribution agent**: Select the **All Subscriptions** tab in the replication monitor and double-click on the subscription row. Under the **Distributor to Subscriber History** tab, observe that distribution agent history is blank, indicating that it isn't started yet:

Figure 3.25: The replication monitor showing the distribution agent history

5. Navigate to the **Undistributed Commands** tab. Observe that there are 1,494 transactions in the distribution database that have not yet been applied at the subscriber:

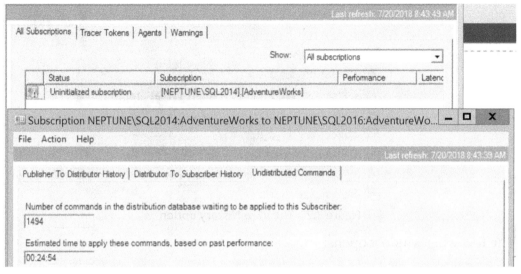

Figure 3.26: The Undistributed Commands tab

> **Note**
>
> An alternate approach to check that the problem is between the distributor and the subscriber is to insert a tracer token.

This confirms that the problem is with the distribution agent.

6. **Review the distribution agent job history**: Connect to the subscriber server in the Object Explorer and expand the **SQL Server Agent** node. Locate the distribution agent job and then right-click and select **View History** to check the job history:

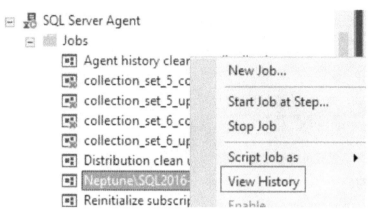

Figure 3.27: The View History option

The following window opens:

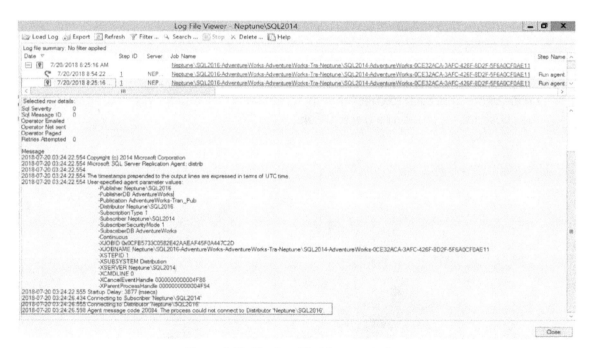

Figure 3.28: The Log File Viewer window

Observe that the error says **The process could not connect to Distributor 'Neptune\SQL2016**.

7. You can also check the error by querying the **MSsubscription_agents** table in the subscriber database. Execute the following query on the subscriber database:

```
SELECT [id]
      ,[publisher]
      ,[publisher_db]
      ,[publication]
      ,[last_sync_status]
      ,[last_sync_summary]
FROM [AdventureWorks].[dbo].[MSsubscription_agents]
```

You should get the following output:

Figure 3.29: Output showing the error

At this point, we know that the distribution agent job on the subscriber server isn't able to connect to the distributor. One cause of this is the network connectivity between the publisher and the subscriber; however, it can be ruled out here as we do have good network connectivity.

8. Now, go to the **Subscription Properties** window to look at the subscription properties and find out how the distribution agent connects to the distributor:

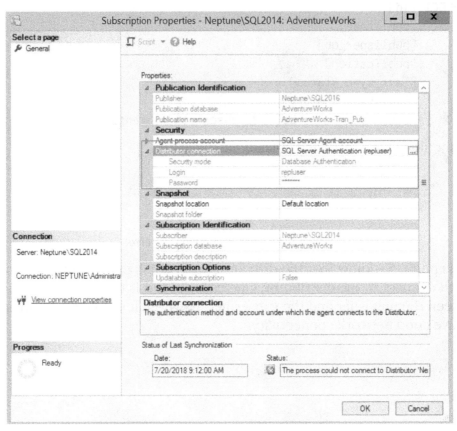

Figure 3.30: The Subscription Properties window

9. You can also view the subscription properties by querying the **MSsubscription_ properties** table or executing the system stored procedure **sp_ helppullsubscription** at the subscriber database. Check for the **distributor_login** and the **distributor_security_mode** column in the table or the procedure output. Execute the following query:

```
SELECT [publisher]
      ,[publisher_db]
      ,[publication]
      ,[distributor]
      ,[distributor_login]
      ,[distributor_password]
      ,[distributor_security_mode]
  FROM [AdventureWorks].[dbo].[MSsubscription_properties]
```

The preceding query returns the following output:

	publisher	publisher_db	publication	distributor	distributor_login	distributor_security_mode	distributor_password
1	Neptune\SQL2016	AdventureWorks	AdventureWorks-Tran_Pub	Neptune\SQL2016	repluser	0	√□╪╬┴╚╝□╜╬╘╞╩╵⑧▓▒▥▦▩▦▦

Figure 3.31: Output showing the subscription properties

The **distributor_security_mode** of **0** indicates SQL authentication.

At this point, the problem seems to be with the authentication; either the password for repluser is wrong or the repluser doesn't exist or doesn't have the correct permission on the distribution instance.

Solution

There are two possible solutions to this problem:

- Change the security mode to Windows authentication, which is **Impersonate SQL Server Agent Service Account** if it has access to the distributor
- Assign relevant permissions to repluser

Solution 1: Modifying the Distributor Security Mode

The distributor security mode can be modified either from SSMS or by T-SQL. To modify it from SSMS, follow these steps:

1. Connect to the subscriber server from the Object Explorer and open the subscription properties, as mentioned earlier.

2. In the **Subscription Properties** window, select the button (with three dots) besides the **SQL Server Authentication (repluser)** text:

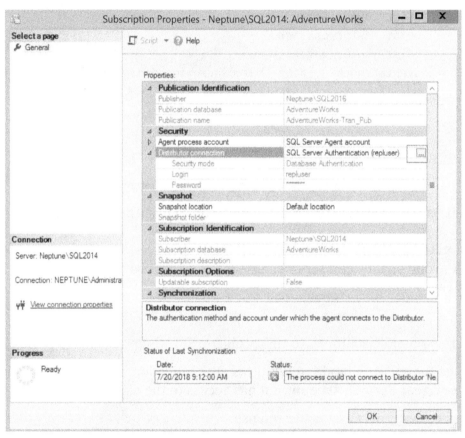

Figure 3.32: The Subscription Properties window

3. In the **Enter Connection Information** dialog box, select **Impersonate agent process account (Window Authentication)** and click on **OK** to continue:

Figure 3.33: The Enter Connection Information dialog box

4. Click **OK** to close the Subscription Properties window.

5. To change the subscription properties using T-SQL, connect to the subscriber database in SSMS, change the query mode to **SQLCMD**, and execute the following query:

```
:setvar Publisher "Neptune\SQL2016"
:setvar Subscriber "Neptune\SQL2014"
:setvar Distributor "Neptune\SQL2016"
:setvar DatabaseName "AdventureWorks"
:setvar PublicationName "AdventureWorks-Tran_Pub"
:setvar Property "distributor_security_mode"
:setvar Value "1"

:CONNECT $(Subscriber)

USE $(DatabaseName)

EXECUTE sp_change_subscription_properties
  @publisher="$(Publisher)",
  @publisher_db="$(DatabaseName)",
```

```
@publication = "$(PublicationName)",
@property= "$(Property)",
@value = "$(Value)"
```

> **Note**
>
> You can also copy the code from the **C:\Code\Lesson03\Problem01\3_ ModifyDistSecurityModeto1.sql** file.

The **sp_change_subscription_properties** procedure is used to set **distributor_ security_mode** to 1, which is Windows authentication. The distribution agent now uses the SQL Server agent service account to connect to the distributor.

6. After you modify the property, navigate to the replication monitor and check the distributor to subscriber history:

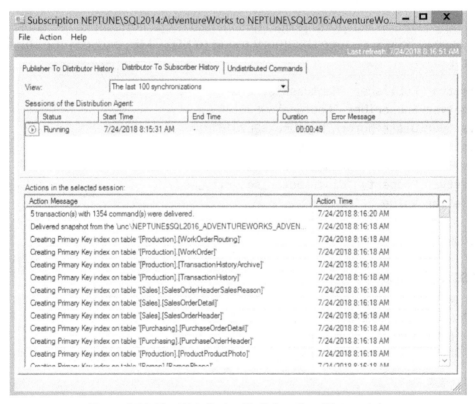

Figure 3.34: The Distributor To Subscriber History tab

Observe that the transactions are now being applied to the subscriber. This was blank earlier.

Solution 2: Giving the Required Permission to repluser

> **Note**
>
> Before applying solution 2, you need to revert to the initial configuration so as to use the repluser to connect to the distributor. You can do this by executing the **C:\ Code\Lesson03\Problem01\4_ModifyDistSecurityModeto0.sql** file. Restart the distributor agent for the change to take effect.

Another solution to this problem is to create and grant the necessary permissions to the repluser. The repluser needs the following permissions:

- Access to the publisher database
- It should be a member of the publication access list

The steps are as follows:

1. To grant the necessary permissions, first navigate to **C:\Code\Lesson03\Problem01** and open **5_GrantPermissionrepluser.sql** in SSMS. Change the query mode to **SQLCMD** and execute the query:

   ```
   :setvar Publisher "Neptune\SQL2016"
   :setvar DatabaseName "AdventureWorks"
   :setvar PublicationName "AdventureWorks-Tran_Pub"
   :setvar Login "repluser"

   :CONNECT $(Publisher)


   USE [master]
   GO
   CREATE LOGIN [repluser] WITH PASSWORD=N'repl@User123',
   DEFAULT_DATABASE=[master], CHECK_EXPIRATION=OFF, CHECK_POLICY=OFF
   GO

   USE $(DatabaseName)

   CREATE USER [repluser] FOR LOGIN [repluser]
   GO
   -- add user to publication access list (PAL)
   EXECUTE sp_grant_publication_access
     @publication = "$(PublicationName)",
   ```

```
@login= "$(Login)"
```

> **Note**
>
> You can also copy the code from the **C:\Code\Lesson03\Problem01\5_
> GrantPermissionrepluser.sql** file.

This query performs the following actions at the publisher: creates a SQL Server login repluser, creates the repluser for the repluser login in the **AdventureWorks** database, and adds the repluser to the publication access list.

2. After the script's execution, verify that the login repluser has been created and has been added as a user to the publisher database (**AdventureWorks**, in our case). To verify that the repluser has been added to the publication access list, check the publication access list in the **Publication Properties** window:

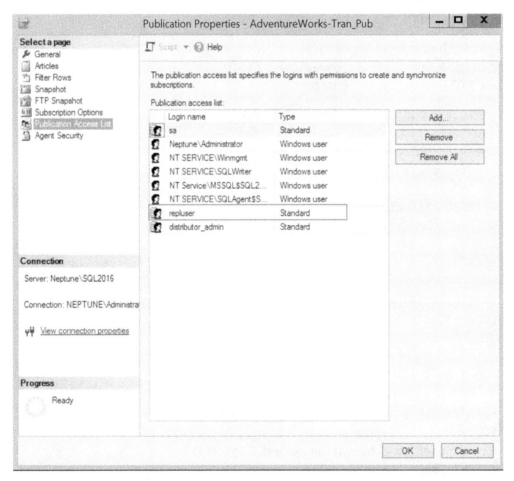

Figure 3.35: The Publication Properties window

You may have to stop and start the distribution agent for the changes to take effect. To verify that replication works, make use of tracer tokens, as explained earlier.

This completes Problem 1.

Exercise 22: Problem 2 – Inactive Subscriptions

The distribution agent fails with the following error:

```
The subscription(s) have been marked inactive and must be reinitialized.
NoSync subscriptions will need to be dropped and recreated.
```

Setup

To reproduce the problem, follow these steps:

1. Navigate to **C:\Code\Lesson03\Problem02** and open **1_MakeSubscriptionInActive. sql** in SSMS. Connect to the distributor and execute the following query:

   ```
   -- Execute the query at the publisher

   UPDATE
       distribution.dbo.MSsubscriptions
   SET STATUS = 0
   ```

   > **Note**
   >
   > You can also copy the code from the **C:\Code\Lesson03\Problem02\1_ MakeSubscriptionInActive.sql** file.

   The **MSsubscriptions** table contains one row for each replicated article. This query sets the replication status to **0**, which is inactive.

In a more practical and real-world scenario, you get this error when subscribers are not synchronized within the distribution retention period or the publisher retention period. The distributor retention period is defined by the **@max_distretention** parameter and has a default value of 72 hours. If the subscription isn't synced within this period, the distribution agent job marks it as inactive. The publisher retention period is defined by the **@retention** parameter, with a default value of 336 hours. If the subscription isn't synced within this time, the subscription is marked as inactive.

The inactive or expired push subscriptions are dropped by the **Expired subscription** clean-up job. However, pull subscriptions are to be removed manually.

> **Note**
>
> Do not run this query in a production environment. It's not advised to modify system tables. Here, it is used for the purpose of explanation.

Troubleshooting

Now, let's verify the replication status:

1. Go to the **Distributor to Subscriber History** tab. We get the error that's shown in the following screenshot:

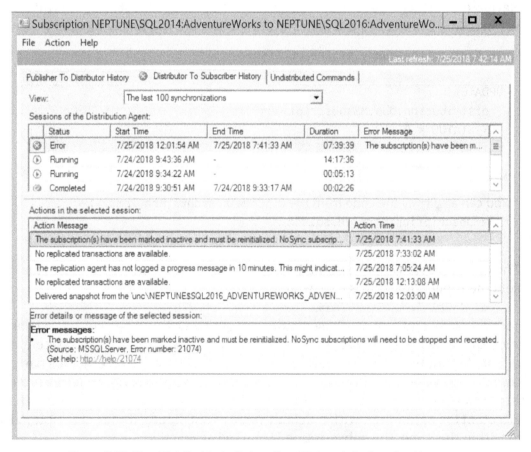

Figure 3.36: The Distributor to Subscriber History tab showing the error

2. You can also query the **MSrepl_errors** table in the distribution database at the publisher to get the error's details. Execute the following query:

```
SELECT
        [time]
        ,[error_type_id]
        ,[error_code]
        ,[error_text]
        ,[xact_seqno]
FROM [distribution].[dbo].[MSrepl_errors]
ORDER BY [time] DESC
```

You should get the following output:

	time	error_type_id	error_code	error_text	xact_seqno
1	2018-07-25 08:00:52.710	0	21074	The subscription(s) have been marked inactive a...	0x00000000000000000000000000000000
2	2018-07-25 07:59:44.577	0	21074	The subscription(s) have been marked inactive a...	0x00000000000000000000000000000000
3	2018-07-25 07:58:41.987	0	21074	The subscription(s) have been marked inactive a...	0x00000000000000000000000000000000

Figure 3.37: The error details

Solution

We can resolve this issue in two ways:

- Reinitializing the subscription
- Modifying the **MSsubscription** table

Solution 1: Reinitializing the Subscription

To reinitialize the subscription, follow these steps:

1. Open the replication monitor and select the **AdventureWorks-Tran_Pub** publication. Under the **All Subscriptions** tab, right-click on the subscription and select **Reinitialize Subscription** from the context menu:

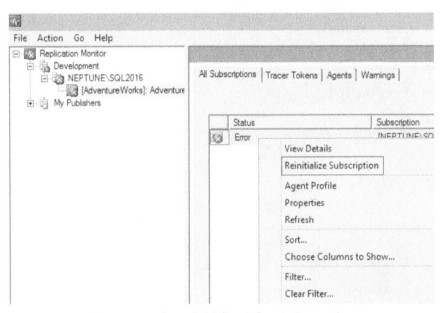

Figure 3.38: The Reinitialize Subscription option

2. In the **Reinitialize Subscription(s)** dialog box, select **Use a new snapshot** and check **Generate the new snapshot now**, if it's not already selected. Click on **Mark For Reinitialization**:

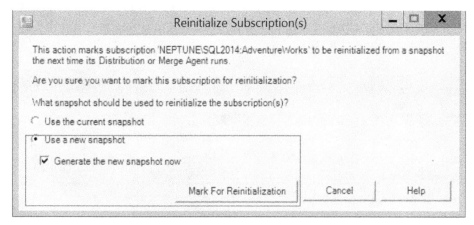

Figure 3.39: The Reinitialize Subscription dialog box

This will start the snapshot agent, which will generate a new snapshot.

3. In the replication monitor, select the **Agents** tab and check the snapshot agent's status:

Figure 3.40: The Agents tab

The snapshot agent is running and will generate a new snapshot. This is required as the subscription hasn't been synced for a long time and may be missing data. Wait for the snapshot to be generated.

4. Once the snapshot has been generated, navigate back to the **All Subscriptions** tab. Observe that the status is now **Running** instead of **Error**. Double-click on the subscription row.

In the resultant dialog box, under the **Distributor to Subscriber History** tab, observe that the distributor agent is now running and has applied the latest snapshot to the subscriber:

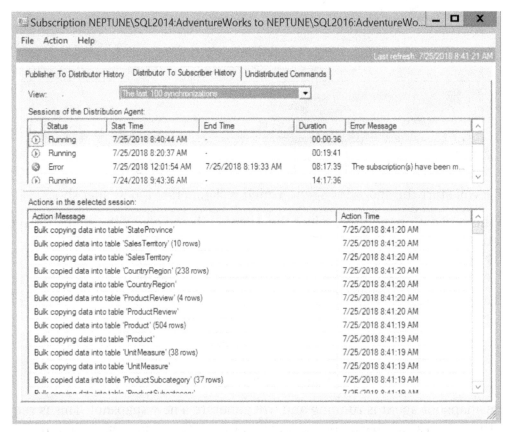

Figure 3.41: The Distributor to Subscriber History tab showing the distributor agent running

This fixes the issue.

Solution 2: Modifying the MSsubscription table

> **Note**
>
> Run the setup script again before you start with solution 2, as the problem has already been fixed by applying solution 1.

It's not at all advised to modify the system tables in a production environment. However, this is one solution that may come in handy if applied correctly. The **MSsubscription** table in the distribution database has one row for each article. It has a status column that can have the following values:

- **status = 0**: This means that the subscription for that article is inactive

- **status = 1**: This means subscribed

- **status = 2**: This means active

The solution is to run an update on the **MSsubscription** table in the publisher/ distributor and set the status to **2** for the given publisher and publication where the status is **0**.

To apply this solution, follow these steps:

1. Query the **MSsubscription** table and check the **status** value for the given publication. The query is to be run at the publisher:

    ```
    SELECT
        s.publisher_db
       ,p.publication
       ,s.article_id
       ,s.status
    FROM distribution.dbo.MSsubscriptions s join
    distribution.dbo.MSpublications p
    ON s.publication_id = p.publication_id
    WHERE p.publication = 'AdventureWorks-Tran_Pub'
    AND s.status=0 AND s.subscriber_db='AdventureWorks'
    ```

You should get the following output:

	publisher_db	publication	article_id	status
13	AdventureWorks	AdventureWorks-Tran_Pub	408	0
14	AdventureWorks	AdventureWorks-Tran_Pub	409	0
15	AdventureWorks	AdventureWorks-Tran_Pub	410	0
16	AdventureWorks	AdventureWorks-Tran_Pub	411	0
17	AdventureWorks	AdventureWorks-Tran_Pub	412	0
18	AdventureWorks	AdventureWorks-Tran_Pub	413	0
19	AdventureWorks	AdventureWorks-Tran_Pub	414	0

Figure 3.42: Checking the status of the publication

The query returns 81 rows.

2. Execute the following query to set **status** to **2** (active) for these rows. The query is to be run at the publisher:

```
UPDATE s SET s.status=2
    FROM distribution.dbo.MSsubscriptions s join
distribution.dbo.MSpublications p
ON s.publication_id = p.publication_id
WHERE p.publication = 'AdventureWorks-Tran_Pub'
AND s.status=0 AND s.subscriber_db='AdventureWorks'
```

You can run the query in *step 1* to check whether the rows have been updated correctly or not. The query in *step 1* returns 0 rows if the update is successful.

Apart from modifying the system table, the solution doesn't guarantee that the subscription will be in sync with the publication. This is because it doesn't apply the snapshot—it changes the status flag, which is picked up by the distribution agent the next time it runs.

To check whether the data is in sync or not, you can use any third-party data/schema comparison tool or the **tablediff** utility, which is a free utility from Microsoft.

> **Note**
>
> To find out more about the tablediff utility, refer to https://docs.microsoft.com/en-us/sql/tools/tablediff-utility?view=sql-server-2017.

Solution 1, though being the correct way to fix the issue, is a time-consuming process for a large database. Solution 2 doesn't apply the snapshot but quickly fixes the replication, allowing the new transactions to go through (new transactions may error out because of data sync issues). The schema and data difference can be fixed later.

This completes problem 2.

Exercise 23: Problem 3 - Missing Replication Stored Procedures

This problem produces the following error:

```
Could not find stored procedure 'sp_MSins_<table_name>'
```

Earlier in this book, we learned that the transactions from the distributor to the subscriber are applied by the insert, update, and delete replication stored procedures.

This error occurs when the replication procedures are missing from the subscriber database.

Setup

1. To reproduce this issue, navigate to `C:\Code\Lesson03\Problem03` and open `1_Setup.sql` in SSMS. Change the query mode to **SQLCMD** and execute the query.

Troubleshooting

1. Open the replication monitor, if not already opened, and check the replication status. You should see the following error:

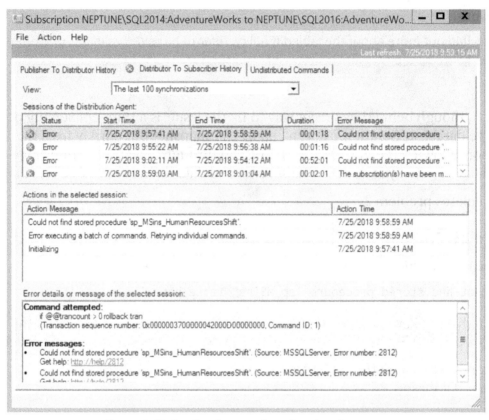

Figure 3.43: Replication monitor showing the error

2. Alternatively, run the following query to get the error details:

```
SELECT
        [time]
        ,[error_type_id]
        ,[error_code]
        ,[error_text]
        ,[xact_seqno]
FROM [distribution].[dbo].[MSrepl_errors]
ORDER BY [time] DESC
```

You should get the following output:

	time	error_code	error_text	xact_seqno
1	2018-07-26 06:55:38.987	2812	Could not find stored procedure 'sp_MSins_HumanResourcesShift'.	0x0000003700000042000D00000000
2	2018-07-26 06:55:38.943		if @@trancount > 0 rollback tran	0x0000003700000042000D00000000
3	2018-07-26 06:55:38.260	2812	Could not find stored procedure 'sp_MSins_HumanResourcesShift'.	0x0000003700000042000D00000000
4	2018-07-26 06:52:47.747	2812	Could not find stored procedure 'sp_MSins_HumanResourcesShift'.	0x0000003700000042000D00000000
5	2018-07-26 06:52:47.737		if @@trancount > 0 rollback tran	0x0000003700000042000D00000000
6	2018-07-26 06:52:47.720	2812	Could not find stored procedure 'sp_MSins_HumanResourcesShift'.	0x0000003700000042000D00000000

Figure 3.44: Output showing the error

Solution

This problem can be solved in the following two ways:

- Reinitializing the subscription will recreate the replication procedures at the subscriber. However, this will also apply the complete database snapshot, which would take time for a bigger database. This solution is therefore not recommended for large databases.

- Recreating the replication procedure.

Solution: Scripting Out the Replication Procedure

Let's look at the second solution. The stored procedure can be recreated by running the system stored procedure **sp_scriptpublicationcustomprocs** in the publisher database. This procedure generates the insert, update, and delete replication procedure for all the articles.

This procedure internally calls the **sp_scriptinsproc**, **sp_scriptdelproc**, and **sp_scriptupdproc** system procedures to get the insert, update, and delete scripts for the replication procedures:

1. To script out all replication procedures, execute the following query at the publisher database. Execute the query in text mode (*Ctrl* + *T* + *E*). This will return the create script for insert, update, and delete procedures for all the articles:

    ```
    USE AdventureWorks
    GO
    EXEC sp_scriptpublicationcustomprocs @publication='AdventureWorks-Tran_
    Pub'
    ```

2. However, as per the error, we are only missing the insert script for the table shift. To script out only the insert script from the replication procedure, execute the following query at the publisher:

    ```
    USE AdventureWorks
    GO
    DECLARE @articleid int;
    SELECT @articleid=article_id FROM distribution.dbo.MSarticles
    WHERE publisher_db='AdventureWorks' and article='Shift'

    EXEC sp_scriptinsproc @artid=@articleid
        ,@publishertype=1
    ```

    You should get the following output:

    ```
    if object_id(N'[sp_MSins_HumanResourcesShift]', 'P') <> 0
    drop proc [sp_MSins_HumanResourcesShift]
    go
    if object_id(N'dbo.MSreplication_objects') is not null
    delete from dbo.MSreplication_objects where object_name = N'sp_MSins_
    HumanResourcesShift'
    go
    create procedure [sp_MSins_HumanResourcesShift]
      @c1 tinyint,@c2 nvarchar(50),@c3 time,@c4 time,@c5 datetime
    as
    begin
    insert into [HumanResources].[Shift](
     [ShiftID]
    ,[Name]
    ```

```
,[StartTime]
,[EndTime]
,[ModifiedDate]
 )
values (
 @c1
,@c2
,@c3
,@c4
,@c5
 )
end
go
if columnproperty(object_id(N'dbo.MSreplication_objects'), N'article',
'AllowsNull') is not null
exec ('insert dbo.MSreplication_objects (object_name, publisher,
publisher_db, publication, article, object_type) values (
+ N''sp_MSins_HumanResourcesShift'' , N''WINDOWS10ENT\SQL2016'' ,
N''AdventureWorks'' , N''AdventureWorks-Tran_Pub'' , N''Shift'' ,''P'')')
```

The script first deletes the entry for **sp_MSins_HumanResourcesShift** from the
MSreplication_objects table. The **MSreplication_objects** table contains entries for
all insert, delete, and update procedures for all the published articles.

> **Note**
>
> Query the **MSreplication_objects** table at the subscriber database for better
> understanding.

The script then creates the **sp_MSins_HumanResourceShift** procedure and inserts an
entry for the procedure in the **MSreplication_objects** table.

3. Copy the preceding query, connect to the subscriber database, and execute it. This will fix the issue. You can verify it in the replication monitor.

> **Note**
>
> Another version of this problem is when the replication insert, update, or delete procedures are missing a parameter. The parameter that's passed to the procedures is the column name from the table, therefore, if there is column mismatch, the procedure errors out.

This completes problem 3.

Data Issues

Data issues are the most common of the issues that may occur in a transactional replication topology. We can't discuss all the data issues; however, we'll discuss the relevant ones and try to establish a methodology to fix all data issues.

Exercise 24: Problem 4 – Row Not Found at the Subscriber

This problem produces the following error:

```
The row was not found at the Subscriber when applying the replicated command.
```

This is one of the most common issues. When a row at the publisher is either deleted or updated, the change is replicated to the subscriber as part of the transactional replication process. However, if the row isn't present at the subscriber, the distribution agent errors out when applying the delete or update command at the subscriber.

Setup

1. To reproduce the error, navigate to **C:\Code\Lesson03\Problem04** and open **1_Setup. sql** in SSMS. Change the query mode to **SQLCMD** and run the query.

Troubleshooting

1. To troubleshoot the problem, open the replication monitor as we did while troubleshooting the previous problems:

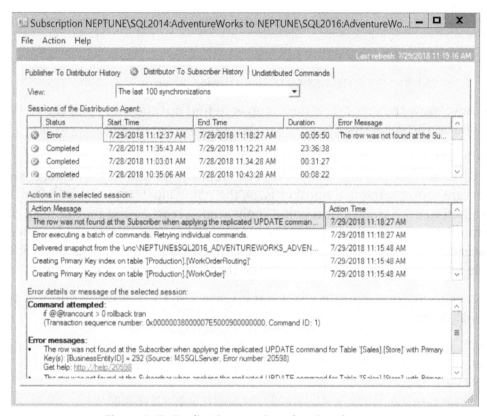

Figure 3.45: Replication monitor showing the error

2. The replication errors out with a **The row was not found at the subscriber** error, as shown in the preceding screenshot. You can also run the following query at the publisher to find out the error:

```
SELECT
        [time]
      ,[error_type_id]
      ,[error_code]
      ,[error_text]
      ,[xact_seqno]
FROM [distribution].[dbo].[MSrepl_errors]
ORDER BY [time] DESC
```

You should get the following output:

	time	error_type_id	error_code	error_text	xact_seqno
1	2018-07-29 11:20:52.403	0	20598	The row was not found at the Subscriber when ap...	0x00000038000007E5000900000000
2	2018-07-29 11:20:52.397	0		if @@trancount > 0 rollback tran	0x00000038000007E5000900000000
3	2018-07-29 11:20:52.377	0	20598	The row was not found at the Subscriber when ap...	0x00000038000007E5000900000000
4	2018-07-29 11:18:28.567	0	20598	The row was not found at the Subscriber when ap...	0x00000038000007E5000900000000
5	2018-07-29 11:18:28.327	0		if @@trancount > 0 rollback tran	0x00000038000007E5000900000000
6	2018-07-29 11:18:28.120	0	20598	The row was not found at the Subscriber when ap...	0x00000038000007E5000900000000

Figure 3.46: Output showing the error

We now know the error. The next step is to find out the table and the row that is missing at the subscriber.

3. To do that, we need the **xact_seqno** value from the previous query result. The **xact_seqno** value can also be found in the replication monitor. The **xact_seqno** or the transaction sequence number is, as the name illustrates, the number that's assigned to each transaction being replicated. A transaction may consist of one or more commands. Each individual command in a transaction is identified by a **command_id**. The transactions to be replicated are stored in the **MSrepl_Commands** table in the distribution database at the distributor/publisher.

To get the command for the given **xact_seqno**, run the following query at the publisher/distributor:

```
USE Distribution
GO
EXECUTE sp_browsereplcmds
   @xact_seqno_start = '0x00000038000007E5000900000000'
    ,@xact_seqno_end =  '0x00000038000007E5000900000000'
```

sp_browsereplcmds lists out the details for the commands being replicated for a given start and end **xact_seqno**. We only have one **xact_seqno**, therefore the start and end **xact_seqno** parameter values are the same in the procedure. You should get the following output:

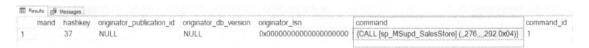

	mand	hashkey	originator_publication_id	originator_db_version	originator_lsn	command	command_id
1		37	NULL	NULL	0x00000000000000000000	{CALL [sp_MSupd_SalesStore] (,,276,,,292.0x04)}	1

Figure 3.47: Output showing the command

`xact_seqno` may be different in your case. `sp_browsereplcmds` returns a lot more information; however, scroll to the right and find the **command** column. Observe that the update procedure for the `Sales.Store` table is being executed and is erroring out.

Now that we have identified the problem, let's look at the possible solutions.

Solution

There are two possible solutions to this problem:

- Skip the errors and fix data inconsistencies
- Insert the missing row at the subscriber

Solution 1 lets us prevent the replication from being stopped whenever a data issue occurs. This is important in a high-transaction **online transaction processing (OLTP)** environment. The error transaction is skipped, and other transactions continue to replicate. However, it requires regular comparison of the data to find and fix the inconsistencies.

Solution 2, on the other hand, makes sure that the data is consistent. However, the replication stops, resulting in delays.

Skipping the Errors

Replication allows you to skip errors by specifying the error numbers. This allows the replication to continue whenever the specified error occurs. This can be done either by modifying the distribution agent job or by changing the distribution agent profile.

Modifying the Distributor Agent Job

To modify the distributor agent job, follow these steps:

1. In SSMS, connect to the subscriber (pull subscription), expand **SQL Server Agent**, right-click the distribution agent job, and select **Properties** from the context menu:

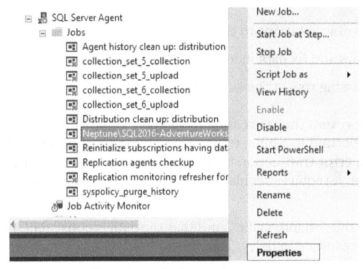

Figure 3.48: The Properties option

2. In the **Job Properties** window, select **Steps** from the left-hand pane. Select the **Run agent** step and click **Edit** at the bottom of the window:

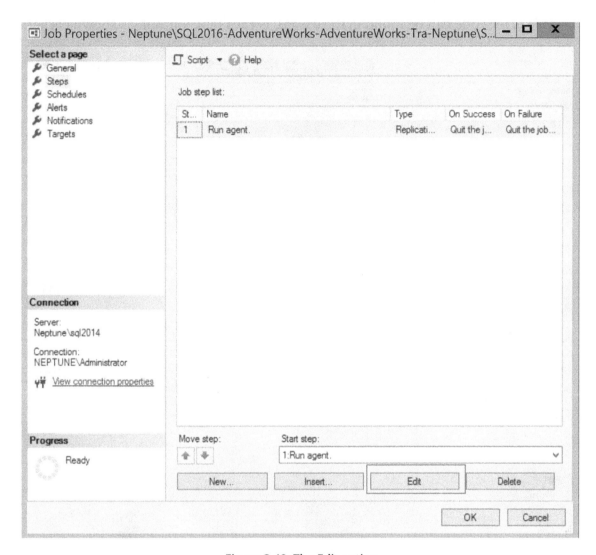

Figure 3.49: The Edit option

3. In the **Command** textbox, add the following parameter at the end:

   ```
   -SkipErrors 20598
   ```

   This error code can be found in the **MSrepl_errors** table output, as shown earlier:

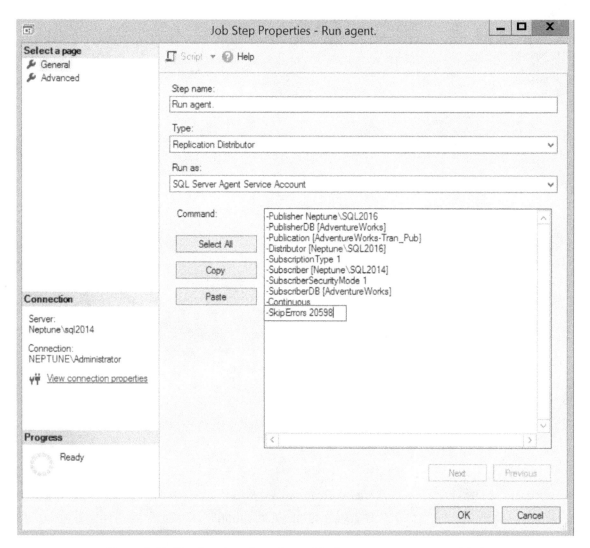

Figure 3.50: The Command textbox with the error parameter added

Click **OK** to save the step and then click **OK** to save the job.

4. The next step is to restart the distribution agent for the new settings to take effect. To restart, right-click on the distribution agent job under the **SQL Server Agent** tab and click on **Stop**. When the job stops successfully, right-click on the job and select **Start** to start the job again.

Once the job restarts successfully, check the replication monitor status; the row has been skipped, and the replication resumes successfully:

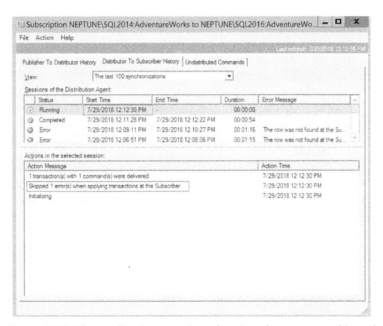

Figure 3.51: The replication monitor showing the row was skipped

Modifying the Distribution Agent Profile

To modify the distribution agent profile, follow these steps:

1. Connect to Object Explorer in SSMS and connect to the publisher. Right-click on the **Replication** node and select **Distributor Properties** from the context menu:

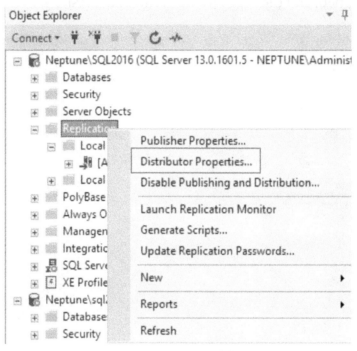

Figure 3.52: The Distributor Properties option

2. In the **Distributor Properties** window, under the **Agent Profiles** section, click on **Profile Defaults**:

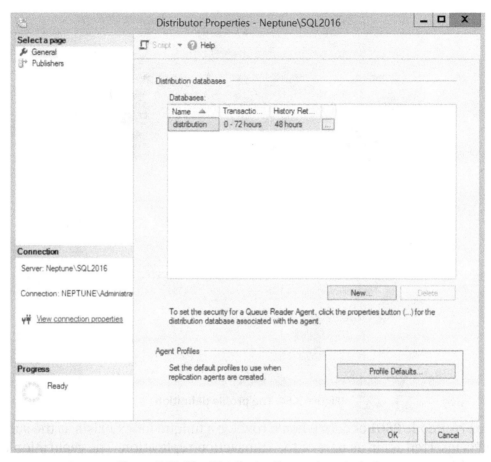

Figure 3.53: The Distributor Properties window

3. In the **Agent Profiles** window, click the button (with three dots) besides the **Continue on data consistency errors** profile.

4. Observe that the profile definition has the **-SkipErrors** parameter defined to skip error codes **2601**, **2627**, and **20598**:

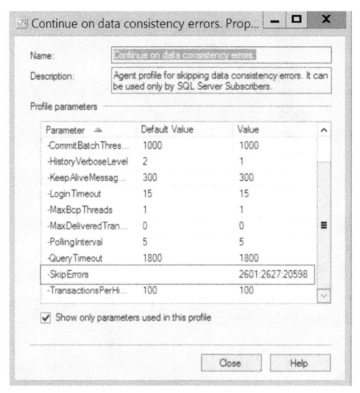

Figure 3.54: The profile definition

The error code **2601** occurs when a row for a unique index exists at the subscriber and is inserted again as part of the transaction replication. The replication errors out with the error `Cannot insert duplicate key row in object <table name> with unique index <index name>`.

The error code **2627** occurs when a row for a given primary key already exists at the subscriber and is inserted again as part of the replication. The replication errors out with the error `Violation of primary key constraint <constraint name>. Cannot insert duplicate key in object <table name>`.

5. Click on **Close** to close the **Continue on data consistency profile** window. In the **Agent Profiles** window, check the **Continue on data consistency errors** profile and uncheck **Default agent profile**.

6. Select **Change Existing Agents** to apply the new profile to all the distribution agents. In the confirmation dialog box, click **Yes** to continue:

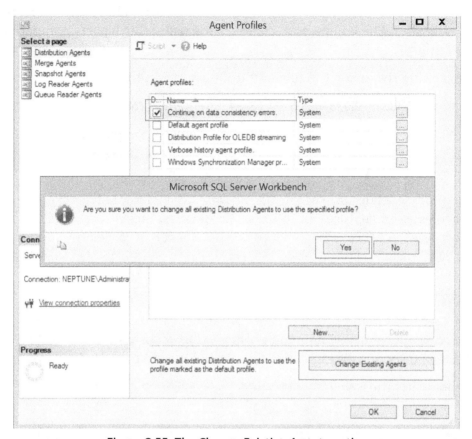

Figure 3.55: The Change Existing Agents option

Click on **OK** to close the **Agent Profiles** window and then click on **OK** to close the distributor properties window. You may have to restart the distribution agent for this change to take effect.

> **Note**
>
> This step will change the profile for all distribution agents. To change specific distribution agent profiles, follow the same steps at the subscriber.

Finding the Missing Row

We now have the replication running, so the next step is to find the missing row at the subscriber. This can be done by comparing the **Sales.Store** table at the subscriber with that of the publisher. The comparison can be made using third-party compare tools or the tablediff utility.

To find the missing row using the tablediff utility, perform the following steps:

1. Navigate to **C:\Code\Lesson03\Problem04** and open **2_Tablediff.txt** in a text editor.

    The following command runs the tablediff utility to compare and generate the T-SQL script to fix the data consistency issue for the **Sales.Store** table. Modify the parameters as per your environment and save the file:

    ```
    "C:\Program Files\Microsoft SQL Server\130\COM\tablediff.exe"
    -sourceserver Neptune\SQL2016 -sourcedatabase AdventureWorks
    -sourcetable Store -sourceschema Sales -destinationServer Neptune\
    SQL2014 -destinationdatabase AdventureWorks -destinationtable Store
    -destinationschema Sales -f "C:\Code\Lesson03\Problem04\SalesStorediff.
    sql"
    ```

2. Open a new command prompt (press Windows + R to open the **Run** window and type **cmd** to open a new command prompt). Copy and paste the modified command from *step 1* into the command prompt. Press *Enter* to execute the command.

    You should get the following output:

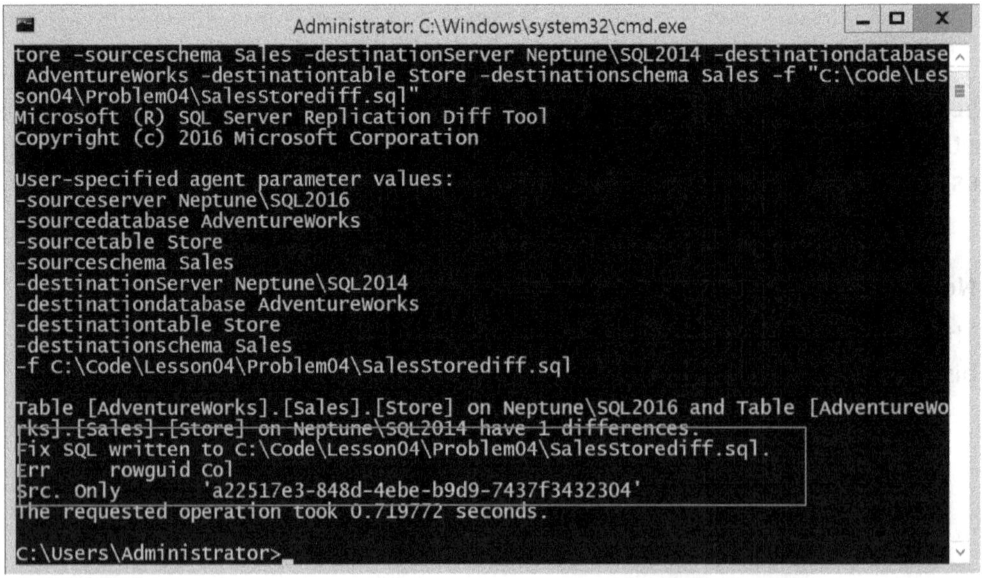

Figure 3.56: The tablediff output

tablediff indicates that there is one row that is at the source and not at the destination. It also generates the T–SQL to sync the source and destination database at the specified location.

3. Navigate to **C:\Code\Lesson03\Problem04** and open **SalesStorediff.sql** in SSMS:

```
-- Host: Neptune\SQL2014
-- Database: [AdventureWorks]
-- Table: [Sales].[Store]
-- Column(s) Demographics are not included in this script because they are
of type(s) text, ntext, varchar(max),
-- nvarchar(max), varbinary(max), image, timestamp, or xml. Columns of
these types cannot be updated by tablediff utility scripts;
-- therefore non-convergence of data can still occur after this script has
been applied.
-- If the tablediff utility output references any of these columns, you
must update the columns manually
-- if you want them to converge.
INSERT INTO [Sales].[Store]
([BusinessEntityID],[ModifiedDate],[Name],[rowguid],[SalesPersonID])
VALUES (292,N'2014-09-12 11:15:07.497',N'Next-Door Bike Store','a22517e3-
848d-4ebe-b9d9-7437f3432304',276)
```

Observe that the script skips the **Demographics** column as it's of the XML datatype and it's not supported by the tablediff utility. The script contains the insert script for the missing row at the subscriber. Connect to the subscriber database and execute the query.

You'll have to manually update the **Demographics** column value to completely sync the data. However, this will solve the row not found at the subscriber issue.

> **Note**
>
> Because of the limitations of the tablediff utility, it's sometimes difficult to sync the data. Moreover, tablediff will be slow on large tables. You should know that almost all data consistency issues can be fixed using the method that's described here. To summarize: find out the reason/error for the data consistency issue and then sync the data.
>
> If the issue is recurring, then find out if there's an application or SQL agent job that's causing data to be deleted/updated at the subscriber.

This completes problem 4.

Performance Issues

As the name suggests, this section talks about common performance issues in transactional replication. Replication performance can be improved not only by appropriately configuring the agent parameters as discussed earlier, but also by following a few of the best practices that will be discussed in this section.

Exercise 25: Problem 5 – Log Reader Agent Takes Time to Scan the Transaction Log

This problem produces the following error:

```
Approximately 500000 log records have been scanned in pass # 4, 0 of which
were marked for replication.
```

This isn't an error; instead, it's an information message that if not considered, can bring down the replication. This message states that the log reader agent has read 500,000 log records that were marked for replication. Ideally, this many log records aren't generated at once in OLTP environments. This means that there is an open and active long-running transaction generating the transactions at large.

The only possible solution to this message is to wait for the transactions to be replicated and to find and stop the runaway transaction, if possible. However, in certain cases, a good replication design can stop the runaway transactions from occurring.

Let's look into this problem.

Setup

1. To reproduce this problem, navigate to **C:\Code\Lesson03\Problem05**. Open **1_ Setup.sql** in SSMS, connect to the publisher database, and execute the query.

Troubleshooting

1. Once this query completes, quickly open the replication monitor to monitor the replication status. In the replication monitor, open the **Subscription** window and navigate to the **Publisher to Distributor History** tab:

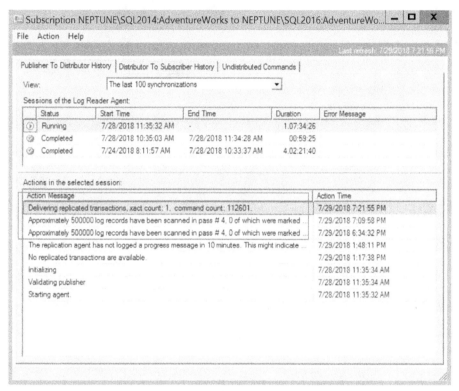

Figure 3.57: The Publisher to Distributor History tab

Observe that it has the following message:

```
Approximately 500000 log records have been scanned in pass # 4, 0 of which
were marked for replication.
```

2. Navigate to the **Distributor to Subscriber History** tab. Observe that it says **Delivering replicated transactions**. This means that the agent is reading the transactions from the distribution database and is applying them to the subscriber:

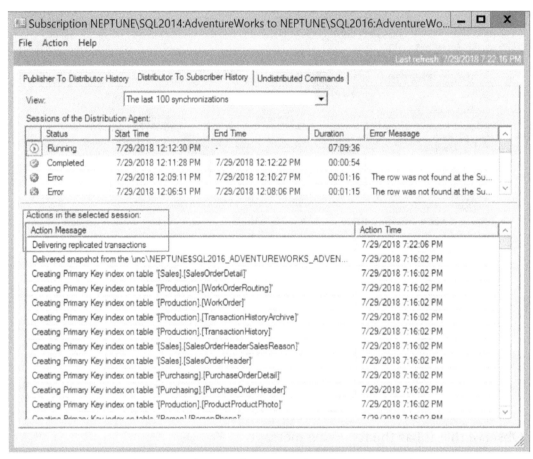

Figure 3.58: The Distributor to Subscriber History tab

3. Quickly navigate to the **Undistributed Commands** tab:

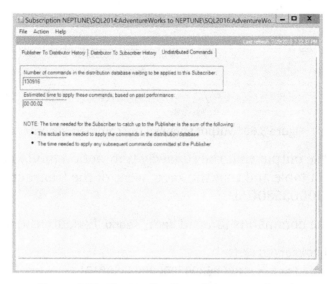

Figure 3.59: The Undistributed Commands tab

Observe that there are 130,916 transactions to be applied to the subscriber. We certainly have a runaway transaction that caused this many log records to be generated. The log reader agent reads the records to be deleted from the transaction log and will insert one row for each row being deleted in the distribution database. This not only increases the distribution database size—it also decreases replication performance.

4. Now, let's work on finding the runaway transaction. Observe that we don't have a **xact_seqno** here to start with. Therefore, let's query the **MSrepl_command** table to get the command count against each **xact_seqno** and the article:

```
SELECT
  rc.xact_seqno,
  a.article,
  COUNT(*) AS CommandCount
FROM MSrepl_commands AS rc WITH(NOLOCK)
join MSarticles a on a.article_id=rc.article_id
GROUP BY rc.xact_seqno,a.article
ORDER BY CommandCount DESC
```

This query returns the following output:

It's clear from the output that the runaway transaction modified the **SalesOrderDetail** table and that the **xact_seqno** of the transaction is **0x0000000800000035800AD**.

5. Now, let's get the commands for said **xact_seqno**. Execute the following query:

```
EXECUTE sp_browsereplcmds
  @xact_seqno_start = '0x0000000800000035800AD'
    ,@xact_seqno_end =  '0x0000000800000035800AD',
    ,@article_id=477
```

The query may take time to complete as it will return 100,000 commands. The **article_id** of **477** is the ID for the **SalesOrderDetail** table. You can get it from the **MSarticles** table:

nmand	hashkey	onginator_publication_id	onginator_db_version	originator_lsn	command	command_id
	54	NULL	NULL	0x00000000000000000000	{CALL [sp_MSdel_SalesSalesOrderDetail] (43659,1)}	1
	55	NULL	NULL	0x00000000000000000000	{CALL [sp_MSdel_SalesSalesOrderDetail] (43659,2)}	2
	56	NULL	NULL	0x00000000000000000000	{CALL [sp_MSdel_SalesSalesOrderDetail] (43659,3)}	3
	57	NULL	NULL	0x00000000000000000000	{CALL [sp_MSdel_SalesSalesOrderDetail] (43659,4)}	4
	58	NULL	NULL	0x00000000000000000000	{CALL [sp_MSdel_SalesSalesOrderDetail] (43659,5)}	5
	59	NULL	NULL	0x00000000000000000000	{CALL [sp_MSdel_SalesSalesOrderDetail] (43659,6)}	6

Figure 3.61: Output showing the commands

There are 100,000 commands to delete rows from the **SalesOrderDetail** table, which means that the runaway transaction deleted 100,000 rows from the **SalesOrderDetail** table. This can be an archival job that moves cold data from transaction tables to the history table or some other activity that's performed as per any particular business requirement.

Now that we know the problem, let's discuss possible solutions.

Solution

A possible solution to this problem or any such request that modifies data in bulk is to wrap up the modification logic or the query in a stored procedure and then replicate the stored procedure. Replicating the stored procedure would result in a single command being logged, and that would be the stored procedure execution instead of 100,000 commands.

Moreover, you should possibly cross-question such requests. It may end up that the modification isn't really required and that there's a much easier way to solve the request.

To fix this issue, follow these steps:

1. Before we go and try out the solution, navigate to **C:\Code\Lesson03\Problem05** and open **2_RestoreSalesOrderDetail.sql** in SSMS.

   This query restores the data that was deleted earlier (in the *Setup* section) into the **SalesOrderDetail** table. The query is to be run at the publisher:

```
USE AdventureWorks
GO
SET IDENTITY_INSERT Sales.SalesOrderDetail ON;
GO
INSERT INTO [Sales].[SalesOrderDetail]
            (SalesOrderID
        ,[SalesOrderDetailID]
        ,[CarrierTrackingNumber]
            ,[OrderQty]
            ,[ProductID]
            ,[SpecialOfferID]
            ,[UnitPrice]
            ,[UnitPriceDiscount]
            ,[rowguid]
            ,[ModifiedDate])
    select
      SalesOrderID
    ,[SalesOrderDetailID]
            ,[CarrierTrackingNumber]
            ,[OrderQty]
            ,[ProductID]
            ,[SpecialOfferID]
            ,[UnitPrice]
            ,[UnitPriceDiscount]
            ,[rowguid]
```

```
        ,[ModifiedDate]
    from salesorderdetail as s
    where s.SalesOrderdetailID not in (select d.SalesOrderDetailID from
sales.salesorderdetail d)
GO
SET IDENTITY_INSERT Sales.SalesOrderDetail OFF;
```

2. Execute the following query at the publisher to create the stored procedure so that you can delete the records from the **SalesOrderDetail** table:

```
USE AdventureWorks
GO
IF OBJECT_ID('Sales.usp_Del_SalesOrderDetail') IS NOT NULL
BEGIN
DROP PROCEDURE Sales.usp_Del_SalesOrderDetail
END;
GO
CREATE PROCEDURE Sales.usp_Del_SalesOrderDetail
AS
WITH Del AS
(
   SELECT TOP(100000) * FROM Sales.SalesOrderDetail
   ORDER BY SalesOrderDetailID, SalesOrderID
)
DELETE FROM Del
```

3. Execute the following query at the publisher database to add the procedure to the replication:

```
USE AdventureWorks
GO
EXEC sp_addarticle
   @publication = 'AdventureWorks-Tran_Pub',
   @article = 'usp_Del_SalesOrderDetail',
   @source_owner = 'Sales',
   @source_object = 'usp_Del_SalesOrderDetail',
   @type = 'Proc Exec',
   @force_invalidate_snapshot=1
GO
```

This query replicates the execution of the stored procedure **usp_del_SalesOrderDetail** to all subscriptions. The **Proc Exec** value for the **type** parameter refers to replicating the procedure execution at all subscriptions.

You'll have to reinitialize the subscription, as explained earlier. Once the subscription has been reinitialized, move on to the next step.

4. Execute the **usp_del_SalesOrderDetail** procedure at the publisher to perform the deletion:

    ```
    USE AdventureWorks
    GO
    EXECUTE Sales.usp_Del_SalesOrderDetail
    ```

    Wait for the procedure to complete execution. This may take some time. Once the procedure completes, verify the row count for the **SalesOrderDetail** table at the publisher and subscriber to make sure that the rows have been deleted from both the publisher and the subscriber.

    Also, check the replication monitor for log scan messages. There won't be any now.

5. Let's look at the **MSrepl_Commands** table to verify the command count for the stored procedure execution:

    ```
    SELECT
      rc.xact_seqno,
      a.article,
      a.article_id,
      COUNT(*) AS CommandCount
    FROM MSrepl_commands AS rc WITH(NOLOCK)
    join MSarticles a on a.article_id=rc.article_id
    WHERE a.article='usp_del_SalesOrderDetail'
    GROUP BY rc.xact_seqno,a.article,a.article_id
    ORDER BY CommandCount
    ```

The query returns the command count for the **usp_del_SalesOrderDetail** procedure:

	xact_seqno	article	article_id	CommandCount
1	0x000000BD000052740005	usp_Del_SalesOrderDetail	479	1
2	0x000000BD000051A701D1	usp_Del_SalesOrderDetail	479	2
3	0x000000BD00003EBF0001	usp_Del_SalesOrderDetail	479	2
4	0x000000BD00004B7A0001	usp_Del_SalesOrderDetail	479	2
5	0x000000BD0000451D0118	usp_Del_SalesOrderDetail	479	2
6	0x000000BD000045FD0091	usp_Del_SalesOrderDetail	479	3
7	0x000000BD0000393F0091	usp_Del_SalesOrderDetail	479	3

Figure 3.62: Output showing the command count

6. There are multiple commands for this procedure. This is because of the snapshot's reinitialization. Copy the **xact_seqno** with **CommandCount** as **1** and execute the following query to check the command:

```
EXECUTE sp_browsereplcmds
  @xact_seqno_start = '0x000000BD000052740005'
   ,@xact_seqno_end =  '0x000000BD000052740005'
   ,@article_id=479
```

You should get the following output:

Figure 3.63: Output showing the command

Observe that instead of 100,000 delete commands, a single call to the stored procedure execution is made. This significantly improves replication performance.

An important point to note here is that replication is intelligent enough to not replicate the delete commands resulting from the execution of the stored procedure at the publisher. It only replicates the stored procedure call and not the individual commands.

Not all scenarios that generate a lot of log records can be covered using this technique, for example, an **alter table** statement on a table with, say, 10 million rows that converts a **varchar** column to a **nvarchar** column. This will generate a lot of log records, and there's no easy way to optimize this.

Moreover, it's more difficult with peer-to-peer replication as it doesn't allow you to switch off the replication schema.

This completes problem 5.

Conflicts in Peer-to-Peer Transactional Replication

As discussed in the previous lesson, P2P transactional replication can result in conflicts. Let's take a look at a conflict example in this section.

> **Note**
>
> You can refer to this link to find out more about conflicts and their types: https://docs.microsoft.com/en-us/sql/relational-databases/replication/transactional/peer-to-peer-conflict-detection-in-peer-to-peer-replication?view=sql-server-2017.

Exercise 26: Problem 6 – Conflicts in P2P Transactional Replication

You will have to set up P2P replication using the scripts in *Lesson 2, Transactional Replication*, for this section.

Setup

To introduce the conflict into the replication, follow these steps:

1. Navigate to `C:\Code\Lesson03\Problem06` and open `1_Setup.sql` and `2_Setup.sql` in SSMS.

2. Connect the query window for `1_Setup.sql` to the publisher and `2_Setup.sql` to the subscriber.

3. Quickly execute the two queries in parallel.

Troubleshooting

Whenever there is a conflict, a message is logged into the SQL Server log. As we discussed earlier, we can also set alerts to be raised whenever a conflict occurs.

The `@p2p_conflictdetection` parameter should be set to **True** to detect the conflicts. In case of a conflict detection, the replication behavior is controlled by the `@p2p_continue_onconflict` parameter. If it's set to **True**, the replication continues; if not, replication stops until the conflict is resolved.

It's advised to set both the parameters to **True**. Our P2P configuration already has the two parameters set to **True**.

When **@p2p_continue_onconflict** is set to **True**, no error is shown in the replication monitor or the **MSrepl_errors** table. The only source of information is the alert; therefore, it's highly advised to configure email alerts for conflict detection.

1. Let's check the SQL Server error log for the conflict error. Execute the following query at the publisher to get the error log. Alternatively, you can view the SQL Error Log UI under the **Management** node in Object Explorer:

    ```
    xp_readerrorlog 0,1,N'conflict'
    ```

    You should get an output similar to the following:

	LogDate	ProcessInfo	Text
1	2018-07-30 08:20:04.570	spid66	A conflict of type 'Update-Update' was detected at peer 1 between peer 2 (incoming), transaction id 0x0000000000002ca6
2	2018-07-30 08:22:54.630	spid66	A conflict of type 'Update-Update' was detected at peer 1 between peer 2 (incoming), transaction id 0x0000000000002cdc
3	2018-07-30 08:23:30.960	spid66	A conflict of type 'Update-Update' was detected at peer 1 between peer 2 (incoming), transaction id 0x0000000000002cf0
4	2018-07-30 08:29:55.990	spid66	A conflict of type 'Update-Update' was detected at peer 1 between peer 2 (incoming), transaction id 0x0000000000002d7e
5	2018-07-30 08:31:26.840	spid66	A conflict of type 'Update-Update' was detected at peer 1 between peer 2 (incoming), transaction id 0x0000000000002dd9
6	2018-07-30 08:32:49.890	spid66	A conflict of type 'Update-Update' was detected at peer 1 between peer 2 (incoming), transaction id 0x0000000000002e2d

Figure 3.64: SQL Server error log

Let's look at the complete error:

```
A conflict of type 'Update-Update' was detected at peer 1 between peer
2 (incoming), transaction id 0x0000000000002ca6  and peer 1 (on disk),
transaction id 0x0000000000002b4e for Table '[Sales].[SalesOrderHeader]'
with Primary Key(s): [SalesOrderID] = 43659,  Current Version
'0x010000004E2B0000000000000', Pre-Version '0x02000000682C0000000000000' and
Post-Version '0x02000000A62C0000000000000'
```

The error says that an update-update conflict occurred when updating the row with the primary key **SalesOrderID** with a value of **43659**. This means that the two transactions, one at the publisher and one at the subscriber, modified the row with **SalesOrderId** as **43659** with different values of the columns.

2. SQL Server provides a GUI interface so that you can view the conflicts and their status. To view the conflict's status, in the Object Explorer (publisher), expand **Replication** and then expand **Local Publications**. Right-click on the publication and select **View Conflicts**:

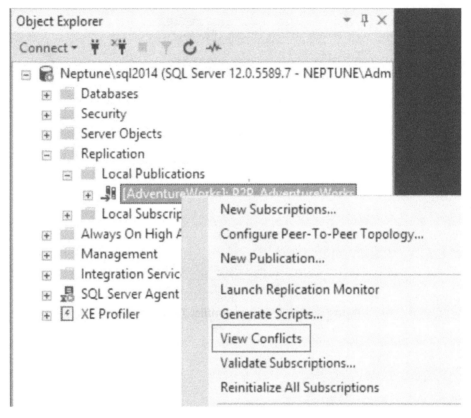

Figure 3.65: The View Conflicts option

3. In the **Select Conflict Table** window, select `SalesOrderHeader` and click on **OK** to continue:

Figure 3.66: The Select Conflict Table window

4. The **Conflict Viewer** window lists all of the conflicts for the selected table. Observe that they are automatically resolved:

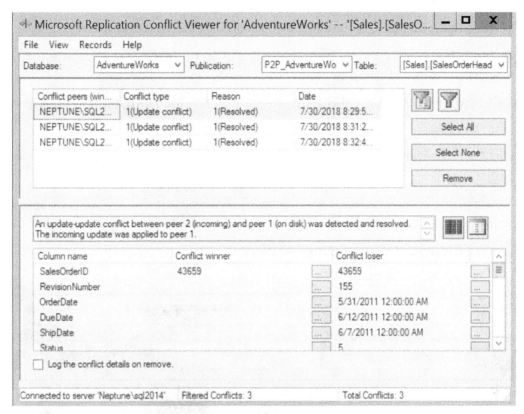

Figure 3.67: The Conflict Viewer window

The **Conflict Viewer** window also tells you about the conflict winner and loser, along with the winning column values.

Solution

As we have already seen, the conflict is automatically resolved by SQL Server. Therefore, we don't need to do much to resolve the conflict. However, if the conflicts are frequent, you will have to find the source and fix it to resolve the issue permanently.

An additional check that can be done here and is also required is to compare the **SalesOrderHeader** table at the publisher and the subscriber:

1. Let's compare the table at both instances. Run the following tablediff command:

    ```
    "C:\Program Files\Microsoft SQL Server\120\COM\tablediff.exe"
    -sourceserver Neptune\SQL2014 -sourcedatabase AdventureWorks
    -sourcetable SalesOrderHeader -sourceschema Sales -destinationServer
    Neptune\SQL2016 -destinationdatabase AdventureWorks -destinationtable
    SalesOrderHeader -destinationschema Sales -f C:\Code\Lesson03\Problem06\
    SalesOrderHeaderSync.sql
    ```

    Here's the output from the tablediff utility:

Figure 3.68: Output of tablediff

You may get a different output.

Observe that it shows a mismatch for the **freight** and the **totaldue** column for the **SalesOrderID** as **43659**. The conflict was resolved automatically; however, the values are not in sync between the publisher and subscriber. The tablediff utility also generates a **SalesOrderHeaderSync.sql** file that contains the query to sync the row:

```
-- Host: Neptune\SQL2016
-- Database: [AdventureWorks]
-- Table: [Sales].[SalesOrderHeader]
-- Column(s) SalesOrderNumber,TotalDue are not included in this script
because they are of type(s) text, ntext, varchar(max), nvarchar(max),
varbinary(max), image, timestamp, or xml. Columns of these types cannot
be updated by tablediff utility scripts; therefore non-convergence of
data can still occur after this script has been applied. If the tablediff
utility output references any of these columns, you must update the
columns manually if you want them to converge.
SET IDENTITY_INSERT [Sales].[SalesOrderHeader] ON
UPDATE [Sales].[SalesOrderHeader] SET [Freight]=500.0000 WHERE
[SalesOrderID] = 43659
SET IDENTITY_INSERT [Sales].[SalesOrderHeader] OFF
```

Observe that the script only updates the **freight** column even though it found the difference for **freight** and **totaldue** column values. This is because the **totaldue** column is a calculated column and is calculated as **isnull(([SubTotal]+[TaxAmt])+[Freight],(0))**. Therefore, once you run the preceding script, the table will be in sync.

This completes the problem.

Activity 4: Troubleshooting Transactional Replication

For this activity, transactional replication should already be configured. You can use the scripts in **C:\Code\Lesson02\Transactional\1_Createpublication.sql** and **C:\Code\Lesson02\Transactional\2_CreateSubscription.sql** to configure transactional replication.

You already have transactional replication configured for the **AdventureWorks** database. The replication was working fine when configured; however, it has suddenly stopped working. You have to find and fix the problem and make transactional replication work for the **AdventureWorks** database.

Setup

Navigate to `C:\Code\Lesson03\Activity` and open `Setup.sql` in SSMS. Change the query mode to **SQLCMD** and execute the query.

This will cause the replication to fail.

The steps to fix this are as follows:

1. Find out the replication fail cause, by using either the replication monitor, replication agent job history, or the `Msrepl_errors` table in the distribution database at the publisher.

2. Take the necessary steps to fix the problem. The replication failure is due to the currency code **TST** being inserted as part of the replication already exists at the subscriber database. Use the `C:\Code\Lesson03\Activity\Fix.sql` script to delete the entry from the subscriber database and fix the issue.

> **Note**
>
> The solution for this activity can be found on page 444.

Summary

This lesson talked about some common real-world transactional replication issues and their solutions. These problems can be broadly classified into data, configuration, and performance problems. In this lesson, we also talked about how to use the replication monitor, replication agent job history, and the `Msrepl_Errors` table to find out replication issues.

This lesson also talked about how to measure replication latency using the tracer tokens in the replication monitor.

In the next lesson, we'll talk about AlwaysOn high availability and disaster recovery.

AlwaysOn Availability Groups

Learning Objectives

By the end of this lesson, you will be able to do the following:

- Describe AlwaysOn availability groups and terminology

- Explain data synchronization in AlwaysOn

- Configure Active Directory Domain Controller

- Configure Windows Server Failover Cluster

- Configure AlwaysOn availability groups using SQL Server Management Studio

- Configure AlwaysOn availability groups on Microsoft Azure

This lesson will teach us how to configure an AlwaysOn availability group using various methods.

Introduction

This lesson introduces SQL Server AlwaysOn **availability groups** (**AGs**) and talks about related concepts and terminology. This lesson also talks about the common AlwaysOn topologies, use cases, and the prerequisites for configuring AlwaysOn AGs.

In this lesson, we then learn the complete process for configuring AlwaysOn AGs and then understand how to review our configuration.

AlwaysOn Availability Group Concepts and Terminology

An AlwaysOn availability group is a group of databases that can fail over from a primary server to a secondary server automatically or manually, as and when required. Commonly known as AlwaysOn AGs, they're the premium high availability and disaster recovery solution available in SQL Server.

Other than being an HA and a DR solution, it can also be used to load-balance read workloads, for maintenance jobs such as backups, and for consistency checks on the secondary databases.

Availability Groups Concepts and Components

A typical AlwaysOn AG topology is shown in the following diagram:

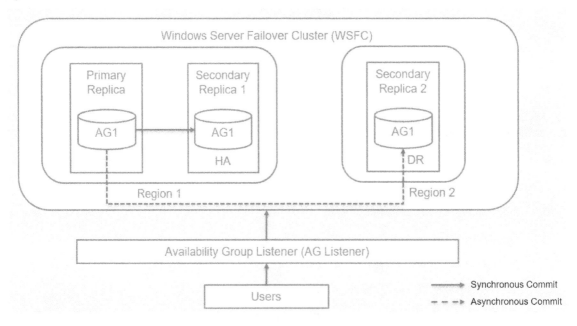

Figure 4.1: Example of an AlwaysOn topology

The given AlwaysOn implementation consists of three replicas or nodes: **Primary Replica**, **Secondary Replica 1**, and **Secondary Replica 2**. The three nodes are part of the same domain name and the same Windows Server Failover Cluster.

An AlwaysOn AG consists of the following components.

Windows Server Failover Cluster

A **Windows Server Failover Cluster** (**WSFC**) consists of two or more servers and is used to provide high availability (or scalability) for applications such as SharePoint, SQL Server, and many more.

WSFC was one of the more common solutions for high availability before AlwaysOn. A typical WSFC for SQL Server (commonly known as **Failover Cluster Instance** (**FCI**)) implementation for HA (without AlwaysOn) is shown in the following diagram:

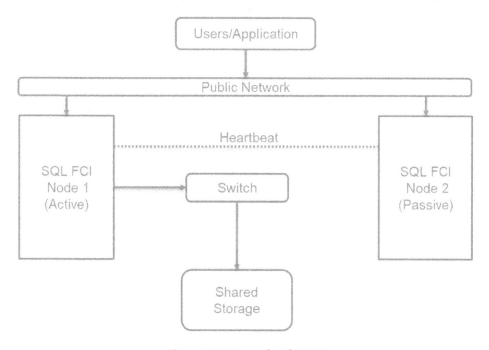

Figure 4.2: Example of WSFC

> **Note**
>
> SQL Server Failover Cluster Instance installation here refers to a SQL Server clustered installation on a Windows Server Failover Cluster.

A typical WSFC implementation consists of two nodes (individual servers): **Node 1** and **Node 2**. The two nodes are part of a Windows Server Failover Cluster. SQL Server is installed on each node (cluster installation and not standalone installation).

The SQL Server database files (.**mdf**, .**ldf**, and .**ndf**) are kept in shared storage accessible from both nodes through a network switch. The two nodes can be within the same data center or in different data centers in the same city, or in a different country altogether.

The users or applications connect to a virtual network name given to the cluster, and are unaware of the server hosting the connections. The heartbeat connection between the two nodes helps to find out whether a node is online. In the case of a failure at **Node 1** (the active node), **Node 2** becomes active automatically and starts accepting user connections. The failover from **Node 1** to **Node 2** (active to passive) is taken care of by WSFC. Once WSFC finds out that **Node 1** is offline, it moves the SQL Server service to **Node 2** automatically. There are a few seconds of downtime involved during the failover:

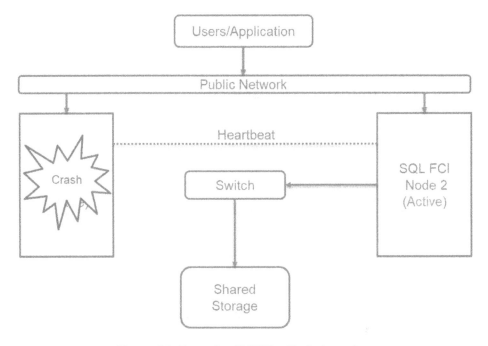

Figure 4.3: Example of WSFC – Node 1 crashes

> **Note**
>
> A complete study of FCI is out of scope for this book. The purpose here is to help understand the basic concept of FCI. WSFC details relevant to AlwaysOn are covered later in this lesson.

The AlwaysOn AG utilizes the failover capability of WSFC to fail over between nodes as and when required.

A major difference between AlwaysOn and FCI is that the FCI uses shared storage, which becomes the single point of failure.

> **Note**
>
> You can read about the difference between FCI and AlwaysOn at https://docs. microsoft.com/en-us/sql/database-engine/availability-groups/windows/failover-clustering-and-always-on-availability-groups-sql-server?view=sql-server-2017.

Availability Group and Availability Database

An availability group or AG is a set of databases that fail together. An availability database is a database that is a part of an availability group. In the example given in *Figure 4.1*, **AG1** is the availability group, which is hosted by the three nodes or replicas: **Primary Replica**, **Secondary Replica 1**, and **Secondary Replica 2**.

> **Note**
>
> Server objects such as logins and SQL Server agent jobs are not part of AGs and do not fail over.

Basic Availability Groups

Basic availability groups, available in the SQL Server Standard edition, uses a subset of availability groups in the SQL Server Enterprise edition.

A basic availability group is essentially a replacement of the database mirroring feature (deprecated) and offers AlwaysOn for one availability database for a maximum of two replicas. The secondary database isn't readable and is only available in the case of failover when the secondary replica takes over as the primary replica.

Basic availability groups have the following limitations:

- Available only with SQL Server 2016 CTP3 Standard edition onward
- Maximum of two replicas: one primary and one secondary
- No read access, database backups, and integrity checks on the secondary replica

- Limited to only one availability database

- Can't be upgraded to advanced availability groups and can't be part of distributed availability groups

Distributed Availability Groups

Introduced in SQL Server 2016, a distributed availability group is a group of two separate availability groups. The two availability groups that are part of a distributed availability group can be on-premises or on the cloud and don't need to be at the same location. The availability groups can be cross domain, that is, in different WSFCs, or can even be cross platform, that is, one availability group can be on Linux and another can be on Windows. If the two availability groups can connect and communicate, they can be part of a distributed availability group.

A distributed availability group can be used for disaster recovery, migrating databases to new hardware or configuration, and for having more than eight read replicas (current limit on read replicas) by spanning multiple availability groups.

Domain Independent Availability Groups

A traditional availability group requires that the availability group replica nodes be part of a WSFC and joined to a single domain. A WSFC uses **Active Directory Domain Service** (**AD DS**). An AD DS defines a domain. A domain is a collection of computers or devices in a network that follow common rules and can be administered as a single unit.

> **Note**
>
> To know more about AD DS, go to https://docs.microsoft.com/en-us/previous-versions/windows/it-pro/windows-server-2003/cc759073(v=ws.10).

Windows Server 2016 introduced a new type of WSFC known as **Active Directory-detached cluster**, a workgroup cluster. A workgroup cluster allows you to deploy an availability group on nodes that are the following:

- Deployed on different domains

- Not joined to any domain

- A combination of domain-joined and non-domain-joined nodes

Such availability groups are referred to as **domain-independent availability groups**.

Availability Replicas

An availability replica is a standalone SQL Server instance that hosts availability groups. There are two types of replicas: primary and secondary.

A primary replica hosts primary databases. The client application connects to the databases at the primary replica for read-write operations. It also replicates the data for the availability databases to the secondary replicas.

A secondary replica hosts the secondary or the replicated copy of the availability databases. A secondary replica can be used for read-only connections or to perform backups and integrity checks. A secondary replica can be configured for the following options:

- **Passive mode**: In passive mode, the secondary replica denies all connections and will only be available in the case of a failover.

- **Active mode**: In active mode, the secondary replica can be used as a read-only replica to load balance read-only queries (read-intent only, allowing connections from clients with `ApplicationIntent` as `ReadOnly` specified in the connection string) and perform backup and integrity checks.

> **Note**
>
> In passive mode, there's no license needed for the SQL Server installation on the secondary replica, provided the secondary replica is only used as part of AlwaysOn and not to host any other databases.

Availability Modes

There are two availability modes:

- **Synchronous commit**: In synchronous or (sync) commit, the primary replica sends the transaction confirmation to the client when it is confirmed that the secondary replica has written (hardened) the transaction log records to the disk. This mode has zero data loss and higher transaction latency. Synchronous mode is the recommended mode for a high availability solution where the nodes are in the same geographical region.

- **Asynchronous commit**: In asynchronous mode, the primary replica sends the transaction confirmation to the client when the transaction log records are hardened at the primary replica and it doesn't wait for the transaction log records to be hardened at the secondary. This mode has a lower transaction latency with data loss. The async mode is recommended for a disaster recovery solution where the nodes are usually in separate geographical locations.

> **Note**
>
> We'll talk about replication or data synchronization between primary and secondary replicas in detail in the *Data Synchronization* section in this lesson.

In the example given in *Figure* 4.1, **Secondary Replica 1** is in synchronous commit and is used for HA. **Secondary Replica 2** is in asynchronous mode and is used for DR.

Availability Group Listeners

An AG listener is the virtual name that the client connects to when connecting to an availability group. It's the server name specified in the client connection string. The AG listener consists of a domain listener name (DNS name), two or more IP addresses, and a listener port.

When an AG listener is created, it becomes the cluster resource in a WSFC and it uses WSFC to fail over to redirect connections to the available or the current primary replica in the case of an availability group failure. The AG listener is therefore the name that the client application understands and connects to, and it automatically connects the client connections to the primary replica.

Failover Modes

An AlwaysOn implementation offers automatic and manual failover modes. Synchronous commit replicas support both manual and automatic failover; however, asynchronous commit replicas only support manual failover:

- **Automatic failover**: An automatic failover occurs when a primary availability group or primary server crashes. The synchronized secondary replica is promoted to the primary replica role with zero data loss.

- **Manual failover**: Manual failover is of two types:

  Manual failover without data loss: This is a planned failover where a synchronous replica is promoted to the primary replica role manually, without data loss. This can be done as part of a Windows or SQL Server patch upgrade, where the secondary replica is patched first and then a manual failover is performed to promote the patched secondary replica as the primary replica. The secondary replica (previous primary) is then patched.

  Manual failover with data loss: This is a forced manual failover with data loss from a primary replica to an asynchronous secondary replica. This can be done in the case of a disaster (disaster recovery), when the primary and the synchronous replica fail and the only active replicas are the asynchronous replicas.

Database-Level Health Detection

Added in SQL Server 2016, database-level health detection fails over an availability group from a primary to secondary replica when any database in an availability group goes offline. For example, if there is a problem in writing to the data file of an availability database on the primary and the database is offline, the availability group will fail over to the secondary.

Flexible Automatic Failover Policy

The flexible failover policy controls the conditions that result in an automatic failover of an availability group. A flexible failover policy can therefore be used to increase or decrease the possibility of an automatic failover to suit the HA and DR business SLA.

A failover policy is defined by two variables: health check timeout threshold and the availability group failure condition level.

Health Check Timeout Threshold

WSFC runs the **sp_server_diagnostic** stored procedure at the primary replica to get diagnostic and health information about SQL Server. The **sp_server_diagnostic** procedure is run every one-third of the health check timeout threshold for an availability group. The default health check timeout value is 30 seconds; therefore, **sp_server_diagnostic** is run every 10 seconds.

If **sp_server_diagnostic** doesn't return any information within 10 seconds, WSFC waits for 30 seconds (full health check timeout value). If it doesn't return any information in 30 seconds, WSFC then determines whether the primary replica is unresponsive based on the failure condition level. If found unresponsive, an automatic failover, if configured, is initiated.

The **sp_server_diagnostic** procedure returns information about the following five components:

- **system**: Includes data on spinlocks, CPU usage, page faults, non-yielding tasks, and server-processing conditions

- **resource**: Includes data on physical and virtual memory, buffer pools, cache, pages, and other memory objects

- **query_processing**: Includes data on worker threads, tasks, wait types, CPU intensive sessions, blocking, and deadlocks

- **io_subsystem**: Includes data on IO

- **events**: Includes data on ring buffer exceptions, ring buffer events on memory buffer, out of memory, security, and connectivity

The **sp_server_diagnostic** procedure returns data for each component and the state of each component. The state can be unknown, clean, warning, or error. The failover condition levels explained next are defined based on the state of the different components returned by the **sp_server_diagnostic** procedure.

Failure Condition Level

There are five failure conditions levels that specify the condition that will cause the automatic failover. They are as follows:

- **Level one (on server down)**: An automatic failover occurs when either the SQL Server is down or the lease of an availability group connecting to WSFC expires. A lease is a signal or a handshake between the SQL Server resource DLL and the SQL Server instance on the primary replica. A lease is governed by a lease timeout, which has a default value of 20 seconds. The SQL Server resource DLL initiates a handshake with the SQL Server instance every one-quarter of the lease timeout value. If the SQL Server instance doesn't signal back to the SQL Server resource DLL within the lease timeout, the lease is expired. When this happens, the SQL Server resource DLL lets WSFC know that the lease has expired and the primary replica doesn't *look alive*. WSFC then initiates the automatic failover as per the AlwaysOn settings.

  > **Note**
  >
  > The SQL Server resource DLL (**SQSRVRES.DLL**) communicates with WSFC and makes it aware of the state of SQL Server resources such as the SQL Server service, the SQL Server agent, and availability groups.

- **Level two (on server unresponsiveness)**: An automatic failover is initiated when any lower level condition is satisfied, the SQL Server instance doesn't connect to the cluster, and the health check timeout expires.

- **Level three (on critical errors)**: An automatic failover is initiated when any lower level condition is satisfied and the system component reports an error.

- **Level four (on moderate server errors)**: An automatic failover is initiated when any lower level condition is satisfied and the resource components report an error.

- **Level five (on any qualified failure)**: An automatic failover is initiated when any lower level condition is satisfied and the `query_processing` component reports an error.

Data Synchronization

We talked about two types of availability modes or synchronization: synchronous commit and asynchronous commit. Let's understand the two modes in detail now.

Synchronous Commit

A synchronous commit configuration is shown in the following diagram:

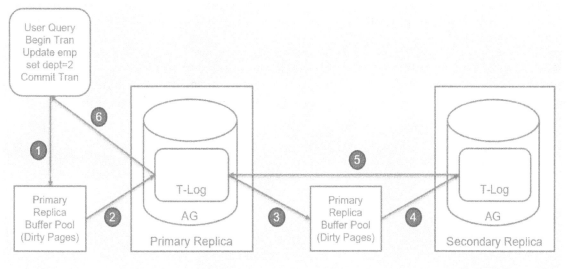

Figure 4.4: Synchronous commit

The synchronous commit works as described here:

1. A user or an application issues an update command against an availability database in the availability group AG. The command modifies the relevant pages in the primary replica buffer pool.

2. The pages in the buffer pool are flushed (or hardened) to the disk in the database transaction log when the transaction commits.

3. The log record is sent to the synchronous replica log cache or (buffer pool).

4. The log record is written to the transaction log on disk (or hardened) at the secondary replica.

5. The secondary replica sends an acknowledgement to the primary replica that the log record is hardened at the secondary.

6. The primary replica informs the clients that the transaction is complete.

There's an additional redo thread that runs at the secondary replica. The redo thread takes the transaction data from the log cache or the transaction log and applies the transactions on the data files (`.mdf` and `.ldf`) at the secondary.

In synchronous commit mode, a transaction takes a longer time to complete as it has to be committed at primary and secondary replicas. A synchronous commit, however, ensures zero data loss.

The primary and secondary replicas always ping each other to check connectivity. If there's a delay of more than 10 seconds in receiving a response, the synchronous replica mode changes to asynchronous. The mode is restored back to synchronous once the connectivity is restored.

Asynchronous Commit

An asynchronous commit configuration is shown in the following diagram:

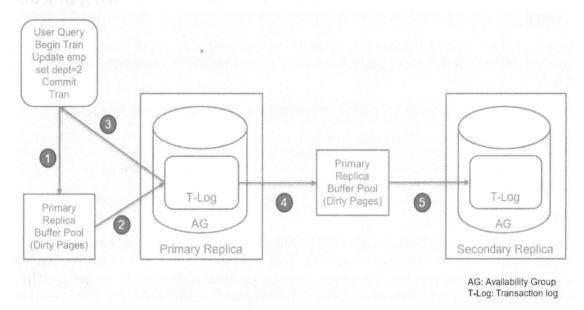

Figure 4.5: Asynchronous commit

The asynchronous commit works as described here:

1. A user or an application issues an update command against an availability database in the availability group AG. The command modifies the relevant pages in the primary replica buffer pool.

2. The pages in the buffer pool are flushed (or hardened) to disk in the database transaction log when the transaction commits.

3. The primary replica informs the clients that the transaction is complete. The primary replica doesn't wait for the log record to be hardened at the secondary replica.

4. The log record is sent to the synchronous replica log cache (or buffer pool).

5. The log record is written to transaction log on disk (or hardened) at the secondary replica.

Similar to synchronous commit, there's an additional redo thread that runs at the secondary replica. The redo thread takes the transaction data from the log cache or the transaction log and applies the transactions on the data files (`.mdf` and `.ldf`) at the secondary.

Asynchronous commit therefore offers better performance as the primary replica doesn't have to wait for the secondary replica to commit the log record before informing the user.

Asynchronous commit, however, may result in data loss during the failover.

Data Synchronization in Different Scenarios

Let's now look at how data synchronization is affected in scenarios such as synchronized secondary replica fails or primary replica fails.

Primary Replica Fails

When a primary replica fails, the automatic failover (if configured) happens and the failover target (synchronized secondary replica) is promoted to the primary replica. The database at the secondary replica starts accepting user connections (read-write). The primary replica takes the role of a synchronized replica when it recovers and is online.

An automatic failover is carried out in the following manner:

1. If the primary replica is running (failover is caused because of an issue with an availability database), the primary database state is changed to disconnected. All clients are also disconnected from the primary replica.

2. The secondary database rolls forward the log records in the recovery queue, if any. The recovery queue consists of all the log records in the secondary database transaction log, which aren't redone at the secondary database.

3. The secondary replica switches to the primary replica and starts accepting client connections. It also rolls back uncommitted transactions (in background) from the transaction log (or performs the undo phase of database recovery).

4. The other secondary replicas, if any, connect to the new primary and start the synchronization process.

5. The primary replica, when available, takes the secondary replica role and starts synchronizing with the new primary.

A planned manual failover is carried out in the following manner:

1. A failover request from primary to synchronized secondary is initiated by a DBA manually.

2. WSFC sends a request to the primary replica to go offline. This ensures that there aren't any new connections during the course of the failover.

3. The secondary databases roll forward the log records in the recovery queue.

4. The secondary replica takes the primary replica role and starts accepting client connections. The original primary replica takes the secondary replica role. Uncommitted transactions are rolled back at the new primary.

5. The databases are in the not-synchronizing state until the new primary replica connects and synchronizes with the original primary replica.

A forced manual failover is carried out in the following manner:

1. A failover request from primary to asynchronized secondary is initiated by a DBA manually.

2. The secondary replica becomes the new primary replica and starts accepting client connections.

3. The original primary replica becomes the secondary replica when it's back online. However, the data synchronization is in a suspended state.

   This is done so that the database at the original primary can be compared against the new primary to find out missing data during the failover. To find out missing data, you can compare the tables in the new primary against the original primary using a third-party comparison tool or the tablediff tool to find out the missing records.

   Once the data is in sync, the data synchronization between the primary and secondary can be started manually.

Secondary Replica Fails

When a synchronous secondary replica fails or is unavailable, its state changes from synchronizing to not synchronizing. The synchronous commit mode is changed to asynchronous commit and the primary replica stops accepting the acknowledgement from the unhealthy secondary replica. This is to make sure that the transactions aren't delayed because of unavailability of acknowledgement from the secondary.

The primary replica, however, maintains the log record, which isn't sent to the unhealthy secondary. This is done to synchronize the secondary replica from where it left off, once it is back online. This results in an increased transaction log size at the primary and at other secondaries as well.

This can be fixed by either fixing the unhealthy secondary replica and bringing it online, or by taking the secondary replica out of the availability group. Once the unhealthy replica is out of the availability group, the primary replica doesn't have to keep the transaction log record and therefore the transaction log can be reused.

When the unhealthy secondary replica is back online, the following happens:

1. It connects to the primary replica and sends the last LSN (or end of log LSN, the last log sequence number in the secondary replica database transaction log) to the primary replica.

2. The primary replica starts sending the log records after the end of log LSN to the secondary replica. The secondary replica changes the state to synchronizing and starts applying the log records as received from the primary. This continues until the LSN at primary and secondary match.
    At this point, the secondary changes the state to synchronized.

3. The primary replica starts waiting for the acknowledgement from the secondary replica and follows the usual process of synchronous commit.

An asynchronous replica, after it recovers from the failure, syncs with the primary replica in the same manner as the synchronous replica. However, in the case of an asynchronous replica, step 3 isn't performed.

The data synchronization state of an asynchronized replica is always synchronizing and is never synchronized. This is because the primary replica doesn't wait for the log record commit acknowledgement at the asynchronous replica and is therefore unaware of the data synchronization status at the secondary replica.

AlwaysOn Availability Groups

In this lesson, we'll configure AlwaysOn AGs on a three node Windows Server Failover Cluster. We'll first look at the prerequisites for the setup and will then do the following:

- Set up four Hyper-V VMs; one VM will act as a domain controller and the other three will be the availability group replicas

- Set up AlwaysOn AGs

The AlwaysOn topology to be configured is shown in the following diagram. This is the same topology as discussed earlier in this lesson:

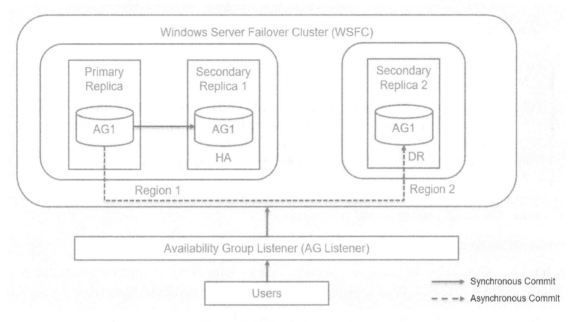

Figure 4.6: AlwaysOn topology

As a part of the AlwaysOn availability setup, we'll also configure a domain controller. In a real-world scenario, configuring a domain controller and Windows Server Failover Cluster is part of a System Administrator's job.

We'll also talk about modifying an existing availability group such as adding/removing a database from an availability group, modifying backup preferences, and adding a new replica.

Prerequisites

In this section, we'll discuss the prerequisites for configuring availability groups. This section talks about the technical prerequisites; however, when deploying an AlwaysOn AG in a production environment, the following should be considered first:

- Number of availability groups to be configured.

- Availability databases to be grouped together in an availability group. For example, critical databases are in one availability group with automatic failover and non-critical databases in another availability group with manual failover.

- Number of synchronous and asynchronous replicas and their locations. Synchronous replicas can be used as reporting databases (offload reads from primary replica), as well as to perform backups and integrity checks.

- Instance failover or enhanced database failover.

> **Note**
>
> A secondary replica being used either as a read or backup replica will incur licensing costs. A passive (only available during failover or when it's changed to a primary) secondary replica doesn't require a license. The cost, therefore, has an important role when deciding on the number of secondary replicas.

Let's now talk about the technical prerequisites.

Operating System

Each replica should be on Windows Server 2008 or later. The recommended version is Window Server 2012 R2. Linux is supported from SQL Server 2017 onward.

In Windows Server 2008 and Windows Server 2012 R2, a cluster can only be created among the nodes joined to the same domain. However, starting from Windows Server 2016, a failover cluster can be created without domain dependency. Therefore, a SQL Server 2016 instance running on Windows Server 2016 can have AlwaysOn set up on nodes in different domains, same domains, or workgroups (no domain).

An AlwaysOn replica cannot be a domain controller. An AlwaysOn replica should have the following patch installed: KB 2654347 (http://go.microsoft.com/fwlink/?LinkId=242896).

SQL Server

A SQL Server instance participating in an availability group should meet the following requirements:

- SQL Server 2012 Enterprise or later is required to configure AlwaysOn. Starting from SQL Server 2016, the Standard edition supports the basic availability group, as discussed earlier.

- Each SQL Server instance should be on a different node of a single WSFC node. A distributed availability group can be on nodes in different WSFCs. An availability group in Windows Server 2016 can be on nodes in different WSFCs or on nodes in workgroups.

- All SQL Server instances in an availability group should be on the same collation.
- All SQL Server instances in an availability group should have the availability group feature enabled.
- It's recommended to use a single SQL Server service account for all the SQL Server instances participating in an availability group.
- If the **FILESTREAM** feature is used, it should be enabled on all SQL Server instances in an availability group.
- If contained databases are used, the contained database authentication server option should be set to **1** on all SQL Server instances participating in an availability group.

Availability Database

A database participating in an availability group should meet the following requirements:

- It should not be a system database.
- It should have a full recovery model with at least one full backup.
- It should not be a part of database mirroring or an existing availability group.
- It should not be a read-only database.

Let's now look at a few important recommendations:

- Each availability group replica should run on the same OS and SQL Server version and configuration.
- Each availability group replica should have the same drive letters. This is to make sure that the database data and log files' paths are consistent across all replicas. If not, then the AlwaysOn setup will error out.
- A dedicated network card should be used for data synchronization between replicas and for WSFC communication.

Let's get started with deploying an AlwaysOn availability group. The AlwaysOn topology that we'll deploy is the one discussed earlier in this lesson. We'll have one primary replica and two secondaries: one for HA and another for DR.

> **Note**
>
> The deployment considers that the replicas are on-premises and not on the cloud. An AlwaysOn setup on Microsoft Azure is discussed later in this lesson.

The deployment consists of the following steps:

1. Creating four Hyper-V VMs: one for the domain controller, one as the primary replica VM, and two as the secondary replica VMs.

2. Configuring Active Directory Domain Controller.

3. Configuring Windows Server Failover Cluster.

4. Installing SQL Server 2016 Developer edition on all replicas.

5. Creating availability groups. This includes enabling the availability group feature in all instances and using the Availability Group Wizard to set up AlwaysOn availability groups.

Steps 1, 2, and 3 are not part of the database administrator profile and are done by system administrators. However, they are prerequisites for AlwaysOn and are therefore included as setup steps.

> **Note**
>
> Although *steps 1, 2,* and *3* are not part of a DBA's job, it's beneficial to know how WSFC and domain controller works.

Let's get started with creating Hyper-V VMs.

Creating Hyper-V VMs

Hyper-V is a virtualization technology built into Windows 8.x and above. Hyper-V allows you to create virtual machines on a Windows 8.x or above host machine. It is useful to demonstrate concepts such as AlwaysOn that require more than one machine for the setup.

In a real-world scenario, the availability group replicas are either physical boxes or on-premises or cloud VMs sized to run **Online Transactional Processing (OLTP)** workloads as per business requirements.

> **Note**
>
> A host machine is the one that will host or contain the virtual machines created as part of this lesson's exercises. Almost all of the PowerShell scripts specified here are to be run on the host machine unless otherwise specified. The host machine should be a physical machine and not a virtual machine. If you plan to use a virtual machine as the host machine, then install Windows Server 2016 and enable nested virtualization to carry out the demos. The PowerShell console should be run in the administrator role.
>
> The **C:\Code** directory contains the code files for this book. If you have copied the code files into a different directory, specify the path accordingly.

Exercise 27: Enabling Hyper-V

Hyper-V is a Windows feature and is not enabled by default. To enable Hyper-V, follow these steps:

1. Open the PowerShell console.

2. In the PowerShell console, change the directory to **C:\Code\Lesson04\On-Premise**.

3. Run the following command:

```
.\1_EnableHyperV.ps1
```

You may have to run the following script to enable script execution for PowerShell in the PowerShell console:

```
Set-ExecutionPolicy Unrestricted
```

Type **Yes** and hit *Enter* in the confirmation message that appears after running the preceding command.

If Hyper-V isn't enabled already, it'll be enabled and the script will ask for a computer reboot to complete the installation:

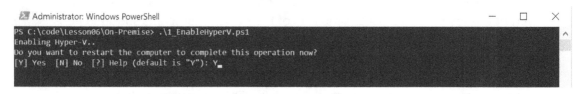

Figure 4.7: Running the 1_EnableHyperV.ps1 script

4. Type **Y** and press *Enter* to restart the computer.

Exercise 28: Downloading Windows Server 2012 R2 Evaluation Edition and Creating the Base VM

The Windows Server 2012 R2 Evaluation edition is to be installed on the primary and secondary replicas and on the domain controller. In this exercise, we'll do that and also create the base VM:

1. To download Windows Server 2012 R2 Evaluation edition, run the following command in a PowerShell console:

```
.\2_GetWin2012R2Eval.ps1 -DownloadLocation "C:\VMs\"
```

This command will download the Windows Server 2012 R2 ISO file in the **C:\ VMs** directory. Once the download starts, you should get the status shown in the following screenshot:

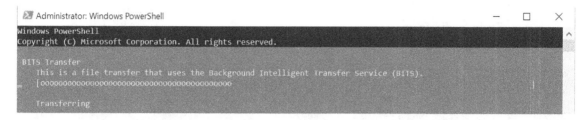

Figure 4.8: Running the 2_GetWin2012R2Eval.ps1 script

> **Note**
>
> The ISO file size is around 4 GB. It may take time to download, depending on your network speed.

2. Once the ISO download is complete, the next step is to create the base VM. The base VM can be used to provision as many VMs as required. For example, if you corrupt a VM during the setup process or do incorrect settings, you can provision a fresh new VM from the base VM. Execute the following command to create a new Hyper-V VM (modify the parameter values as per your environment and press *Enter*):

```
.\3_ProvisionBaseVM.ps1 -VMpath C:\VMs\AlwaysOn -VMName DPLBase -ISOPath
"C:\VMs\Win2012R2EvalEdition.iso"
```

This command accepts the following parameters:

VMPath: This is the path where the VM files are to be saved. Do not create a folder with the **VM** name. The PowerShell script automatically creates a folder with the **VM** name inside the **VMPath** you specify. You will still have to create an AlwaysOn folder inside the **C:\VMs** folder.

VMName: This is the name of the VM. The default name is **DPLBase**. You can change it if you wish to.

ISOPath: This is the full path to the Windows Server 2012 R2 ISO file, including the ISO file name.

You should get the following output:

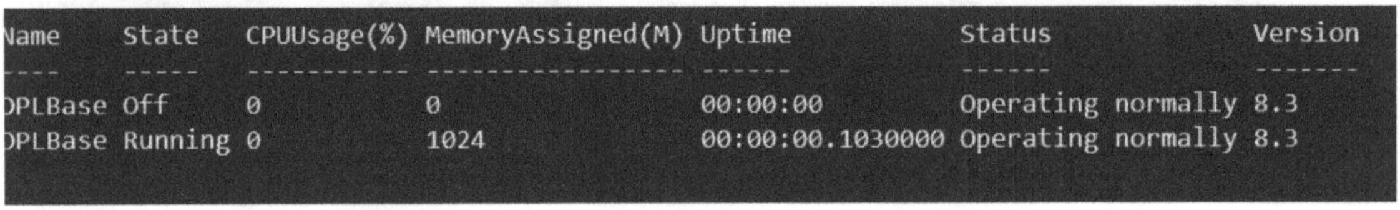

```
Name      State     CPUUsage(%) MemoryAssigned(M) Uptime                Status              Version
----      -----     ----------- ----------------- -------               ------              -------
DPLBase Off       0           0                 00:00:00              Operating normally 8.3
DPLBase Running 0             1024              00:00:00.1030000 Operating normally 8.3
```

Figure 4.9: Running the 3_ProvisionBaseVM.ps1 script

The VM **DPLBase** is created and is running.

The next step is to connect to the VM and install the Windows Server 2012 R2 Evaluation edition.

Exercise 29: Installing the Windows Server 2012 R2 Evaluation Edition

To install the Windows Server 2012 R2 Evaluation edition in the newly created VM, follow these steps:

1. Press Windows + R to open the **Run** command window. In the **Run** command window, type `virtmgmt.msc` and press *Enter* or click on **Ok** to open the Hyper-V Manager console.

    Notice that it lists the **DPLBase** VM created earlier:

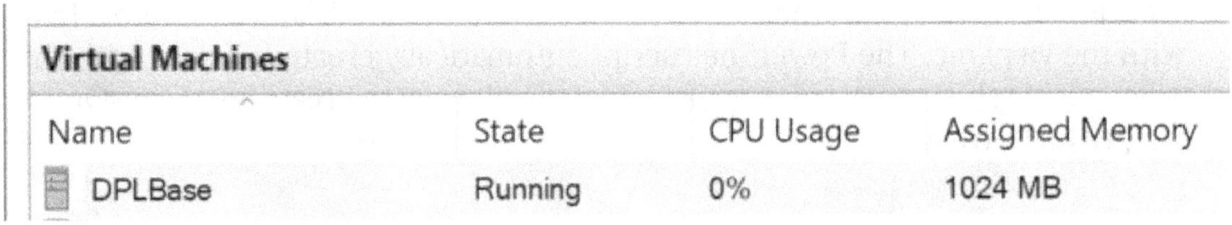

Virtual Machines

Name	State	CPU Usage	Assigned Memory
DPLBase	Running	0%	1024 MB

Figure 4.10: The Hyper-V Manager console

2. Right-click on the VM and select **Connect** from the context menu:

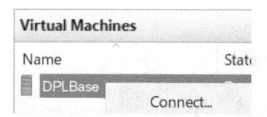

Figure 4.11: The Connect option

3. In the **Virtual Machine Connection** window, install Windows Server 2012 R2 as shown in the following screenshot. Provide the language, time, and keyboard values as per your environment, and click on **Next** to continue:

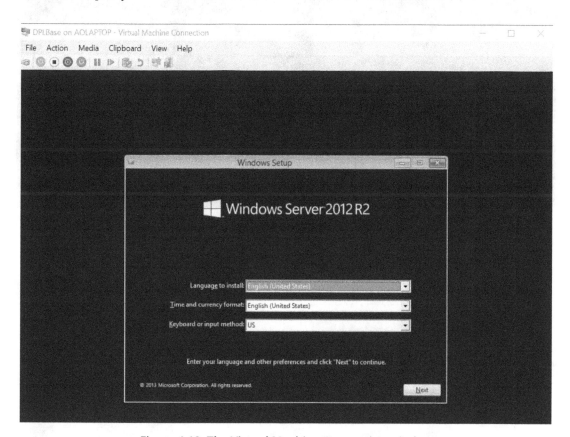

Figure 4.12: The Virtual Machine Connection window

4. In the **Windows Setup** window, click on **Install now** to continue:

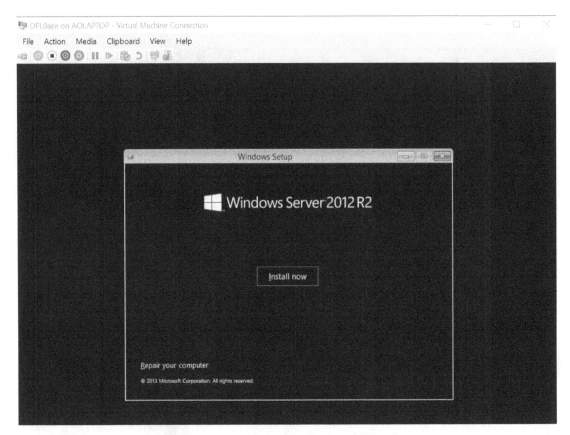

Figure 4.13: The Windows Setup window

5. In the **Windows Setup** window, select either **Windows Server 2012 R2 Standard Evaluation** or **Windows Server 2012 R2 Datacenter Evaluation** editions (select Server with a GUI and not the core version) and click on **Next** to continue:

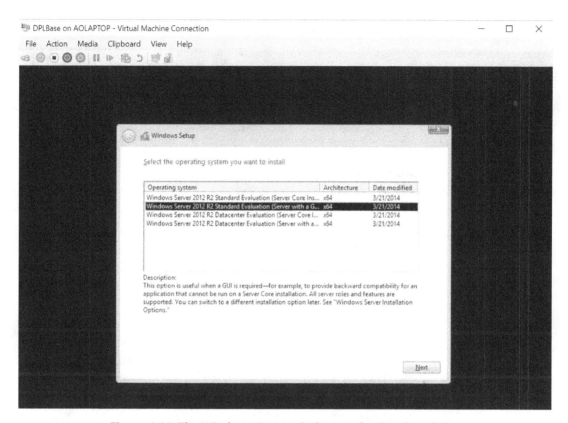

Figure 4.14: The Windows Setup window – selecting the edition

6. In the next window, check **I accept the license terms** and click on **Next** to continue:

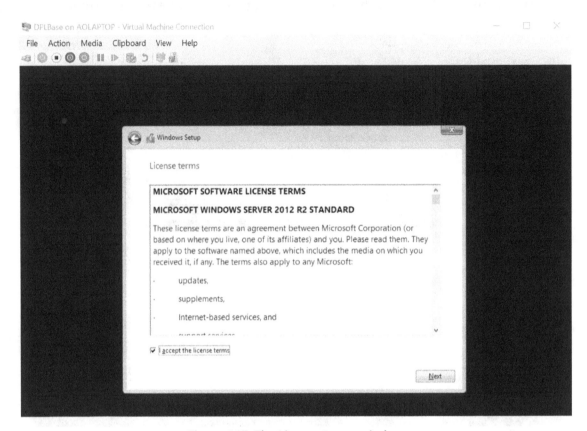

Figure 4.15: The License terms window

7. In the next window, select **Custom: Install Windows only (advanced)**:

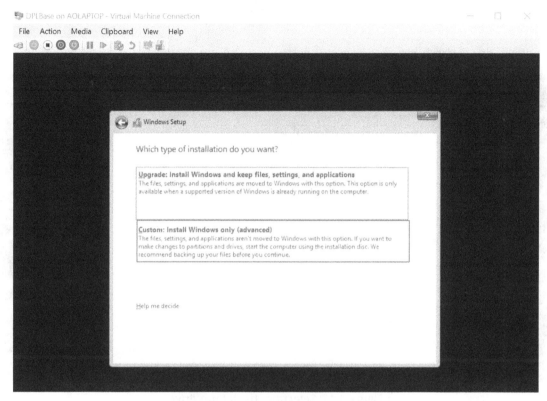

Figure 4.16: Selecting the type of installation

8. In the next window, select the default drive (already selected) and click on **Next** to continue:

Figure 4.17: Selecting the default drive

The Windows setup now has all the information to start the installation and will start installing Windows Server 2012 R2 Evaluation edition. It'll take some time for the installation to complete. When the installation completes, you'll be asked to provide the administrator's password. Provide the password and click on **Finish**:

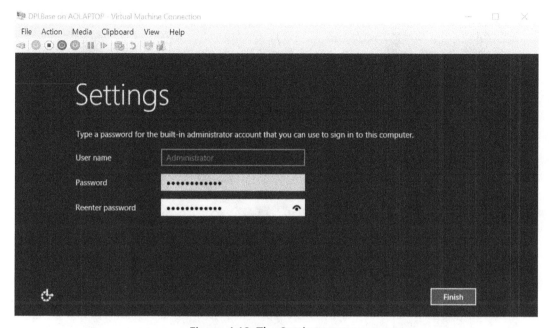

Figure 4.18: The Settings screen

9. The next step is to log in to the base virtual machine and install .NET Framework 3.5 and 4.0. To do that, select the *Ctrl* + *Alt* + *Delete* icon from the **Virtual Machine Connection** window's top menu:

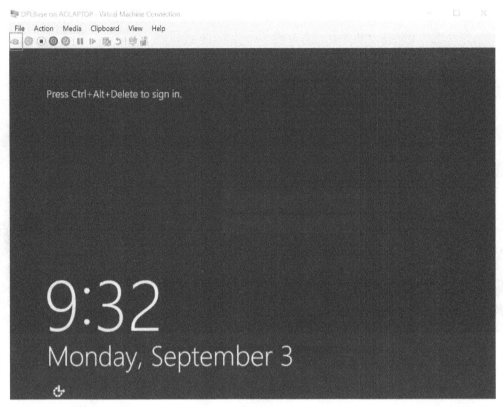

Figure 4.19: Signing in

10. In the login window, provide the password and press *Enter* to log into Windows.

11. Open a new PowerShell console (in the VM and not the host machine) and execute the following command to install .NET 3.5:

```
Install-WindowsFeature Net-Framework-core -source D:\sources\sxs
```

The source location is the location in the DVD drive attached to the VM. You should get the following output confirming that .NET 3.5 is successfully installed:

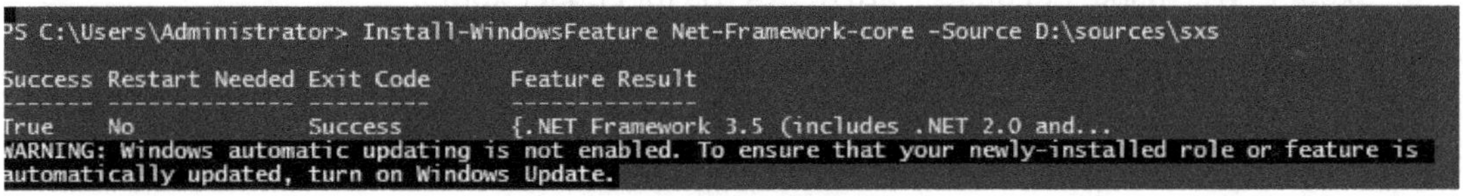

```
PS C:\Users\Administrator> Install-WindowsFeature Net-Framework-core -Source D:\sources\sxs

Success Restart Needed Exit Code       Feature Result
------- -------------- ---------       --------------
True    No             Success         {.NET Framework 3.5 (includes .NET 2.0 and...
WARNING: Windows automatic updating is not enabled. To ensure that your newly-installed role or feature is
automatically updated, turn on Windows Update.
```

Figure 4.20: Installing .NET 3.5

The next step is to run **sysprep** and generalize the Windows installation so that it can be used to create other VMs.

12. From the PowerShell window, execute the following command to sysprep the Windows installation:

    ```
    C:\Windows\System32\Sysprep\Sysprep.exe /oobe /generalize /shutdown
    ```

This command executes **sysprep.exe** with the following parameters:

/oobe: Out of box experience allows users to customize the Windows operating system, name the computer, and create users when the current VM is used as a base VM when creating a new VM.

/generalize: Removes unique system information, clears event logs and restore points, and resets the **security ID (SID)**.

/shutdown: Shuts down the computer when the sysprep command runs successfully.

This allows you to create new VMs using the base VMs and still specify different Windows settings. The command will ask you to select the VM window size when connecting from the host machine. Select **Large** and click on **Connect** to continue. When sysprep is complete, the VM will shut down.

The next step is to export the base VM. Any new VM to be created will be created by importing the base VM.

13. To export the VM, connect to a PowerShell console and execute the following command on the host:

```
Export-VM -Name DPLBase -Path C:\VMs\DPLBaseExport
```

The **Export-VM** command accepts two parameters:

Name: This is the name of the VM to export, **DPLBase** in this case.

Path: This is the directory to export the VM to.

Modify the parameters and run the export command. Once the export is complete, you should be able to see the following at the export path:

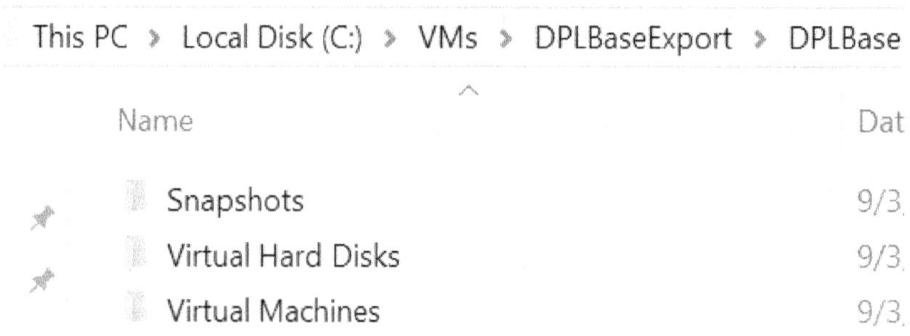

This PC > Local Disk (C:) > VMs > DPLBaseExport > DPLBase	
Name	Dat
Snapshots	9/3
Virtual Hard Disks	9/3
Virtual Machines	9/3

Figure 4.21: Folders at the export path

14. At this point in time, you can delete the **DPLBase** VM, if you wish to. To delete the VM, change the directory in the PowerShell window to **C:\Code\Lesson04\Common** and execute the following PowerShell command:

```
.\RemoveVM.ps1 -VMName DPLBase
```

This command removes the VM from Hyper-V and the **DPLBase** folder in the **C:\ VMs\AlwaysOn** directory.

Exercise 30: Provisioning VMs Using the Base VM

The next step is to provision the following four VMs from the base VM:

- **DPLDC**: This will be used as the Active Directory Domain Controller.
- **DPLPR**: This is the primary replica.
- **DPLHA**: This is the secondary replica used for high availability.
- **DPLDR**: This is another secondary replica used for disaster recovery.

Let's start with creating the new VMs:

1. To create the new VMs using the base VM, change the directory to **C:\Code\ Lesson04\On-Premise** and execute the following PowerShell script:

   ```
   .\4_ProvisionVMs.ps1 -BaseVMPath "C:\VMs\DPLBaseExport\DPLBase\Virtual
   Machines\8829DF48-1187-4C79-8502-B5E21F19E133.vmcx" -NewVMBasePath "C:\
   VMs\AlwaysOn\" -BaseVMName DPLBase
   ```

   This PowerShell script takes three parameters:

   BaseVMPath: This is the full path to the **.vmcx** file of the base VM created earlier. You'll find it in the folder you exported the base VM to. The virtual machine **.vmcx** filename will be different in your case.

   NewVMBasePath: This is the path where the files for the new VMs will be created.

   BaseVMName: This is the name of the base VM.

   You should get the following output from the PowerShell script:

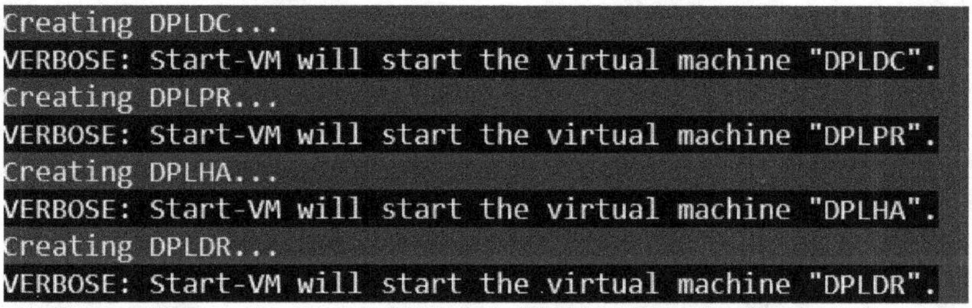

Figure 4.22: Running the 4_ProvisionVMs.ps1 script

The PowerShell script creates four VMs, as seen in Hyper-V Manager. In addition to creating the VMs, the PowerShell script also creates a Hyper-V VM switch, DPLPrivate. The DPLPrivate switch is attached to all the VMs. This is done to make sure that the VMs are connected to one another:

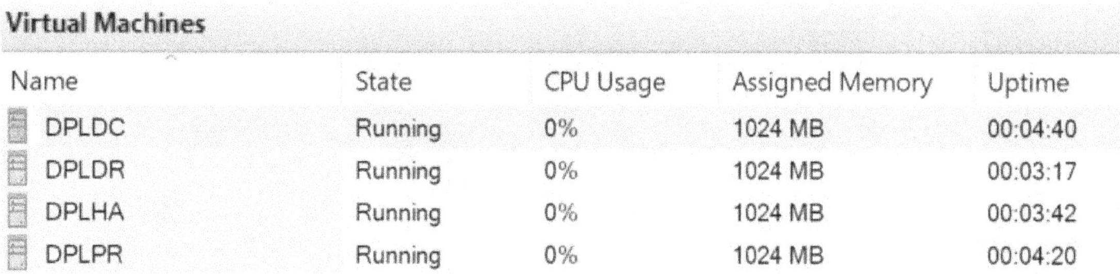

Virtual Machines

Name	State	CPU Usage	Assigned Memory	Uptime
DPLDC	Running	0%	1024 MB	00:04:40
DPLDR	Running	0%	1024 MB	00:03:17
DPLHA	Running	0%	1024 MB	00:03:42
DPLPR	Running	0%	1024 MB	00:04:20

Figure 4.23: The 4 created VMs

2. The next step is to configure Windows settings in the VMs. To do this, follow this process for each VM: Press Windows + R to open the **Run** command window. Enter `virtmgmt.msc` in the **Run** command window and press *Enter*.

3. In Hyper-V Manager, right-click on the **DPLDC** VM and select **Connect to**. When connected, provide the settings shown in the following screenshot; modify the settings as per your country and language:

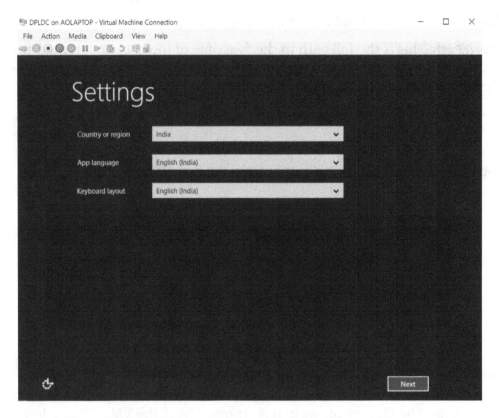

Figure 4.24: The Settings window – selecting country and language

4. In the next window, provide the administrator password and click on **Finish**:

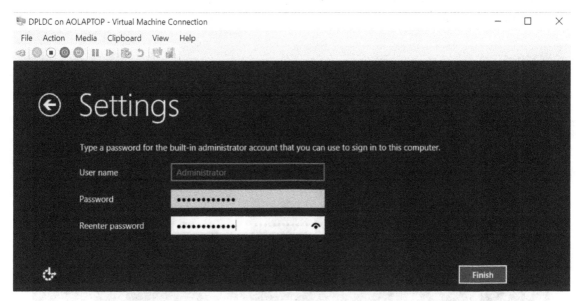

Figure 4.25: The Settings window – adding the username and password

5. When the settings are complete, you'll see a login screen, as shown in the following screenshot. Select the *Ctrl + Alt + Delete* icon from the top menu or from the **Action** menu:

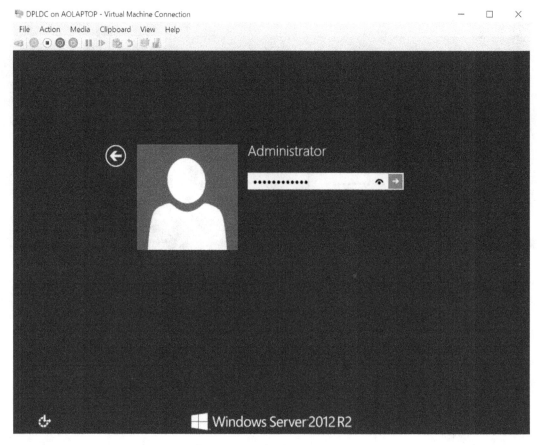

Figure 4.26: The login screen

6. Enter the administrator password and press *Enter* to continue. This completes the Windows Server 2012 R2 setup on the VM.

7. The next step is to remove the Windows Server 2012 R2 Evaluation edition ISO from the VM DVD drive. If you don't do this, you'll get the following error whenever the VM reboots:

```
Press any key to boot from CD or DVD....
```

Figure 4.27: The error if ISO is not removed

To do this, navigate to the **C:\Code\Lesson04\On-Premise** directory and run the following PowerShell script:

```
.\4.1_RemoveWindowsISO.ps1
```

If you still get the message **Press any key to boot from CD or DVD**, don't press any key. You'll be directed to the Windows login screen.

8. The next step is to log into the VM and change the following VM settings: Disable the firewall, change the network profile to public, and modify the IP address.

    To do this, navigate to the **C:\Code\Lesson04\On-Premise** directory and copy the **5_ ModifySettings.ps1** PowerShell script in the VM you wish to modify the settings of.

    > **Note**
    >
    > If you are unable to copy the PowerShell script from the host machine to the VM, restart the VM and try again.

9. Execute the following command to modify the settings. Make sure that the PowerShell script is run against the VM and not the host machine:

    ```
    .\5_ModifySettings.ps1 - VMName DPLDC -IPAddress 192.168.1.20
    ```

    This command will set the IP address of the DPLDC VM to **192.168.1.20** and change the computer name to DPLDC (the same as the VM name). This will cause the VM to restart.

    Run this script against each VM. The script to be executed at each VM is given here:

    DPLPR:

    ```
    .\5_ModifySettings.ps1 -VMName DPLPR -IPAddress "192.168.1.3, 192.168.1.4, 192.168.1.5"
    ```

    DPLHA:

    ```
    .\5_ModifySettings.ps1 -VMName DPLHA -IPAddress "192.168.1.6,192.168.1.7, 192.168.1.8"
    ```

DPLDR:

```
.\5_ModifySettings.ps1 -VMName DPLDR -IPAddress "192.168.1.9,192.168.1.10,
192.168.1.11"
```

You may get the following error when executing this PowerShell script. Ignore it as it is because the default gateway can't be set multiple times and the script tries to do that:

```
New-NetIPAddress : Instance DefaultGateway already exists
At C:\Scripts\5_ModifySettings.ps1:25 char:1
+ New-NetIPAddress -IPAddress $ipa -DefaultGateway 192.168.1.1 -AddressFamily IPv4 ...
+
    + CategoryInfo          : InvalidArgument: (MSFT_NetIPAddress:ROOT/StandardCimv2/MSFT_NetIPAddress) [New-NetIPAddr
   ess], CimException
    + FullyQualifiedErrorId : Windows System Error 87,New-NetIPAddress

New-NetIPAddress : Instance DefaultGateway already exists
At C:\Scripts\5_ModifySettings.ps1:25 char:1
```

Figure 4.28: The error on executing the 5_ModifySettings.ps1 script

Although you can have whatever IP you wish to, having similar IPs will help you understand the AlwaysOn setup explained later in this lesson.

This completes the VM setup. Disconnect the VM and repeat the steps for the other VMs. When you have finished modifying the settings for all VMs, make sure that the VMs are connected to one another. You can verify this by running the **ping** command. The next step is to set up the domain controller on the DPLDC VM.

Active Directory Domain Controller

ADDC is implemented in almost every organization that has a Windows workstation. In day-to-day work, ADDC is used to authenticate users into their laptops, Outlook, and other applications. For example, let's say John works in an organization named ABC *Consulting*. He'd usually log in to his work laptop using his AD account **ABC\John**. Usually, AD-DC is configured and managed by system administrators; however, a system administrator does have experience with ADDC.

ADDC is required as a prerequisite for configuring AlwaysOn availability groups on Windows Server 2012 R2.

Exercise 31: Configuring Active Directory Domain Controller

To configure ADDC on the DPLDC VM, follow these steps:

1. Connect to the DPLDC VM that is the domain controller. ADDS is to be installed on this VM.

2. Once connected, navigate to the **C:\Code\Lesson04\Common** folder (on your host/ local machine) and copy the PowerShell script **CreateDomain.ps1** to the **C:\Scripts** folder in the DPLDC VM.

3. In the DPLDC VM, open a PowerShell console (as an administrator) and run the following command:

   ```
   C:\Scripts\CreateDomain.ps1 -DomainName dpl.com
   ```

   The script will install Active Directory and will then promote DPLDC as a domain controller for the **dpl.com** domain. You'll be asked to provide **safemodedomainadminpassword**. You can give another domain name; however, it's advised to keep it the same, as it's used later in this lesson. The script will also modify the DNS for the **DPLPrivate** network to **127.0.0.1**.

   Once the ADDS installation completes, the computer will automatically restart.

4. When the VM comes back, verify the computer name by running the following PowerShell command:

   ```
   [System.Net.Dns]::GetHostByName($env:computerName)
   ```

   You should get the following output:

Figure 4.29: Verifying the computer name

5. The next step is to join the rest of the VMs (DPLPR, DPLHA, and DPLDR) to the **dpl.com** domain. To do that, follow the next steps on DPLPR, DPLHA, and DPLDR. On your host machine, navigate to the **C:\Code\Lesson04\Common** folder. Copy the **JoinDomain.ps1** script to the **C:\Scripts** folder on the VM.

6. In the VM, open a new PowerShell console window and execute the following command (modify this command to provide your domain admin password, the password of the **DPL\Administrator** user of the DPLDC VM):

```
C:\Scripts\JoinDomain.ps1 -domain dpl.com -domainadminpassword Pass$$word
-DNSIPAddress 192.168.1.20
```

The script modifies the DNS IP address of the VM, joins the machine to the domain, and restarts the VM.

7. Once the VM is back, execute the following PowerShell command to verify that it's joined to the domain:

```
[System.net.Dns]::GetHostByName($env:computerName)
```

You should get the following output:

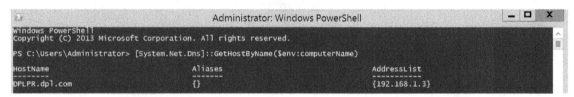

Figure 4.30: Verifying that the machine has joined the domain

You need to follow these steps for DPLPR, DPLHA, and DPLDR. Do make sure that the servers can connect to each other. You can do this by using the Ping utility.

> **Note**
>
> Once all of the VMs are in the domain, use the domain login, **DPL\Administrator**, to log in or connect to the VMs instead of the individual VM administrator account.

The next step is to install the SQL Server 2016 Developer edition on the replicas (DPLPR, DPLHA, and DPLDR) and configure Windows Server Failover Cluster.

Installing the SQL Server Developer Edition

SQL Server 2016 or SQL Server 2017 Developer editions can be used for configuring AlwaysOn. In our case, we will download and install the SQL Server 2016 Developer edition.

Exercise 32: Downloading and Installing the SQL Server 2016 Developer Edition

To download and install the SQL Server 2016 Developer edition, follow these steps on your host machine:

1. Create a Visual Studio Dev Essentials account if you don't have it already at https://visualstudio.microsoft.com/dev-essentials/.

2. Join the *Dev Essentials* program and log in to dev essentials using the link once you have created your account:

3. Select **Downloads** from the top menu:

Figure 4.31: The Downloads option

4. On the **Downloads** page, under **Servers**, select **SQL Server 2016 with Service Pack 1**:

Servers

SQL Server 2016 with Service Pack 1

SQL Server 2017

Figure 4.32: The Servers section

5. On the **Downloads** page, select the **Download** button besides **SQL Server 2016 Developer with Service Pack 1** to download the Developer edition ISO file:

Figure 4.33: The Download button

6. When the download completes, execute the following PowerShell command to attach the ISO to Hyper-V VMs:

```
.\SetDvDDrive.ps1 -SQLISOPath C:\VMs\en_sql_server_2016_developer_x64_
dvd_8777069.iso
```

The **SQLISOPath** is the full SQL Server ISO download path. The script will attach the ISO as a DVD drive to the VMs. The DVD drive is used to install SQL Server on the availability group replicas.

7. You can also provide the DVD drive from the Hyper-V Manager console. In Hyper-V Manager, right-click on the VM and selects Settings from the context menu:

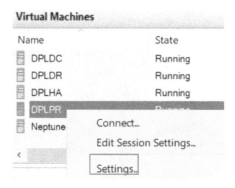

Figure 4.34: The Settings option

8. In the VM settings window, locate **IDE Controller 1 | DVD Drive** and provide the ISO path under the **Image file** option:

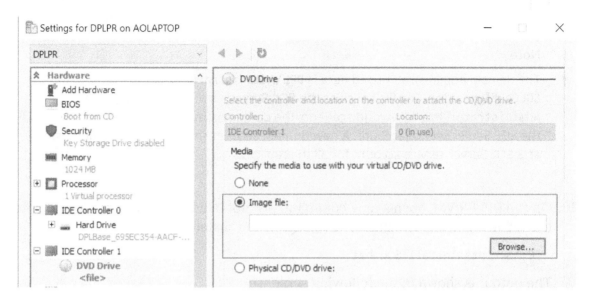

Figure 4.35: The Settings page

9. The next step is to install the SQL Server 2016 Developer edition on all the availability replicas. Copy the **Install-SQL.bat** and **SQLConfiguration.ini** files from **C:\Code\Lesson04\Common** to the **C:\Scripts** folder in the DPLPR VM.

The **Install-SQL.bat** file calls **setup.exe** in the SQL Server 2016 ISO file with **SQLConfiguration.ini** as the configuration file. The **SQLConfiguration.ini** file specifies the installation configuration. The **Install-SQL.bat** code is shown here:

```
D:\Setup.exe /SQLSVCPASSWORD="Awesome@1234" /SAPWD="SQL@2016" /
ConfigurationFile=C:\Scripts\SQLConfiguration.INI /Q /
IAcceptSQLServerLicenseTerms
```

You may have to change the path of the **SQLConfiguration.ini** file if you didn't copy the file in the **C:\Scripts** folder and the **/SQLSVCPASSWORD**, which is the password of the domain administrator.

Note that this command is not to be run. It's mentioned here to explain what parameters should be changed before running the **Install-SQL.bat** file in the next step.

> **Note**
>
> The domain administrator used here is **DPL\Administrator**. The **SQLConfiguration.ini** file specifies the SQL Server service account to be **DPL\ Administrator**. In a real-world scenario, the domain administrator shouldn't be the SQL Server service account. A new domain account should be created and used as a SQL Server service account for all the replicas.

10. On the DPLPR VM, open a new command prompt in administrator mode and enter the following to start an unattended SQL Server installation:

    ```
    C:\Scripts\Install-SQL.bat
    ```

    The output is shown in the following screenshot:

Figure 4.36: Installing SQL Server on a VM

SQL Server installation will take time as the VM runs on only one CPU and 1 GB RAM. If you wish to see the installation progress, remove the **/Q** switch in the **Install-SQL.bat** file. Once the script finishes, it'll ask you to restart the VM to complete the installation.

Install SQL Server on DPLHA and DPLDR, following the preceding steps. Do not install SQL Server on DPLDC.

11. The next step is to install SQL Server Management Studio (SSMS) on one of the three VMs (DPLPR, DPLHA, or DPLDR).

> **Note**
>
> Starting from SQL Server 2016, SSMS isn't part of the regular SQL Server installation and is available as a separate installation.

Execute the following PowerShell command to download SSMS on your host machine:

```
C:\Code\Lesson04\Common\GetSSMS2017.ps1 -DownloadLocation C:\VMs
```

Copy the SSMS setup file **SSMS-Setup-ENU.exe** from the **C:\VMs** folder on your host machine to the DPLPR VM's **Scripts** folder. Double-click on the **SSMS-Setup-ENU.exe** setup file and follow the instructions to install SSMS.

12. After SSMS installation, the next step is to open SSMS and connect to SQL Server on all of the availability replicas from DPLPR. Note that you need to log in to the VMs using the **DPL\Administrator** domain account.

In DPLPR (or the VM you installed SSMS), press Windows + R to open the **Run** command window. Type **SSMS** in the **Run** command window and press *Enter* to open SSMS.

13. In SSMS, press F8 to open the Object Explorer. In the Object Explorer, select **Connect** and then select **Database Engine**:

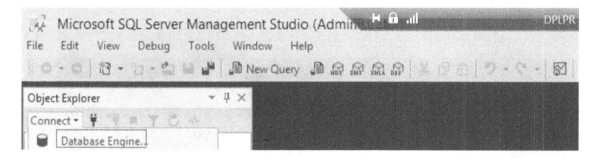

Figure 4.37: The Database Engine option

14. In the **Connect to Server** dialog box, enter **DPLPR** as **Server name** and the **Authentication** option as **Windows Authentication**, and click on **Connect**:

Figure 4.38: The Connect to Server window

15. Connect to DPLHA and DPLDR following the same method:

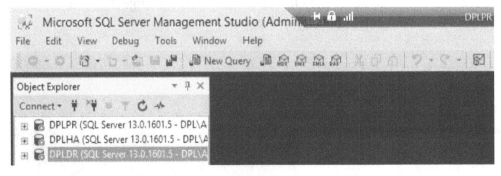

Figure 4.39: Connecting to the other VMs

You should be able to connect to all three replicas; if not, review the earlier steps.

> **Note**
>
> The demo considers the replicas to be standalone SQL Server installations. However, a cluster installation can also be part of AlwaysOn. You can also upgrade to SQL Server 2016 SP2 from here: https://www.microsoft.com/en-us/download/details.aspx?id=56836.

Exercise 33: Restoring Sample Databases

The next step is to restore sample databases to be used as availability databases. Follow these steps to install the required databases:

1. Download **AdventureWorks2016.bak** from https://github.com/Microsoft/sql-server-samples/releases/tag/adventureworks.

2. Copy and paste the backup file downloaded in *step 1* to the **C:\Scripts** folder in the DPLPR VM.

3. Execute the following PowerShell command (at DPLPR) to create the directory structure on the replicas for the database:

```
#DPLPR
New-Item -Path \\DPLPR\C$\Database\Data -type directory -Force
New-Item -Path \\DPLPR\C$\Database\Log -type directory -Force
#DPLHA
New-Item -Path \\DPLHA\C$\Database\Data -type directory -Force
New-Item -Path \\DPLHA\C$\Database\Log -type directory -Force
#DPLDR
New-Item -Path \\DPLDR\C$\Database\Data -type directory -Force
New-Item -Path \\DPLDR\C$\Database\Log -type directory -Force
```

As mentioned earlier, the database data and log file path on the secondary replicas should be the same as in the primary replica. These commands create folders named **Data** and **Log** under the **Database** folder in the **C** drive on all the replicas.

4. Once the folder structure is created, execute the following query in SSMS against the DPLPR server to install the databases:

```
USE [master]
GO
RESTORE DATABASE [Sales]
FROM  DISK = N'C:\Scripts\AdventureWorks2016.bak'
WITH  FILE = 1,
MOVE N'AdventureWorks2016_Data' TO N'C:\Database\Data\Sales_Data.mdf',
MOVE N'AdventureWorks2016_Log' TO N'C:\Database\Log\Sales_Log.ldf',
NOUNLOAD,  STATS = 5
GO
RESTORE DATABASE [Finance]
FROM  DISK = N'C:\Scripts\AdventureWorks2016.bak'
WITH  FILE = 1,
MOVE N'AdventureWorks2016_Data' TO N'C:\Database\Data\Finance_Data.mdf',
MOVE N'AdventureWorks2016_Log' TO N'C:\Database\Log\Finance_Log.ldf',
NOUNLOAD,  STATS = 5
GO
```

This query creates two databases named **Sales** and **Finance** from the **AdventureWorks2016.bak** file. After the restore, you should see the databases listed under the DPLPR server:

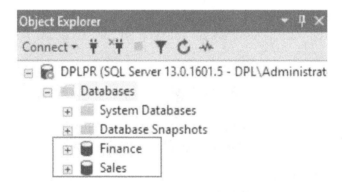

Figure 4.40: The 2 created databases

The data and log files for the **Sales** and **Finance** databases are restored at **C:\Database\Data** and **C:\Database\Log** folders respectively.

Here are the data files:

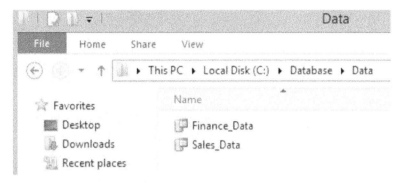

Figure 4.41: The data files

Here are the log files:

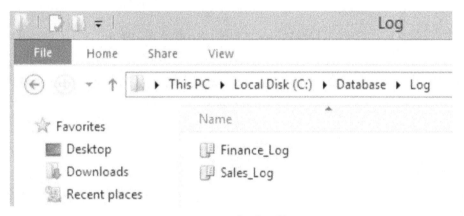

Figure 4.42: The log files

5. The next step is to change the recovery mode of the **Sales** and **Finance** databases to full and take a full backup. As discussed earlier, this is one of the requirements for a database to be added to an availability group.

Create a new folder, **Backup**, in **C** drive and enable sharing on the folder. This shared folder is required later in this lesson. Execute the following query in SSMS to change the recovery mode to full and take a full backup:

```
USE Master
GO
ALTER DATABASE [Sales] SET RECOVERY FULL
GO
```

```
ALTER DATABASE [Finance] SET RECOVERY FULL
GO
BACKUP DATABASE [Sales] TO DISK='C:\Backup\Sales.bak' WITH COMPRESSION,
STATS=10,INIT
GO
BACKUP DATABASE [Finance] TO DISK='C:\Backup\Finance.bak' WITH
COMPRESSION, STATS=10,INIT
```

We now have the SQL Server 2016 Developer edition and databases ready.

Windows Server Failover Cluster

The next step is to configure Windows Server Failover Cluster.

Exercise 34: Configuring Windows Server Failover Cluster

To configure Windows Server Failover Cluster on the replicas, follow these steps:

1. The first step is to install the failover clustering Windows feature on all replicas, DPLPR, DPLHA, and DPLDR.

    Navigate to the **C:\Code\Lesson04\Common** directory and copy the **Install-FailoverCluster.ps1** PowerShell script to the **C:\Scripts** directory in DPLPR VM. When connected to DPLPR, execute the following command to enable the failover clustering feature on all the replicas:

    ```
    C:\Scripts\Install-FailoverCluster.ps1
    ```

2. To verify the installation on a particular VM, execute the following PowerShell command:

    ```
    Get-WindowsFeature *clus* -ComputerName DPLHA
    ```

    You should get the output shown in the following screenshot:

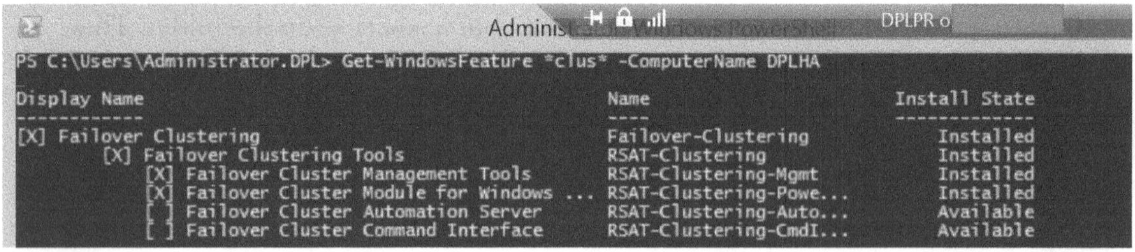

Figure 4.43: Verifying the installation

    Modify the **-ComputerName** parameter in this command and verify for the DPLPR and DPLDR VMs.

3. The next step is to validate the cluster configuration on the nodes. The cluster validation lists out the critical errors and warnings, if there are any, that will be encountered when creating the cluster. If the cluster validation fails, you'll have to fix the errors and re-run the validations.

To run the validation, execute the following PowerShell command in DPLPR VM:

```
Test-Cluster -Node DPLPR,DPLHA,DPLDR
```

This command performs cluster validation on the three replicas. You should get an output similar to the one shown in the following screenshot:

```
PS C:\Users\Administrator.DPL> Test-Cluster -Node DPLPR,DPLHA,DPLDR
WARNING: Storage - Validate Disk Access Latency: The test reported some warnings..
WARNING: Storage - Validate Microsoft MPIO-based disks: The test reported some warnings..
WARNING: Storage - Validate SCSI device Vital Product Data (VPD): The test reported some warnings..
WARNING: Storage - Validate SCSI-3 Persistent Reservation: The test reported some warnings..
WARNING: Storage - Validate Storage Spaces Persistent Reservation: The test reported some warnings..
WARNING: Storage - Validate Disk Arbitration: The test reported some warnings..
WARNING: Storage - Validate Multiple Arbitration: The test reported some warnings..
WARNING: Storage - Validate Disk Failover: The test reported some warnings..
WARNING: Storage - Validate File System: The test reported some warnings..
WARNING: Storage - Validate Simultaneous Failover: The test reported some warnings..
WARNING: Network - Validate Network Communication: The test reported some warnings..
WARNING:
Test Result:
ClusterConditionallyApproved
Testing has completed successfully. The configuration appears to be suitable for clustering. However, you should
review the report because it may contain warnings which you should address to attain the highest availability.
Test report file path: C:\Users\Administrator.DPL\AppData\Local\Temp\2\Validation Report 2018.09.21 At 09.44.22.xml.mht

Mode                LastWriteTime     Length Name
----                -------------     ------ ----
-a---        21-09-2018     09:48     548183 Validation Report 2018.09.21 At 09.44.22.xml.mht
```

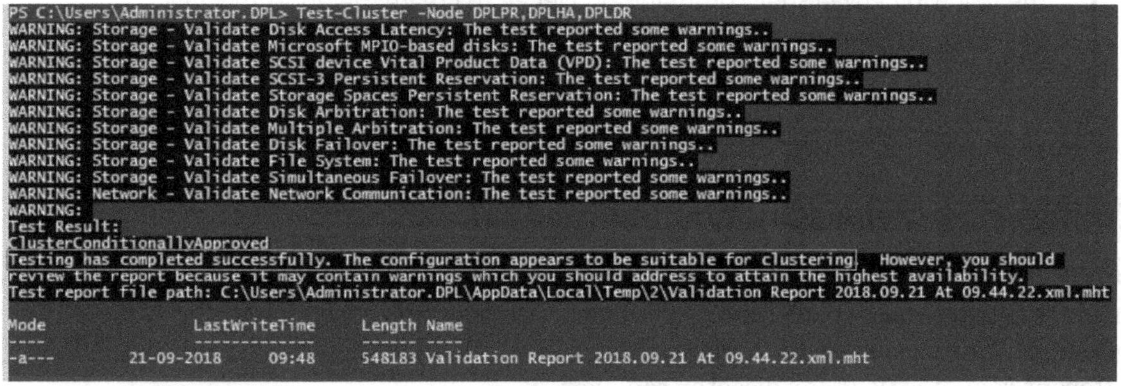

Figure 4.44: Performing cluster validation

You can review the report if you are working in a production environment. However, for demo purposes, let's leave it as it is, as there are no major errors and validations are successful.

4. The next step is to create WSFC. To do this, run the following PowerShell command at the DPLPR VM:

```
New-Cluster -Name DPLAO -Node DPLPR,DPLHA,DPLDR -StaticAddress
192.168.1.15 -NoStorage
```

This command creates a WSFC cluster named DPLAO with three nodes: DPLPR, DPLHA, and DPLDR with a static IP address of **192.168.1.15**.

You should get output similar to that shown in the following screenshot:

```
PS C:\Users\Administrator.DPL> New-Cluster -Name DPLAO -Node DPLPR,DPLHA,DPLDR -StaticAddress 192.168.1.15 -NoStorage
Report file location: C:\Windows\cluster\Reports\Create Cluster Wizard DPLAO on 2018.09.22 At 07.38.31.mht

Name
----
DPLAO
```

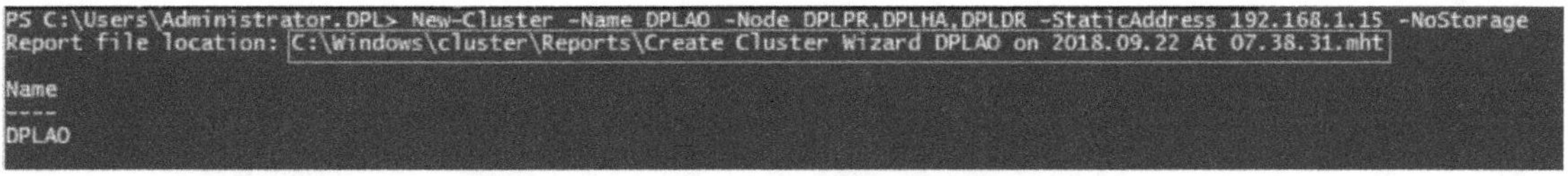

Figure 4.45: Creating the WSFC cluster

This command also generates a report with the steps carried out to create the cluster. You can review the report if you wish to.

> **Note**
>
> A **quorum** is required for WSFC. However, it's skipped here for the sake of brevity. If you wish to set up a quorum, create a new VM, say, DPLFS (FS stands for file share). Assign it an IP address, say `192.168.1.16`, and join it to the **DPL** domain. Create a shared folder, say `witness`. The `witness` folder should be accessible from all of the other VMs (DPLPR, DPLHA, and DPLDR). Execute the following PowerShell command on DPLPR to create the quorum:
>
> `Set-ClusterQuorum -NodeAndFileShareMajority "\\DPLFS\Witness"`.

The next step is to configure the AlwaysOn availability groups.

Configuring AlwaysOn Availability Groups

Earlier in this lesson, we discussed a typical AlwaysOn topology consisting of a primary replica and two secondary replicas. One secondary replica in the same region (geographic area) is used for high availability and another secondary replica in a different region is used for disaster recovery.

We'll now configure the same topology. However, the replicas used in the demos are not in a different subnet. In a real-world scenario, the replicas will be in different subnets; however, they'll be under the same domain and part of one WSFC.

Let's get started with configuring AlwaysOn AG.

Exercise 35: Enabling the AlwaysOn AG Feature

The first step is to enable the AlwaysOn feature for SQL Server instances at each replica. To do this, follow these steps:

1. Connect to the DPLPR VM and open SQL Server 2016 Configuration Manager.

2. Select **SQL Server Services** from the left-hand pane to list out the available SQL Server services. In the right-hand pane, right-click on **SQL Server (MSSQLServer)** and select **Properties** from the context menu:

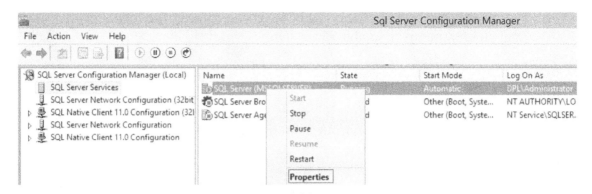

Figure 4.46: The Properties option

3. In the **Properties** window, select the **AlwaysOn High Availability** tab and check the **Enable AlwaysOn Availability Groups** checkbox. Notice that it automatically detects the WSFC name that the replica belongs to. Click **OK** to apply and close the **Properties** window:

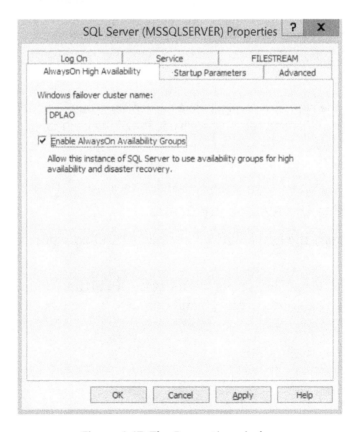

Figure 4.47: The Properties window

The SQL Server service needs to be restarted for the change to take effect.

4. Follow this process on DPLHA and DPLDR, or you can run the following PowerShell commands to enable AlwaysOn:

```
Enable-SqlAlwaysOn -ServerInstance DPLPR
Enable-SqlAlwaysOn -ServerInstance DPLHA
Enable-SqlAlwaysOn -ServerInstance DPLDR
```

You should get the following output from these commands:

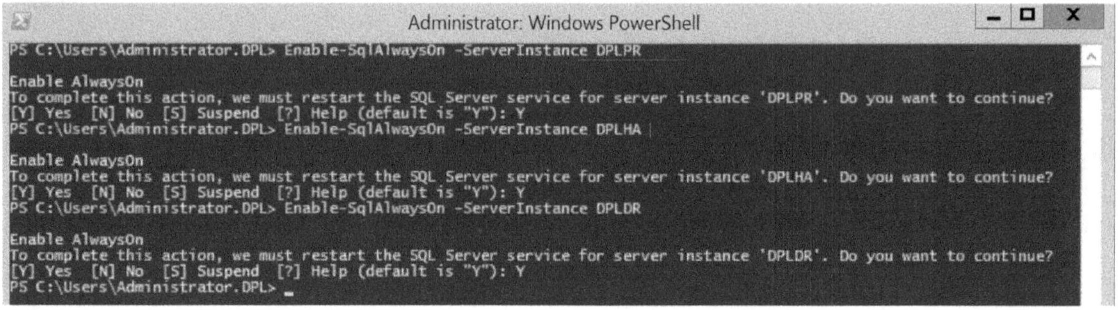

Figure 4.48: Enabling AlwaysOn on the other VMs

> **Note**
>
> We'll first use the wizard to configure the availability group to understand the different components and settings. We'll use PowerShell to manage and maintain the availability group in the next lesson.

Exercise 36: Creating the Availability Group

The next step is to start the availability group wizard and configure the rest of the settings:

1. To create a new availability group, connect to DPLPR and open SSMS. In SSMS, open the Object Explorer (press F8) and connect to the DPLPR SQL Server instance.

2. In the Object Explorer, right-click on **Always On High Availability** and select **New Availability Group Wizard** from the context menu:

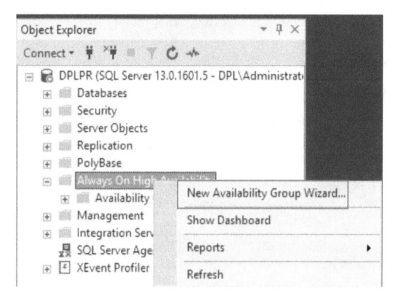

Figure 4.49: The New Availability Group Wizard option

3. In the **Introduction** window, read through the steps to create an availability group, then select **Next** to continue:

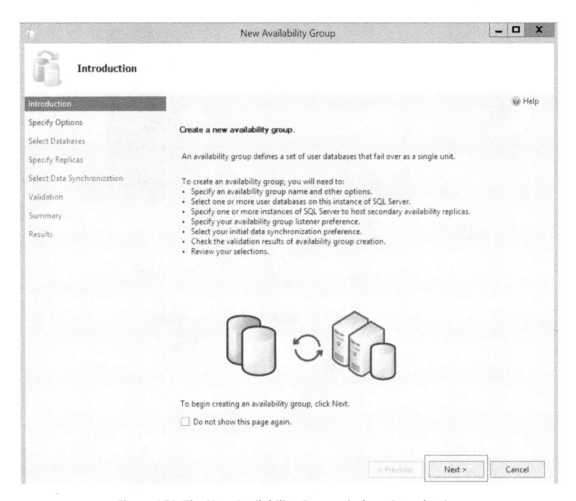

Figure 4.50: The New Availability Group window - introduction

4. In the **Specify Availability Group Options** window, provide the availability group name as **DPLAG**. The cluster type is already selected as **Windows Server Failover Cluster**.

   Check the **Database Level Health Detection** option. When selected, the failover happens if an availability database in an availability group crashes. This is the enhanced database failover option discussed earlier.

The **Per Database DTC Support** option, when checked, provides distributed transaction support for availability databases. DTC support wasn't there before SQL Server 2016:

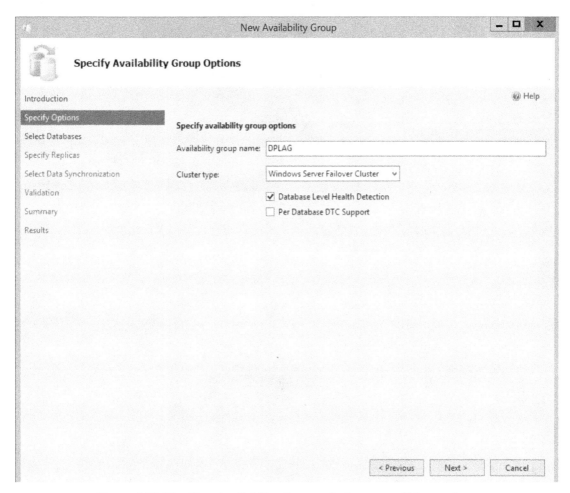

Figure 4.51: The New Availability Group window – specifying options

Click **Next** to continue.

5. In the **Select Databases** window, notice that the two databases **Sales** and **Finance** are listed, and they meet the prerequisites to be part of an availability group. Select the two databases:

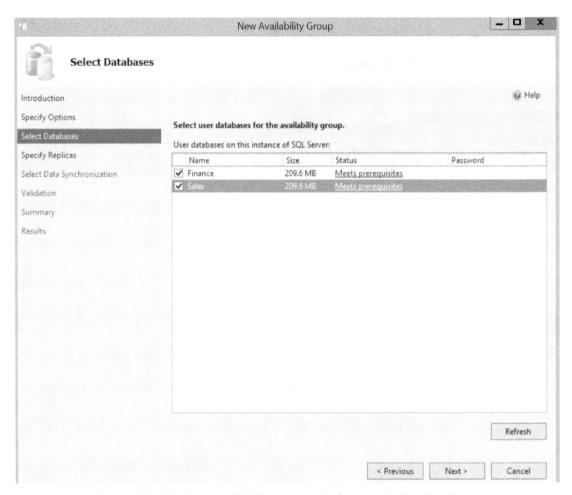

Figure 4.52: The New Availability Group window – selecting databases

Click **Next** to continue.

6. In the **Specify Replicas** window, we can specify the secondary replicas, endpoints, backup preferences, listeners, and read-only routing.

We'll first specify the secondary replicas. The primary replica, DPLPR, is already listed under the **Availability Replicas** section. To add the secondary replicas, click on the **Add Replica** button:

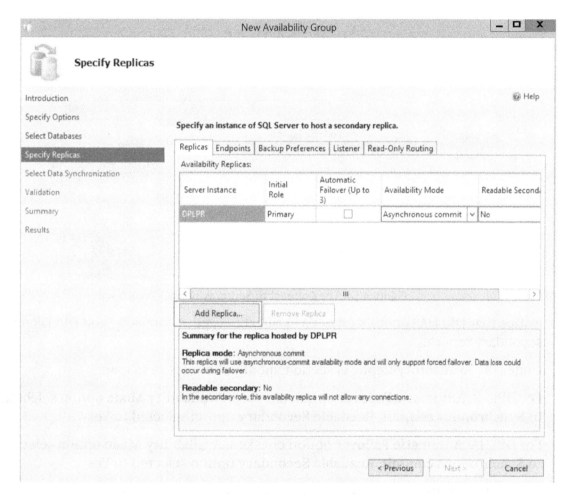

Figure 4.53: The New Availability Group window – specifying replicas

7. In the **Connect to Server** dialog box, enter DPLHA as the **Server name** option and leave the **Authentication** option as default. Click on **Connect** to connect to the DPLHA SQL Server instance:

Figure 4.54: The Connect to Server window

8. Notice that DPLHA is not listed as an availability replica. Similarly, add DPLDR as a secondary replica.

9. Under the **Availability Replicas** section, modify the roles as follows:

    For DPLPR: **Automatic Failover** option checked, **Availability Mode** option selected to **Synchronous commit**, **Readable Secondary** option selected to **Yes**

    For DPLHA: **Automatic Failover** option checked, **Availability Mode** option selected to **Synchronous commit**, **Readable Secondary** option selected to **Yes**

    For DPLDR: **Automatic Failover** option unchecked, **Availability Mode** option selected to **Asynchronous commit**, **Readable Secondary** option selected to **Read-intent only**

DPLPR and DPLHA will be in synchronous mode (high availability) and DPLPR and DPLDR will be in asynchronous mode (disaster recovery):

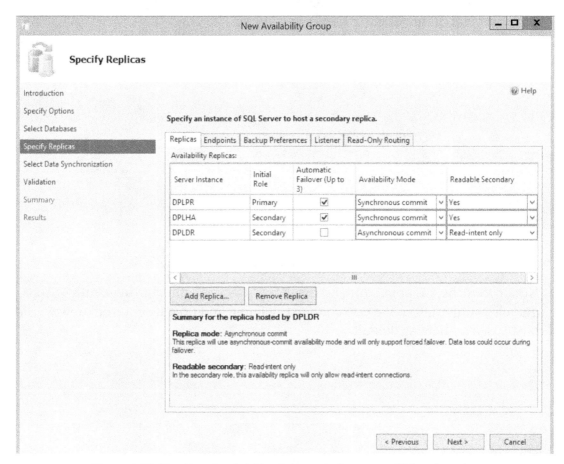

Figure 4.55: The New Availability Group window – modifying the roles

10. Endpoints are the database mirroring endpoints used by the instances to listen to AlwaysOn AG messages from other replicas. The endpoints are created by default when configuring AlwaysOn AG using the **Availability Group** wizard. Select the **Endpoints** tab in the **Specify Replicas** window:

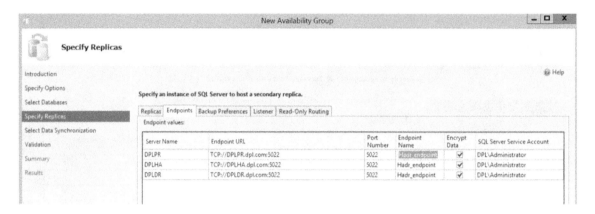

Figure 4.56: The Endpoints tab

Notice that the endpoints for the three replicas are listed automatically with the default configuration. We can change the name and port if required; however, it's best to leave them as default.

11. The **Backup Preferences** tab specifies the replica responsible for performing backups for the availability databases. Select the **Backup Preferences** tab in the **Specify Replicas** window:

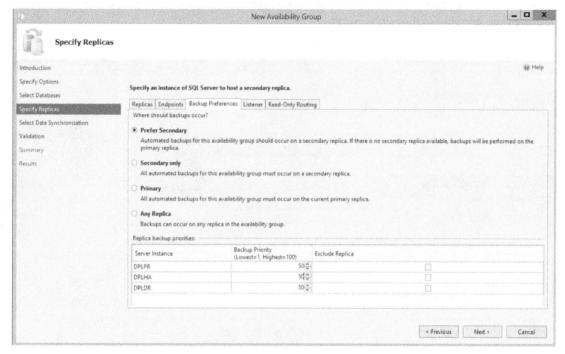

Figure 4.57: The Backup Preferences tab

Notice that the default option is **Prefer Secondary**: that is, the automatic backups are to be performed at secondary replicas when available. If a secondary replica isn't available, then the backups are performed at the primary replica.

> **Note**
>
> Backup preferences are covered in detail in the next lesson.

12. An availability group listener is a virtual network name to which the client connects to access the availability databases. To create a listener, select the **Listener** tab in the **Specify Replicas** window.

13. Select the **Create an availability group listener** option and provide the listener name as **DPLAGL** and port as **1433**:

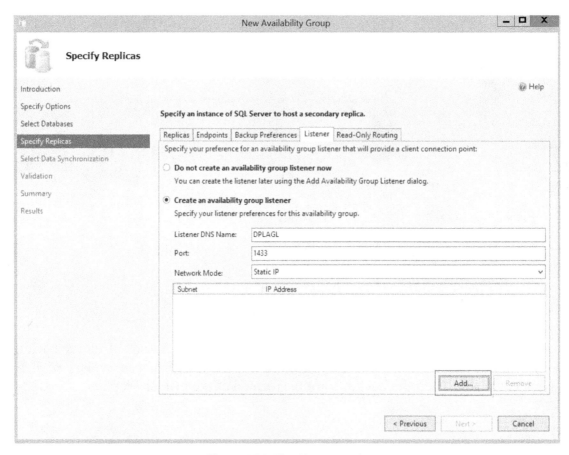

Figure 4.58: The Listener tab

14. It is recommended to add a static IP address for the listener in a multi-subnet environment: that is, when each availability replica is in a different subnet. To provide the static IP address, in the same **Listener** tab, set the **Network Mode** option to **Static IP** and click on the **Add** button.

15. In the **Add IP Address** dialog box, notice that the **Subnet** dropdown lists only one subnet `192.168.1.0/24`. In the case of a multi-subnet environment, it'll list the different subnets the replica belongs to. In the **IPv4 Address** textbox, enter `192.168.1.17` and press **OK** to exit the dialog box:

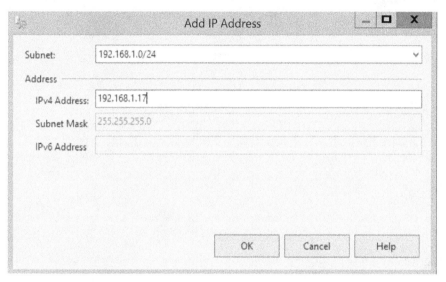

Figure 4.59: The Add IP Address window

The listener configuration should be as shown in the following screenshot:

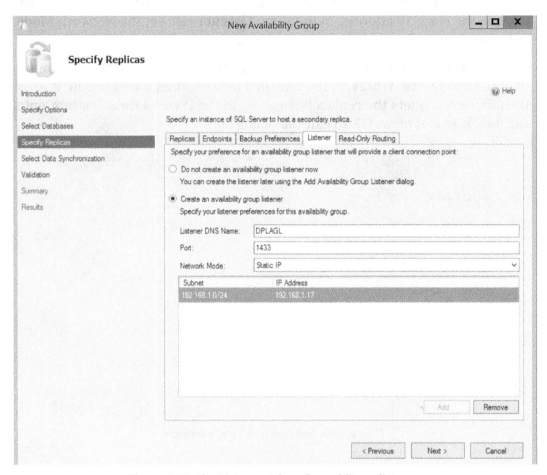

Figure 4.60: The Listener tab – after adding a listener

16. Read-only routing allows SQL Server to direct read-only requests to readable secondary replicas. We'll not be configuring read-only routing as part of our AlwaysOn configuration. Read-only routing is covered in detail in the next lesson. Click on **Next** to continue the wizard:

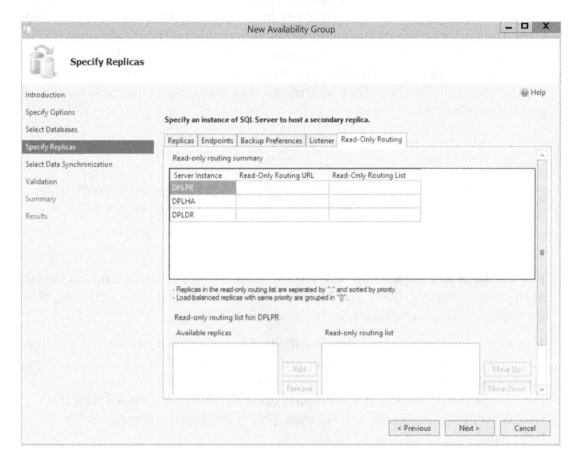

Figure 4.61: The Read-Only Routing tab

17. The **Select Initial Data Synchronization** window provides four different options to perform the initial sync:

Automatic Seeding: The database is created automatically on all the secondary replicas and the data from the primary replica is streamed through the endpoints to the secondary replicas. Automatic seeding was first introduced in SQL Server 2016. The performance of automatic seeding depends on the database size, network speed, and the distance between the replicas. An important point to note about automatic seeding is that the transaction log at the primary replica continues to grow and can only be truncated by taking a full database backup after automatic seeding is complete.

> **Note**
>
> Trace flag **9567** can be enabled on the primary replica to enable data stream compression. This speeds up the automatic seeding process but comes with the cost of high CPU usage.

Full database and log backup: The wizard takes the full database and log backup of the availability databases and restores it on all the available secondaries. This method should be avoided if the databases are very large.

Join only: This assumes that the availability databases have already been restored on all secondaries and the databases are only to be joined to the availability group. To manually restore the databases on secondaries, take the full and log databases at the primary and restore the databases with the **No Recovery** option on the secondaries. This is the preferred method for large databases.

Skip initial data synchronization: This skips the initial sync. We'll have to manually restore and then join the databases to the availability group.

Select the **Automatic Seeding** option and click on **Next** to continue:

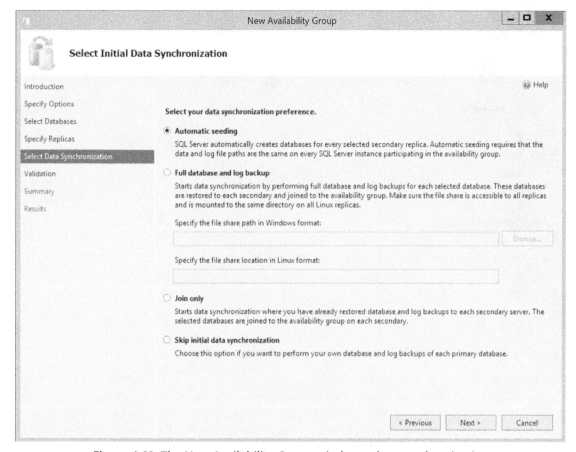

Figure 4.62: The New Availability Group window – data synchronization

18. The wizard validates the provided configuration values and highlights issues, if any. If there are validation errors, we'll have to fix and re-run the validation to continue the wizard. Observe that all of the validations are successful. Click **Next** to continue:

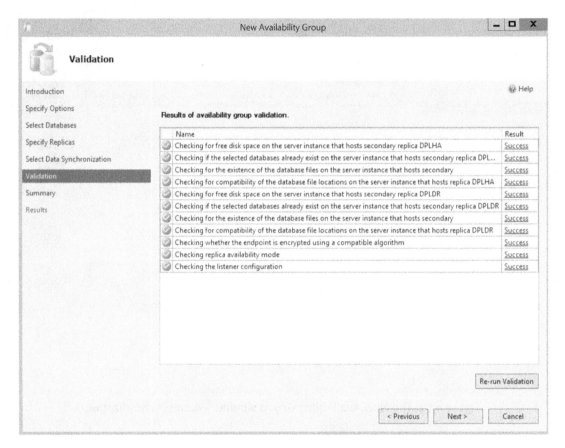

Figure 4.63: The New Availability Group window – validation

19. In the **Summary** window, review the configuration. Before we click on **Finish**, let's script out the configuration. Click the down arrow besides the **Script** button and select **File**:

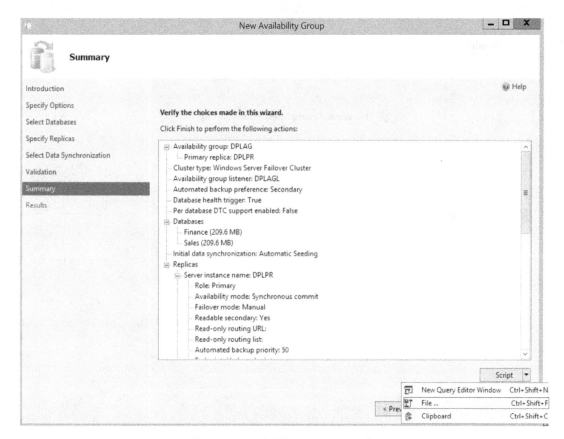

Figure 4.64: The New Availability Group window – summary

Save the T-SQL script to a file at a location of your choice.

20. Click on **Finish** to complete the wizard. The wizard creates the availability group with the provided configuration settings:

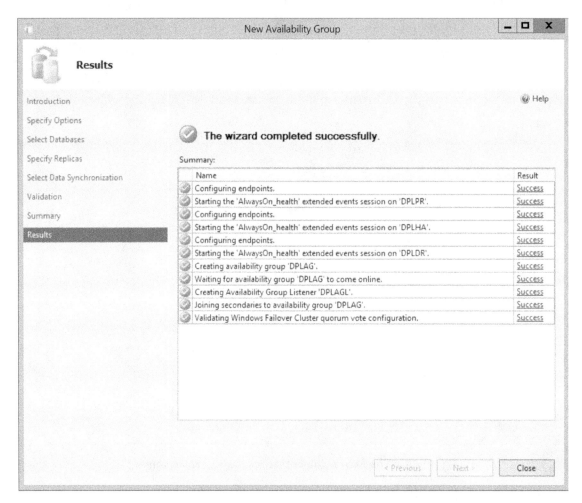

Figure 4.65: The New Availability Group window – results

Click on **Close** to close the wizard.

21. Press *Ctrl + N* to open a new query window. Connect to DPLPR and run the following query to verify the status of automatic seeding:

```
SELECT
    has.start_time
    ,has.completion_time
    ,ags.name
    ,db.database_name
    ,has.current_state
    ,has.performed_seeding
    ,has.failure_state
    ,has.failure_state_desc
FROM sys.dm_hadr_automatic_seeding as has
JOIN sys.availability_databases_cluster as db
    ON has.ag_db_id = db.group_database_id
JOIN sys.availability_groups as ags
    ON has.ag_id = ags.group_id
```

You should get output similar to what is shown in the following screenshot:

	start_time	completion_time	name	database_name	current_state	performed_seeding	failure_state	failure_state_desc
1	2018-09-23 13:11:11.633	NULL	DPLAG	Finance	SEEDING	1	NULL	NULL
2	2018-09-23 13:11:12.460	NULL	DPLAG	Finance	SEEDING	1	NULL	NULL
3	2018-09-23 13:11:11.637	NULL	DPLAG	Sales	SEEDING	1	NULL	NULL
4	2018-09-23 13:11:12.460	2018-09-23 13:11:47.350	DPLAG	Sales	COMPLETED	1	NULL	NULL

Figure 4.66: Verifying the status of automatic seeding

The **current_state** column gives the seeding status. Observe that the seeding for the **Sales** database for one secondary replica is completed.

We have successfully configured an AlwaysOn availability group. In the next section, we'll review the configuration and look at the resources created as part of the AlwaysOn AG creation.

Exercise 37: Reviewing an AlwaysOn AG Configuration

Let's connect to the AlwaysOn AG listener and review the availability group replicas, databases, and the listener. Follow these steps:

1. Press F8 to open the Object Explorer in SSMS. Enter **DPLAGL** as the **Server name** option and select **Windows Authentication** as the **Authentication** type.

2. Click on **Connect** to connect to the availability group:

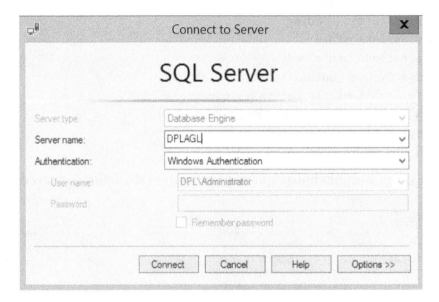

Figure 4.67: The Connect to Server window

3. Expand the **Databases** node in the Object Explorer:

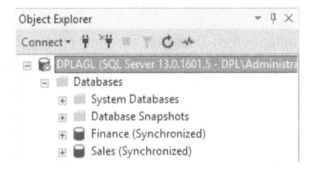

Figure 4.68: The synchronized databases

Observe that the **Finance** and **Sales** databases have **Synchronized** status. This means that the changes are being replicated to the secondaries.

4. Expand the **Always On High Availability** node in the Object Explorer:

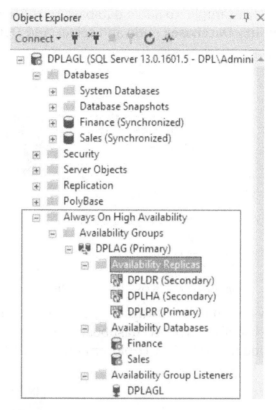

Figure 4.69: The three replicas, two availability databases, and one availability group listener

Observe that there are three availability replicas: DPLDR, DPLHA, and DPLPR. Each replica has a postfix specifying its role in the availability group. There are two availability databases: **Finance** and **Sales**. There is also one availability group listener: DPLAGL.

5. You can modify the properties of an availability group from the Object Explorer. To modify any property of a resource, right-click and select the available option from the context menu. For example, to add a database to the availability group, right-click on the **Availability Databases** node and select **Add Database**:

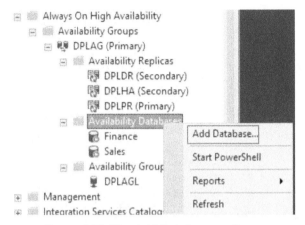

Figure 4.70: The Add Database option

6. Another way to view and manage AlwaysOn AG resources is through the AlwaysOn dashboard. To open the AlwaysOn AG dashboard, right-click on the **Always On High Availability** node in the Object Explorer and select **Show Dashboard**:

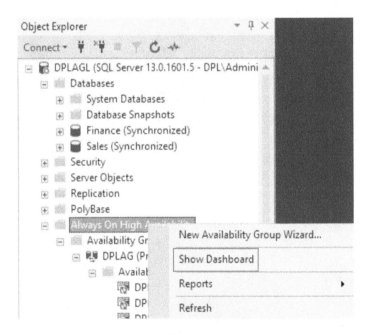

Figure 4.71: The Show Dashboard option

7. The dashboard lists all of the available availability groups. Select the **DPLAG** availability group:

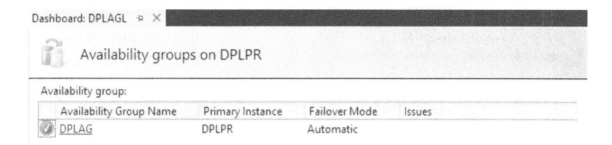

Figure 4.72: Dashboard listing the AG

This opens the DPLAG dashboard:

Figure 4.73: The DPLAG dashboard

The dashboard provides the status of the availability group and also allows you to monitor the AG. The dashboard also allows you to manually fail over to available replicas as and when required.

8. WSFC provides failover capability and that is because the availability group is created as a cluster role. To view the WSFC configuration, press Windows + R to open the **Run** command window. Enter `cluadmin.msc` in the **Run** command window and press *Enter* to open the Failover Cluster Manager.

9. In the Failover Cluster Manager window, expand the **DPLAO.dpl.com** node and select **Roles**:

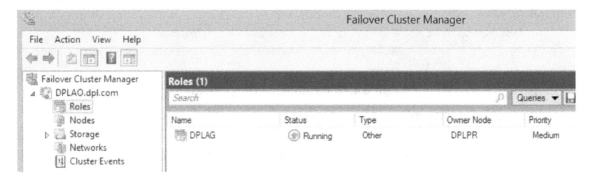

Figure 4.74: The Roles option

Observe that the DPLAG availability group is listed as a role. The owner node of DPLAG is DPLPR, which is the primary replica.

10. Select the **DPLAG** role to see the resource information in the bottom status window:

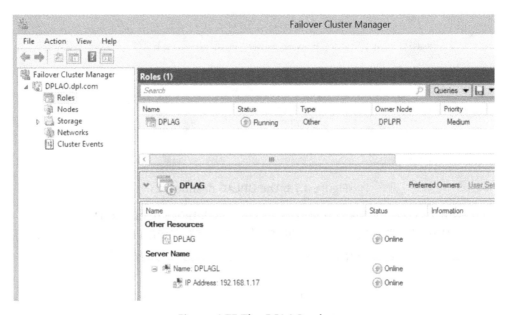

Figure 4.75 The DPLAG role

The availability group role can also be added from the Failover Cluster Manager; however, it is recommended to create it using SQL Server. Moreover, you can fail over or move the DPLAG role to any of the available secondaries from Failover Cluster Manager.

AlwaysOn Availability Groups on Microsoft Azure

Azure is a cloud platform offering from Microsoft that has a vast set of services for organizations to build and deploy applications. Deploying a SQL Server AlwaysOn availability group on Microsoft Azure is not a lot different than deploying it on-premises. The requirements, components, and prerequisites remain the same; however, the implementation differs.

Exercise 38: Configuring an AlwaysOn Availability Group on Microsoft Azure

To configure a two-node AlwaysOn AG on Azure, we still need a domain controller, a primary replica, a secondary replica, and an AlwaysOn listener. However, the VMs are provisioned on Azure and Azure VMs require a load balancer. An AlwaysOn AG on Azure can either be configured manually or automatically by using the SQL Server AlwaysOn Cluster template.

In this exercise, we'll configure an AlwaysOn AG using the SQL Server AlwaysOn Cluster template. Follow these steps to configure an AlwaysOn AG on Microsoft Azure.

> **Note**
>
> You will need an Azure account for this exercise. If you don't have one, create a free account here: https://azure.microsoft.com/en-in/free/.

1. Open https://portal.azure.com and log in using your Azure account.

2. Under **Microsoft Azure**, select **Create a resource**:

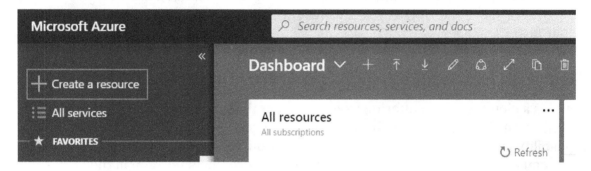

Figure 4.76: The Create a resource option

3. In the **New** blade, type `SQL Server AlwaysOn` in the search box and hit *Enter*:

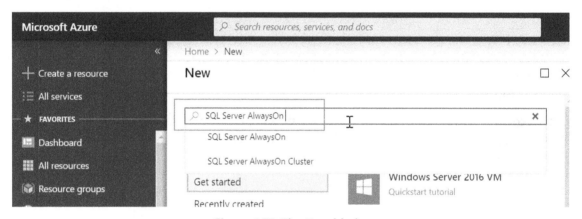

Figure 4.77: The New blade

4. In the **Everything** blade, select **SQL Server AlwaysOn Cluster**:

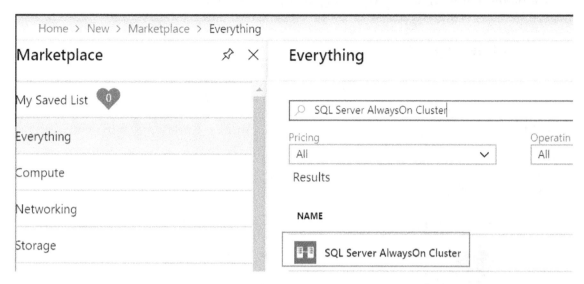

Figure 4.78: The Everything blade

5. This opens the **SQL Server AlwaysOn Cluster** blade. Scroll down to locate the topology that is to be deployed as part of this template:

Figure 4.79: The SQL Server AlwaysOn Cluster blade

The template deploys two nodes (one primary replica and one secondary replica): an AlwaysOn AG with a domain controller, and a file share witness. All the VMs (DC-1, DC-2, SQL-1, FSW, and SQL-2) created as part of the deployment are in the same Azure region. The domain controller and the availability nodes are in two different subnets within one virtual private network. There is an internal load balancer, ILB, which holds the IP address of the AG listener.

Click the **Create** button to continue.

6. Configure the basic settings, as shown in the following screenshot:

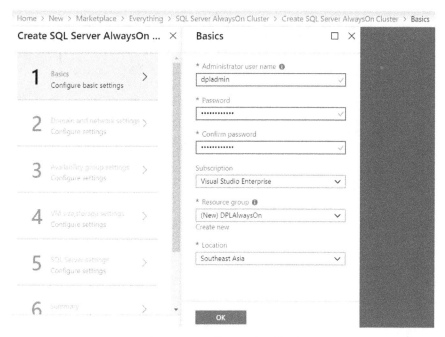

Figure 4.80: The Basics blade

Provide the domain administrator user name and password. Select the subscription. The template expects an empty resource group. If you don't have an existing empty resource group, create a new one by clicking on the **Create new** link.

Choose the location and click on **OK** to continue.

7. Configure the domain and network settings, as shown in the following screenshot:

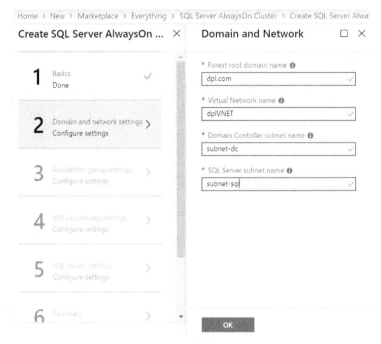

Figure 4.81: The Domain and network settings blade

Provide the domain name, virtual network name, and the subnet name for the domain controller and for the SQL Server VMs.

8. Configure the availability group and listener settings, as shown in the following screenshot:

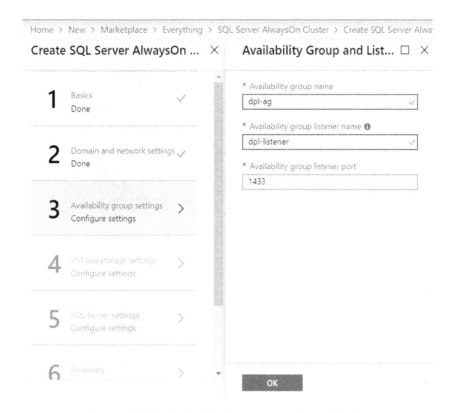

Figure 4.82: The Availability group settings blade

Provide the availability group name, listener name, and the port.

9. Configure the virtual machine size and storage settings, as shown in the following screenshot:

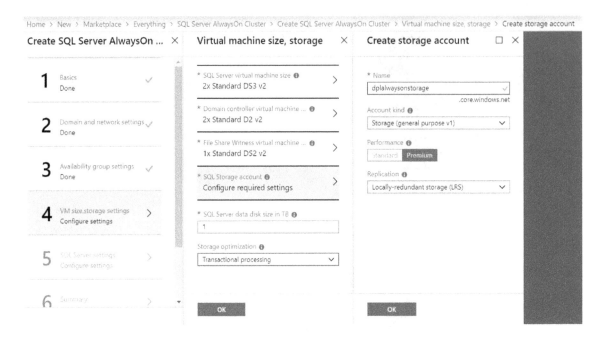

Figure 4.83: The VM size, storage settings blade

This blade provides us with the recommended VM size for the domain controller, file share witness, and the availability replicas.

However, Microsoft Azure has a wide variety of VMs to support different types of workloads. If you are setting up a production SQL Server environment, it's recommended to find out the VM size that best suits your application needs. Configure a new storage account to hold the virtual hard disks (VHDs) for the Azure VMs. The template also provides options to optimize the storage for transactional processing, data warehousing, or general workload. Let's select **Transactional processing** for the **Storage optimization** option.

Click **OK** to continue.

10. Configure the SQL Server settings as shown in the following screenshot:

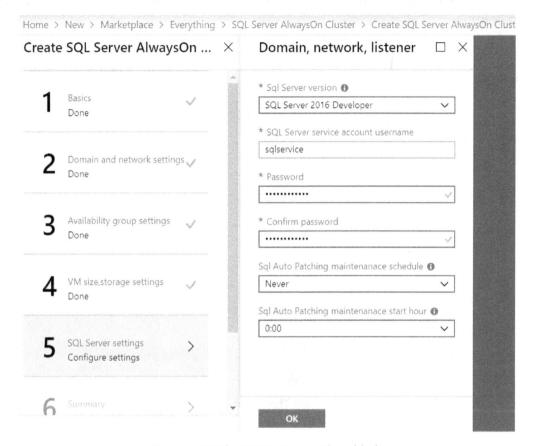

Figure 4.84: The SQL Server settings blade

Select the SQL Server 2016/2017 Developer edition as SQL Server version. Provide the SQL Server service account name and password. Set the SQL auto patching maintenance schedule to **Never**.

Click **OK** to continue.

11. The **Summary** blade will summarize all of the configurations made so far. The configurations will also be re-validated. If there are no validation errors, click **OK** to continue:

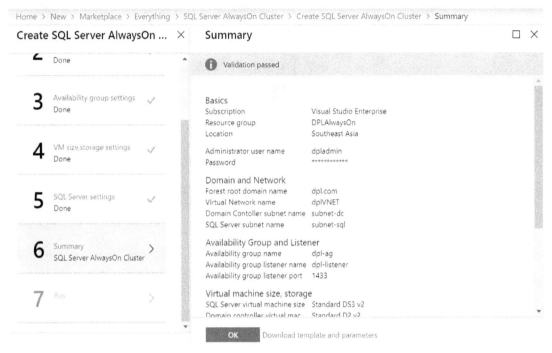

Figure 4.85: The Summary blade

12. In the **Buy** blade, accept the terms and services and click on the **Create** button to start the deployment:

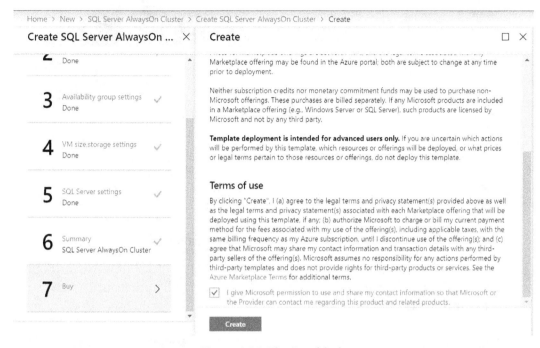

Figure 4.86: The Buy blade

The deployment notification will appear in the **Notifications** section (bell icon) in the top menu:

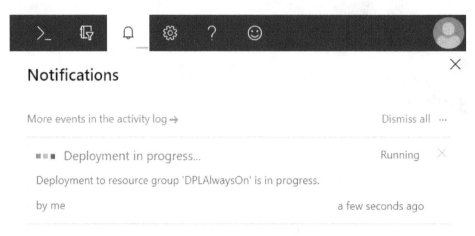

Figure 4.87: The Notifications section

It may take up to an hour for the deployment to complete. Once the deployment completes, the **Deployment succeeded** notification will appear under the **Notifications** section:

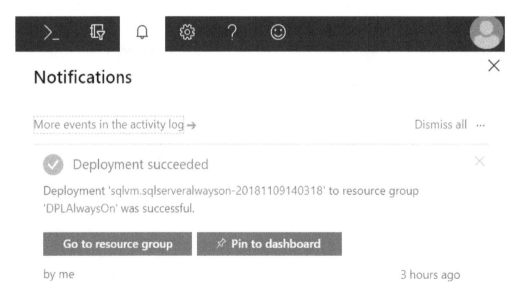

Figure 4.88: The Deployment succeeded notification

This completes the configuration. Let's look at the components created as part of the deployment.

> **Note**
>
> The automatic deployment configures AlwaysOn; however, the availability databases are to be added manually.

You can click on the **Go to resource group** button to review the objects created as part of the deployment. The **DPLAlwaysOn** resource group blade is shown in the following screenshot:

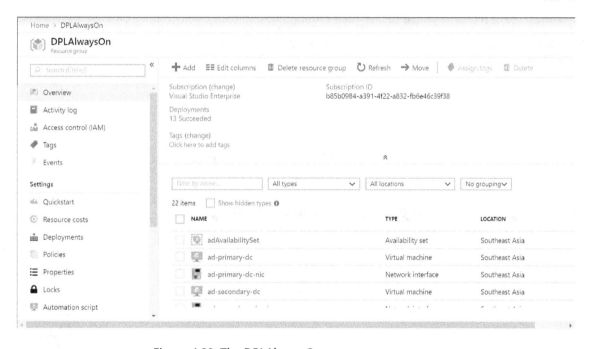

Figure 4.89: The DPLAlwaysOn resource group page

In the resource group blade, you can click on the **No grouping** dropdown and use **Group by type** as the grouping option:

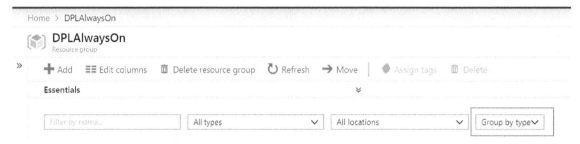

Figure 4.90: The DPLAlwaysOn resource group page – the group-by option

Virtual Networks

An Azure virtual network allows the VMs to securely communicate with one another. All the VMs created as part of the deployment belong to one virtual network:

Figure 4.91: The virtual networks page

Virtual Machines

The following VMs are created as part of the deployment:

Figure 4.92: The virtual machines page

The **ad-primary-dc** and **ad-secondary-dc** VMs are the two domain controller VMs (primary and secondary). The **sqlserver-0** and **sqlserver-1** VMs are the primary and the secondary availability replicas. The **cluster-fsw** VM is the file share witness.

Storage Accounts

The following storage accounts are created as part of the deployment:

STORAGE ACCOUNT		
dplalwaysonstorage	Storage account	Southeast Asia
dplalwaysonstoragedc	Storage account	Southeast Asia
jqqduykfwl3m4diag	Storage account	Southeast Asia
jqqduykfwl3m4fsw	Storage account	Southeast Asia

Figure 4.93: The storage accounts page

The **dplalwaysonstorage** storage account contains the availability replica VMs' VHDs. You can go to **dplalwaysonstorage | Blobs | vhds** to view the content of the VHD container:

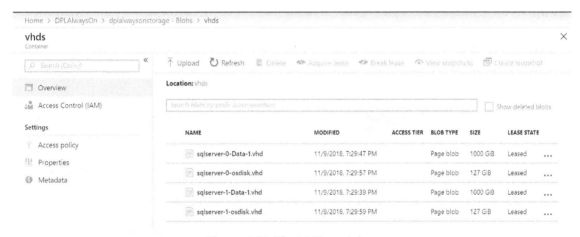

Figure 4.94: The VHD container

There's one OS and data disk for each availability replica VM. The OS disk contains the OS binaries and the data disks store the SQL Server data and log files. Multiple data disks can be added to a VM. However, the AlwaysOn template has a provision to add one data disk only.

The **dplalwaysonstoragedc** storage account contains the VHDs for the domain controller VM. The **dplalwaysonstoragefsw** storage account contains the VHDs for the file share witness VM. The **jqqduykfwl3m4diag** storage account contains the log files.

Public IP Addresses

The following public IP addresses are created as part of the deployment:

Figure 4.95: The public IP addresses page

backupDCIPjqqdu and **primaryDCIPjqqd** are the domain controller VMs' public IP addresses. **sql0Ipjqqduykfw** and **sql1Pjqqduykfw** are the availability replicas' public IP addresses. Click on **sql0ijqqduykfw** to open the overview page:

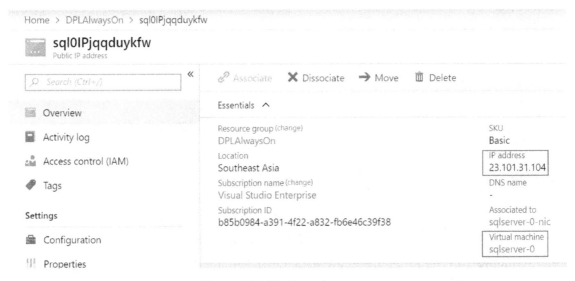

Figure 4.96: The overview page

Observe that the IP address is assigned to the **sqlserver-0** VM. You can look into the other IP addresses in the same manner. The IP addresses for the VMs will be different in your case.

Network Interfaces

A network interface is a software equivalent of the physical network interface card in an on-premises system. The following network interfaces are created as part of the deployment:

NETWORK INTERFACE		
ad-primary-dc-nic	Network interface	Southeast Asia
ad-secondary-dc-nic	Network interface	Southeast Asia
cluster-fsw-nic	Network interface	Southeast Asia
sqlserver-0-nic	Network interface	Southeast Asia
sqlserver-1-nic	Network interface	Southeast Asia

Figure 4.97: The network interfaces page

There's one network interface for each virtual machine.

Load Balancers

A load balancer is used to store the IP address of the listener. The following load balancer is created as part of the deployment:

LOAD BALANCER		
sqlLoadBalancer	Load balancer	Southeast Asia

Figure 4.98: The Load Balancer page

You can click on **sqlLoadBalancer** to view its details:

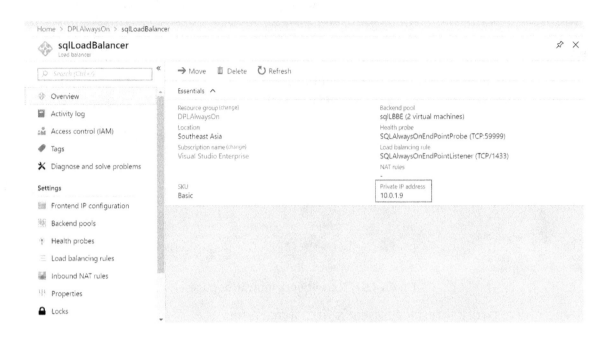

Figure 4.99: The sqlLoadBalancer overview page

The load balancer has two virtual machines and has a private IP address `10.0.1.9`.

The **Backend pools** option available in the left-hand pane opens its overview page:

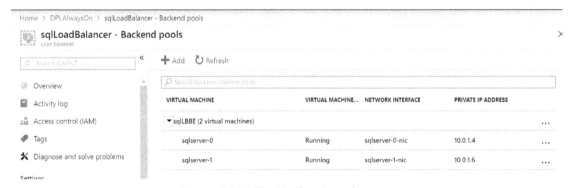

Figure 4.100: The Backend pools page

The **Backend pools** page has the availability group replica VMs. The private IPs of the VMs are `10.0.1.4` and `10.0.1.6`.

The **Load balancing rules** option available in the left-hand pane opens its overview page:

Figure 4.101: The Load balancing rules page

You can select the **SQLAlwaysOnEndPointListener** rule to view its details:

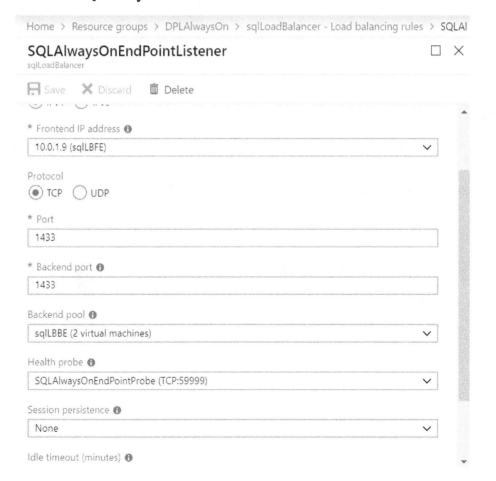

Figure 4.102: The SQLAlwaysOnEndPointListener rule

The frontend IP address is the availability group listener's IP address. The backend pool contains the **sqlserver-0** and **sqlserver-1** virtual machines. The health probe is used by Azure to find out which SQL Server instance owns the availability group listener. The traffic is routed to the SQL Server instance that owns the listener.

Availability Sets

An availability set is similar to Windows Server Failover Cluster. An availability set contains two or more VMs, domain controllers in this case. If one of the domain controller VM fails, the other VM works as the domain controller. There are two availability sets created as part of the deployment:

AVAILABILITY SET

☐	adAvailabilitySet	Availability set
☐	sqlAvailabilitySet	Availability set

Figure 4.103: The Availability Sets page

The **adAvailablitySet** is for the domain controller VMs and the **sqlAvailabilitySet** is for the SQL VMs.

Exercise 39: Reviewing Our Availability Group Configuration

Now that we have reviewed the objects created, let's log into the SQL Server VMs and review the availability group configuration.

1. To log into the VM, locate and click on **sqlserver-1** on the **DPLAlwaysOn** blade.

2. In the **sqlserver-1 | Overview** blade, click on the **Connect** button:

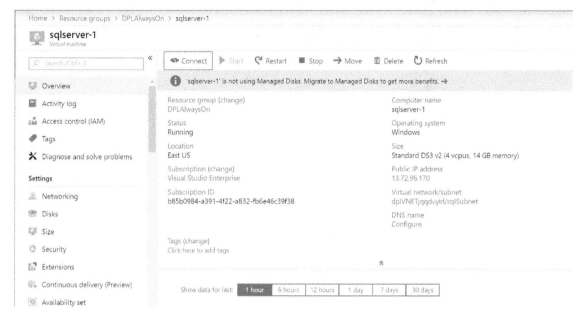

Figure 4.104: The Connect button

3. In the **Connect to virtual machine** blade, under the **RDP** tab, click on the **Download RDP File** button to download the remote desktop file:

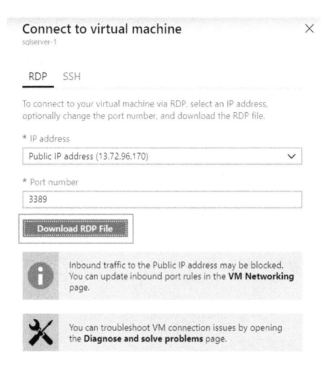

Figure 4.105: The Connect to virtual machine window

A file, `sqlserver-1.rdp`, will be downloaded to the system's default `Downloads` folder.

4. Locate and double-click on the **sqlserver-1.rdp** file. In the **Remote Desktop Connection** dialog box, click on **Connect**:

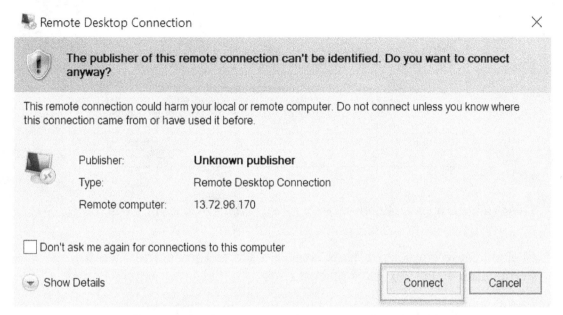

Figure 4.106: The Remote Desktop Connection window

5. In the **Enter your credentials** dialog box, provide the domain administrator user name and password. This should be the same as provided in *step 6* in *Exercise 38: Configuring an AlwaysOn Availability Group on Microsoft Azure*:

Figure 4.107: The Enter your credentials dialog box

Note that you may get the following error when connecting to the **sqlserver-1** or **sqlserver-0** VM:

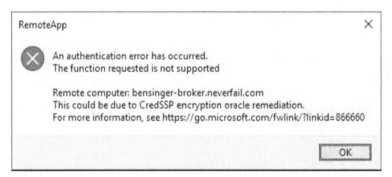

Figure 4.108: The error

This is a known issue. Refer to https://www.netwoven.com/2018/05/15/solved-credssp-encryption-oracle-remediation/ for how to fix it.

6. Click on **OK** to connect to the **sqlserver-1** VM. In the **Remote Desktop Connection** dialog box, click on **Yes**:

Figure 4.109: The Remote Desktop Connection dialog box

You'll be connected to the **sqlserver-1** VM.

7. When connected to the VM, open SQL Server Management Studio and connect to the **sqlserver-1** SQL Server instance. In the Object Explorer, expand **Always On High Availability** | **Availability Groups** and right-click on the **dpl-ag** availability group. Select **Show Dashboard** from the context menu:

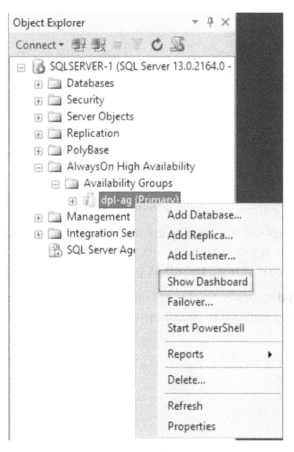

Figure 4.110: The Show Dashboard option

This will open the AlwaysOn availability group dashboard for the dpl-ag availability group:

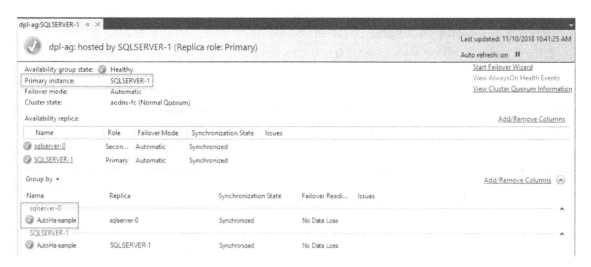

Figure 4.111: The AlwaysOn availability group dashboard for the dpl-ag availability group

Observe that the dpl-ag availability group has two replicas, **sqlserver-1** and **sqlserver-0**, in synchronous availability mode. A sample database, **AutoHA-sample**, has been added to the dpl-ag group as part of the AlwaysOn template.

You can now add databases to the dpl-ag availability group (we will cover this in *Lesson 5, Managing AlwaysOn Availability Groups*).

8. Let's look at the listener configuration. In the Object Explorer, expand **Always On High Availability** | **Availability Groups** | **dpl-ag** | **Availability Group Listeners**. Right-click on **dpl-listener** and select **Properties** from the context menu:

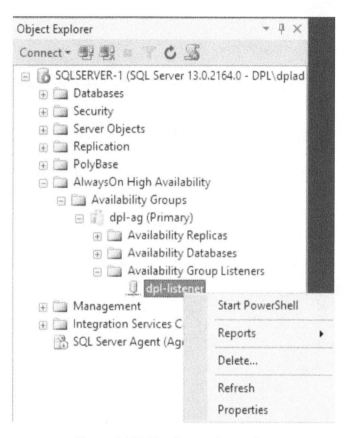

Figure 4.112: The Properties option

This will open the **Listener Properties** window:

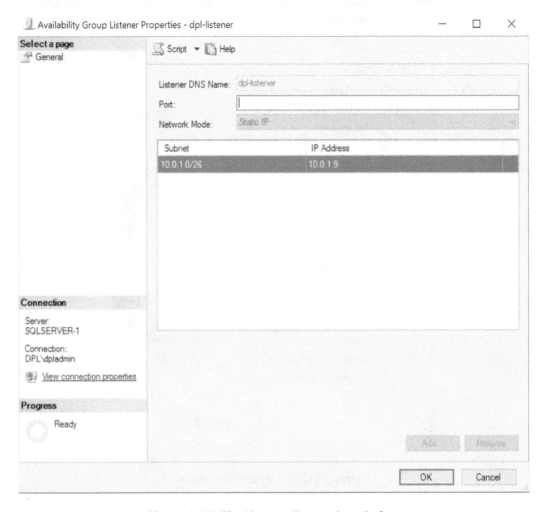

Figure 4.113: The Listener Properties window

Observe that the listener IP address is the same as the one given as the frontend IP address in the load balancer.

This completes our review of the configuration.

Configuring AlwaysOn in Microsoft Azure using the template is fast and easy, compared to setting it up on-premises. However, it has the following limitations:

- It expects a new virtual network and can't be created in an existing virtual network.

- The VMs created are publicly exposed. Extra work is required to secure the VMs.

> **Note**
>
> To know more about securing VMs, visit https://azure.microsoft.com/en-in/services/virtual-machines/security/.

- The template doesn't have an option to add extra disks at the time of creation. Each VM has an OS disk and a data disk. More disks need to be added manually if the database files are to be kept on separate disks.

- The template doesn't provide a way to name the Windows Failover Cluster.

- The template creates two availability replicas. If more than two availability replicas are required, it should be done manually.

The template is a good choice to quickly set up development environments. However, it's advised to configure AlwaysOn AG manually for production environments.

Exercise 40: Deleting the AlwaysOn Configuration

In this exercise, we will delete our DPLAlwaysOn resource group:

1. To delete the AlwaysOn deployment, select **Delete resource group** from the **DPLAlwaysOn** resource group blade:

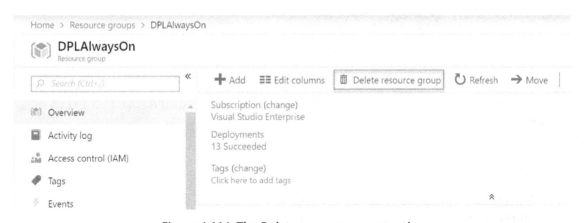

Figure 4.114: The Delete resource group option

2. In the delete confirmation page, type the resource group name in the **TYPE THE RESOURCE GROUP NAME** text box and click on the **Delete** button:

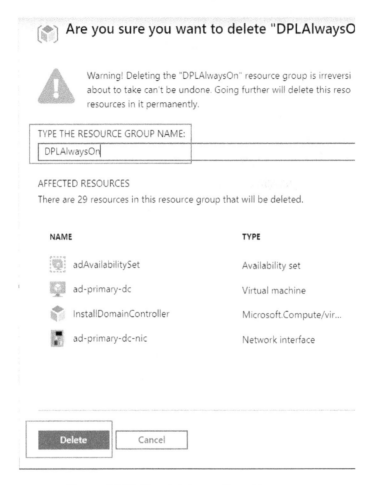

Figure 4.115: The delete confirmation page

Deleting a resource group also deletes all of the associated Azure resources or services.

> **Note**
>
> An AlwaysOn AG also allows you to add an Azure VM as a secondary replica in an on-premises AlwaysOn AG configuration. This requires a site-to-site VPN to be configured between the on-premises network and Azure to get the connectivity.

Summary

In this lesson, we have covered AlwaysOn AGs in detail. We first started by discussing the common concepts and terminologies associated with AlwaysOn. We then talked about the prerequisites to configure an AlwaysOn AG. This lesson also talked about provisioning Hyper-V VMs as a part of the infrastructure setup to configure AlwaysOn AG.

Further on, we learned how to create an Active Directory Domain Controller, a Windows Server Failover Cluster, and the AlwaysOn AG. The AlwaysOn AG is configured with three replicas: one primary and two secondary. Finally, we talked about the different resources created as part of the AlwaysOn AG configuration.

In the next lesson, we'll learn to manage and monitor AlwaysOn AG.

5

Managing AlwaysOn Availability Groups

Learning Objectives

By the end of this lesson, you will be able to do the following:

- Perform automatic and manual failover

- Perform various management tasks against an availability group

- Monitor an AlwaysOn availability group

- Detect common AlwaysOn availability group problems and implement their solutions

This lesson will show us how to manage and maintain an AlwaysOn AG. We will also learn how to troubleshoot an AG.

Introduction

In the previous lesson, we configured a three-node AlwaysOn **availability group** (**AG**) with one primary and two secondary nodes.

However, configuring an AlwaysOn AG is half the task. In this lesson, we'll learn to manage and maintain AlwaysOn availability groups. We'll also learn to troubleshoot AG to find and fix problems when they occur.

AlwaysOn AG Failover

A failover can be of two types:

- An automatic failover, triggered as a result of the primary instance being unavailable or the availability databases being unavailable (when database level health detection is enabled)

- A manual failover to a synchronous (zero data loss) or an asynchronous (data loss) replica

Let's now look at automatic and manual failover in detail.

Automatic Failover

In a real-world scenario, an automatic failover is triggered when a primary instance is unavailable, or any of the availability databases are unavailable (when database-level health detection is enabled).

Let's simulate a primary node failure and verify the automatic failover works. However, before that, let's just verify the configuration. To do this, you can open the Failover Cluster Manager and verify that all nodes are active and DPLPR is the owner of the DPLAG role.

> **Note**
>
> Connect to the DPLHA VM as we will shut down the DPLPR VM to simulate failure and trigger automatic failover.

Also, make sure that the DPLDC VM is up and running.

The following screenshot shows nodes:

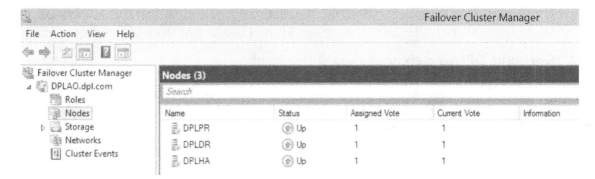

Figure 5.1: Failover Cluster Manager - nodes

The following screenshot shows roles:

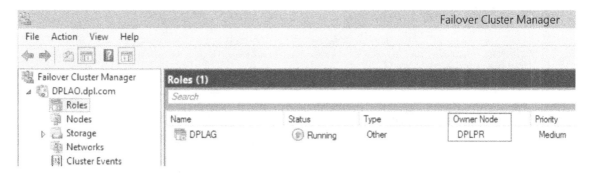

Figure 5.2: Failover Cluster Manager - roles

Let's now verify that AlwaysOn is working well and that all the replicas are synchronizing or are in a synchronized state.

Exercise 41: Automatic Failover

In this exercise, we will verify that our automatic failover is successfully running:

1. Open SSMS and connect to the DPLAGL listener. Right-click on the **Always On High Availability** node, and then select **Show Dashboard** from the context menu.

2. Select the **DPLAG** resource group in the dashboard:

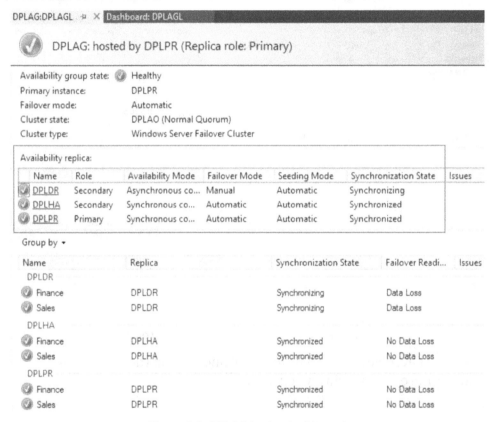

Figure 5.3: DPLAG in the dashboard

As the dashboard says, the availability group status is good. Notice that it also lists the type of failover that can be done at each node.

3. To simulate a primary replica failure, execute the following command on the host machine to stop the primary replica. You can also stop the DPLPR VM from the Hyper-V manager. Right-click on **DPLPR** in the Hyper-V VM and select **Shutdown**:

```
Stop-VM
```

4. While the VM is being stopped, connect to DPLHA and open Failover Cluster Manager, if not already opened. Select the **Nodes** section under the **DPLAO.dpl. com** cluster. Observe that the DPLPR status has changed to **Down**:

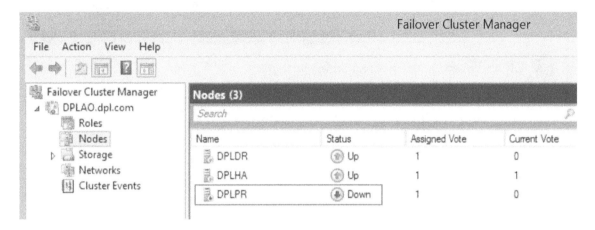

Figure 5.4: DPLPR is down

5. Select the **Roles** section and verify the DPLAG role owner. It should be DPLHA as a result of the automatic failover:

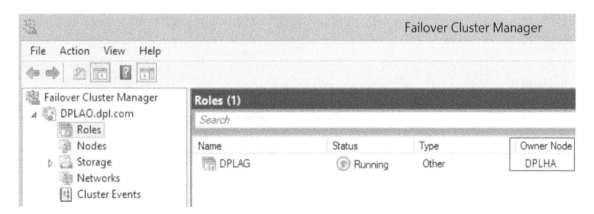

Figure 5.5: DPLAG role owner

The automatic failover completed successfully and the DPLAG availability group role was moved to DPLHA.

6. Open SSMS and connect to the DPLAGL listener.

> **Note**
>
> You may have to install SSMS on DPLHA if not already installed.

7. In the Object Explorer, right-click on the **Always On High Availability** node and select **Show Dashboard**:

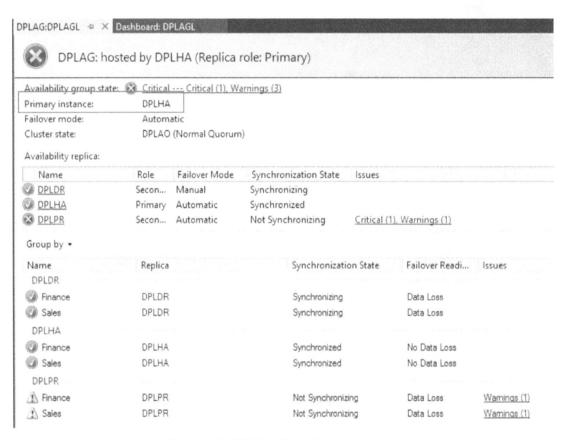

Figure 5.6: DPLHA is the primary instance

Notice that the primary instance is now DPLHA, as DPLPR isn't available. This means that the automatic failover was successful.

> **Note**
>
> There will be temporary unavailability during the failover. The connectivity is restored once the failover is complete.

8. Let's start the DPLPR VM and observe the AlwaysOn AG status. To start the VM, run the following PowerShell command on the host machine:

```
Start-VM -Name DPLPR
```

As the VM is starting, observe the node status in Failover Cluster Manager. As soon as the node is up, it is automatically joined to the cluster.

The node is joining:

Figure 5.7: DPLPR is joining

The node is up:

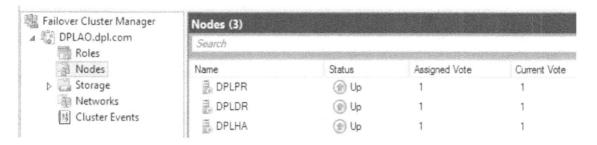

Figure 5.8: DPLPR is up

The node now shows the **Up** status. Let's check the AlwaysOn AG dashboard status:

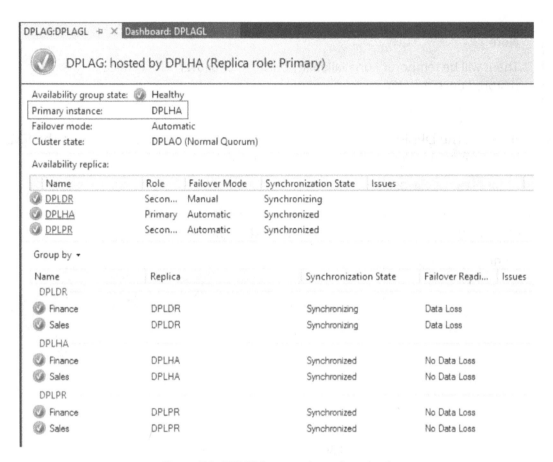

Figure 5.9: DPLPR is up and synchronized

The DPLPR is up and is synchronized. The synchronization may take some time depending on the amount of data to be synchronized. Notice that though the DPLPR node is up, the primary node is still DPLHA.

Manual Failover

Manual failover can be either with or without data loss. We'll see both in this section.

Exercise 42: Manual Failover without Data Loss

Let's do a manual failover from DPLHA to DPLPR. The failover, either manual or automatic, between two synchronous replicas will be without data loss.

Manual failover can be done using the AlwaysOn dashboard, T-SQL, or PowerShell. To do it using the dashboard, select the **Start Failover Wizard** link at the top-right corner of the dashboard and follow the wizard.

Let's see how to do it using T-SQL:

1. You'll have to change the SQL Server query mode to **SQLCMD**. To do so, select the **Query** menu option from the top menu and then select **SQLCMD Mode**:

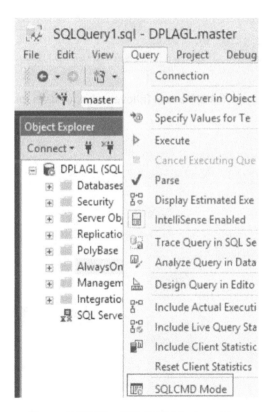

Figure 5.10: The SQLCMD Mode option

2. To perform a manual failover using T-SQL, execute the following script:

```
:Connect DPLPR
ALTER AVAILABILITY GROUP [DPLAG] FAILOVER;
```

The query connects to the DPLPR SQL Server instance and then runs the failover command to failover to DPLPR. This query needs to be run at the replica to which the failover is to be done.

You should get a similar output to this:

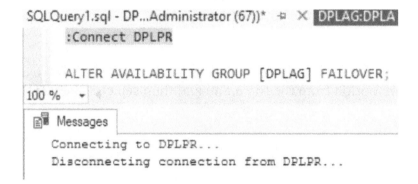

Figure 5.11: Manual failover without data loss

3. Switch to the dashboard and verify the primary replica:

DPLAG: hosted by DPLPR (Replica role: Primary)

Last updated: 29-09-2018 15:0

Auto refresh: on ❚❚

Availability group state:	✓ Healthy
Primary instance:	DPLPR
Failover mode:	Automatic
Cluster state:	DPLAO (Normal Quorum)

Start Failover Wizard
View Always On Health Event
View Cluster Quorum Inform

Availability replica:

Add/Remove Colum

Name	Role	Failover Mode	Synchronization State	Issues
DPLDR	Secon...	Manual	Synchronizing	
DPLHA	Secon...	Automatic	Synchronized	
DPLPR	Primary	Automatic	Synchronized	

Group by ▾

Add/Remove Columns

Name	Replica	Synchronization State	Failover Readi...	Issues
DPLDR				
Finance	DPLDR	Synchronizing	Data Loss	
Sales	DPLDR	Synchronizing	Data Loss	
DPLHA				
Finance	DPLHA	Synchronized	No Data Loss	
Sales	DPLHA	Synchronized	No Data Loss	
DPLPR				
Finance	DPLPR	Synchronized	No Data Loss	
Sales	DPLPR	Synchronized	No Data Loss	

Figure 5.12: DPLPR is now the primary instance

Notice that the primary instance is now DPLPR.

Exercise 43: Manual Failover with Data Loss

Manual failover with data loss is between two asynchronous replicas. Let's failover to DPLDR from DPLPR. You can do this using the dashboard, T-SQL, or PowerShell.

To do this using the dashboard, select the **Start Failover Wizard** in the top-right corner of the dashboard and follow the wizard.

We'll see how to do this using T-SQL:

1. To perform a manual failover using T-SQL, open a new query in SSMS, change the query mode to **SQLCMD**, and execute the following query:

   ```
   :Connect DPLDR
   ALTER AVAILABILITY GROUP [DPLAG] FORCE_FAILOVER_ALLOW_DATA_LOSS;
   ```

   The query first connects to the DPLDR node and then runs the failover command. Observe that unlike the command used for manual failover without data loss, the command here specifies the FORCE_FAILOVER_ALLOW_DATA_LOSS option.

   You should get the following output:

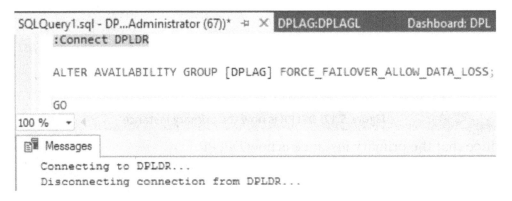

Figure 5.13: Manual failover with data loss

2. Check the dashboard to verify the primary instance:

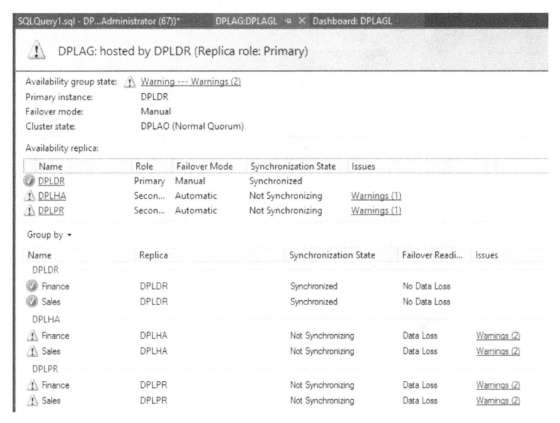

Figure 5.14: DPLDR is now the primary instance

Notice that the primary instance is now DPLDR. However, the databases at DPLHA and DPLPR are in the **Not Synchronizing** state.

3. To further investigate the issue, check the availability database's status in the Object Explorer. Connect to DPLPR in SSMS. In the Object Explorer, expand **Always On High Availability | Availability Groups | Availability Databases**:

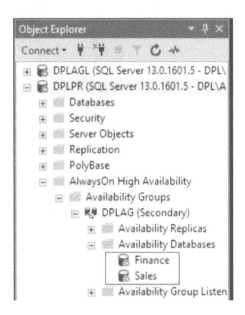

Figure 5.15: Data movement is paused

4. Observe the blue pause icon on the databases. This indicates that the data movement for the databases is paused. To resume the data movement, right-click on the database and select **Resume Data Movement**:

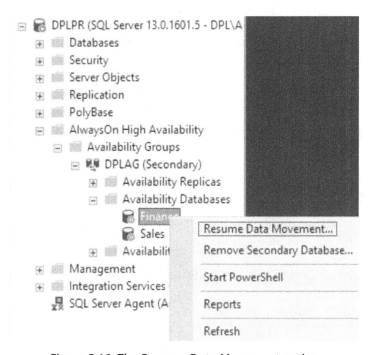

Figure 5.16: The Resume Data Movement option

You can also execute the following T-SQL script in a new query window on the DPLPR instance to resume the data movement:

```
ALTER DATABASE [Finance] SET HADR RESUME
GO
ALTER DATABASE [Sales] SET HADR RESUME
```

5. Refresh the **Availability Databases** nodes. The blue pause icon changes to a green play icon, inferring that the data movement has resumed. Execute the preceding T-SQL script on DPLHA to resume the data movement on the DPLHA instance.

6. Refresh the dashboard. The databases are now in the synchronizing state.

   The enabling data movement step is only required when the failover is to or from an asynchronous replica.

7. Execute the following queries in **SQLCMD** mode to failover to the DPLPR instance and switch to the original AlwaysOn configuration:

   Fail over to DPLPR from DPLDR:

   ```
   :Connect DPLPR
   ALTER AVAILABILITY GROUP [DPLAG] FORCE_FAILOVER_ALLOW_DATA_LOSS;
   GO
   ```

   Resume data movement at DPLHA and DPLDR:

   ```
   :Connect DPLHA
   ALTER DATABASE [Finance] SET HADR RESUME
   GO
   ALTER DATABASE [Sales] SET HADR RESUME
   GO
   :Connect DPLDR
   ALTER DATABASE [Finance] SET HADR RESUME
   GO
   ALTER DATABASE [Sales] SET HADR RESUME
   ```

The dashboard should show the following status after running these queries:

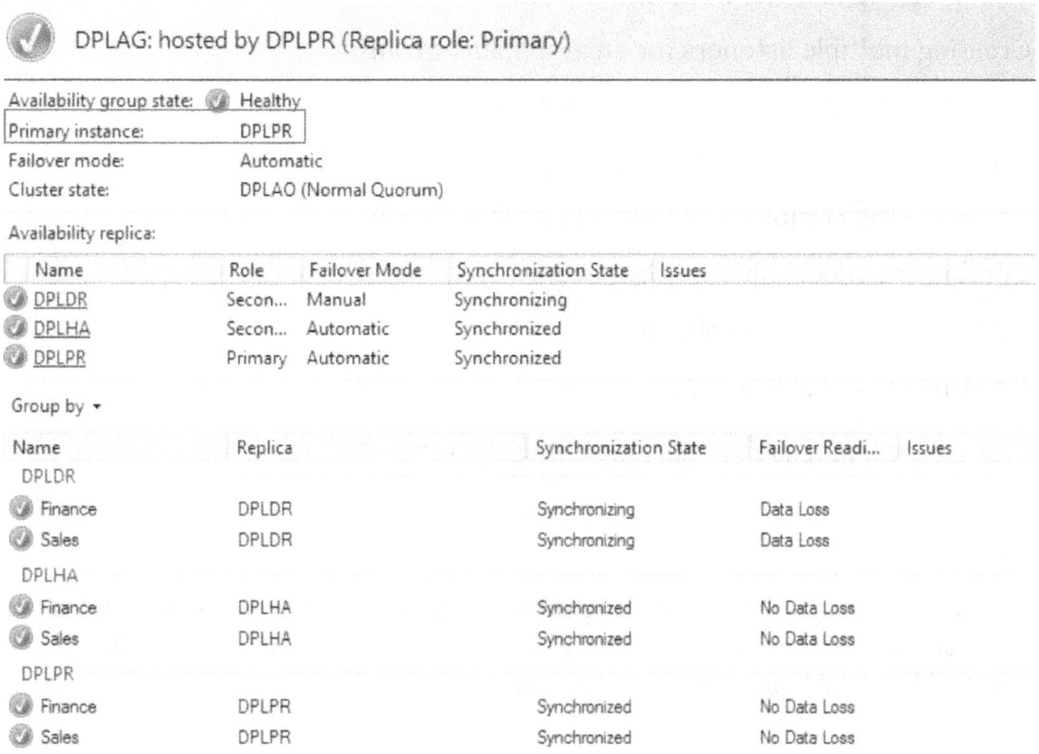

Figure 5.17: DPLPR is the primary instance again

Managing AlwaysOn Availability Groups

In this section, you'll learn about the various management tasks that you will have to perform once an AlwaysOn availability group is up and running. These include the following tasks:

- Removing a database from an existing availability group
- Adding a new database to an existing availability group
- Adding a new replica to an existing availability group
- Removing a replica from an existing availability group

- Changing the availability mode of a replica

- Changing the failover mode of a replica

- Creating multiple listeners for an availability group

- Creating multiple availability groups on one SQL Server instance

- Configuring backup on secondary replicas

- Changing the compression of an availability group

- Configuring read-only routing

- Taking an availability group offline

- Deleting an availability group and listener

Let's look into the details of these tasks.

> **Note**
>
> All of these tasks will be done using either T-SQL or PowerShell. However, these can also be performed using Object Explorer in SSMS or from the AlwaysOn Availability Dashboard. This is not covered in this book.

Removing a Database from an Existing Availability Group

A database can be removed from an availability group under the following conditions:

- The business requirement changes and the database is no longer a part of the application or is obsolete.

- The database synchronization is suspended due to an error. This would cause the transaction log of the database to grow. It is better to remove the database from the availability group and add it back once the issue is resolved.

A database can be removed from the primary replica as well as the secondary replica.

Exercise 44: Removing a Database from the Secondary Replica

If a database is removed from the secondary replica, the data movement to that secondary replica is stopped. The other replicas continue to receive the data from the primary replica for that database. In this exercise, we will remove the **Sales** database from the secondary replica, DPLHA:

1. Connect to the secondary replica, DPLHA, and execute the following query in SSMS:

   ```
   -- Remove Sales database from the availability group
   ALTER DATABASE [Sales] SET HADR OFF;
   ```

2. Connect to DPLAGL in the Object Explorer in SSMS and open the AlwaysOn Availability Dashboard:

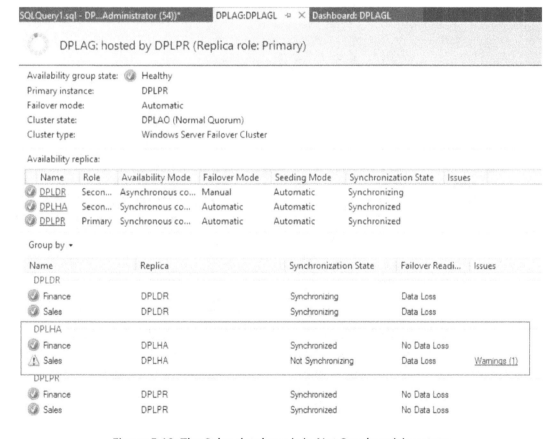

Figure 5.18: The Sales database is in Not Synchronizing state

Observe that the **Sales** database for the DPLHA instance is in a **Not Synchronizing** state, as it has been removed from the availability group.

3. Connect to the DPLHA instance in Object Explorer in SSMS. Expand the **Databases** node:

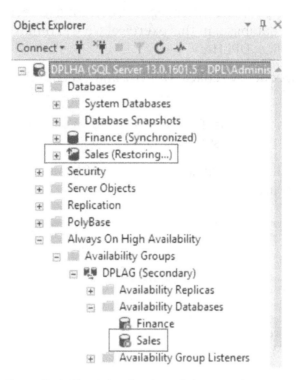

Figure 5.19: The Sales database is in restoring state

Observe that the **Sales** database is in a restoring state. Moreover, there is a red cross on the **Sales** database under the **Availability Databases** node, indicating that the database is not a part of the availability group.

4. To add the **Sales** database to the availability group on DPLHA, connect to DPLHA and execute the following query:

```
-- Add Sales database to the availability group
ALTER DATABASE [Sales] SET HADR SET AVAILABILITY GROUP = DPLAG;
```

Exercise 45: Removing a Database from the Primary Replica

If the database is removed from the primary replica, it is removed from all of the secondary replicas. In this exercise, we will remove the **Sales** database from the primary replica, DPLPR:

1. To remove a database from the primary replica, connect to DPLPR (primary replica) and execute the following command:

    ```
    -- Remove Sales database from the primary replica
    ALTER AVAILABILITY GROUP [DPLAG] REMOVE DATABASE [Sales];
    ```

2. Check the status in the dashboard:

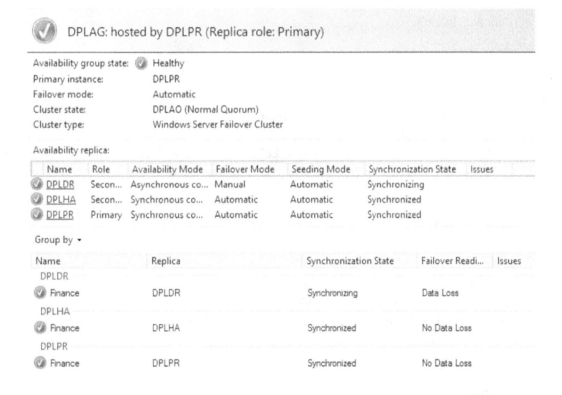

Figure 5.20: The Sales database is removed

Observe that the **Sales** database is not the part of the availability group when removed from the primary replica. The **Sales** database is in an online state at the primary replica, DPLPR, and is in a restoring state on the secondary replicas, DPLHA and DPLDR.

Exercise 46: Adding a Database to an Availability Group

In the previous exercise, we removed the **Sales** database from the availability replica, DPLAG. Let's now add it back to the availability group:

1. The **Sales** database needs to be removed from DPLDR and DPLHA before we can add it to the availability group. To do so, execute the following query on DPLHA and DPLDR:

   ```
   DROP DATABASE [Sales];
   ```

2. To add the **Sales** database to the availability group, execute the following query in **SQLCMD** mode in SSMS:

   ```
   -- Connect to DPLAGL
   :Connect DPLAGL

   USE [master]

   GO
   -- Enable Automatic Seeding for DPLDR
   ALTER AVAILABILITY GROUP [DPLAG]
   MODIFY REPLICA ON N'DPLDR' WITH (SEEDING_MODE = AUTOMATIC)

   GO

   USE [master]

   GO

   GO
   -- Enable Automatic Seeding for DPLHA
   ALTER AVAILABILITY GROUP [DPLAG]
   MODIFY REPLICA ON N'DPLHA' WITH (SEEDING_MODE = AUTOMATIC)

   GO

   USE [master]

   GO
   -- Add Sales database to the availability group DPLAG
   ALTER AVAILABILITY GROUP [DPLAG]
   ADD DATABASE [Sales];

   GO
   ```

```
-- Connect to replica DPLDR
:Connect DPLDR


-- Give permissions to DPLAG to create database on DPLDR
-- This is required for Automatic Seeding
ALTER AVAILABILITY GROUP [DPLAG] GRANT CREATE ANY DATABASE;


GO


-- Connect to replica DPLHA
:Connect DPLHA


-- Give permissions to DPLAG to create database on DPLHA
-- This is required for Automatic Seeding
ALTER AVAILABILITY GROUP [DPLAG] GRANT CREATE ANY DATABASE;
```

This T-SQL script enables automatic seeding as the initial synchronization mechanism for DPLHA and DPLDR, adds the **Sales** database to the DPLAG availability group, and gives rights to the DPLAG availability group to create databases on DPLHA and DPLDR.

The script will differ if the initial synchronization method selected is different than automatic seeding.

3. Check the dashboard and verify the **Sales** database was successfully added:

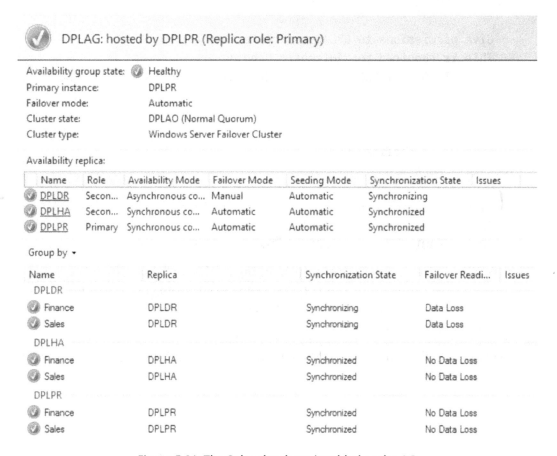

Figure 5.21: The Sales database is added to the AG

Observe that the **Sales** database is now part of the DPLAG availability group.

Exercise 47: Removing a Replica from an Availability Group

A replica can be removed from an availability group if it's no longer required:

1. To remove a replica DPLDR from the DPLAG availability group, connect to DPLAGL on DPLPR or DPLHA, and execute the following query:

    ```
    -- Remove DPLDR from the availability group DPLAG
    ALTER AVAILABILITY GROUP [DPLAG] REMOVE REPLICA ON 'DPLDR';
    ```

2. Check the availability group status on the dashboard:

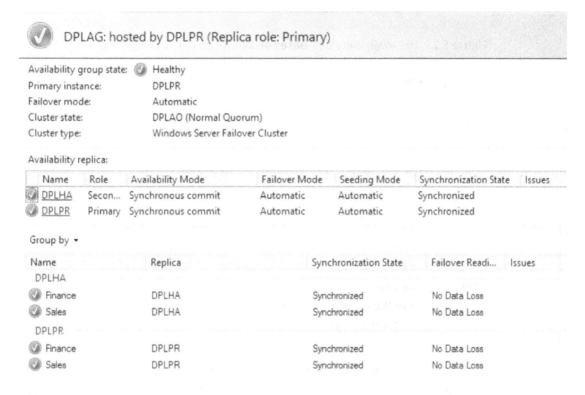

Figure 5.22: DPLDR is removed

Observe that we only have two replicas in the DPLAG availability group and DPLDR is successfully removed.

The availability databases on the removed replica, DPLDR, go to a restoring state:

Figure 5.23: The availability databases on DPLDR go to restoring state

Exercise 48: Adding a Replica to an Availability Group

A new secondary replica can be added to an existing availability group. The replica should satisfy all the prerequisites mentioned in the *Prerequisites* section in *Lesson 4, AlwaysOn Availability Groups*.

Let's add DPLDR to the DPLAG availability group.

> **Note**
>
> We do not need to delete the databases on DPLDR. The existing databases are already in a restoring state and can be joined back to the DPLAG availability group. However, this may not work if there are log backups being done on the primary/secondary replica. To make it work, restore the log backups from the time the replica was taken out of the availability group until the last log backup available.

1. Connect to the DPLPR instance, open a new query window, change the query mode to **SQLCMD**, and execute the following query to add DPLDR to the DPLAG availability group:

   ```
   :Connect DPLAGL

   ALTER AVAILABILITY GROUP [DPLAG]
   ADD REPLICA ON N'DPLDR'
   WITH
   (
   ```

```
    ENDPOINT_URL = N'TCP://DPLDR.dpl.com:5022',
    FAILOVER_MODE = MANUAL,
    AVAILABILITY_MODE = ASYNCHRONOUS_COMMIT,
    BACKUP_PRIORITY = 50, -- optional
    SEEDING_MODE = AUTOMATIC,
    SECONDARY_ROLE(ALLOW_CONNECTIONS = READ_ONLY));

GO

Waitfor delay '00:00:10'

GO

:Connect DPLDR


ALTER AVAILABILITY GROUP [DPLAG] JOIN;

GO

ALTER DATABASE [Sales] SET HADR AVAILABILITY GROUP = [DPLAG]
GO

ALTER DATABASE [Finance] SET HADR AVAILABILITY GROUP = [DPLAG]
```

This query performs the following operations:

It connects to DPLAGL and adds the DPLDR replica to DPLAG using the **ALTER AVAILABILITY GROUP** command. The **ALTER AVAILABILITY GROUP** command requires the endpoint URL (database mirroring endpoint). Availability mode and failover mode are also required when adding a new replica; the remaining parameters are optional.

> **Note**
>
> This script can also be executed on the current primary instance.

It connects to DPLDR and joins the DPLDR instance to the DPLAG availability group using the **ALTER AVAILABILITY GROUP** command.

It adds the **Sales** and **Finance** databases on DPLDR to the DPLAG availability group using the **ALTER DATABASE SET HADR** command.

This step should be run when the database already exists on the secondary replica. The database can be manually created on the secondary replica by restoring full and log backups (taken from the primary replica).

> **Note**
>
> Refer to the following link for details on the **ALTER AVAILABILITY GROUP** command: https://docs.microsoft.com/en-us/sql/t-sql/statements/alter-availability-group-transact-sql?view=sql-server-2017.

2. Check the AlwaysOn dashboard to verify that the replica has been successfully added:

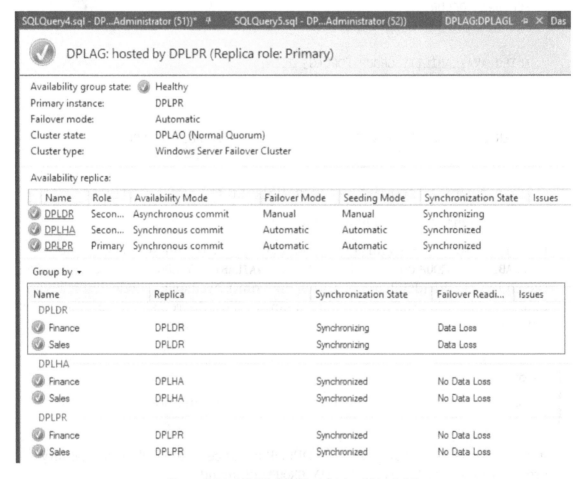

Figure 5.24: DPLDR is added to the DPLAG AG

Observe that DPLDR has been successfully added to the DPLAG availability group.

We added a replica which was earlier a part of the DPLAG group and already has databases created.

When adding a fresh node to an existing availability group, make sure that the new secondary replica meets all the prerequisites mentioned in the *Prerequisites* section in *Lesson 4, AlwaysOn Availability Groups*. Moreover, if you choose manual seeding mode, make sure to prepare the database on the secondary replica. To do so, follow these steps:

1. Suspend any scheduled log backups of the availability databases on the primary/ secondary instance until the replica is added to the availability group.

2. Take a full backup and a log backup of the availability databases on the primary instance.

3. Restore the full and log backups of the availability databases on the secondary instance using the **WITH NORECOVERY** option. The restored databases should be in the **Restoring** state.

> **Note**
>
> To get the T-SQL script to add a new replica with different synchronization options, use the GUI to add the replica. Choose the desired synchronization option from the following: **Automatic Seeding**, **Backup and Restore**, **Join Only**, or **Skip Initial Sync**. At the last step in the GUI, select **Script to file** in the bottom-right of the window.

Exercise 49: Changing the Availability Mode of a Replica

In this exercise, we will change the availability mode of DPLDR:

1. To change the availability mode of a replica DPLDR from asynchronous to synchronous, connect to DPLAGL and run the following query:

```
USE [master]
GO
ALTER AVAILABILITY GROUP [DPLAG]
MODIFY REPLICA ON N'DPLDR' WITH (AVAILABILITY_MODE = SYNCHRONOUS_COMMIT)
GO
```

2. Check the dashboard for the change made:

 DPLAG: hosted by DPLPR (Replica role: Primary)

Availability group state:	Healthy
Primary instance:	DPLPR
Failover mode:	Automatic
Cluster state:	DPLAO (Normal Quorum)
Cluster type:	Windows Server Failover Cluster

Availability replica:

Name	Role	Availability Mode	Failover Mode	Seeding Mode	Synchronization State
DPLDR	Secon...	Synchronous commit	Manual	Manual	Synchronized
DPLHA	Secon...	Synchronous commit	Automatic	Automatic	Synchronized
DPLPR	Primary	Synchronous commit	Automatic	Automatic	Synchronized

Group by ▾

Name	Replica	Synchronization State	Failover Readi...
DPLDR			
Finance	DPLDR	Synchronized	No Data Loss
Sales	DPLDR	Synchronized	No Data Loss
DPLHA			
Finance	DPLHA	Synchronized	No Data Loss
Sales	DPLHA	Synchronized	No Data Loss
DPLPR			
Finance	DPLPR	Synchronized	No Data Loss
Sales	DPLPR	Synchronized	No Data Loss

Figure 5.25: Availability mode of DPLDR has changed

Observe that the availability mode of DPLDR has successfully changed to **Synchronous commit**.

3. To change it back to asynchronous, run the following query:

```
USE [master]
GO
ALTER AVAILABILITY GROUP [DPLAG]
MODIFY REPLICA ON N'DPLDR' WITH (AVAILABILITY_MODE = ASYNCHRONOUS_COMMIT)
GO
```

Exercise 50: Changing the Failover Mode of a Replica

In this exercise, we will change the failover mode of DPLHA to manual and then revert it to automatic:

1. To change the failover mode of a replica DPLHA, connect to DPLAGL or the primary instance and execute the following query:

```
USE [master]
GO
ALTER AVAILABILITY GROUP [DPLAG]
MODIFY REPLICA ON N'DPLHA' WITH (FAILOVER_MODE = MANUAL)
GO
```

2. Check the dashboard for the changes made:

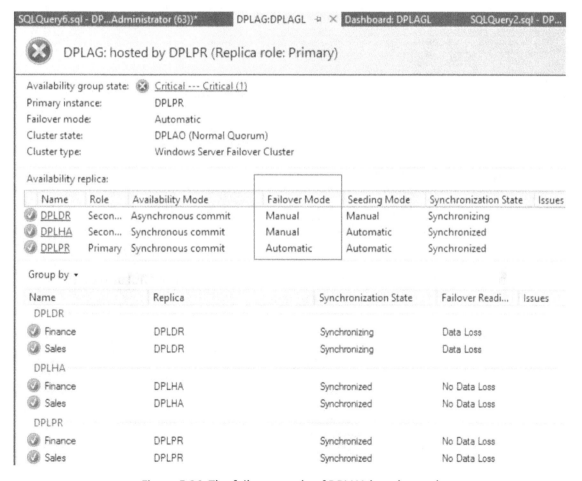

Figure 5.26: The failover mode of DPLHA has changed

3. Observe that the failover mode of DPLHA has been changed to **Manual**. However, the **Availability group state** is now **Critical**. To find out more about the problem, click on **Critical**, next to **Availability group state** at the top of the dashboard:

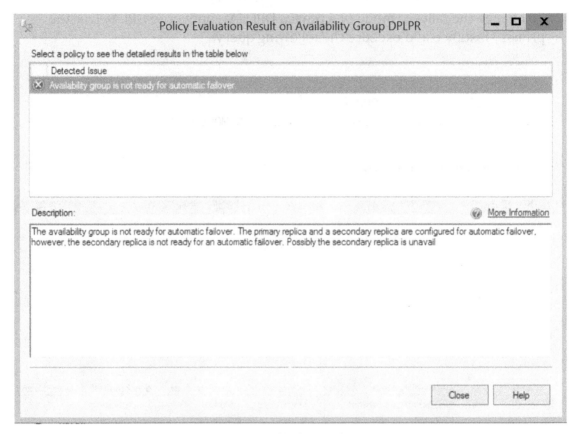

Figure 5.27: The detected issue

The problem states that the availability group isn't ready for automatic failover as no replica is configured for automatic failure.

4. To change the failover mode of DPLHA to automatic, execute the following query:

```
USE [master]
GO
ALTER AVAILABILITY GROUP [DPLAG]
MODIFY REPLICA ON N'DPLHA' WITH (FAILOVER_MODE = AUTOMATIC)
GO
```

> **Note**
>
> The failover mode of an asynchronous replica cannot be changed to automatic.

Exercise 51: Creating Multiple Listeners for the Same Availability Group

Often, multiple listeners might be needed for the same availability group. One such example is applications using different instance names in the connection string to connect to databases that are now part of the availability group.

Let's say that the **Sales** and **Finance** databases were on a different SQL instance, DPLAPP, before being added to the DPLAG availability group. There's a legacy application that connects to DPLAPP and it's not possible to modify the instance name in the legacy application.

Any additional listener has to be added from Failover Cluster Manager and can't be added from SSMS or T-SQL.

To add a new listener, DPLAPP, for the DPLAG availability group, follow these steps:

> **Note**
>
> You can perform these steps on any of the VMs: DPLPR, DPLHA, or DPLDR.

1. Press Windows + R to open the **Run** command window. Type `cluadmin.msc` in the **Run** command window and press *Enter* to open the Failover Cluster Manager console.

2. In the Failover Cluster Manager console, expand **DPLAO.dpl.com** and select **Roles**. Right-click on the **DPLAG** role, select **Add Resource**, and then select **Client Access Point**:

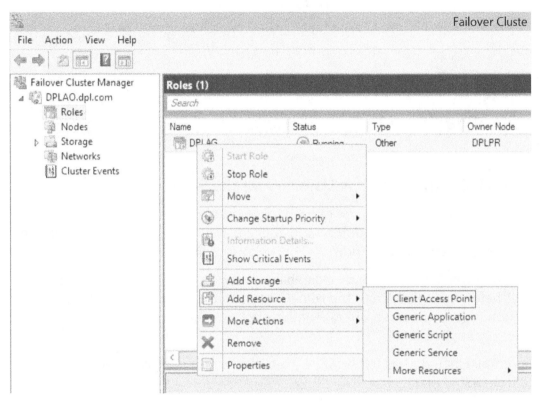

Figure 5.28: The Client Access Point option

3. In the **New Resource Wizard** window, enter DPLAPP as the client access point name. In the IP grid, enter 192.168.1.23 as the IP address:

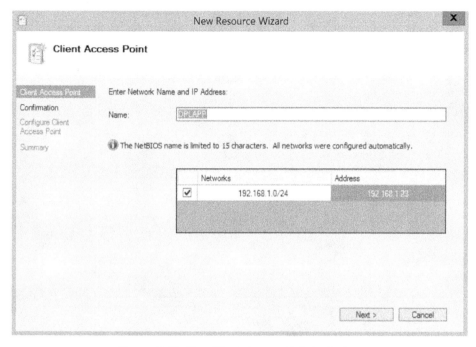

Figure 5.29: The Client Access Point window

Click **Next** to continue.

4. In the **Confirmation** window, verify the client access point (listener) name and the IP address:

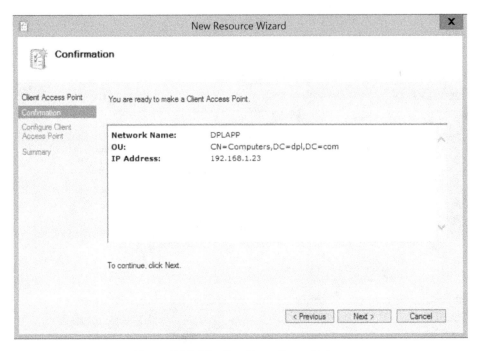

Figure 5.30: The Confirmation window

Click **Next** to continue.

The listener will be created, and a summary window displays the result:

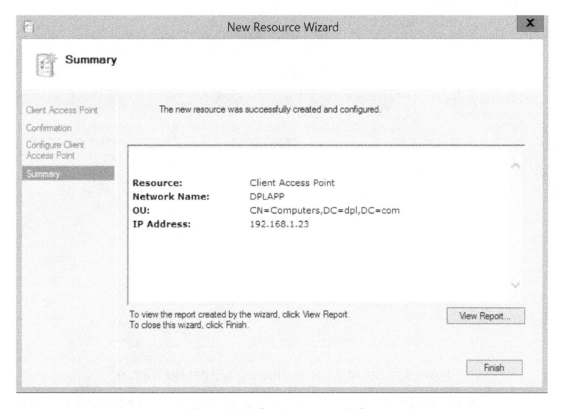

Figure 5.31: The Summary window

5. Click on **Finish** to complete the wizard. You'll be taken back to the Failover Cluster Manager console:

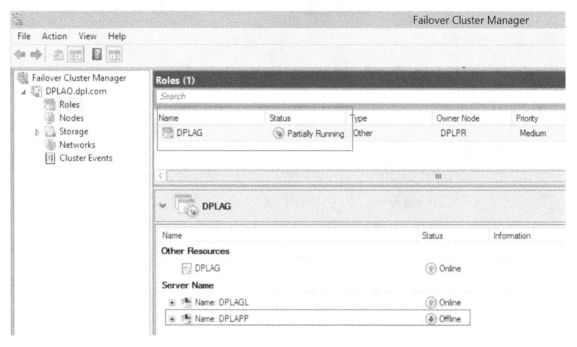

Figure 5.32: DPLAG is partially running and DPLAPP is offline

Observe that the DPLAG status is **Partially Running**. This is because it has two listeners, DPLAGL and DPLAPP, and DPLAPP is offline.

6. To bring DPLAPP online, go to the resource tab at the bottom of the window. Right-click on the **DPLAPP** resource and select **Bring Online** from the context menu:

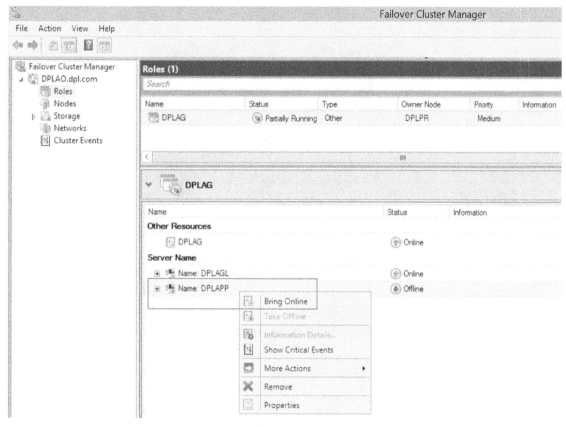

Figure 5.33: The Bring Online option

The Failover Cluster Manager will show the following status once DPLAPP is online:

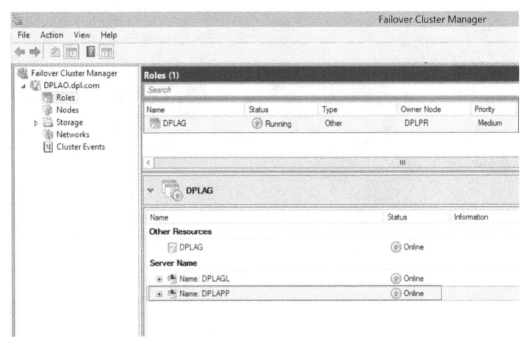

Figure 5.34: DPLAPP is online and DPLAG is running

Observe that once DPLAPP is online, the status of DPLAG is changed to **Running** from **Partially Running**.

7. The next step is to modify the dependency setting for DPLAG. To do that, right-click on **DPLAG** under **Other Resources** in the bottom pane and select **Properties**:

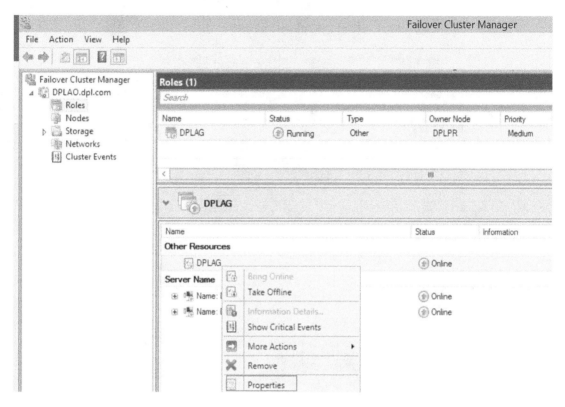

Figure 5.35: The Properties option

In the **DPLAG Properties** window, modify the dependencies as shown in the following screenshot:

Figure 5.36: The Dependencies tab

The **Dependencies** tab lists the resources that should be brought online before DPLAG is brought online. The **OR** condition makes sure that if there is a problem with any one of the access points and it's not online, DPLAG will be online as one access point or listener is online.

Click **OK** to continue.

This completes the setup at the Failover Cluster Manager console. The next step is to check that the listener is listed in SQL Server with the correct properties.

8. Connect to DPLAGL or the primary SQL instance and execute the following query to list the listeners. You can also verify the listeners in the Object Explorer:

```
USE Master
GO
select * from  sys.availability_group_listeners
GO
```

You should get output that is similar to this:

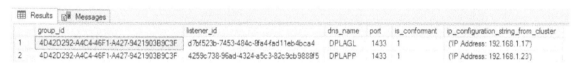

Figure 5.37: Listing the listeners

group_id and **listener_id** will be different in your case.

9. Notice that the port is undefined for the DPLAPP listener. Execute the following query to set the port for DPLAPP to **1433**:

```
ALTER AVAILABILITY GROUP [DPLAG] MODIFY LISTENER 'DPLAPP' (PORT = 1433)
```

Check the listener status again by querying the **sys.availability_group_listeners** DMV:

	group_id	listener_id	dns_name	port	is_conformant	ip_configuration_string_from_cluster
1	4D42D292-A4C4-46F1-A427-9421903B9C3F	d7bf523b-7453-484c-8fa4-fad11eb4bca4	DPLAGL	1433	1	('IP Address: 192.168.1.17')
2	4D42D292-A4C4-46F1-A427-9421903B9C3F	4259c738-96ad-4324-a5c3-82c9cb9888f5	DPLAPP	1433	1	('IP Address: 192.168.1.23')

Figure 5.38: Setting the port for DPLAPP

Observe that the port is set to **1433** for the DPLAPP listener.

10. The next step is to connect to the DPLAPP listener and verify it's working. To do so, select **Connect** in the Object Explorer and provide **DPLAPP** as the server name. Set the **Authentication** type as **Windows Authentication**:

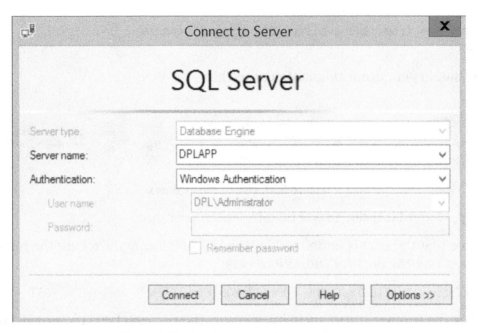

Figure 5.39: The Connect to Server window

Click **Connect** to continue.

11. When connected, expand the **Databases** node and go to **AlwaysOn High Availability | Availability Groups | DPLAG | Availability Group Listeners**:

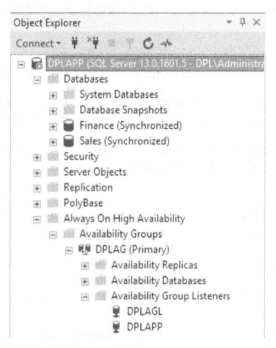

Figure 5.40: The DPLAG availability group showing two listeners

Observe that it connects to the primary instance. The DPLAG availability group now has two listeners listed under the **Availability Group Listeners** node.

Exercise 52: Configuring Backups on the Secondary Replica

An important benefit of implementing AlwaysOn, other than HA and DR, is that AlwaysOn allows you to take database backups on the secondary replicas. Backing up is a resource intensive operation; therefore, performing backups on the secondary instance avoids performance issues on the primary instance during backups.

AlwaysOn has the following backup preferences:

- **Preferred Secondary**: In this, backups are performed at the secondary replica. If no secondary replica is available, then the backups are performed at the primary replica. This is the default option.

  Copy-only full backups and log backups are allowed at secondary replicas. Differential backups can't be performed on secondary replicas.

- **Secondary Only**: In this, backups are performed on the secondary replica. If no secondary replica is available, backups are not performed.

- **Primary**: In this, backups are performed only at the primary replica. Choose this option if you plan to take a differential backup, which is not supported on the secondary replica.

- **Any Replica**: In this, backups can be performed on any replica. This option, however, considers the backup priority of the replicas when performing backups.

- **Backup priority**: The backup priority specifies the priority for performing the backups on a given replica, with 1 being the lowest and 100 being the highest priority. A priority of 0 signifies that the replica is not to be used to take backups.

The backup preference and priority can be configured or changed after creating the availability group:

1. To change the backup preference to Primary, connect to DPLAGL and execute the following query:

```
USE [master]
GO
ALTER AVAILABILITY GROUP [DPLAG] SET(
AUTOMATED_BACKUP_PREFERENCE = PRIMARY
);
GO
```

The valid values for the **AUTOMATED_BACKUP_PREFERENCE** parameter are **Primary** (Primary), **Secondary_Only**, **Secondary** (Preferred Secondary), and **None** (Any Replica).

2. To change the backup priority, connect to the DPLAGL and execute the following query:

```
USE [master]
GO
ALTER AVAILABILITY GROUP [DPLAG]
MODIFY REPLICA ON N'DPLDR' WITH (BACKUP_PRIORITY = 3
GO
USE [master]
GO
ALTER AVAILABILITY GROUP [DPLAG]
MODIFY REPLICA ON N'DPLHA' WITH (BACKUP_PRIORITY = 2)
GO
USE [master]
GO
ALTER AVAILABILITY GROUP [DPLAG]
MODIFY REPLICA ON N'DPLPR' WITH (BACKUP_PRIORITY = 1)
GO
```

This query sets the backup priority of the DPLDR instance to 3, of the DPLHA instance to 2, and of the DPLPR instance to 1.

This means that with backup preference set to Preferred Secondary, the backups will be first performed on DPLDR (highest priority). If DPLDR is unavailable, then the backups will be performed on DPLHA. If none of the secondary replicas are available, then the backup will be performed on DPLPR, the primary instance.

You must be wondering, given the backup preference and the priority, how these settings can be utilized to find out whether the replica the backup is being run on is the preferred or the right replica.

This is done using the **sys.fn_hadr_backup_is_preferred_replica** function. The function returns **1** if the replica is the preferred replica. Therefore, when setting up a backup job for AlwaysOn, all you need to do is add a check to find out whether the replica the backup job is running on is a preferred replica. If it isn't, then skip the backup and if it is, then perform the backup.

This can be tested with a simple backup command that performs the backing up of the **Sales** database. This can be done by opening a new query window in SSMS and executing the following query one by one on the DPLPR, DPLHA, and DPLDR SQL instances. This query uses the **sys.fn_hadr_backup_is_preferred_replica** function to verify the replica is a preferred replica; if it is, then it performs the backup of the **Sales** database:

```
IF (sys.fn_hadr_backup_is_preferred_replica('Sales') = 1)

BEGIN

  SELECT @@SERVERNAME AS 'Preferred Replica'


  BACKUP DATABASE Sales TO DISK = '\\DPLPR\Backup\Sales.bak' WITH COPY_ONLY

END
```

The backup preference of the availability group DPLAG is Preferred Secondary. The highest priority replica is DPLDR. Therefore, the query will not give any results on DPLPR and DPLHA. The backup will be performed at DPLDR:

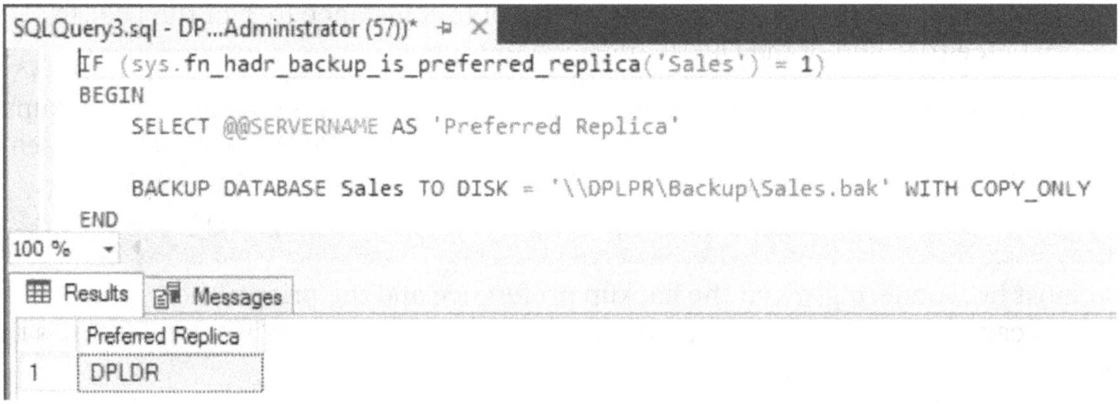

Figure 5.41: Backup is performed at DPLDR

Note that for this query to run, you need to create a folder named **Backup** on DPLPR and modify the sharing settings to share the **Backup** folder with **DPL\Administrator**:

```
SQLQuery3.sql - DP...Administrator (57))*    ☐ ✕
      IF (sys.fn_hadr_backup_is_preferred_replica('Sales') = 1)
      BEGIN
          SELECT @@SERVERNAME AS 'Preferred Replica'

          BACKUP DATABASE Sales TO DISK = '\\DPLPR\Backup\Sales.bak' WITH COPY_ONLY
      END
100 %    ▾

 ⊞ Results   ⊟ Messages

  (1 row affected)
  Processed 26248 pages for database 'Sales', file 'AdventureWorks2016_Data' on file 5.
  Processed 2 pages for database 'Sales', file 'AdventureWorks2016_Log' on file 5.
  BACKUP DATABASE successfully processed 26250 pages in 6.320 seconds (32.448 MB/sec).
```

Figure 5.42: Output of the query

With this check in place, the backup job can be created on all replicas; however, it'll only run on the preferred replica. Let's say if DPLDR is unavailable, then the backup job will run on DPLHA. If both DPLDR and DPLHA are unavailable, the job will run on DPLPR.

Exercise 53: Configuring Readable Secondaries

An important benefit of AlwaysOn AGs is they allow you to offload read queries to the secondary replica. This helps to speed up the performance of the primary instance by reducing read-write contention. There may be some daily or weekly reports that are required to be run and are resource intensive. Such reports can be run on secondary replicas instead of the primary instance.

The **allow_connections** property of a replica defines whether or not the secondary server is used for read queries. The **allow_connections** property is to be defined for each replica participating in an AlwaysOn AG and can have one of the following three values:

- **ALL**: An application can connect to a secondary instance and execute read queries against it.

- **NO**: Secondary replicas don't accept read connections and will only accept connections in the case of a failover, that is, when it takes the role of a primary instance.

- **READ_ONLY**: Applications with `ApplicationIntent` set to `ReadOnly` in the configuration string can read from the secondary replica.

> **Note**
>
> `ApplicationIntent` is a parameter in the application connection string. The `ReadOnly` value tells SQL Server that the connection will only send read queries. It is only required to connect to replicas with the readable configuration set to `ReadOnly`.

Let's look at readable secondary configuration for DPLAG:

1. Connect to DPLAGL and execute the following query:

    ```
    SELECT replica_server_name, secondary_role_allow_connections_desc FROM
    sys.availability_replicas
    ```

    You should get the following output:

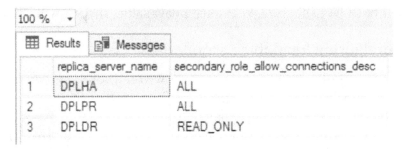

Figure 5.43: Secondary configurations for DPLAG

The secondary replica DPLHA will acknowledge any read connection; however, the replica DPLDR will only acknowledge connections with `ApplicationIntent` set to `ReadOnly`.

2. Let's connect to DPLDR in SSMS and run a read query against the **Sales** database. Open SSMS and connect to DPLDR. Open a new query window and execute the following query against the **Sales** database:

```
Use Sales
GO
SELECT  TOP(10) * FROM Sales.SalesOrderHeader
```

You'll get the following error:

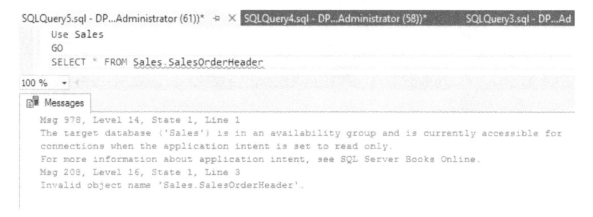

Figure 5.44: Error related to ApplicationIntent

The error mentions that the **Sales** database can only be accessed if, and only if, **ApplicationIntent** is set to **ReadOnly**.

3. To rectify this, right-click anywhere in the query editor, select **Connection**, and then select **Change Connection**:

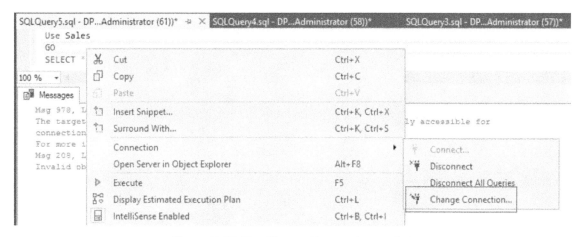

Figure 5.45: The Change Connection option

4. In the **Connect to Database Engine** dialog box, provide the server name as **DPLDR** and the **Authentication** type as **Windows Authentication**.

5. Select **Options** at the bottom-right of the **Connect to Database Engine** dialog box:

Figure 5.46: The Connect to Database Engine window

6. Select the **Additional Connection Parameters** tab and specify
   `ApplicationIntent=ReadOnly`:

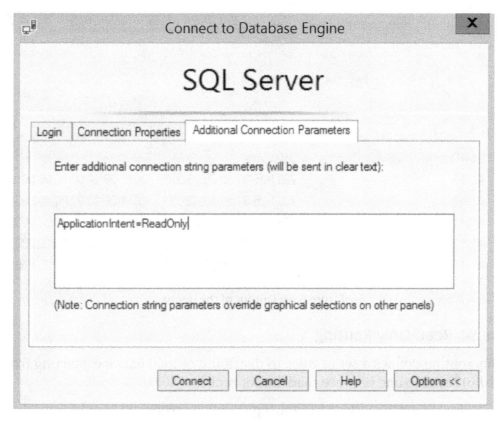

Figure 5.47: The Additional Connection Parameters tab

Select **Connect** to continue.

7. When connected, execute the query once again. You should get the output shown here:

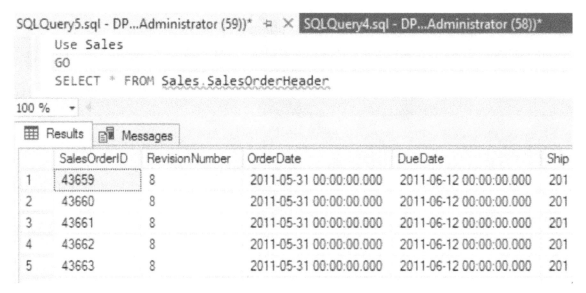

Figure 5.48: Output of the query

Exercise 54: Read-Only Routing

Read-only routing defines a set of rules to distribute or load balance (starting from SQL Server 2016) reads to one or more read-intent replicas.

For read-only routing to work, the following should be true:

- **ApplicationIntent** should be set to **ReadOnly** for the incoming connections.

- The **allow_connections** property of the secondary replica should be either **ALL** or **READ_ONLY**.

- Each replica must have **READ_ONLY_ROUTING_URL** and **READ_ONLY_ROUTING_LIST** defined.

Configuring read-only routing is a two-step process:

1. The first step defines the read-only routing URL for each secondary replica. The read-only routing URL helps to route the read request to a readable secondary. It is of the following form: `tcp://replica-address:port`.

    `replica-address` can either be the fully qualified domain name of the replica instance or its IP address. The `port` is the port number to which SQL Server listens to at that replica instance.

2. The second and last step is to define the routing list. The routing list tells SQL Server the order in which to distribute the read queries.

Let's see this in practice:

1. To configure the read-only routing URL for each replica, DPLPR, DPLDR, and DPLHA, open a new query in SSMS, connect to the DPLAGL listener, and execute the following queries:

    ```
    Use Master
    GO
    ALTER AVAILABILITY GROUP [DPLAG]
    MODIFY REPLICA ON N'DPLDR'
    WITH (SECONDARY_ROLE(READ_ONLY_ROUTING_URL = N'tcp://DPLDR:1433'))
    GO
    ALTER AVAILABILITY GROUP [DPLAG]
    MODIFY REPLICA ON N'DPLHA'
    WITH (SECONDARY_ROLE(READ_ONLY_ROUTING_URL = N'tcp://DPLHA:1433'))
    GO
    ALTER AVAILABILITY GROUP [DPLAG]
    MODIFY REPLICA ON N'DPLPR'
    WITH (SECONDARY_ROLE(READ_ONLY_ROUTING_URL = N'tcp://DPLPR:1433'))
    GO
    ```

2. A read-only routing list is a comma-separated list of replica instances that the read traffic should be sent to. For example: the routing list **(DPLHA, DPLDR, DPLPR)** will send the read traffic first to DPLHA; if DPLHA isn't available, then to DPLDR; and if DPLDR isn't available, then to DPLPR. Essentially, the read traffic is sent to the first available replica.

Starting from SQL Server 2016, the read traffic can be load balanced among a set of replicas. For example, the routing list **((DPLHA, DPLDR), DPLPR)** will load balance the reads between DPLHA and DPLPR in a round-robin manner. The load balanced replicas are defined within an extra bracket. There can be more than one load balanced set, such as **((Replica 1, Replica 2, Replica 3), (Replica 4, Replica 5)**.

To configure the read-only routing list, connect to the DPLAGL listener and execute the following queries:

```
ALTER AVAILABILITY GROUP [DPLAG]
MODIFY REPLICA ON N'DPLPR'
WITH (PRIMARY_ROLE(READ_ONLY_ROUTING_LIST =
((N'DPLHA',N'DPLDR'),N'DPLPR')))
GO
ALTER AVAILABILITY GROUP [DPLAG]
MODIFY REPLICA ON N'DPLDR'
WITH (PRIMARY_ROLE(READ_ONLY_ROUTING_LIST =
((N'DPLHA',N'DPLPR'),N'DPLDR')))
GO
ALTER AVAILABILITY GROUP [DPLAG]
MODIFY REPLICA ON N'DPLHA'
WITH (PRIMARY_ROLE(READ_ONLY_ROUTING_LIST =
((N'DPLPR',N'DPLDR'),N'DPLHA')))
GO
```

3. The following query lists out the read-only routing settings for an availability group. Execute this query next:

```
SELECT
    ag.name AvailabilityGroup,
    ar1.replica_server_name as PrimaryServer,
    routinglist.routing_priority as RoutingPriority,
    ar2.replica_server_name as ReadReplica
FROM sys.availability_read_only_routing_lists routinglist
INNER JOIN sys.availability_replicas ar1 on routinglist.replica_id = ar1.replica_id
INNER JOIN sys.availability_replicas ar2 on routinglist.read_only_replica_id = ar2.replica_id
INNER JOIN sys.availability_groups ag on ar1.group_id = ag.group_id
ORDER BY AvailabilityGroup,PrimaryServer,RoutingPriority
```

The **sys.availability_read_only_routing_lists** DMV provides information about the routing lists configured for the availability groups. The **sys.availabiltiy_groups** and **sys.availability_replicas** DMVs provide information about the availability groups and the availability replicas respectively.

You should get the following output after running the previous query:

	AvailabilityGroup	PrimaryServer	RoutingPriority	ReadReplica
1	DPLAG	DPLDR	1	DPLHA
2	DPLAG	DPLDR	1	DPLPR
3	DPLAG	DPLDR	2	DPLDR
4	DPLAG	DPLHA	1	DPLPR
5	DPLAG	DPLHA	1	DPLDR
6	DPLAG	DPLHA	2	DPLHA
7	DPLAG	DPLPR	1	DPLHA
8	DPLAG	DPLPR	1	DPLDR
9	DPLAG	DPLPR	2	DPLPR

Figure 5.49: Listing the read-only routing settings

The **RoutingPriority** value **1** for both DPLHA and DPLPR with DPLDR as the primary replica indicates that the read requests will be load balanced between the two secondaries.

4. Let's see the read-only routing lists in action. To simulate read requests, run the following PowerShell command:

```
Write-Host "Press CTRL + C to terminate the script.." -ForegroundColor
Green
while(1 -eq 1)
{
    $ConnectionString = "Data Source=DPLAGL;Initial
Catalog=Sales;integrated security=true;ApplicationIntent=ReadOnly"
    $SqlConnection = new-object system.data.SqlClient.
SQLConnection($ConnectionString)
    $query = "Select @@ServerName AS [ConnectedToServer] "
    $Sqlcommand = new-object system.data.sqlclient.
sqlcommand($query,$SqlConnection)
    $SqlConnection.Open()
    $Sqlcommand.ExecuteScalar()
    $SqlConnection.close()
   Start-Sleep -Seconds 2
}
```

> **Note**
>
> This command is part of the **1_ReadWorkload.ps1** script at **C:\Code\Lesson05**.

This script does the following: it first opens a connection to DPLAGL with **ReadOnly** intent. The connection string is specified in the **$ConnectionString** variable. Then, it executes the **Select @@Servername** query to return the name of the server. Finally, it closes the connection.

> **Note**
>
> You will have to copy the **1_ReadWorkload.ps1** script to the VM you wish to run it on. You can run it on any replica, DPLPR, DPLHA, or DPLDR.

5. Open two new PowerShell console windows and run the following PowerShell command to execute the **1_ReadWorkload.ps1** script:

```
PowerShell.exe -File C:\Scripts\ReadWorkload.ps1
```

The following screenshot shows the output for both PowerShell windows:

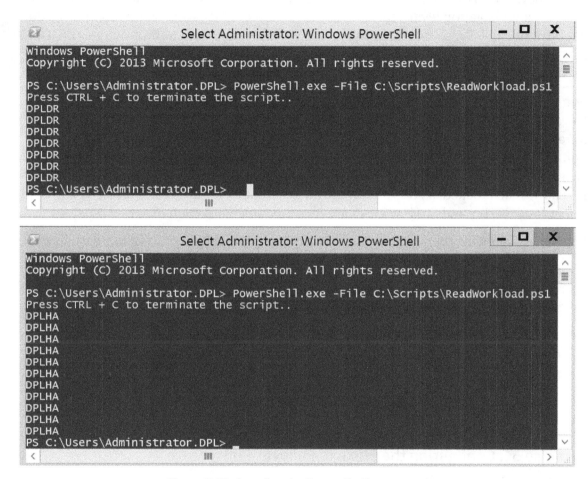

Figure 5.50: Running the PowerShell command

Notice that in the first PowerShell console window, the read requests are directed to DPLDR and in the second PowerShell console window, the reads are directed to DPLHA. The read requests are therefore load balanced as per the routing list.

An important thing to consider is the impact of the read workload on the secondary replicas. As discussed in *Lesson 4, AlwaysOn Availability Groups*, a REDO thread at the secondary replica constantly reads and applies the transactions to the database. Therefore, the REDO thread does consume resources.

Read queries don't interfere with the REDO thread, as the read queries are run under the snapshot isolation level and don't acquire shared locks. However, read queries do acquire the SCH-S (schema stability) lock. Therefore, any data definition query (DDL) that alters an existing table results in blocking between the read query and the REDO thread.

For example, let's say a query is reading from a table, **Sales.SalesOrderHeader**, on the secondary replica. At the same time, an **Alter table** statement is issued on the **SalesOrderHeader** table on the primary replica to change the datatype of an existing column. The REDO thread requires a SCH-M (schema modification) lock on the **SalesOrderHeader** table to replicate the **Alter table** change on the replica. The REDO thread will be blocked, as there is already a SCH-S lock on the table (taken by the read query) and SCH-S and SCH-M locks are incompatible with each other.

When this happens, there will be delay in replication and it'll result in increase in the size of the redo queue.

To remove read-only routing for a replica, say DPLDR, you can connect to the DPLAGL listener and the following query can be executed:

```
ALTER AVAILABILITY GROUP [DPLAG]

MODIFY REPLICA ON N'DPLDR' WITH (PRIMARY_ROLE(READ_ONLY_ROUTING_LIST =
NONE))
```

Observe that the **READ_ONLY_ROUTING_LIST** value is set to **NONE** to remove read-only routing for the DPLDR replica.

Exercise 55: Configuring the Flexible Failover Policy

The flexible failover policy controls when an automatic failover occurs by modifying the variables on which a failover depends. These variables are health check timeout, lease timeout, and failure condition level. The variables are discussed in detail in the *Flexible Automatic Failover Policy* part of the *Availability Groups Concepts and Components* section in *Lesson 4, AlwaysOn Availability Groups*.

The health check timeout and the failover condition level can be modified using T-SQL, Failover Cluster Manager, or PowerShell. However, lease timeout can be modified from Failover Cluster Manager or PowerShell only:

1. To modify health check timeout, execute the following query when connected to the DPLAGL listener or the primary instance:

    ```
    ALTER AVAILABILITY GROUP DPLAG SET (HEALTH_CHECK_TIMEOUT = 60000)
    ```

2. To modify failover condition level, execute the following query when connected to the DPLAGL listener or the primary instance:

    ```
    ALTER AVAILABILITY GROUP DPLAG SET (FAILURE_CONDITION_LEVEL = 1);
    ```

3. To fetch the failover condition level and health check timeout values for an AG, execute the following T-SQL query when connected to the DPLAGL listener or the primary instance:

    ```
    SELECT
        Name AS AvailabilityGroup,
        failure_condition_level,
        health_check_timeout
    FROM sys.availability_groups
    ```

    You should get the following output:

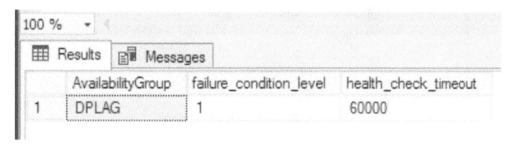

Figure 5.51: The failover condition level and health check timeout values

4. Next, we'll modify the lease timeout using the Failover Cluster Manager console (you should be connected to DPLPR, DPLDR, or DPLHA). Press Windows + R to open the **Run** command window. In the **Run** command window, type `cluadmin.msc` and press *Enter* to open the Failover Cluster Manager console.

5. In the Failover Cluster Manager console, expand **DPLAO.dpl.com** and select **Roles**. Right-click on **DPLAG** under **Other Resources** in the bottom tab and select **Properties** from the context menu:

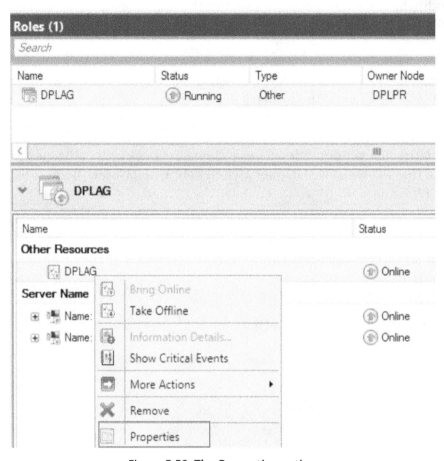

Figure 5.52: The Properties option

6. In the **DPLAG Properties** dialog box, select the **Properties** tab:

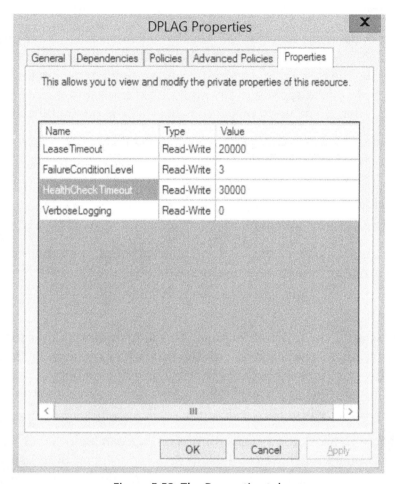

Figure 5.53: The Properties tab

Observe that it lists the **LeaseTimeout**, **FailureConditionLevel**, and **HealthCheckTimeout** values in milliseconds.

7. Change the lease timeout value to say 30000 (30 seconds) and click on **OK** to apply the changes and close the **DPLAG Properties** dialog box.

Availability Database Synchronization States

An availability database can have the following synchronization states:

- **Initializing**: A database recovery process broadly consists of four phases: discovery, analysis, redo, and undo. In the discovery and analysis phase, the transaction log file is scanned to get the transactions to be applied during the redo phase. The redo phase applies all the committed transactions from the transaction log to the database. The undo phase rolls back all the uncommitted transactions.

  The initializing state indicates that the transaction log required by the secondary to catch up to the primary database's undo LSN is being replicated and hardened.

  A failover during the initializing phase renders the secondary database as unusable. This is because the secondary is not up to the mark with the primary and it's in the process of being initialized.

- **Reverting**: This indicates a phase in the undo process when the secondary is actively getting the data from the primary database. A database may go to the reverting state following a failover. This is because the database is synced to the new primary.

- **Synchronizing**: At the primary instance, this state indicates that the availability database is ready to synchronize with the secondary replicas. At the secondary instance, this state indicates that replication is going on between the primary and secondary instances. An availability database for an asynchronous replica will always be in the synchronizing state.

  An availability database for a synchronous replica can be in the synchronizing state until the secondary database catches up with the primary database. After that, the state is changed to synchronized. This can happen during initial synchronization or because of network delay between primary and the secondary instance.

- **Not synchronizing**: At the primary instance, this state indicates that the availability database isn't ready to synchronize the data with secondary replicas. At the secondary instance, this state indicates that the secondary database can't synchronize with the primary instance. This may be because of the following reasons: a connection issue, the data movement for the availability database is suspended, or the availability database is transitioning to a different state because of an initial setup or role switch.

- **Synchronized**: At the primary instance, this state indicates that at least one secondary instance is synchronized. At the secondary instance, this state indicates that the database is synchronized with the primary instance.

  The synchronized state is only applicable to the secondary instance with synchronous availability mode.

Monitoring AlwaysOn Availability Groups

Monitoring an AlwaysOn availability group is important to quickly find problems before or when they occur, and then take corrective actions. Monitoring an AlwaysOn AG can be done using the AlwaysOn dashboard, T-SQL, PowerShell, Performance Monitor, or other third-party monitoring tools.

In this section, we'll learn how to use different methods to monitor AGs and configure monitoring alerts.

The AlwaysOn AG Dashboard

In the previous lesson, we have seen how to use the dashboard to monitor the AlwaysOn AG, listener, replica, and synchronization status. However, the dashboard can be used to monitor the real-time health metrics of an AlwaysOn AG too.

The dashboard has hidden columns that can be used to get details on an AlwaysOn AG. The hidden columns are added by selecting the **Add/Remove Columns** link next to the **Group by** section on the dashboard:

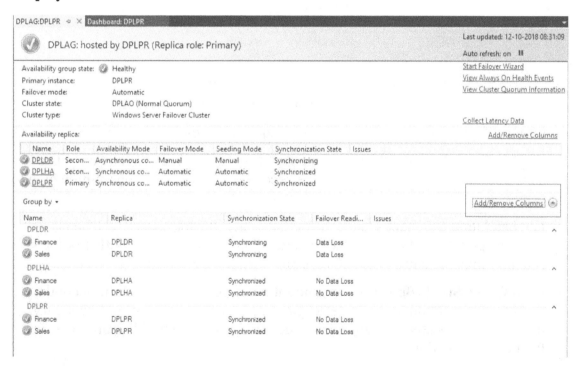

Figure 5.54: The Add/Remove Columns link

The following hidden columns are available to add to the dashboard:

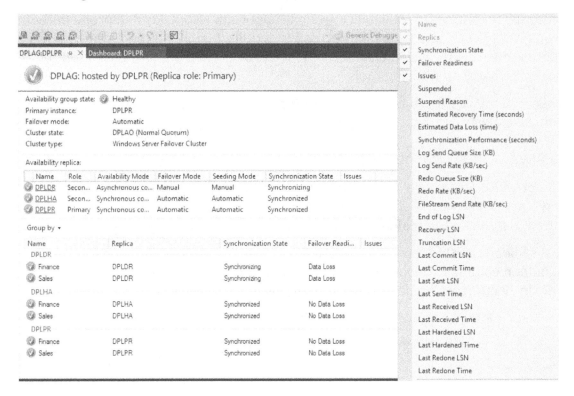

Figure 5.55: The hidden columns

Let's discuss a few of the important columns required for monitoring an AlwaysOn AG:

- **Log Send Queue Size (KB)**: This is the amount of records in KB that are yet to be sent from the primary database to the secondary database. A consistently high log send queue size indicates a problem and requires further investigation.

- **Log Send Rate (KB/sec)**: This is the rate at which the log records are being sent from the primary database to the secondary database. A consistently low log send rate may indicate a problem and requires further investigation.

- **Redo Queue Size (KB)**: This is the amount of log records in KB in the secondary database transaction log that are yet to be redone or applied at the secondary database. A consistently high redo queue size indicates a problem and requires further investigation.

- **Redo Rate (KB/sec)**: This is the rate at which the transactions are redone at the secondary database. A consistently low redo rate indicates a problem and requires further investigation.

- **Estimated Data Loss (time)**: This is the time in seconds the data at the secondary database is behind the primary database. This is an important metric to monitor the RPO. It's the time difference between the last transaction in the transaction log of the primary database and the last transaction in the transaction log of the secondary database.

  This should be zero for a synchronous replica and as low as possible for an asynchronous replica.

- **Estimated Recovery Time (seconds)**: This is the time in seconds it takes for the secondary database to catch up to the primary database. This is an important metric to monitor the RTO.

- **Last Commit LSN**: This is the last committed transaction log LSN for an availability database.

- **Last Commit Time**: This is the last committed transaction log LSN time for an availability database.

> **Note**
>
> To know about the remaining hidden columns, go to https://docs.microsoft.com/en-us/sql/database-engine/availability-groups/windows/use-the-always-on-dashboard-sql-server-management-studio?view=sql-server-2017.

Exercise 56: Collecting Latency Data Using the AlwaysOn AG Dashboard

The AlwaysOn dashboard can be used to collect AlwaysOn AG latency data. This feature is available from SQL Server 2016 SP1 onward.

The prerequisites for collecting latency data are as follows:

- SQL Server 2016 Service Pack 1 or above

- SQL Server Agent must be running on all the availability replicas.

To collect latency data, follow these steps:

1. Open SSMS and connect to any availability replica. In the Object Explorer, right-click on **Always On High Availability** and select **Show Dashboard** from the context menu. Select **DPLAG** under the **Availability group** section:

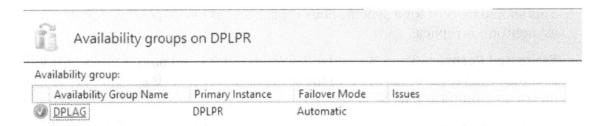

Figure 5.56: AGs on DPLPR

2. Click on the **Collect Latency Data** link on the right-hand side of the dashboard to start the data collection.

   The **Collect latency Data** option, when enabled, creates a SQL Server agent job, `AlwaysOn_Latency_Data_Collection`, on all availability replicas and creates the Primary Replica Latency and Secondary Replica Latency reports on all availability group replicas.

SQL Server Agent Job

The SQL Server agent job has the following seven steps:

- **Step 1 Collect AG Information**: This step creates the `LatencyCollectionStatus` table in `tempdb`.

- **Step 2 Create XE Session**: This step creates and starts an extended event session for AlwaysOn AG data collection.

- **Step 3 Wait For Collection**: This step waits for two minutes for the data to be collected.

- **Step 4 End XE Session**: This step stops the extended event session created in step 2.

- **Step 5 Extract XE Data**: The extended event data is extracted and inserted into multiple tables in `tempdb`.

- **Step 6 Create Result Set**: The data from step 5 is summarized and prepared for the reports.

- **Step 7 Drop XE Session**: The extended event session from step 2 is dropped:

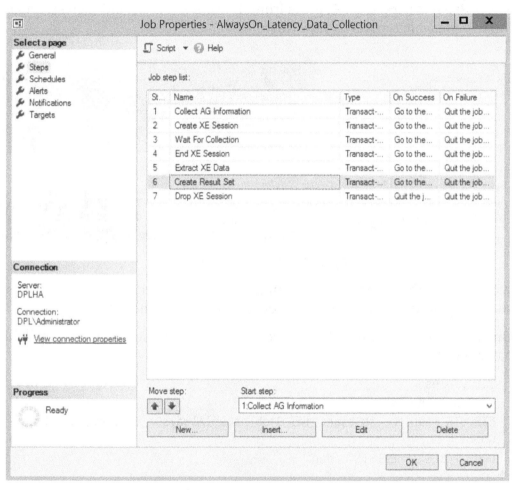

Figure 5.57: Steps in the SQL Server agent job

Exercise 57: Configuring Reports

The reports are accessible from the Object Explorer. To configure them, follow these steps:

1. Connect to any availability group replica, expand **Always On High Availability |
   Availability Groups**, and then right-click on **DPLAG**.

2. Select **Reports | Standard Reports** from the context menu and then select any of
   the two available reports to view them:

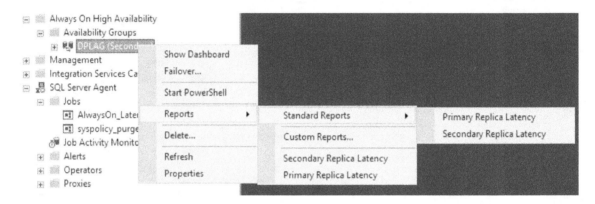

Figure 5.58: The reports options

We now have the job and reports configured to collect the latency data. Let's do some transactions and run the latency jobs to capture the data.

3. Open a query window in SSMS and connect to the DPLAGL listener. Copy and paste the following query:

```
USE [Sales]
-- Start the Data Collection Job
EXECUTE msdb.dbo.sp_start_job @job_name='AlwaysOn_Latency_Data_Collection'
GO
DROP TABLE IF EXISTS Orders
GO
CREATE TABLE Orders
(
  OrderID int identity,
  OrderQty int,
  Price int
)
GO
DECLARE @i int = 1
WHILE(@i<=50000)
```

```
BEGIN
  INSERT INTO Orders VALUES(@i,@i*2)
  SET @i = @i + 1;
  WAITFOR DELAY '00:00:01'
END
```

This query does the following: it starts the **AlwaysOn_Latency_Data_Collection** job on the primary instance. Then, it creates and inserts data in the **Orders** table to simulate transactions.

4. Open another query window and connect to the DPLHA replica. Copy and paste the following query into the query window:

```
EXECUTE msdb.dbo.sp_start_job @job_name='AlwaysOn_Latency_Data_Collection'
```

This query will start the **AlwaysOn_Latency_Data_Collection** job on the DPLHA secondary replica.

5. Execute the two queries and wait for four-five minutes for the queries to run and for the latency data collection job to collect and summarize the data.

This completes the exercise.

Primary Replica Latency Report

To view the primary replica latency report, you can connect to DPLAGL or the primary instance in the Object Explorer within SSMS and open the **Primary Replica Latency** report as explained in the previous exercise.

The report has three sections: Data Collection Time, Latency Graph, and Primary Replica Statistics.

Data Collection Time

This section lists the time the data was collected, along with the lists of the availability replicas and their roles at the time of data collection:

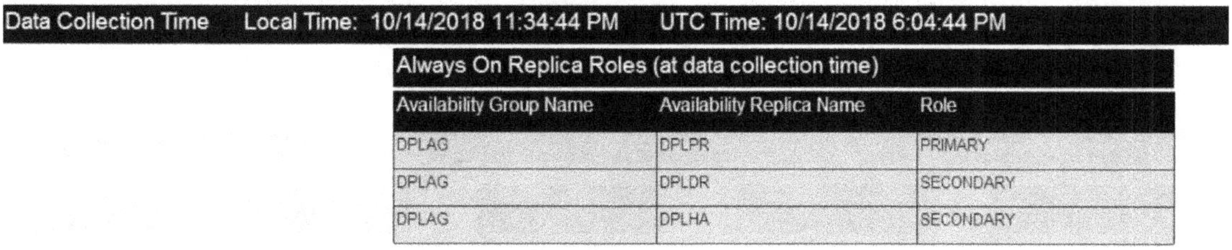

Data Collection Time	Local Time: 10/14/2018 11:34:44 PM	UTC Time: 10/14/2018 6:04:44 PM
Always On Replica Roles (at data collection time)		
Availability Group Name	Availability Replica Name	Role
DPLAG	DPLPR	PRIMARY
DPLAG	DPLDR	SECONDARY
DPLAG	DPLHA	SECONDARY

Figure 5.59: The Data Collection Time section

Latency Graph

The primary replica latency report has two latency graphs: **Primary Replica Commit Time** and **Primary Replica Remote Harden Time**:

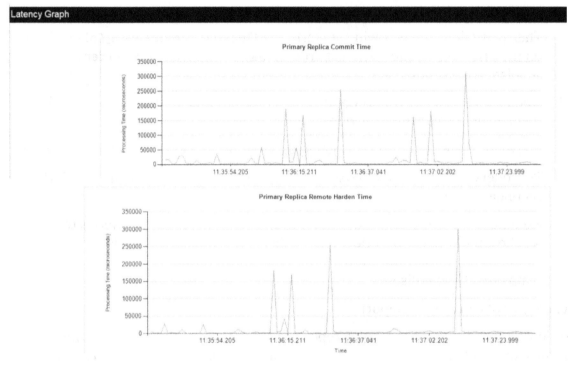

Figure 5.60: The Latency Graph section

> **Note**
>
> The terms in the graph are explained in the next section. Also, the numbers and graph will vary in your case.

Primary Replica Statistics

This section lists the following primary replica statistics:

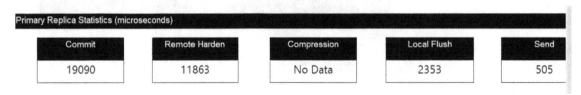

Commit	Remote Harden	Compression	Local Flush	Send
19090	11863	No Data	2353	505

Figure 5.61: The Primary Replica Statistics section

Let's see them one by one:

- **Commit**: This is the average time taken to commit a transaction on the primary replica in microseconds. The primary replica takes 19,090 microseconds or 0.019090 seconds to commit a transaction.

- **Remote Harden**: This is the time duration between sending the log block from the primary replica and getting the acknowledgement for that log block from all synchronous replicas. The remote harden time doesn't include the network time taken to send and receive the log records.

> **Note**
>
> The more secondary replicas there are, the longer the remote harden time. In SQL Server 2017, the **REQUIRED_SYNCHRONIZED_SECONDARIES_TO_COMMIT** parameter was introduced. This specifies the number of secondary replicas required to commit before the primary replica commits a transaction. It is an effective way to reduce the remote harden time for an environment with more than one secondary replicas. It can be modified using the **ALTER AVAILABILITY GROUP** replica command.

- **Compression**: This is the time taken to compress the log records before sending them to the secondary replica. Starting from SQL Server 2016, log records are only compressed for asynchronous replicas.

- **Local Flush**: This is the average time spent in flushing the log records from the log cache to the transaction log file at the primary replica. A higher log flush time indicates a problem and should be investigated further.

- **Send**: This is the time spent in sending the log records to the log capture queue at the primary replica. A higher send time indicates a problem and should be investigated further.

Secondary Replica Latency Report

To view the secondary replica latency report, you can connect to DPLHA and open the **Secondary Latency Report** as explained in the previous exercise.

The secondary replica also has three sections: Data Collection Time, Latency Graph, and Secondary Replica Statistics.

Data Collection Time

This section states the local and the UTC collection start date and time. It also states the replica for which the report is generated:

Figure 5.62: The Data Collection Time section

Latency Graph

This displays the graph for the replica send time over the duration of the data collection:

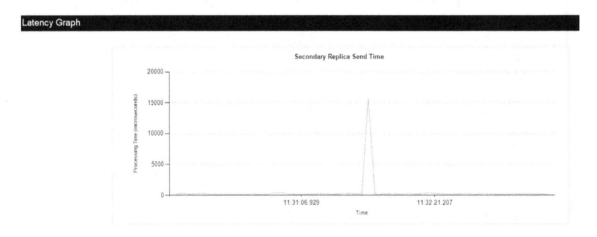

Figure 5.63: The Latency Graph section

> **Note**
>
> The replica send time statistic is explained in the next section.

Secondary Replica Statistics

This report provides the following statistics:

Figure 5.64: The Secondary Replica Statistics section

- **Local Flush**: This is the average time taken to harden the log record to the transaction log at the secondary instance.

- **Decompression**: This is the time taken to decompress the log records after they are received from the primary instance. Starting from SQL Server 2016, the log records are only compressed for asynchronous replicas. DPLHA is a synchronous replica and the decompression time is therefore negligible.

- **Receive**: This is the time spent in receiving the log records.

- **Send**: This is the time spent in sending the acknowledgement message to the primary replica. This doesn't include the network transit time from the secondary replica to the primary replica.

> **Note**
>
> For more details on AlwaysOn latency reports, visit https://blogs.msdn.microsoft.com/sql_server_team/new-in-ssms-always-on-availability-group-latency-reports/.

Monitoring AlwaysOn AG Using T-SQL

The AlwaysOn AG dashboard gives a nice and easy-to-use interface to monitor an AlwaysOn AG. However, it cannot be used to set up alerts. For this, we use T-SQL. In this section, we'll learn to monitor AlwaysOn AG using catalog views, dynamic management views, and dynamic management functions.

Monitoring Availability Replica States

The following T-SQL query can be used to monitor replica states:

```
SELECT
    ag.name AS AvailabilityGroup,
    ar.replica_server_name AS ReplicaName,
    ars.role_desc AS Role,
    ars.operational_state_desc
FROM
sys.availability_groups ag join sys.availability_replicas ar
on ag.group_id=ar.group_id
join sys.dm_hadr_availability_replica_states ars
on ar.replica_id=ars.replica_id
```

When this query is run against the primary replica, it returns the state of the primary and the secondary replicas. When it is run against the secondary replica, it returns the state of that particular secondary replica.

You should get the following output when the query is run on DPLPR:

	AvailabilityGroup	ReplicaName	Role	operational_state_desc
1	DPLAG	DPLHA	SECONDARY	NULL
2	DPLAG	DPLPR	PRIMARY	ONLINE
3	DPLAG	DPLDR	SECONDARY	NULL

Figure 5.65: Output on DPLPR

You should get the following output when it is run on DPLHA:

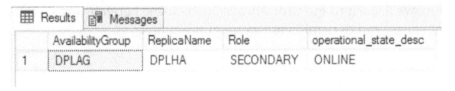

	AvailabilityGroup	ReplicaName	Role	operational_state_desc
1	DPLAG	DPLHA	SECONDARY	ONLINE

Figure 5.66: Output on DPLHA

This query gets the data from the following three DMVs:

- `sys.availability_groups` returns the configuration details for the availability groups. Each availability group is identified by a unique identifier, `group_id`.

- `sys.availability_replicas` returns the configuration details for the availability group replicas. Each replica is identified by a unique identifier, `replica_id`. Each replica is mapped to its corresponding availability group using the `group_id` availability group.

- `sys.dm_hadr_availability_replica_states` returns information on the replica states. A replica is identified by the combination of the `replica_id` and `group_id` columns.

The **Role** column returns the current availability role of the replica. It can have any one of the following three values: **PRIMARY**, **SECONDARY**, and **RESOLVING**. The **RESOLVING** value is usually used when a replica is in a transient state from primary to secondary or vice versa.

The **operational_state_desc** column can have following values:

- **PENDING_FAILOVER**: This is when the failover is being performed for an availability group.

- **OFFLINE**: This is when there is no primary replica available in an availability group.

- **ONLINE**: This is when the replica is online.

- **FAILED**: This is when the replica can't read or write from the WSFC cluster.

- **NULL**: This is when the replica is a remote replica.

When configuring email alerts, we can send an email whenever the role or operational state of an availability replica is changed.

> **Note**
>
> Email alerts can be set up using database mail and the SQL Server agent. First, configure the database mail with the correct SMTP settings. Then, create a SQL Server agent job with the preceding query and send an email whenever the `operational_state_desc` of an availability replica is either `PENDING` or `FAILED`.

Monitoring Availability Databases' Synchronization Status

The following T-SQL query can be used to monitor the health of availability databases:

```
SELECT
    ag.name AS AvailabilityGroup,
    ar.replica_server_name AS ReplicaName,
    d.name AS DatabaseName,
    drs.database_state_desc,
    drs.synchronization_state_desc,
    drs.synchronization_health_desc
FROM
sys.availability_groups ag join sys.availability_replicas ar
on ag.group_id=ar.group_id
join sys.dm_hadr_database_replica_states drs
on ar.replica_id=drs.replica_id
join sys.databases d
on d.database_id=drs.database_id
```

When run against the primary replica, you should get the following output:

	AvailabilityGroup	ReplicaName	DatabaseName	database_state_desc	synchronization_state_desc	synchronization_health_desc
1	DPLAG	DPLDR	Sales	NULL	SYNCHRONIZING	HEALTHY
2	DPLAG	DPLHA	Sales	NULL	SYNCHRONIZED	HEALTHY
3	DPLAG	DPLPR	Sales	ONLINE	SYNCHRONIZED	HEALTHY
4	DPLAG	DPLDR	Finance	NULL	SYNCHRONIZING	HEALTHY
5	DPLAG	DPLHA	Finance	NULL	SYNCHRONIZED	HEALTHY
6	DPLAG	DPLPR	Finance	ONLINE	SYNCHRONIZED	HEALTHY

Figure 5.67: Output on the primary replica

Observe that the **database_state_desc** column for the DPLHA and DPLDR replicas is **NULL**. This doesn't mean that the database is offline or unavailable. This is because the instance DPLPR can't determine the database state of a database on DPLHA, DPLDR, or any other secondary replica.

When the query is run against the DPLHA secondary replica, you should get the following output:

	AvailabilityGroup	ReplicaName	DatabaseName	database_state_desc	synchronization_state_desc	synchronization_health_desc
1	DPLAG	DPLHA	Finance	ONLINE	SYNCHRONIZED	HEALTHY
2	DPLAG	DPLHA	Sales	ONLINE	SYNCHRONIZED	HEALTHY

Figure 5.68: Output on the secondary replica

Observe that the database state of DPLHA is online.

The `sys.dm_hadr_database_replica_states` DMV returns the database health information of the availability databases in an availability group.

The **synchronization_health_desc** column can have the following values:

- **HEALTHY**: This is when the synchronization state is either **SYNCHRONIZED** or **SYNCHRONIZING**.

- **NOT_HEALTHY**: This is when the synchronization state is **NOT SYNCHRONIZING**.

- **PARTIALLY_HEALTHY**: This is when the synchronization state of a synchronous replica is **SYNCHRONIZING**. This can happen during initialization, role switch, or in case of slow network connectivity.

When setting up email alerts, you can trigger an email when the **synchronization_health_desc** column value changes to **NOT_HEALTHY** or **PARTIALLY_HEALTHY**.

> **Note**
>
> An availability database at the secondary replica can also become unhealthy if the database state is not online. Therefore, when troubleshooting such errors, it is worth looking at the database state at the secondary replica.

Monitoring the AlwaysOn AG Current Workload

The following T-SQL query can be used on the primary instance to monitor the current workload of an availability group:

```
SELECT
    ag.name AS AvailabilityGroup,
    ar.replica_server_name AS ReplicaName,
    ars.role_desc,
    ars.operational_state_desc,
    d.name AS DatabaseName,
    drs.database_state_desc,
    drs.synchronization_state_desc,
    drs.synchronization_health_desc,
    drs.log_send_queue_size,
    drs.log_send_rate,
    drs.redo_queue_size,
    drs.redo_rate,
    drs.secondary_lag_seconds

FROM
sys.availability_groups ag join sys.availability_replicas ar
on ag.group_id=ar.group_id
join sys.dm_hadr_availability_replica_states ars
on ars.replica_id=ars.replica_id
join sys.dm_hadr_database_replica_states drs
on ar.replica_id=drs.replica_id and drs.replica_id = ars.replica_id
join sys.databases d
on d.database_id=drs.database_id
```

The query gets the data from the DMVs discussed earlier; however, it gets the following additional columns from the **sys.dm_hadr_database_replica_states** DMV:

- **log_send_queue_size**: This is the log records in KB yet to be sent to the secondary replicas.

- **log_send_rate**: This is the rate in KB/sec at which the log records are being sent to secondary replicas.

- **redo_queue_size**: This is the log records in KB at the secondary replica transaction log that are yet to be redone.

- **redo_rate**: This is the rate in KB/sec at which the log records are being redone at the secondary replica.

- **secondary_lag_seconds**: This is the number of seconds a secondary replica is behind the primary replica in data replication.

> **Note**
>
> The preceding query's output can be recorded in a table, say, every 15 seconds. That table can then be used to analyze the issues or trends with the preceding metrics to predict or troubleshoot issues.
>
> A complete list of AlwaysOn AG DMVs is given here: https://docs.microsoft.com/en-us/sql/relational-databases/system-dynamic-management-views/always-on-availability-groups-dynamic-management-views-functions?view=sql-server-2017.

Monitoring an AlwaysOn AG Using PowerShell

PowerShell provides the following cmdlets to get the AlwaysOn AG health status:

- **Test-SqlAvailabilityGroup**: This returns the health status of the availability group as **Healthy** or **Error**. The following PowerShell command returns the status of the DPLAG availability group. It should be executed on the primary instance:

  ```
  PS C:\Users\Administrator.DPL> Get-ChildItem "SQLServer:\SQL\DPLPR\
  DEFAULT\AvailabilityGroups" | Test-SqlAvailabilityGroup
  ```

You should get the following output:

```
PS C:\Users\Administrator.DPL> Get-ChildItem "SQLServer:\SQL\DPLPR\DEFAULT\AvailabilityGroups" | Test-SqlAvailabilityGr
up -NoRefresh

HealthState          Name
-----------          ----
Healthy              DPLAG
```

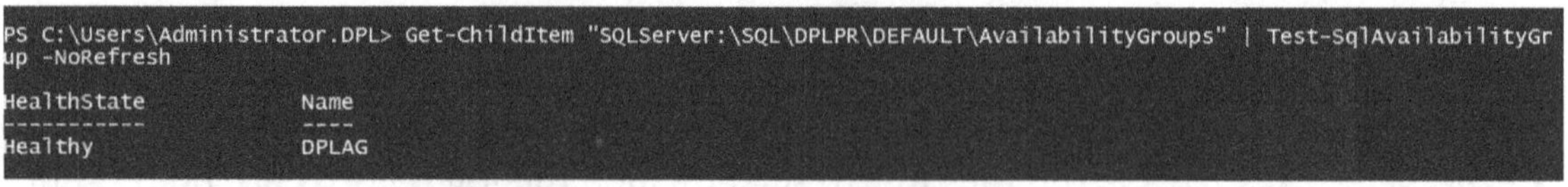

Figure 5.69: Output of Test-SqlAvailabilityGroup

- **Test-SqlAvailabilityReplica**: This returns the health status of an availability group replica as **Healthy** or **Error**. The following PowerShell command returns the status of all availability replicas in the DPLAG availability group:

   Get-ChildItem SQLServer:\SQL\DPLPR\DEFAULT\AvailabilityGroups\DPLAG\
   AvailabilityReplicas" | Test-SqlAvailabilityReplica

   You should get the following output:

```
PS C:\Users\Administrator.DPL> Get-ChildItem "SQLServer:\SQL\DPLPR\DEFAULT\AvailabilityGroups\DPLAG\AvailabilityReplicas
" | Test-SqlAvailabilityReplica

HealthState          AvailabilityGroup     Name
-----------          -----------------     ----
Healthy              DPLAG                 DPLDR
Healthy              DPLAG                 DPLHA
Healthy              DPLAG                 DPLPR
```

Figure 5.70: Output of Test-SqlAvailabilityReplica

- **Test-SqlDatabaseReplicaState**: This returns the health status of all the availability databases for the given availability replica in an availability group. The following PowerShell command returns the status of all availability databases across all availability replicas in the DPLAG availability group:

   PS C:\Users\Administrator.DPL> Get-ChildItem "SQLSERVER:\SQL\DPLPR\
   DEFAULT\AvailabilityGroups\DPLAG\DatabaseReplicaStates" | Test-
   SqlDatabaseReplicaState

You should get the following output:

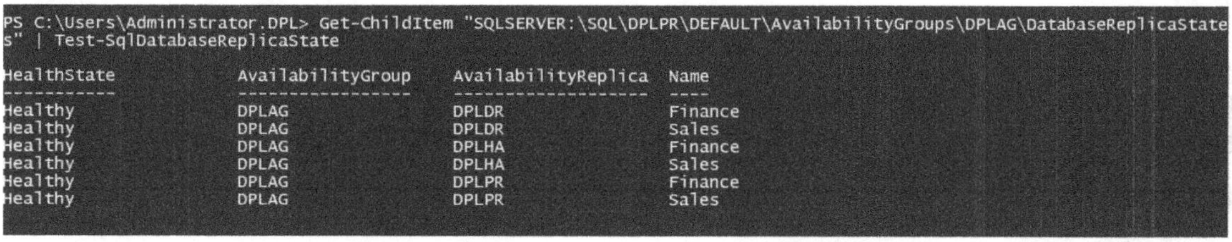

```
PS C:\Users\Administrator.DPL> Get-ChildItem "SQLSERVER:\SQL\DPLPR\DEFAULT\AvailabilityGroups\DPLAG\DatabaseReplicaState
s" | Test-SqlDatabaseReplicaState

HealthState          AvailabilityGroup    AvailabilityReplica   Name
-----------          -----------------    -------------------   ----
Healthy              DPLAG                DPLDR                 Finance
Healthy              DPLAG                DPLDR                 Sales
Healthy              DPLAG                DPLHA                 Finance
Healthy              DPLAG                DPLHA                 Sales
Healthy              DPLAG                DPLPR                 Finance
Healthy              DPLAG                DPLPR                 Sales
```

Figure 5.71: Output of Test-SqlDatabaseReplicaState

> **Note**
>
> To only get the status of the databases at the DPLHA replica, provide the replica as DPLHA instead of DPLPR and execute the command at the DPLHA replica.

The cmdlets can be used to set up automatic email alerts whenever the **HealthState** value returned for an availability group, availability replica, or availability database is **Error** and not **Healthy**.

> **Note**
>
> An AlwaysOn AG can also be monitored using Performance Monitor counters and wait statistics. However, these topics aren't covered in this book.

Troubleshooting AlwaysOn Availability Groups

In this section, we'll look at some of the common AlwaysOn AG problems and their solutions.

Exercise 58: Problem 1 - DDL Queries Block the Redo Thread on the Secondary Replica

This is one of the most common issues you can come across in an AlwaysOn AG environment: the DDL queries on the primary replica block the redo thread on the secondary replica.

Setup

To simulate the problem, follow these steps:

1. Navigate to the **C:\Code\Lesson05** folder and open **3_CreateTableOrders.sql** in SSMS. Connect to the DPLPR instance and execute this query:

```sql
-- To be executed at DPLPR
-- Creates a sample Orders table and populates it with dummy data
USE Sales
GO
DROP TABLE IF EXISTS Orders
GO
CREATE TABLE Orders
(
  OrderID int identity,
  OrderQty int,
  Price int,
  [Description] varchar(100)
)
GO
WITH cte0 AS (SELECT 0 g UNION ALL SELECT 0)
    ,cte1 AS (SELECT 0 g FROM cte0 a CROSS JOIN cte0 b)
    ,cte2 AS (SELECT 0 g FROM cte1 a CROSS JOIN cte1 b)
    ,cte3 AS (SELECT 0 g FROM cte2 a CROSS JOIN cte2 b)
    ,cte4 AS (SELECT 0 g FROM cte3 a CROSS JOIN cte3 b)
    ,numbers as (Select ROW_NUMBER() OVER(ORDER BY (SELECT NULL)) as num
FROM cte4)
INSERT INTO Orders
(
  OrderQty,
  Price,
  [Description]
)
SELECT
  num AS OrderQty,
  num *2 AS Price,
```

```
'SomeDescription' AS [Description]
FROM numbers
```

This query creates an **Orders** table and populates it with dummy data. Wait for the query to complete.

2. Navigate to the **C:\Code\Lesson05** folder and open **4_LargeReport.sql** in SSMS. Connect to the DPLDR SQL instance:

```
-- To be run at DPLDR
-- Simulates a large report that runs at secondary replica
USE Sales
GO
SELECT
  COUNT_BIG(*)
FROM orders a, orders b, orders c, orders d
```

This query simulates a large hourly report that runs at the secondary replica DPLDR. Execute the query.

3. Navigate to the **C:\Code\Lesson05** folder and open **7_AlterTableOrders.sql** in SSMS. Connect to DPLPR:

```
-- To be run at DPLPR
-- Simulate DDL activity at DPLPR
USE [Sales]
GO
ALTER TABLE orders ALTER COLUMN [description] NVARCHAR(1000)
GO
ALTER TABLE orders ALTER COLUMN [description] VARCHAR(500)
GO
ALTER TABLE orders ALTER COLUMN [description] NVARCHAR(1000)
GO
ALTER TABLE orders ALTER COLUMN [description] VARCHAR(500)
GO
ALTER TABLE orders ALTER COLUMN [description] NVARCHAR(500)
GO
ALTER TABLE orders ALTER COLUMN [description] VARCHAR(500)
GO
ALTER TABLE orders ALTER COLUMN [description] NVARCHAR(500)
GO
ALTER TABLE orders ALTER COLUMN [description] NVARCHAR(1000)
GO
ALTER TABLE orders ALTER COLUMN [description] VARCHAR(500)
GO
```

```
ALTER TABLE orders ALTER COLUMN [description] NVARCHAR(1000)
GO
ALTER TABLE orders ALTER COLUMN [description] VARCHAR(500)
GO
ALTER TABLE orders ALTER COLUMN [description] NVARCHAR(500)
GO
ALTER TABLE orders ALTER COLUMN [description] VARCHAR(500)
GO
ALTER TABLE orders ALTER COLUMN [description] NVARCHAR(500)
GO
ALTER TABLE orders ALTER COLUMN [description] NVARCHAR(1000)
GO
ALTER TABLE orders ALTER COLUMN [description] VARCHAR(500)
GO
ALTER TABLE orders ALTER COLUMN [description] NVARCHAR(1000)
GO
ALTER TABLE orders ALTER COLUMN [description] VARCHAR(500)
GO
ALTER TABLE orders ALTER COLUMN [description] NVARCHAR(500)
GO
ALTER TABLE orders ALTER COLUMN [description] VARCHAR(500)
GO
ALTER TABLE orders ALTER COLUMN [description] NVARCHAR(500)
GO
ALTER TABLE orders ALTER COLUMN [description] NVARCHAR(1000)
GO
ALTER TABLE orders ALTER COLUMN [description] VARCHAR(500)
GO
ALTER TABLE orders ALTER COLUMN [description] NVARCHAR(1000)
GO
ALTER TABLE orders ALTER COLUMN [description] VARCHAR(500)
GO
ALTER TABLE orders ALTER COLUMN [description] NVARCHAR(500)
GO
ALTER TABLE orders ALTER COLUMN [description] VARCHAR(500)
GO
ALTER TABLE orders ALTER COLUMN [description] NVARCHAR(500)
GO
ALTER TABLE orders ALTER COLUMN [description] NVARCHAR(1000)
GO
ALTER TABLE orders ALTER COLUMN [description] VARCHAR(500)
GO
```

```
ALTER TABLE orders ALTER COLUMN [description] NVARCHAR(1000)
GO
ALTER TABLE orders ALTER COLUMN [description] VARCHAR(500)
GO
ALTER TABLE orders ALTER COLUMN [description] NVARCHAR(500)
GO
ALTER TABLE orders ALTER COLUMN [description] VARCHAR(500)
GO
ALTER TABLE orders ALTER COLUMN [description] NVARCHAR(500)
GO
ALTER TABLE orders ALTER COLUMN [description] NVARCHAR(1000)
GO
ALTER TABLE orders ALTER COLUMN [description] VARCHAR(500)
GO
ALTER TABLE orders ALTER COLUMN [description] NVARCHAR(1000)
GO
ALTER TABLE orders ALTER COLUMN [description] VARCHAR(500)
GO
ALTER TABLE orders ALTER COLUMN [description] NVARCHAR(500)
GO
ALTER TABLE orders ALTER COLUMN [description] VARCHAR(500)
GO
ALTER TABLE orders ALTER COLUMN [description] NVARCHAR(500)
GO
ALTER TABLE orders ALTER COLUMN [description] NVARCHAR(1000)
GO
ALTER TABLE orders ALTER COLUMN [description] VARCHAR(500)
GO
ALTER TABLE orders ALTER COLUMN [description] NVARCHAR(1000)
GO
ALTER TABLE orders ALTER COLUMN [description] VARCHAR(500)
GO
ALTER TABLE orders ALTER COLUMN [description] NVARCHAR(500)
GO
ALTER TABLE orders ALTER COLUMN [description] VARCHAR(500)
GO
ALTER TABLE orders ALTER COLUMN [description] NVARCHAR(500)
GO
ALTER TABLE orders ALTER COLUMN [description] NVARCHAR(1000)
GO
ALTER TABLE orders ALTER COLUMN [description] VARCHAR(500)
GO
```

```
ALTER TABLE orders ALTER COLUMN [description] NVARCHAR(1000)
GO
ALTER TABLE orders ALTER COLUMN [description] VARCHAR(500)
GO
ALTER TABLE orders ALTER COLUMN [description] NVARCHAR(500)
GO
ALTER TABLE orders ALTER COLUMN [description] VARCHAR(500)
GO
ALTER TABLE orders ALTER COLUMN [description] NVARCHAR(500)
```

Execute this query. This query will take a long time to complete.

4. Navigate to the **C:\Code\Lesson05** folder and open **5_GetBlockedProcessDetails.sql** in SSMS. Connect to the DPLDR instance:

```
-- To be run at DPLDR
-- Returns blocked process details
SELECT
    session_id AS blocked_session_id,
    blocking_Session_id,
    command as blocked_session_command,
    wait_type as blocked_session_wait_type,
    db_name(database_id) AS database_name,
    wait_resource
FROM sys.dm_exec_requests where blocking_session_id>0
```

Execute this query. You should get the following output:

Figure 5.72: Output of the query

Observe that system session 33 is blocked by session 53. Session 53 is the one running the **4_LargeReport.sql** query. Session 53 is waiting on the LCK_M_ SCH_M wait type. LCK_M_SCH_M occurs when a session is waiting on a resource (table) to get a schema modification lock, but the resource already has an incompatible lock granted to another session.

In this case, session 33, which is the REDO thread, is waiting to acquire a schema modification lock on the **orders** table (specified by the **wait_resource** column, object ID 68195293); however, the **orders** table already has a SCH-S lock granted to session 53.

> **Note**
>
> To learn more about the locks in SQL Server, visit https://technet.microsoft.com/ en-us/library/jj856598(v=sql.110).aspx#Lock_Engine.

SCH-S is a schema stability lock and is incompatible with the LCK_M_SCH_M lock. Therefore, the REDO thread is blocked. The REDO thread will be blocked until the large report completes.

Solution

1. Navigate to **C:\Code\Lesson05** and open **6_MonitorAlwaysOnWorkload.sql** in SSMS. Connect to the DPLDR instance:

```
-- To be run at DPLDR
-- Monitor the redo queue at the secondary replica
SELECT
   ag.name AS AvailabilityGroup,
   ar.replica_server_name AS ReplicaName,
   ars.role_desc,
   d.name AS DatabaseName,
   drs.log_send_queue_size,
   drs.log_send_rate,
   drs.redo_queue_size,
   drs.redo_rate,
   drs.secondary_lag_seconds
FROM
sys.availability_groups ag join sys.availability_replicas ar
on ag.group_id=ar.group_id
```

```
join sys.dm_hadr_availability_replica_states ars
on ars.replica_id=ars.replica_id
join sys.dm_hadr_database_replica_states drs
on ar.replica_id=drs.replica_id and drs.replica_id = ars.replica_id
join sys.databases d
on d.database_id=drs.database_id
```

Execute the query. You should get the following results:

100 %

Results | Messages

	AvailabilityGroup	ReplicaName	role_desc	DatabaseName	log_send_queue_size	log_send_rate	redo_queue_size	redo_rate
1	DPLAG	DPLDR	SECONDARY	Sales	535876	10417	2728988	289
2	DPLAG	DPLDR	SECONDARY	Finance	0	0	0	0

Figure 5.73: Running the query once

2. Observe the redo queue size. Execute the query multiple times and observe the increase in the redo queue size. Note that the redo rate, however, remains constant:

> **Note**
>
> The redo queue size and redo rate value will be different in your case.

100 %

Results | Messages

	AvailabilityGroup	ReplicaName	role_desc	DatabaseName	log_send_queue_size	log_send_rate	redo_queue_size	redo_rate
1	DPLAG	DPLDR	SECONDARY	Sales	NULL	10131	2828076	289
2	DPLAG	DPLDR	SECONDARY	Finance	0	0	0	0

Figure 5.74: Running the query multiple times

3. Navigate to the query window running **4_LargeReport.sql**. Press the stop button in the top menu to stop the execution:

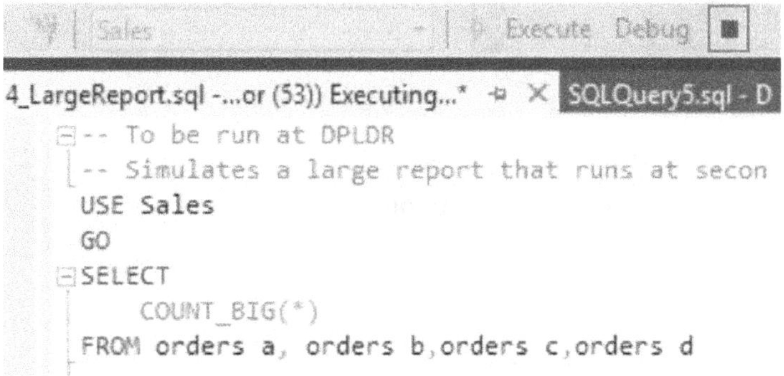

Figure 5.75: The stop button

4. Switch to the **5_GetBlockedProcessDetails.sql** query window and execute it to get the blocked processes:

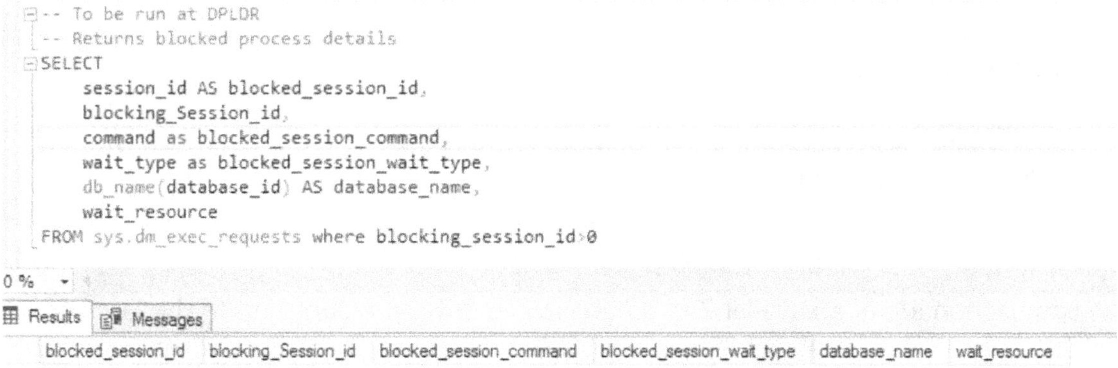

Figure 5.76: The blocked processes are cleared

Observe that the blockings have been cleared. This is the result of stopping the **4_LargeReport.sql** query at DPLDR.

5. Switch to **6_MonitorAlwaysOnWorkload.sql** and execute the query multiple times:

	AvailabilityGroup	ReplicaName	role_desc	DatabaseName	log_send_queue_size	log_send_rate	redo_queue_size	redo_rate
1	DPLAG	DPLDR	SECONDARY	Sales	0	3840	1275588	4912
2	DPLAG	DPLDR	SECONDARY	Finance	0	0	0	0

Figure 5.77: Running the query once

After running the query multiple times, we should see this:

	AvailabilityGroup	ReplicaName	role_desc	DatabaseName	log_send_queue_size	log_send_rate	redo_queue_size	redo_rate
1	DPLAG	DPLDR	SECONDARY	Sales	0	3840	898780	4508
2	DPLAG	DPLDR	SECONDARY	Finance	0	0	0	0

Figure 5.78: Running the query multiple times

Observe that the redo queue size starts decreasing and the redo rate starts increasing. The redo thread will be close to zero after a while.

In a busy system, it is recommended to configure alerts on the blocking and the redo queue size to proactively find the issue.

Exercise 59: Problem 2 - Transaction Log is Growing

The transaction log of an availability database can only be cleared up to the last commit LSN at the secondary replicas. Therefore, if for any reason there isn't any replication from the primary replica to any one of the secondary replicas, the transaction log at the primary log won't be cleared and will keep growing.

If the problem is not resolved, the transaction log will fill the disk it's hosted on and the availability database at the primary replica. This will cause the applications to fail with the **Transaction log for the database <database name> is full** issue.

Setup

To simulate the problem, follow these steps:

1. Connect to DPLPR and execute the following query:

```
USE [master]
GO
ALTER DATABASE [Sales] MODIFY FILE ( NAME = N'AdventureWorks2016_Log',
MAXSIZE = 500MB1GB )
GO
```

This query sets the maximum size of the **Sales** database transaction log to 500 MB. This is to simulate the disk full issue, which can happen if the transaction log outgrows the disk capacity.

2. Connect to DPLDR and execute the following query:

```
ALTER DATABASE [Sales] SET HADR SUSPEND
```

This query will stop the **Sales** database data synchronization from DPLPR to DPLDR.

3. Navigate to **C:\Code\Lesson05** and open **9_MonitorLSNCommitTime.sql** in SSMS. Connect to DPLPR. This query monitors the AlwaysOn workload:

```
-- To be run at DPLPR
-- Monitor the redo queue at the secondary replica
SELECT
   ag.name AS AvailabilityGroup,
   ar.replica_server_name AS ReplicaName,
   ars.role_desc,
   d.name AS DatabaseName,
   drs.log_send_queue_size,
   drs.log_send_rate,
   drs.redo_queue_size,
   drs.redo_rate,
   drs.last_commit_lsn,
   drs.last_commit_time,
   drs.secondary_lag_seconds
FROM
sys.availability_groups ag join sys.availability_replicas ar
on ag.group_id=ar.group_id
join sys.dm_hadr_availability_replica_states ars
on ars.replica_id=ars.replica_id
join sys.dm_hadr_database_replica_states drs
```

```
on ar.replica_id=drs.replica_id and drs.replica_id = ars.replica_id
join sys.databases d
on d.database_id=drs.database_id
WHERE d.name = 'Sales'
```

Execute the query to note the current values:

	AvailabilityGroup	ReplicaName	role_desc	DatabaseName	log_send_queue_size	log_send_rate	redo_queue_size	redo_rate	last_commit_lsn	last_commit_time	secondary_lag_seconds
1	DPLAG	DPLHA	SECONDARY	Sales	0	8526	0	2933	70700002404000001	2018-10-21 17:54:03.520	0
2	DPLAG	DPLPR	PRIMARY	Sales	NULL	NULL	NULL	NULL	70700002404000001	2018-10-21 17:54:03.520	NULL
3	DPLAG	DPLDR	SECONDARY	Sales	NULL	6869	0	4338	70700002404000001	2018-10-21 17:54:03.520	0

Figure 5.79: The last_commit_lsn and last_commit_time values

Observe that the **last_commit_lsn** and **last_commit_time** values are the same across all replicas, indicating that the replicas are in sync.

> **Note**
>
> The **last_commit_lsn** and **last_commit_time** values for a synchronous replicas should always be the same if there isn't any lag. However, the **last_commit_lsn** and **last_commit_time** values for an asynchronous replica may differ.

4. Navigate to **C:\Code\Lesson05** and open **8_CreateTableComments.sql** in SSMS. This query creates a **Comments** table in the **Sales** database and inserts data into it. This will cause the transaction log of the database to grow:

```
-- To be executed at DPLPR
-- Creates a sample Comments table and populates it with dummy data
USE Sales
GO
DROP TABLE IF EXISTS Comments
GO
CREATE TABLE Comments
(
  ID int,
  comment char(8000)
)
```

```
GO
WITH cte0 AS (SELECT 0 g UNION ALL SELECT 0)
    ,cte1 AS (SELECT 0 g FROM cte0 a CROSS JOIN cte0 b)
    ,cte2 AS (SELECT 0 g FROM cte1 a CROSS JOIN cte1 b)
    ,cte3 AS (SELECT 0 g FROM cte2 a CROSS JOIN cte2 b)
  ,cte4 AS (SELECT 0 g FROM cte2 a CROSS JOIN cte3 b)
  ,cte5 AS (SELECT 0 g FROM cte2 a CROSS JOIN cte4 b)
  ,cte6 AS (SELECT 0 g FROM cte2 a CROSS JOIN cte5 b)
  ,cte7 AS (SELECT 0 g FROM cte2 a CROSS JOIN cte6 b)
  ,cte8 AS (SELECT 0 g FROM cte2 a CROSS JOIN cte7 b)
    ,numbers as (Select ROW_NUMBER() OVER(ORDER BY (SELECT NULL)) as num
FROM cte7)
INSERT INTO Comments
(
  ID, comment
)
SELECT
  num AS ID,
  'Some comment' AS [comment]
FROM numbers
```

Execute the query and wait until the query errors out with the following error:

```
Msg 9002, Level 17, State 9, Line 13
The transaction log for database 'Sales' is full due to 'AVAILABILITY_
REPLICA'.
```

In a real-world environment, the error will be logged by the application and if the alerts are configured, the alert email will be sent out to a mailing list. The alert will also be logged in the SQL Server error logs. If the proper database monitoring is in place, an alert email will be sent to the DBAs.

> **Note**
>
> Any attempt to truncate or shrink the transaction log will fail at this point in time. The transaction log can't be truncated until all the records are replicated to the secondaries. The transaction log can only be truncated up to the **last_commit_lsn** of the DPLDR replica. The LSNs at the primary after the **last_commit_lsn** at the DPLDR are not replicated to DPLDR and therefore can't be removed from the transaction log.

Solution

1. The alert clearly states that the transaction log is full due to **AVAILABILITY_REPLICA**. However, it may happen that the reason for the transaction log being full isn't mentioned in the error. In such cases, execute the following query to find the cause of the full transaction log issue. The query is to be run at the primary replica:

```
SELECT
    log_reuse_wait_desc
FROM sys.databases WHERE name='Sales'
```

You should get the following output:

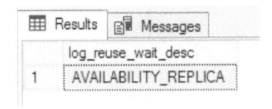

Figure 5.80: Finding the cause of the full transaction log issue

2. The next step is to verify the AlwaysOn availability state. To do this, execute the **9_MonitorLSNCommitTime.sql** query at DPLPR, DPLDR, and DPLHA.

Here's the output from the three replicas:

DPLDR:

Figure 5.81: Output at DPLDR

DPLHA:

Figure 5.82: Output at DPLHA

DPLPR:

	AvailabilityGroup	ReplicaName	role_desc	operational_state_desc	DatabaseName	log_send_queue_size	redo_queue_size	last_commit_lsn	last_commit_time	secondary_lag_seconds	synchronization_health_
1	DPLAG	DPLHA	SECONDARY	NULL	Sales	60	0	84900000157440020	2018-10-21 18:10:54.043	0	HEALTHY
2	DPLAG	DPLPR	PRIMARY	ONLINE	Sales	NULL	NULL	84900000157440020	2018-10-21 18:10:54.043	NULL	HEALTHY
3	DPLAG	DPLDR	SECONDARY	NULL	Sales	NULL	46828	77500000302960064	2018-10-21 18:06:41.453	5102	NOT_HEALTHY

Figure 5.83: Output at DPLPR

Observe that **Sales** database synchronization is not healthy for the DPLDR replica. Moreover, the DPLDR replica is 5102 seconds behind the DPLPR primary replica. The DPLHA replica is online and is synchronized with the DPLPR primary replica.

3. The next step would be to check whether the synchronization is suspended at the DPLDR replica. To do that, connect to DPLDR in the Object Explorer and navigate to **Always On High Availability | Availability Groups | DPLAG | Availability Databases**:

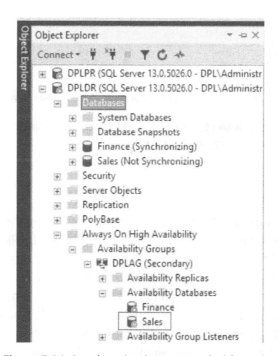

Figure 5.84: Synchronization suspended for Sales

4. Observe that the synchronization is suspended for the **Sales** database. To start the synchronization, connect to DPLDR and execute the following query to resume data synchronization:

```
ALTER DATABASE [Sales] set HADR Resume
```

5. Execute the **9_MonitorLSNCommitTime.sql** query to verify the AlwaysOn status:

Figure 5.85: Verifying the AlwaysOn status

6. Observe that the data synchronization status for the DPLDR replica is now healthy. Run the query multiple times to verify that the data has been successfully replicated to DPLDR:

Figure 5.86: The last_commit_lsn and last_commit_time values are same at all replicas

Observe that the **last_commit_lsn** and **last_commit_time** values are the same at all replicas after the data synchronization.

> **Note**
>
> If data synchronization is not resumed even after executing the preceding command, it's advised to take the database out of the availability group from the faulty replica. This will allow the transaction log to truncate during the next scheduled log backup. You can then find and fix the problem with the faulty replica. Once the problem is fixed, add the database back to the availability group. For example, consider that the disk at the secondary replica hosting the **Sales** database goes out of space, stopping the data synchronization. Adding a new disk or extending the disk capacity will take time. Therefore, it's better to get the database out of the availability group at DPLDR, extend the disk, and add the database back to the availability group. In a real-world environment, transaction log backups are scheduled to occur at specified time intervals. The backup not only helps in restoring the data whenever required, but also in truncating the transaction log.

The full transaction log problem can also occur if there is a delay in sending a transaction log harden acknowledgement from the synchronous secondary to the primary replica. This can happen for reasons such as a slow network, high resource utilization at the secondary slowing down the REDO thread, or high workload on the primary.

Exercise 60: Problem 3 - Replica Database in the Resolving State

A secondary replica can be in the resolving state in the following scenarios:

- During an automatic failover when the role switch is being performed. The secondary replica is promoted to primary replica when the primary replica is unavailable.

- During an unsuccessful failover. For example, let's say that the synchronous secondary replica isn't healthy and the primary replica goes down at the same time. When this happens, the secondary replicas will be in the resolving state. When the primary replica comes back online, the secondary replica will resume its role.

Setup

To simulate an unsuccessful failover, follow these steps:

1. Open a new query window in SSMS and execute the following query at DPLHA:

   ```
   ALTER DATABASE [Sales] set HADR SUSPEND
   ```

   This query will suspend the data synchronization for the **Sales** database between DPLPR and DPLHA. This will cause the data synchronization to go into the not healthy state.

2. Navigate to **C:\Code\Lesson05** and open **8_CreateTableComments.sql**. This is the same query used in the previous problem. It creates a new **Comments** table and populates it with data. Execute the query on DPLPR and wait for it to terminate with the full transaction log issue.

3. Navigate to **C:\Code\Lesson05** and open **9_MonitorLSNCommitTime.sql**. The script is the same as used in the previous problem. It returns the AlwaysOn health status. Execute the query at DPLPR. You should get a similar output:

	AvailabilityGroup	ReplicaName	role_desc	operational_state_desc	DatabaseName	log_send_queue_size	redo_queue_size	last_commit_lsn	last_commit_time	secondary_lag_seconds	synchronization_health
1	DPLAG	DPLHA	SECONDARY	NULL	Sales	NULL	0	10210000031408000009	2018-10-21 23:30:18.487	143	NOT_HEALTHY
2	DPLAG	DPLPR	PRIMARY	ONLINE	Sales	NULL	NULL	10720000001360016	2018-10-21 23:30:51.050	NULL	HEALTHY
3	DPLAG	DPLDR	SECONDARY	NULL	Sales	0	105592	10610000019376000061	2018-10-21 23:30:49.083	0	HEALTHY

Figure 5.87: The AlwaysOn health status

Observe that the replica DPLHA is not healthy and is 143 seconds behind the primary replica (as indicated by **secondary_log_seconds**).

4. Let's now force the automatic failover. To do that, stop the SQL Server services at the primary replica, DPLPR, by running the following command in the command prompt. You should be connected to the DPLPR virtual machine:

```
net stop MSSQLServer
```

You should get the following output:

Figure 5.88: Forcing the automatic failover

The SQL Server service at DPLPR is stopped. This will trigger the automatic failover from DPLPR to DPLHA. However, the data synchronization state at DPLHA is not healthy.

5. Let's now check the AlwaysOn status by executing the **9_MonitorLSNCommitTime.sql** script. The script is to be executed at the DPLDR and DPLHA SQL instances.

You should get the following output:

DPLDR:

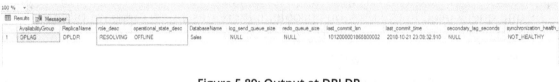

Figure 5.89: Output at DPLDR

DPLHA:

Figure 5.90: Output at DPLHA

Observe that both the secondary replicas are in the resolving state. The automatic failover is therefore unsuccessful. Let's check the DPLAG role status in the Failover Cluster Manager.

6. Press Windows + R to open the **Run** command window. Type `cluadmin.msc` in the **Run** command window and hit *Enter*. In the Failover Cluster Manager console, expand **DPLAO.dpl.com** and select **Roles**:

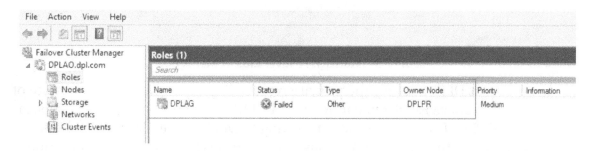

Figure 5.91: The role status is Failed

Observe that the role status is **Failed** and there is no active owner of the role.

Solution

In such cases, we have the following options to recover from the problem:

- Fix the primary replica and bring it online.

- Perform a manual failover to any of the available secondary replicas (DPLDR in this case).

Let's go with the second solution:

1. To perform a manual failover, execute the following query. Remember, it'll be a manual failover with data loss:

```
-- To be executed at DPLDR
-- force failover with data loss
ALTER AVAILABILITY GROUP [DPLAG] FORCE_FAILOVER_ALLOW_DATA_LOSS;
```

When the query completes, check the AlwaysOn status at the DPLDR SQL instance. You should get the following output:

	AvailabilityGroup	ReplicaName	role_desc	operational_state_desc	DatabaseName	log_send_queue_size	redo_queue_size	last_commit_lsn	last_commit_time	secondary_lag_seconds	synchronization_healt
1	DPLAG	DPLHA	SECONDARY	NULL	Sales	NULL	0	0	NULL	NULL	NOT_HEALTHY
2	DPLAG	DPLPR	SECONDARY	NULL	Sales	NULL	0	0	NULL	NULL	NOT_HEALTHY
3	DPLAG	DPLDR	PRIMARY	ONLINE	Sales	NULL	NULL	1072000000013600016	2018-10-21 23:30:51.050	NULL	HEALTHY

Figure 5.92: Data synchronization status for DPLHA is unhealthy

Here's the status at the Failover Cluster Manager:

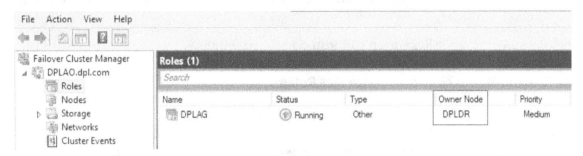

Figure 5.93: Status at Failover Cluster Manager

Observe that DPLDR is now the primary replica. The data synchronization state of the DPLHA replica is still unhealthy. Once DPLDR switches to the primary replica role, the DPLAGL listener will start resolving to DPLDR. The AlwaysOn AG will start accepting the client connections. This is because the data synchronization for the **Sales** database is suspended.

> **Note**
>
> The data synchronization state of the **Finance** database will also be suspended at DPLHA. This is because of the manual failover.

2. Execute the following query at DPLHA to resume the data movement for the **Sales** and **Finance** database:

```
ALTER DATABASE [Sales] set HADR RESUME
GO
ALTER DATABASE [Finance] SET HADR RESUME
```

Let's verify the AlwaysOn AG status at the DPLDR SQL instance:

	AvailabilityGroup	ReplicaName	role_desc	operational_state_desc	DatabaseName	log_send_queue_size	redo_queue_size	last_commit_lsn	last_commit_time	secondary_lag_seconds	synchronization_healt
1	DPLAG	DPLHA	SECONDARY	NULL	Sales	332756	201052	1035000001103200057	2018-10-21 23:30:36.597	1187	HEALTHY
2	DPLAG	DPLPR	SECONDARY	NULL	Sales	NULL	0	0	NULL	NULL	NOT_HEALTHY
3	DPLAG	DPLDR	PRIMARY	ONLINE	Sales	NULL	NULL	1072000000013600016	2018-10-21 23:30:51.050	NULL	HEALTHY

Figure 5.94: Data synchronization status for DPLHA changes to healthy

Observe that the data synchronization status for DPLHA changes to healthy. However, it's still unhealthy for the DPLPR replica.

3. Let's start the SQL Server services at DPLPR. Execute the following command on the command prompt to start the SQL Server services:

```
net start mssqlserver
```

```
C:\Users\Administrator.DPL>net start mssqlserver
The SQL Server (MSSQLSERVER) service is starting.
The SQL Server (MSSQLSERVER) service was started successfully.

C:\Users\Administrator.DPL>_
```

Figure 5.95: Starting the SQL Server services at DPLPR

As the replica DPLPR comes online, it'll take the role of the secondary replica.

4. Run the following command to resume data synchronization for the **Sales** and **Finance** database at DPLPR:

```
ALTER DATABASE [Sales] SET HADR RESUME
GO
ALTER DATABASE [Finance] SET HADR RESUME
```

Let's verify the AlwaysOn AG status at the DPLDR SQL instance:

	AvailabilityGroup	ReplicaName	role_desc	operational_state_desc	DatabaseName	log_send_queue_size	redo_queue_size	last_commit_lsn	last_commit_time	secondary_lag_seconds	synchronization_health
1	DPLAG	DPLHA	SECONDARY	NULL	Sales	0	0	107200000013600016	2018-10-21 23:30:51.050	0	HEALTHY
2	DPLAG	DPLPR	SECONDARY	NULL	Sales	0	0	0	NULL	0	HEALTHY
3	DPLAG	DPLDR	PRIMARY	ONLINE	Sales	NULL	NULL	107200000013600016	2018-10-21 23:30:51.050	NULL	HEALTHY

Figure 5.96: Verifying the AlwaysOn AG status at DPLDR

The DPLPR replica is back online and is synchronizing to the DPLDR primary replica. It is, however, recommended to failback to DPLPR as the primary replica. This is because at this point in time, there isn't any replica with synchronous availability mode.

There are many different issues that can happen in an AlwaysOn AG environment. When troubleshooting problems, start by looking at the AlwaysOn AG state, SQL Server, and failover cluster logs. Find out the root cause and take appropriate actions. It is of utmost importance to set up email alerts to find and fix issues quickly.

Activity 5: Manual Failover

You manage an AlwaysOn environment with three nodes: DPLPR (primary replica), DPLHA (synchronous secondary), and DPLDR (asynchronous secondary). The infrastructure team has to install Windows updates on the three replicas. DPLHA and DPLDR have already been patched. To patch DPLPR, you have been asked to manually failover to DPLHA. Once the Windows update installation is complete on DPLPR, you should fail back to DPLPR from DPLHA.

To failover to DPLHA, you can use the AlwaysOn dashboard *or* run the T-SQL commands as described under the *Manual Failover* section earlier in this lesson. The steps to do this are as follows:

1. Failover from DPLPR to DPLHA.

2. Verify that the failover is complete on DPLHA.

3. Fall back to DPLPR.

> **Note**
>
> The solution for this activity can be found on page 446.

Activity 6: Adding a New Database to an Existing Availability Group

You manage a three-node availability group, DPLAG, that has DPLPR (primary replica), DPLHA (synchronous secondary), and DPLDR (asynchronous node). The business requires you to add a new database, **Customer**. The **Customer** database is large in size and you'll have to add it by manually restoring the backups on the secondary.

Setup

Execute the following query to restore the **Customer** database on DPLPR, the primary replica:

```
USE [master]

RESTORE DATABASE [Customer] FROM  DISK = N'C:\Code\Customer.bak' WITH  FILE
= 1,  NOUNLOAD,  STATS = 5
```

The steps are as follows:

1. Add the `Customer` database to the availability group at DPLPR.

2. Take a full backup of the `Customer` database at DPLPR.

3. Take a log backup of the `Customer` database at DPLPR.

4. Restore the full backup of the `Customer` database with the **NORECOVERY** option at DPLHA and DPLDR.

5. Restore the log backup of the `Customer` database with the **NORECOVERY** option at DPLHA and DPLDR.

6. Join the `Customer` database at DPLHA and DPLDR to the DPLAG availability group using T-SQL or the Object Explorer in SSMS.

> **Note**
>
> The solution for this activity can be found on page 447.

Summary

In this lesson, we talked about managing and maintaining an AlwaysOn Availability group. The lesson covered automatic failover and manual failover with and without data loss. We saw how to perform a number of maintenance and management tasks related to an AlwaysOn AG. We saw how to monitor an AlwaysOn AG, and finally we looked at common AlwaysOn problems and their solutions.

In the next lesson, we'll learn how to use log shipping as a disaster recovery solution.

Configuring and Managing Log Shipping

Learning Objectives

By the end of this lesson, you will be able to do the following:

- Describe log shipping
- Configure log shipping
- Manage and monitor log shipping

This lesson will teach us how to configure log shipping. We will then see how to manage and troubleshoot it.

Introduction

Log shipping is one of the oldest disaster recovery solutions available in SQL Server. Log shipping automatically ships the transaction log backups of the specified database from a primary instance to one or more secondary instances. The secondary instances restore the transaction log backups individually, thereby maintaining a copy of the primary database.

In this lesson, we'll learn to configure, manage, and monitor log shipping.

A typical log shipping configuration consists of a primary SQL Server instance and one or more secondary SQL Server instance. The following diagram shows a log shipping configuration with a primary SQL Server instance, **P**, and two secondary SQL Server instances: **S1** and **S2**:

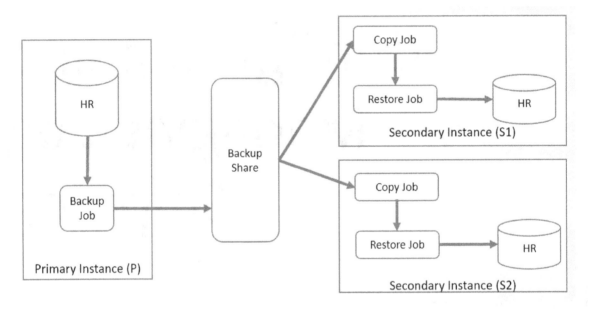

Figure 6.1: A log shipping configuration

The steps performed to log ship the **HR** database shown in the diagram are as follows:

1. A SQL Server agent backup job at the primary instance **P** performs a transaction log backup of the **HR** database and copies it to the backup share location.

    The backup share is a shared folder accessible by all SQL Server instances participating in log shipping.

2. The secondary instances **S1** and **S2** run a copy job to copy the transaction log backup of the **HR** database from the backup share to a local folder.

3. The secondary instances **S1** and **S2** then run a restore job to restore the transaction log backup from the local copy to their corresponding local HR database.

An optional monitor instance can be used to track the status and history of the jobs. If the monitor server is available, the primary and secondary instances share the job status with the monitor instance.

Log Shipping Use Cases

Log shipping has the following use cases:

*   The primary use of log shipping is to maintain one or more DR SQL Server instances.

*   An important use case is database migration from one SQL Server instance to another. This can be done by configuring log shipping between the current and the new SQL Server instances and performing failover to the new instances as and when required.

*   The secondary databases can be read between two restore jobs. Log shipping can therefore be used to offload reads.

*   Log shipping can be used to recover from a bad update. There's a delay when the primary job backs up the log and the secondary instances copy and restore the backup. This delay is configurable. A longer delay can be helpful to recover from a bad update at the primary instance.

Configuring Log Shipping

In this section, we'll learn to configure log shipping using SQL Server Management Studio. We'll be using the DPLPR, DPLDR, and DPLHA Hyper-V machines prepared in *Lesson 4, AlwaysOn Availability Groups*.

> **Note**
>
> Execute the **C:\Code\Lesson05\10_Delete_AG_DPLAG.sql** script to delete the DPLAG availability group. The script also deletes the **Sales** and **Finance** databases at DPLHA and DPLDR.

We'll log ship the **Sales** database from the primary instance, DPLPR, to the secondary instance, DPLHA.

Exercise 61: Configuring Log Shipping

To configure the log shipping setup, follow these steps:

1. Connect to the VM DPLPR. Copy the **C:\Code\Lesson06\CreateFolders.ps1** script to the **C:\Scripts** folder on DPLPR. Open a new PowerShell window on DPLPR and run the following command:

   ```
   C:\Scripts\CreateFolders.ps1
   ```

   The script creates a new **Logshipshare** directory in the **C** drive and shares it with read access to the **DPL\Administrator** user and a new directory, **C:\DPLPRTlogs**, at the secondary instance DPLHA. This is used to store the transaction log backups copied from the backup share **\\DPLPR\Logshipshare** folder.

2. To verify that the shared folder is accessible, connect to DPLHA. Press Windows + R to open the **Run** command window. Type **\\DPLPR\Logshipshare** and press *Enter*.

   You should be able to connect to the shared folder.

3. For log shipping to work, the database should be in either full or bulk-logged recovery model. To verify the recovery model of the **Sales** database, open SSMS and connect to DPLPR. Open a new query window and execute the following query:

```
-- If the recovery_model_desc is SIMPLE
-- Change the recovery model to FULL
IF EXISTS (
SELECT
  1
FROM sys.databases
WHERE name='sales'
AND recovery_model=3
)
BEGIN
ALTER DATABASE [Sales] SET RECOVERY FULL
END
GO
SELECT
   recovery_model,recovery_model_desc
FROM sys.databases
WHERE name='sales'
```

This script changes the recovery model of the **Sales** database to **FULL** if the current recovery model is **Simple**.

You should get the following output:

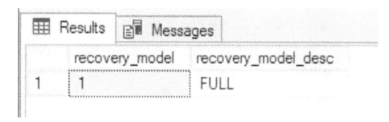

Figure 6.2: Changing the recovery model of the Sales database

The next step is to configure log shipping using the log shipping wizard.

4. In SSMS, connect to Object Explorer (DPLPR) and expand **Databases**. Right-click on the **Sales** database and select **Properties**:

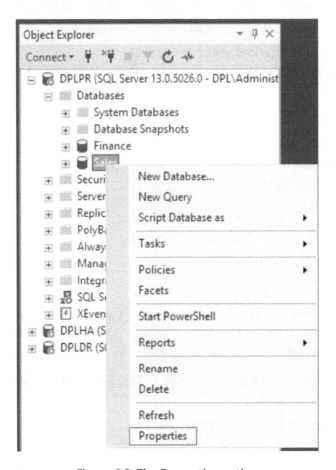

Figure 6.3: The Properties option

5. In the **Database Properties – Sales** dialog box, under **Select a page**, select **Transaction Log Shipping**.

> **Note**
>
> Another way to get to this page is to right-click on the **Sales** database and then select **Tasks | Ship Transaction Logs**.

6. On the **Transaction Log Shipping** page, check the **Enable this as a primary database in a log shipping configuration** option:

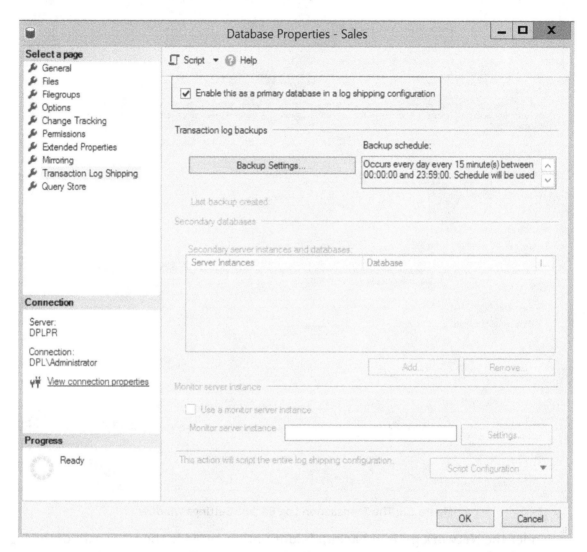

Figure 6.4: The Transaction Log Shipping page

7. Under the **Transaction log backups** section, click on the **Backup Settings** button. In the **Transaction Log Backup Settings** dialog box, do the following:

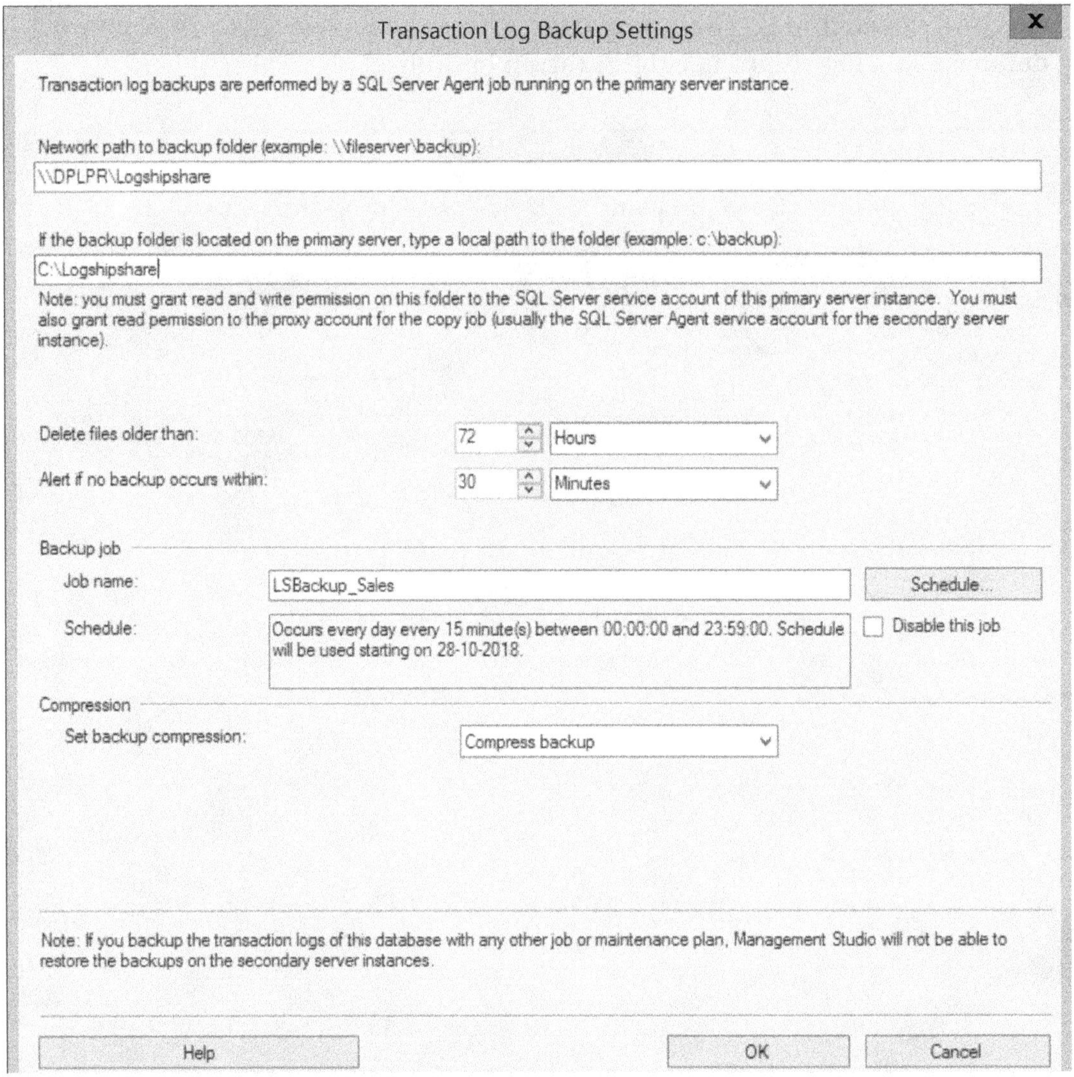

Figure 6.5: The Transaction Log Backup Settings window

Under the **Network path to backup folder** option, provide the UNC path of the log shipping backup share folder created in *step 1* (**\\DPLPR\Logshipshare**).

Under the **If the backup folder is located on the primary server, type the local path to the folder** option, provide the local path of the **Logshipshare** folder (**C:\Logshipshare**).

> **Note**
>
> If the backup share folder is not on the primary instance, leave it as blank.

Modify the **Alert if no backup occurs within** setting's time to **30** minutes.

Under **Backup job**, besides **Job name**, click on the **Schedule** button. In the **Job Schedule Properties** window, under the **Daily frequency** section, modify the **Occurs every** option from **15** minutes to **1** minute:

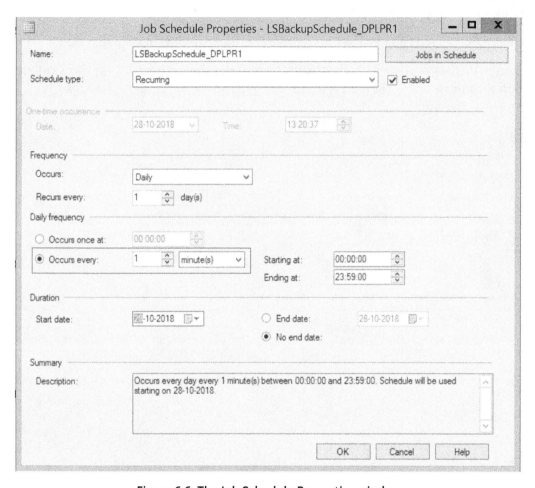

Figure 6.6: The Job Schedule Properties window

Note

In a real-world scenario, the job schedule depends on the RTO and RPO specified by the business. However, it's set to 1 minute here to save time.

Under **Compression**, select **Compress backup**.

Leave the **Delete files older than**, **Job name**, and **Schedule** settings as default.

The **LSBackup_Sales** backup job will be created at the primary instance DPLPR. The job will run every one minute and will take the **Sales** database transaction log backup in the **C:\Logshipshare** folder.

Click **OK** to save the settings and close the **Backup Settings** dialog box.

8. Under the **Secondary server instances and databases** section on the **Transaction Log Shipping** page, click on **Add**. In the **Secondary Database Settings** dialog box, do the following:

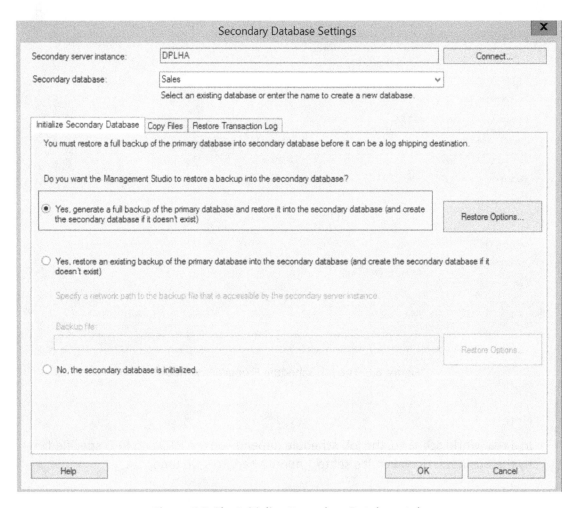

Figure 6.7: The Initialize Secondary Database tab

Besides **Secondary server instance**, click on **Connect**. In the **Connect to Server** dialog box, connect to DPLHA with `DPL\Administrator` and **Windows Authentication**:

Figure 6.8: The Connect to Server window

Under **Secondary databases**, select **Sales**.

In the **Initialize Secondary Database** tab, select the first option: **Yes, generate a full backup of the primary database and restore it on the secondary database (and create the secondary database if it doesn't exist)**.

With this selected, the wizard will initialize the log ship database. The secondary database files (data and log files) are created in the same location as the data and log files of the master database.

To change the data and log file path, select the **Restore Options** button. Provide the folder for data and log files, as shown here:

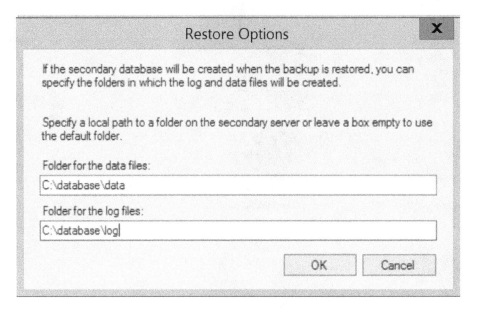

Figure 6.9: The Restore Options window

The specified location should exist on the secondary instance.

> **Note**
>
> If the data and log files are spread across multiple folders, it's advised to restore the database manually at the secondary server and select the **No, the secondary database is initialized** option in the **Secondary Database Settings** dialog box.

Click **OK** to save the settings and close the **Restore Options** dialog box.

9. Select the **Copy Files** tab. This tab configures the SQL agent copy job at the secondary server:

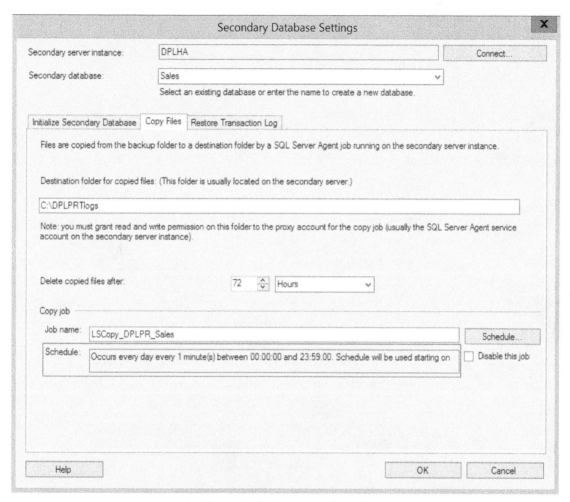

Figure 6.10: The Copy Files tab

Under **Destination folder for copied files**, specify the local folder as `C:\DPLPRTlogs`. The backup files will be copied to this folder from the backup share, which is `\\DPLPR\Logshipshare`. The folder is created in *step* 1.

In the **Copy job** section, against **Job name**, select the **Schedule** button. In the **New Job Schedule** dialog box, under **Daily frequency**, change the **Occurs every** option from **15** minutes to **1** minute:

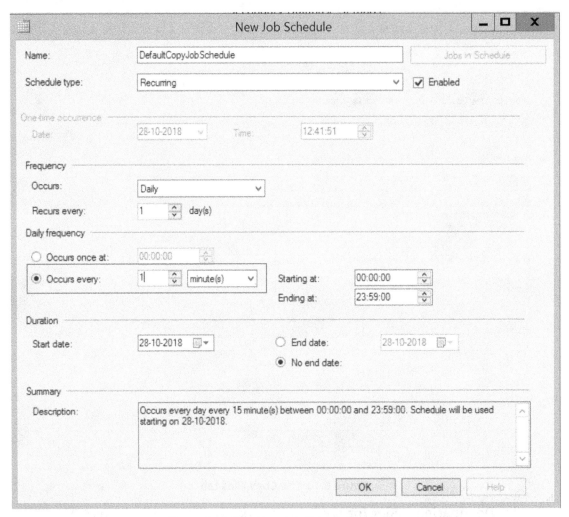

Figure 6.11: The New Job Schedule window

In a real-world scenario, the schedule depends on the RTO and RPO; however, for demo purposes, it's kept at the minimum to save time.

Click **OK** to save the schedule and close the **New Job Schedule** dialog box.

Leave the rest of the settings as default.

The copy job, `LSCopy_DPLPR_Sales`, will be created at the secondary instance DPLHA. The job will run every one minute and will copy the new transaction log backups from `\\DPLPR\Logshipshare` to the local `C:\DPLPRTlogs` folder.

10. Select the **Restore Transaction Log** tab. This tab specifies the configuration
    settings for the restore job:

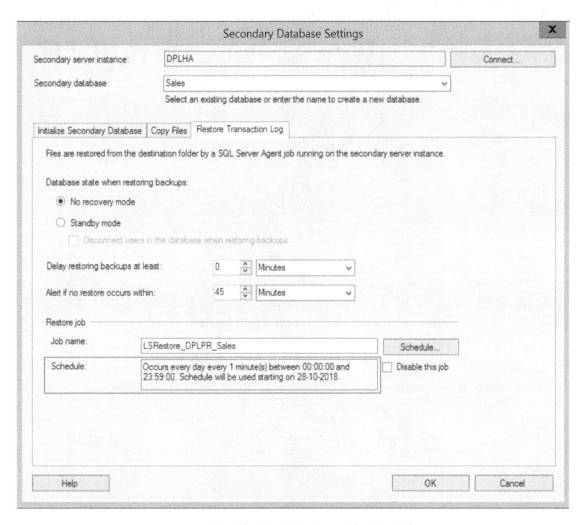

Figure 6.12: The Restore Transaction Log tab

Under **Database state when restoring backups**, select **No recovery mode**. The
No recovery mode option doesn't allow read connections to be made to the
secondary database. The **Standby mode** option allows the read connections to be
made to the secondary database. However, the read and restore operations can't
be done in parallel. Therefore, if you select the **Disconnect users in the database
when restoring backups** option, the read queries are killed when restoring the
backups. If this option is unchecked, the restore operation can only happen if
there are no read connections to the secondary database.

Under the **Restore job** section, select the **Schedule** button. In the **New Job Schedule** dialog box, under **Daily frequency**, change the **Occurs every** option from **15** minutes to **1** minute:

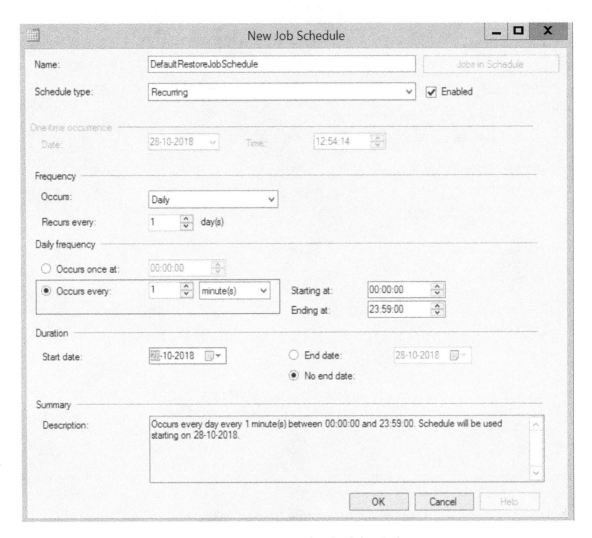

Figure 6.13: The New Job Schedule window

Click on **OK** to save the settings and close the **New Job Schedule** window.

Leave the rest of the options as default. Click on **OK** to save the settings and close the **Secondary Database Settings** dialog box.

11. Select the **Script Configuration** dropdown at the bottom of the window and then select **Script Configuration to File**:

Figure 6.14: The Script Configuration to File option

Save the script in the `C:\Script` folder as `LogShip_Sales_DPLPR_To_DPLHA.sql`. It is advised to script out the configuration in a production environment. The script can either be used later to set up log shipping with the same configuration or to verify the log shipping configuration:

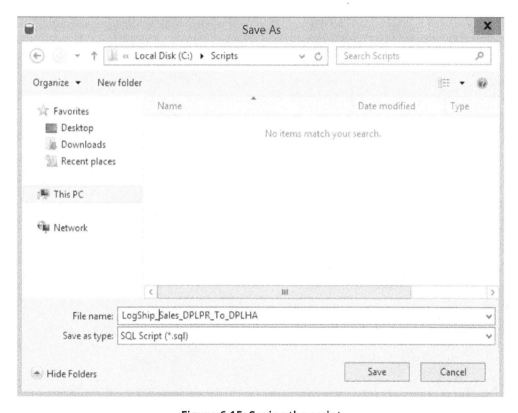

Figure 6.15: Saving the script

This completes the log shipping configuration.

12. One last thing is to verify that the SQL Server agent service is running on the primary and secondary instances. If not, execute the following command in a PowerShell console to start the SQL Server agent service:

```
net start SQLServerAgent
Invoke-Command -ComputerName DPLHA -ScriptBlock {net start SQLServerAgent}
```

The SQL Server agent service should be running under the **DPL\Administrator** account for the log shipping agent job to run. To change the SQL Server agent service account, follow these steps on the primary and the secondary server.

13. Press Windows + R to open the **Run** command window. In the **Run** command window, enter **SQLServerManager13.msc** and press *Enter* to open the SQL Server Configuration Manager.

14. In SQL Server Configuration Manager, right-click on the **SQL Server Agent** service and select **Properties** from the context menu:

Figure 6.16: The Properties option

15. In the **Properties** window, select **This account**, and provide the **Account Name** as `DPL\Administrator` and the password. Click **Apply** to save the settings:

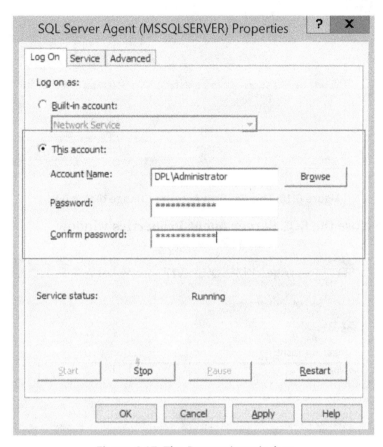

Figure 6.17: The Properties window

16. In the **Confirm Account Change** dialog box, click **Yes**. This will change the **Log on as** account to `DPL\Administrator` and will restart the SQL Server Agent service:

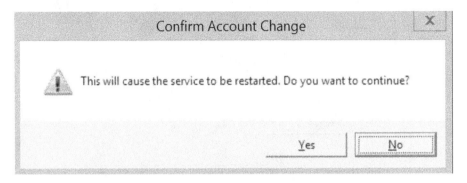

Figure 6.18: The Confirm Account Change dialog box

17. Click **OK** to close the **SQL Server Agent Properties** window:

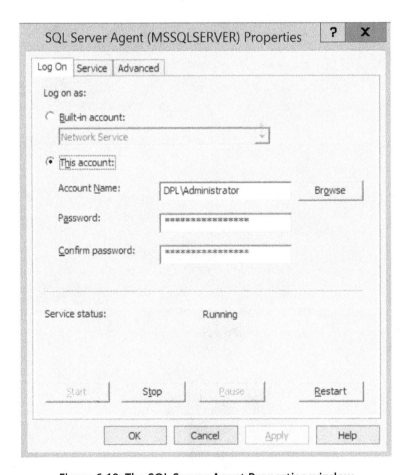

Figure 6.19: The SQL Server Agent Properties window

A **Save Log Shipping Configuration** dialog box will open. The SSMS will perform the following steps:

Back up the `Sales` database at the primary instance, DPLPR. The backup file will be placed in the `\\DPLPR\Logshipshare` folder.

Restore the `Sales` database at the secondary instance, DPLDR. The restore is done using the **With NORECOVERY** option. This is because additional transaction log backups can then be applied to the secondary database.

Create the copy job, restore job, and alert job at the secondary instance, DPLHA.

Create the backup and alert job at the primary instance, DPLPR.

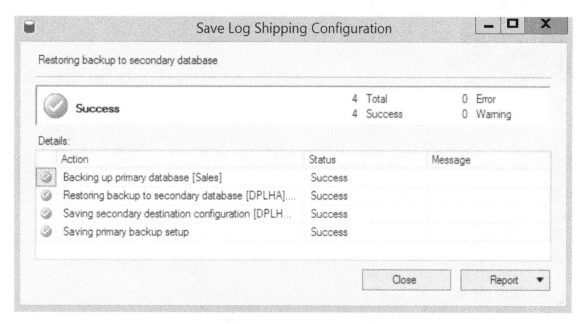

Figure 6.20: The Save Log Shipping Configuration window

18. Click on **Close** to close the **Save Log Shipping Configuration** window.

This completes the log shipping setup.

The log shipping SQL Server agent jobs perform the backup, copy, and restore operations using the log shipping utility `sqllogship.exe`. `sqllogship.exe` is an independent executable file that comes free with the SQL Server installation.

The SQL agent jobs are used only to schedule the **sqllogship.exe** command. For example, the backup job runs the following command to perform the transaction log backup:

```
"c:\Program Files\Microsoft SQL Server\130\Tools\Binn\sqllogship.exe"
-Backup CAEEC8A4-0643-46ED-8511-42B6585C0754 -server DPLPR
```

This command has two parameters: the backup ID and the server. The backup ID comes from the **log_shipping_monitor_primary** system table in the **msdb** database.

The table contains the log shipping configuration information for the individual log shipped databases at the primary instances. **sqllogship.exe** uses this information to perform the transaction log backup of the primary database.

The **sqllogship.exe** comes free with SQL Server installation.

> **Note**
>
> You can log in to the DPLHA secondary instance and verify the SQL agent jobs and the databases created as part of the log shipping configuration.

Managing and Monitoring Log Shipping

In this section, we'll learn to do the following:

- Add or remove a secondary instance to/from an existing log shipping configuration.
- Add or remove a database to/from an existing log shipping configuration.
- Monitor log shipping.
- Change the database restoring state at the secondary.
- Perform failover from the primary instance to the secondary instance.

Exercise 62: Adding a New Secondary Instance to an Existing Log Shipping Configuration

To add a new secondary instance, follow these steps:

1. Connect Object Explorer to the DPLPR instance. Expand the **Databases** node, right-click on the **Sales** database, and select **Properties**. In the **Database Properties - Sales** window, under **Select a page**, select the **Transaction Log Shipping** page.

2. Under the **Secondary databases** section, click on **Add** to add a new secondary server instance to log ship the **Sales** database:

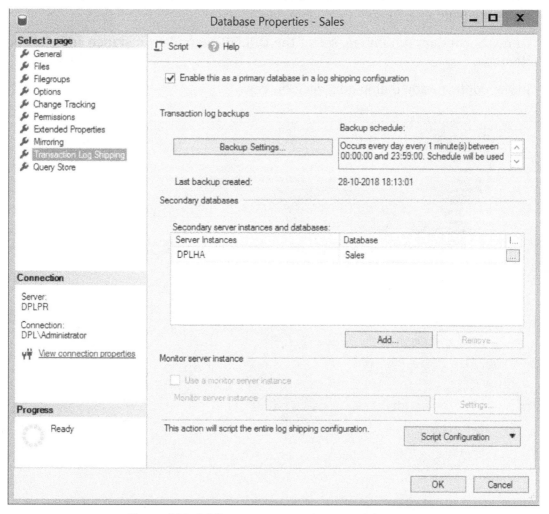

Figure 6.21: Adding a new secondary server instance

3. Follow *steps 8 to 11* from *Exercise 61: Configuring Log Shipping* to add the secondary instance DPLDR to the log shipping configuration.

Exercise 63: Removing a Secondary Instance from an Existing Log Shipping Configuration

To remove a secondary instance from an existing log shipping configuration, follow these steps:

1. Connect Object Explorer to the DPLPR instance. Expand the **Databases** node, right-click on the **Sales** database, and select **Properties**. In the **Database Properties – Sales** window, under **Select a page**, select the **Transaction Log Shipping** page.

2. Under **Secondary databases**, select the **DPLDR** secondary instance and click on **Remove**.

   In the confirmation dialog box, click on **Yes**:

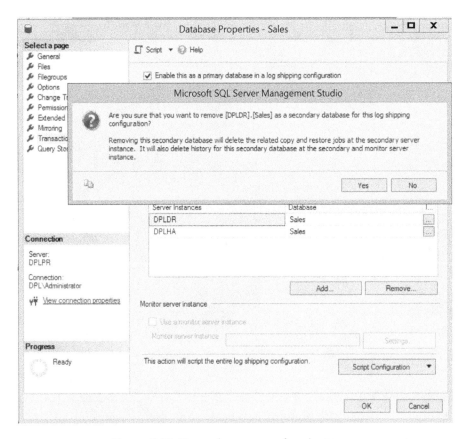

Figure 6.22: Removing a secondary instance

3. Click on **OK** to remove the DPLDR secondary instance:

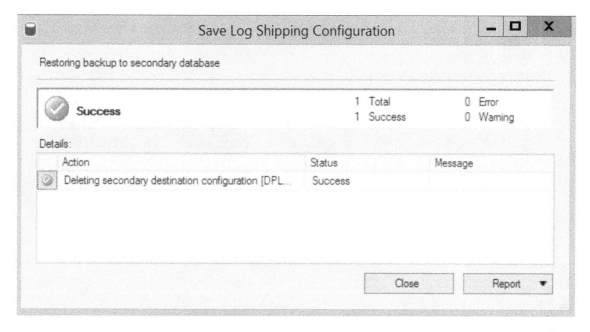

Figure 6.23: The Save Log Shipping Configuration dialog box

Click on **Close** to close the **Save Log Shipping Configuration** dialog box.

Removing a secondary instance removes the copy and restore jobs. It also removes the job history and the log shipping history.

Exercise 64: Adding a Database to a Log Shipping Configuration

To log ship a new database, say **Finance**, follow these steps:

1. Execute the following query at the primary instance to make sure that the **Finance** database is in full recovery model:

```
-- If the recovery_model_desc is SIMPLE
-- Change the recovery model to FULL
IF EXISTS (
SELECT
  1
FROM sys.databases
WHERE name='sales'
AND recovery_model=3
)
BEGIN
ALTER DATABASE [Sales] SET RECOVERY FULL
```

```
END
GO
SELECT
   recovery_model,recovery_model_desc
FROM sys.databases
WHERE name='finance'
```

2. Connect Object Explorer to the DPLPR instance. Expand the **Databases** node, right-click on the **Finance** database, and select **Properties**. In the **Database Properties – Finance** window, under **Select a page**, select the **Transaction Log Shipping** page:

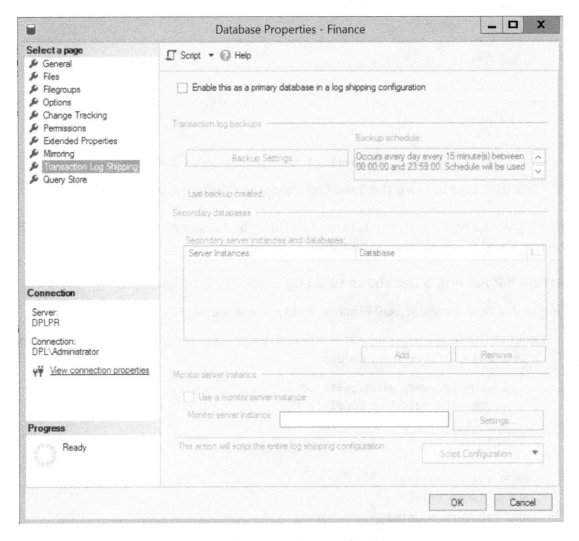

Figure 6.24: The Transaction Log Shipping page

3. Follow *steps 6 to 11* in *Exercise 61: Configuring Log Shipping* to configure the **Finance** database for log shipping. Notice that each database has its own backup and copy and restore jobs.

   When log shipping multiple databases, it's advised to store the transaction log backup for each database in its specific folder. For example, when setting up log shipping for the **Finance** database, create a new backup share as **\\DPLPR\ Logshipshare\Finance**.

   At the secondary instance, create a new folder, **C:\DPLPRTlogs\Finance**, to copy the transaction log backup of the **Finance** database from the backup share **\\DPLPR\ Logshipshare\Finance** folder.

Exercise 65: Removing a Log Shipped Database

To remove log shipping for the **Sales** database, follow these steps:

1. In SSMS, connect to the DPLPR instance in the Object Explorer. Expand **Databases**, right-click on the **Sales** database, and select **Properties**.

2. In the **Database Properties – Sales** dialog box, under **Select a page**, select the **Transaction Log Shipping** page.

   Uncheck the **Enable this as a primary database in a log shipping configuration** option.

In the confirmation dialog box, click **Yes** to continue:

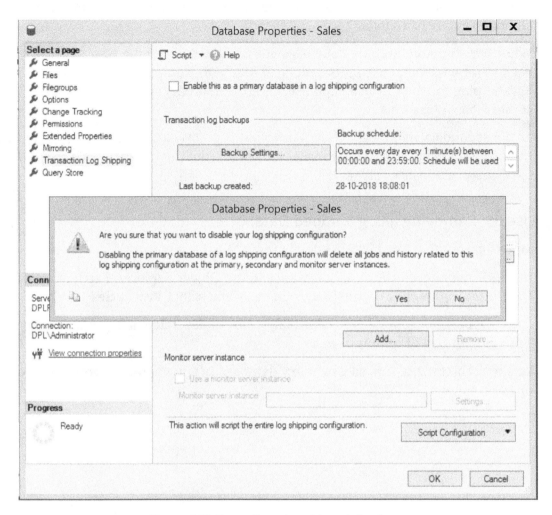

Figure 6.25: Removing a log shipped database

3. Click **OK** to remove log shipping. This will remove the SQL agent jobs and history created as part of the log shipping configuration from the primary and secondary instances.

Monitoring Log Shipping

Log shipping configuration can be monitored in the following ways:

- Configuring email alerts for the log shipping SQL agent jobs
- Using T-SQL to set up custom monitoring

Exercise 66: Configuring Email Alerts for the Log Shipping SQL Agent Jobs

We have already learned that log shipping is carried out by a set of SQL agent jobs. Therefore, the best way to monitor log shipping is to set up email alerts when any of the SQL agent jobs fails.

To configure email alerts on the SQL Server agent backup job, **LSBackup_Sales**, at the primary instance, follow these steps:

1. Configure the database mail. Follow the steps mentioned at https://docs. microsoft.com/en-us/sql/relational-databases/database-mail/configure-database-mail?view=sql-server-2017#DBWizard to configure the database email.

   Use the SMTP settings of your organization.

   > **Note**
   >
   > If you don't have access to your organization's SMTP, you can use the Gmail SMTP to configure the database email. The SMTP is **smtp.gmail.com** and the port number is **587**. This is an optional step. Do this if you have time.

2. Create the operator as follows:

   ```
   use [msdb]
   GO
   EXEC msdb.dbo.sp_add_operator @name=N'DBA',
       @enabled=1,
       @pager_days=0,
       @email_address=N'ahmad@dataplatformlabs.com'
   ```

3. In the Object Explorer (after connecting to DPLPR), expand **SQL Server Agent** | **Jobs**. Right-click on the **LSBackup_Sales** job and select **Properties**:

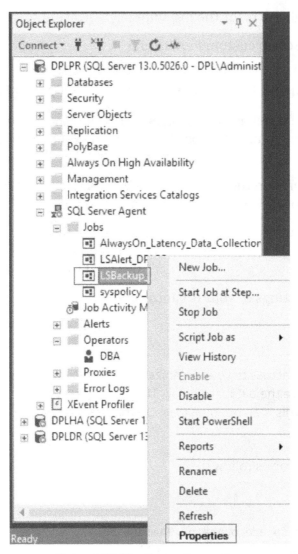

Figure 6.26: The Properties option

4. In the **Job Properties – LSBackup_Sales** window, under **Select a page**, select the **Notifications** page.

   Check **E-mail**, select **DBA** from the operator dropdown list, and select **When the job fails**:

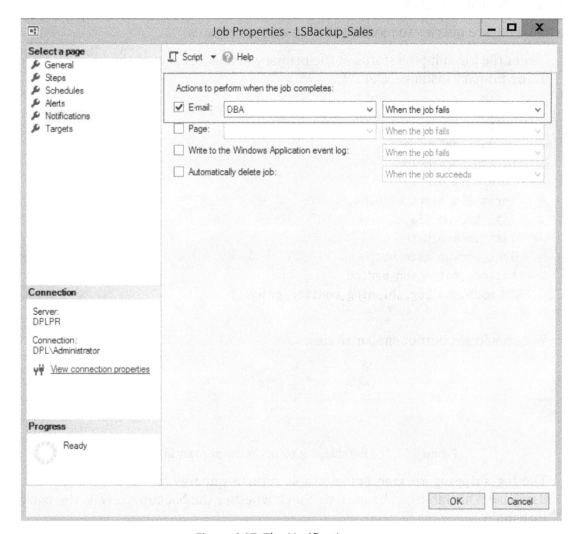

Figure 6.27: The Notifications page

Whenever the LSBackup_Sales job fails, an email notification will be sent out to all the email IDs specified in the DBA operator.

5. Click **OK** to save and close the window.

You can set up email notifications for all the log shipping SQL Server agent jobs.

Exercise 67: Using T-SQL to Set Up Custom Monitoring

A set of history tables maintain the log ship metadata and the history at the primary and secondary instances. The tables can be queried to get log shipping metadata and health status. In addition to this, a set of procedures is also provided to get the log ship metadata and health status.

The following are queries to monitor the log shipping status:

1. To get the log shipping status at the primary instance, execute the following query at the primary instance, DPLPR:

    ```
    SELECT
        primary_server,
        primary_database,
        backup_threshold,
        threshold_alert,
        threshold_alert_enabled,
        last_backup_file,
        last_backup_date,
        last_backup_date_utc,
        history_retention_period
    FROM msdb.dbo.log_shipping_monitor_primary
    GO
    ```

    You should get output similar to this:

	primary_server	primary_database	backup_threshold	threshold_alert	threshold_alert_enabled	last_backup_file	last_backup_date	last_backup_date_utc	history_retention_period
1	DPLPR	Finance	60	14420	1	C:\Logshipshare\Finance_20181028141902.trn	2018-10-28 19:49:02.517	2018-10-28 14:19:02.517	5760
2	DPLPR	Sales	30	14420	1	C:\Logshipshare\Sales_20181028141902.trn	2018-10-28 19:49:02.517	2018-10-28 14:19:02.517	5760

Figure 6.28: The log shipping status at the primary instance

The **log_shipping_monitor_primary** table returns one row for each log ship database. This table can be used to check whether the backup exceeds the backup threshold.

2. Execute the following query, which will return a row if the backup time exceeds the backup threshold:

```
SELECT
      primary_server
      ,primary_database
      ,ISNULL(threshold_alert, 14420)
      ,backup_threshold
      ,DATEDIFF(MINUTE, last_backup_date_utc, GETUTCDATE())
FROM msdb.dbo.log_shipping_monitor_primary
WHERE threshold_alert_enabled = 1
AND DATEDIFF(MINUTE, last_backup_date_utc, GETUTCDATE()) > backup_
threshold
```

The **sp_help_log_shipping_monitor_primary** procedure queries return the same information as the **log_shipping_monitor_primary** table. The query is listed here:

```
USE master
GO
EXECUTE  sp_help_log_shipping_monitor_primary
        @primary_server='DPLPR',
        @primary_database='Sales'
```

3. To get the log shipping status at the secondary instance, execute the following query at the secondary instance, DPLHA:

```
SELECT
    secondary_server,
    secondary_database,
    primary_server,
    primary_database,
    restore_threshold,
    threshold_alert,
    threshold_alert_enabled,
    last_copied_date,
    last_copied_date_utc,
    last_copied_file,
    last_restored_date,
    last_restored_date_utc,
    last_restored_latency
FROM msdb.dbo.log_shipping_monitor_secondary
```

The **log_shipping_monitor_secondary** table returns one row for each log shipped database at the secondary instance.

The output is useful for troubleshooting log shipping issues related to copy or restore jobs:

Figure 6.29: The log shipping status at the secondary instance

4. The `sp_help_log_shipping_monitor_secondary` procedure can also be used to get the log shipping status at the secondary server for a given database. Execute this query on our DPLHA secondary server:

```
USE master
GO
EXECUTE  sp_help_log_shipping_monitor_secondary
         @secondary_server='DPLHA',
         @secondary_database='Sales'
```

5. To get the log shipping job history, execute the following query, which returns the detailed steps performed by a log shipping job. This query can be executed on both primary and secondary servers:

```
SELECT
    database_name,
    message,
    log_time
FROM msdb.dbo.log_shipping_monitor_history_detail
ORDER BY log_time desc
```

You should get the following output:

	database_name	message	log_time
1	Finance	The backup operation was successful. Primary Database: 'Finance', Log Backup File: 'C:\Logshipshare\Finance_20181029020101.trn'	2018-10-29 07:31:01.907
2	Sales	The backup operation was successful. Primary Database: 'Sales', Log Backup File: 'C:\Logshipshare\Sales_20181029020101.trn'	2018-10-29 07:31:01.890
3	Sales	Deleting old log backup files. Primary Database: 'Sales'	2018-10-29 07:31:01.843
4	Finance	Deleting old log backup files. Primary Database: 'Finance'	2018-10-29 07:31:01.843
5	Finance	Backing up transaction log. Primary Database: 'Finance', Log Backup File: 'C:\Logshipshare\Finance_20181029020101.trn'	2018-10-29 07:31:01.560
6	Sales	Backing up transaction log. Primary Database: 'Sales', Log Backup File: 'C:\Logshipshare\Sales_20181029020101.trn'	2018-10-29 07:31:01.560
7	Sales	Retrieved backup settings. Primary Database: 'Sales', Backup Directory: 'C:\Logshipshare', Backup Retention Period: 4320 minute(s), Backup C...	2018-10-29 07:31:01.297
8	Finance	Retrieved backup settings. Primary Database: 'Finance', Backup Directory: 'C:\Logshipshare', Backup Retention Period: 4320 minute(s), Backu...	2018-10-29 07:31:01.297
9	NULL	Retrieving backup settings. Primary ID: '0f81218f-13f6-4563-9546-1fb8ea050da9'	2018-10-29 07:31:01.280
10	NULL	Retrieving backup settings. Primary ID: '41e0e90e-a611-4ed5-a963-d29c5513f36b'	2018-10-29 07:31:01.280

Figure 6.30: Log shipping job history

The `log_shipping_monitor_history_details` table returns the steps performed by the log shipping job. The information is helpful in troubleshooting log shipping failures.

You can also get the history details by looking at the individual job history.

6. To get log shipping errors, execute the following query, which returns the errors in the log shipping agent jobs, if any. The query can be executed on either a primary or a secondary server:

```
SELECT
  CASE agent_type
    WHEN 0 THEN 'Backup Job'
    WHEN 1 THEN 'Copy Job'
    WHEN 2 THEN 'Restore Job'
  END
  session_id,
  message,
  source,
  log_time
FROM msdb.dbo.log_shipping_monitor_error_detail order by log_time desc
```

Here's an example output from the query:

	session_id	message	source	log_time
1	Copy Job	Access to the path '\\DPLPR\Logshipshare' is den...	mscorlib	2018-10-29 08:14:02.247
2	Copy Job	Access to the path '\\dplpr\Logshipshare' is denied.	mscorlib	2018-10-29 08:14:02.217
3	Copy Job	Access to the path '\\DPLPR\Logshipshare' is den...	mscorlib	2018-10-29 08:13:02.240
4	Copy Job	Access to the path '\\dplpr\Logshipshare' is denied.	mscorlib	2018-10-29 08:13:02.207
5	Copy Job	Access to the path '\\dplpr\Logshipshare' is denied.	mscorlib	2018-10-29 08:12:02.137
6	Copy Job	Access to the path '\\DPLPR\Logshipshare' is den...	mscorlib	2018-10-29 08:12:02.137
7	Copy Job	Access to the path '\\DPLPR\Logshipshare' is den...	mscorlib	2018-10-29 08:11:02.130

Figure 6.31: Log shipping errors

Note

You may not get the same errors.

7. To get the log shipping database configuration, execute the following query, which returns the log shipping configuration details for all the log shipped databases on the primary server:

```
SELECT
    primary_database,
    backup_directory,
    backup_share,
    backup_retention_period,
    backup_job_id,
    last_backup_file,
    last_backup_date,
    backup_compression
FROM msdb.dbo.log_shipping_primary_databases
```

Here's the output:

	primary_database	backup_directory	backup_share	backup_retention_period	backup_job_id	last_backup_file	last_backup_date	backup_compression
1	Finance	C:\Logshipshare	\\dplpr\Logshipshare	4320	4DBA996B-FF30-4B10-9331-6402B290B35E	C:\Logshipshare\Finance_20181029022001.trn	2018-10-29 07:50:02.003	1
2	Sales	C:\Logshipshare	\\DPLPR\Logshipshare	4320	5C0CE5B9-86AF-4369-BAEC-9ED22E1F145F	C:\Logshipshare\Sales_20181029022001.trn	2018-10-29 07:50:01.957	1

Figure 6.32: Log shipping database configuration

This information can also be obtained by running the following stored procedure on the primary server:

```
USE master
GO
EXECUTE sp_help_log_shipping_primary_database @database='Sales'
```

8. To get the log shipping report, we can use the **sp_help_log_shipping_monitor** procedure, which returns the status and log shipping health status. The procedure is also used in the transaction log shipping standard server report.

To open the report, in the Object Explorer, right-click on DPLPR. From the context menu, select **Reports | Standard Reports | Transaction Log Shipping Status**:

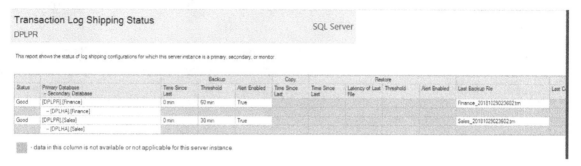

Figure 6.33: Report output from DPLPR

Here's the report output from the secondary server, DPLHA:

Figure 6.34: Report output from DPLHA

> **Note**
>
> To get details on the log shipping system tables, refer to https://docs.microsoft.com/en-us/sql/relational-databases/system-tables/log-shipping-tables-transact-sql?view=sql-server-2017.

Exercise 68: Changing the Database State at the Secondary

Earlier in this lesson, we learned that the secondary database can be in one of two states: No Recovery mode and Standby mode. In this exercise, we will see how to change the secondary database state.

1. Standby mode allows users to read from the secondary database in between two restore jobs. We configured log shipping in No Recovery mode. To change it to Standby mode, execute the following query:

```
-- To be run at the secondary - DPLHA
-- Get the restore mode
-- 0 = NoRecovery, 1=Standby
Use master
GO
SELECT
    secondary_database,
    restore_mode,
    disconnect_users,
    last_restored_file
FROM msdb.dbo.log_shipping_secondary_databases
GO
-- Modify the restore mode
-- @restore_mode = 1 = Standby
-- @disconnect_users = 1 = will disconnect users during a restore
operation
EXEC sp_change_log_shipping_secondary_database
  @secondary_database = 'Sales',
  @restore_mode = 1,
  @disconnect_users = 1
GO
-- Get the restore mode
SELECT
    secondary_database,
    restore_mode,
    disconnect_users,
    last_restored_file
FROM msdb.dbo.log_shipping_secondary_databases
```

The **sp_change_log_shipping_secondary_database** procedure is used to change the secondary database settings.

> **Note**
>
> To know more about the **sp_change_log_shipping_secondary_database** procedure, refer to https://docs.microsoft.com/en-us/sql/relational-databases/system-stored-procedures/sp-change-log-shipping-secondary-database-transact-sql?view=sql-server-2017.

You should get the following output:

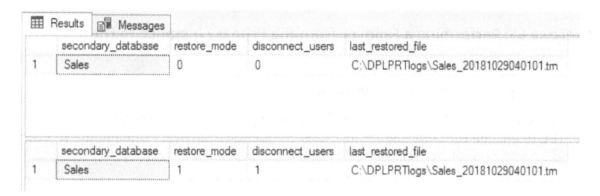

	secondary_database	restore_mode	disconnect_users	last_restored_file
1	Sales	0	0	C:\DPLPRTlogs\Sales_20181029040101.tm

	secondary_database	restore_mode	disconnect_users	last_restored_file
1	Sales	1	1	C:\DPLPRTlogs\Sales_20181029040101.tm

Figure 6.35: Restore mode changed to Standby – query output

2. Restore mode is changed to Standby. However, the database state doesn't change instantly. The configuration change will be applied after the next restore job runs successfully. Wait for the restore job at the DPLHA SQL instance to complete and then refresh the Object Explorer:

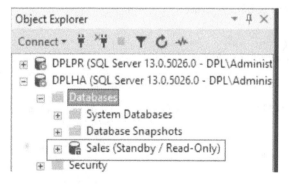

Figure 6.36: Restore mode changed to Standby – in the GUI

The restore job is scheduled to be run every one minute, and therefore you don't have to wait long for the change to be effective. However, in a real-world scenario, you have to manually run the restore job to restore the latest transaction log backup and modify the database state to Standby.

3. Revert to the No Recovery database state by executing the following query:

```
USE master
GO
EXEC sp_change_log_shipping_secondary_database
  @secondary_database = 'Sales',
  @restore_mode = 0,
  @disconnect_users = 0
GO
```

Exercise 69: Performing a Failover from the Primary Instance to the Secondary Instance

Log shipping doesn't provide automatic failover. A failover has to be done manually.

Before we proceed to failover, execute the following query at the secondary instance, DPLHA, to change the copy and restore jobs' frequency from every one minute to every 15 minutes. This will help to better understand the failover process:

```
USE msdb;

GO

DECLARE @scheduleid int;

SELECT

@scheduleid=schedule_id

FROM sysjobs j join sysjobschedules s ON j.job_id=s.job_id

WHERE j.name='LSRestore_DPLPR_Sales'


EXEC msdb.dbo.sp_update_schedule

@schedule_id=@scheduleid,

@freq_subday_interval=15

GO

DECLARE @scheduleid int;

SELECT

@scheduleid=schedule_id
```

```
FROM sysjobs j join sysjobschedules s ON j.job_id=s.job_id
WHERE j.name='LSCopy_DPLPR_Sales'


EXEC msdb.dbo.sp_update_schedule
@schedule_id=@scheduleid,
@freq_subday_interval=15
GO
```

To fail over from the primary instance, DPLPR, to the secondary instance, DPLHA, follow these steps:

1. To simulate a failure at DPLPR, open a new command line or a PowerShell console and execute the following command. This will stop the SQL Server services at DPLPR:

    ```
    net stop mssqlserver
    ```

2. Copy the leftover backup files from the backup share to the local folder at the secondary instance, DPLHA.

    To do this, open SSMS and connect to the DPLHA SQL instance. Execute the following query to manually start the copy job at the secondary instance:

    ```
    EXECUTE msdb.dbo.sp_start_job @job_name='LSCopy_DPLPR_Sales'
    ```

    > **Note**
    >
    > There may not be any leftover backup files; however, this step is important to make sure that all of the backup files are copied.

    You can either wait for the copy job to run at the scheduled time and copy the leftover files or start the copy job manually. Wait for the copy job to complete. You can monitor the copy job progress in **Job Activity Monitor** under the **SQL Server Agent** node in the Object Explorer.

3. Restore the leftover transaction logs on the secondary instance. To do this, connect to the DPLHA SQL instance in SSMS and execute the following query:

    ```
    EXECUTE msdb.dbo.sp_start_job @job_name='LSRestore_DPLPR_Sales'
    ```

    You can monitor the restore job progress in **Job Activity Monitor** under the **SQL Server Agent** node in the Object Explorer.

4. To verify that all the copied files have been restored successfully, execute the following query at the DPLHA SQL instance:

```
SELECT
    sd.secondary_database,
    s.last_copied_file,
    sd.last_restored_file
FROM msdb.dbo.log_shipping_secondary_databases sd
JOIN  msdb.dbo.log_shipping_secondary s ON sd.secondary_id=s.secondary_id
WHERE primary_server='DPLPR' AND primary_database='Sales'
```

The output will be as follows:

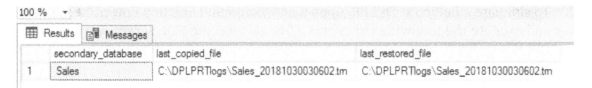

Figure 6.37: Verifying all copied files have been restored successfully

Observe that the **last_copied_file** and **last_restored_file** values are the same. This means that all the copied files have been restored successfully.

> **Note**
>
> If the primary database is accessible, it's advised to take a tail log backup with the **NORecovery** option. This changes the primary database state to restoring, which in turn allows transaction log backups to be restored from the new primary database.
>
> Moreover, restoring the tail log backup of the primary database to the secondary database brings the two databases completely in sync.

5. The secondary database is now in sync with the primary database; however, it's still in the restoring state and is not accessible to users.

   The next step is to bring the secondary database online and make it accessible to the user. To do this, open a new query window in SSMS, connect to the DPLHA SQL instance, and execute the following query:

```
USE master
GO
RESTORE DATABASE [Sales] WITH RECOVERY
```

The following screenshot shows the secondary database state before running the query:

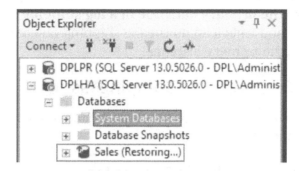

Figure 6.38: The secondary database state before running the query

The following screenshot shows the secondary database state after running the query:

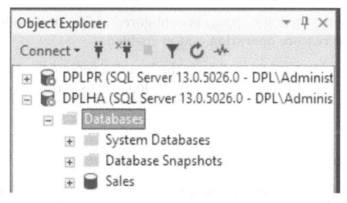

Figure 6.39: The secondary database state after running the query

The database is now available to users.

This completes the failover process. As a post-failover task, you can do the following:

- Verify that all the server logins at the primary instance do also exist at the secondary instance. If not, then the applications when moved to the secondary database will not be able to connect to the secondary database.

- Disable the log shipping copy, restore, and alert jobs at the secondary.

Log shipping doesn't copy the server logins from the primary to the secondary instance. The logins at the primary should therefore have to be created explicitly at the secondary.

To get to the original state, which is DPLPR as the primary instance, start the SQL Server services at the primary. When the instance is up, right-click on the **Sales** database and select **Properties**. Select the **Transaction Log Shipping** page and uncheck **Enable this database as the primary database in a log shipping configuration**. This will disable the log shipping and will clean up the log shipping objects. Reconfigure the log shipping with DPLPR as the primary instance.

Troubleshooting Common Log Shipping Issues

In this section, we'll look at few of the common problems that can occur in a log shipping environment and their solutions.

Exercise 70: Problem 1 – Middle of a Restore Error

Consider the following error:

```
Msg 927, Level 14, State 6, Line 9

Database 'Sales' cannot be opened. It is in the middle of a restore.
```

This issue occurs when the log shipping is configured in Standby mode with the **Disconnect users at restore operation** option enabled.

When a user transaction tries to read from the Standby secondary database, and at that time the restore job is restoring the transaction log, the user transaction terminates with this error.

Setup

To simulate the error, follow these steps:

1. Execute the following query to change the database state of the **Sales** database at the secondary DPLHA, from NoRecovery to Standby mode. The query is the same as mentioned in the *Changing the Database State at the Secondary* section:

```
-- To be run at the secondary - DPLHA
-- Get the restore mode
-- 0 = NoRecovery, 1=Standby
Use master
GO
SELECT
    secondary_database,
    restore_mode,
    disconnect_users,
    last_restored_file
FROM msdb.dbo.log_shipping_secondary_databases
GO
```

```
-- Modify the restore mode
-- @restore_mode = 1 = Standby
-- @disconnect_users = 1 = will disconnect users during a restore
operation
EXEC sp_change_log_shipping_secondary_database
  @secondary_database = 'Sales',
  @restore_mode = 1,
  @disconnect_users = 1
GO
-- Get the restore mode
SELECT
    secondary_database,
    restore_mode,
    disconnect_users,
    last_restored_file
FROM msdb.dbo.log_shipping_secondary_databases
```

You should get the following output:

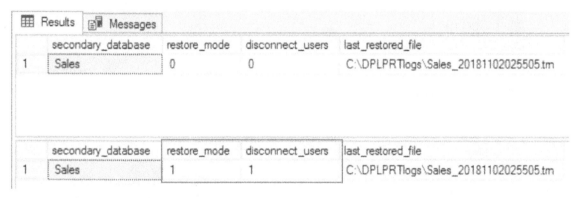

Figure 6.40: Changing the database state of the Sales database – query output

Wait for the restore job to run and the **Sales** database state should change to the **Standby** state:

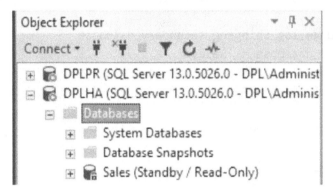

Figure 6.41: Changing the database state of the Sales database - GUI

2. Execute the following query to read data from the **Sales** database at the secondary instance, DPLHA:

```
WHILE(1=1)
BEGIN
SELECT COUNT(*) FROM Sales.Sales.SalesOrderDetail
WAITFOR DELAY '00:00:10'
END
```

This code will query the **SalesOrderDetail** table in the **Sales** database every 10 seconds. You should get the following output:

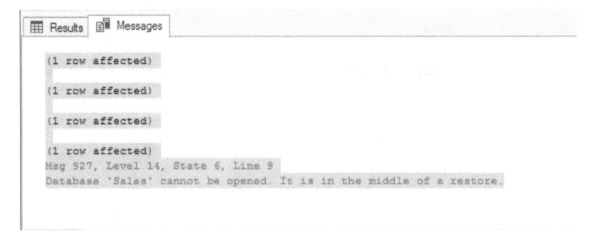

Figure 6.42: The middle-of-a-restore error

When the error occurs, the user connection is disconnected and the error is returned to the application. There is no effect on the log shipping.

Solution

This isn't exactly a problem; it's a behavior. A database is unavailable to users when it's being restored.

A workaround for this is to change the restore schedule to occur every 30 minutes or one hour. The application should connect to the standby database based on the restore job schedule. Another workaround is to add retry logic in the application. A transaction log restore usually doesn't take long to complete. The retry logic will try to read, say, every five minutes, if the error occurs during the read operation.

Exercise 71: Problem 2 – Directory Lookup for File Failed

Consider the following error:

```
*** Error: Directory lookup for the file "C:\SalesDataFile\Sales_Data.ndf"
failed with the operating system error 2(The system cannot find the file
specified.).

File 'Sales_Data' cannot be restored to 'C:\SalesDataFile\Sales_Data.ndf'.
Use WITH MOVE to identify a valid location for the file.
```

The problem occurs when a new data or log file is added to the primary database. The issue is not quite understandable from the error description; however, the **Use WITH MOVE to identify a valid location for the file** string gives an indication that a new file has been added to the primary database.

The new file location is not present at the secondary. For example, let's say that a new data file is added to the **Sales** database at the **C:\SalesDataFile** folder. However, the folder doesn't exist on the secondary. In this case, the restore job fails with this error.

Setup

To simulate the problem, follow these steps:

1. Connect to the DPLPR VM and create a new folder, **SalesDataFile**, in the **C** drive.

2. Execute the following query at the DPLPR instance to add a new data file in the **Sales** database:

```
USE [master]
GO
ALTER DATABASE [Sales] ADD FILE
(
  NAME = N'Sales_Data',
  FILENAME = N'C:\SalesDataFile\Sales_Data.ndf' ,
```

```
    SIZE = 8192KB ,
    FILEGROWTH = 65536KB
) TO FILEGROUP [PRIMARY]
GO
```

This query will add a new data file, **Sales_Data.ndf**, at the location **C:\ SalesDataFile**.

3. Connect to DPLHA in the Object Explorer and view the restore job history:

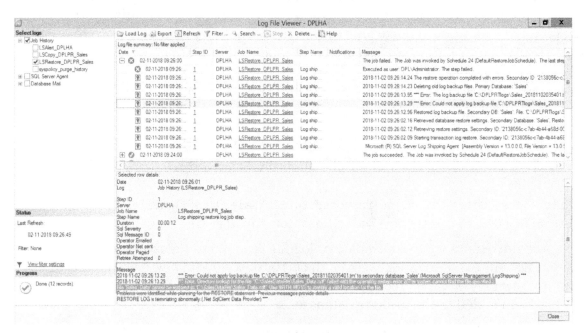

Figure 6.43: The restore job history

The restore job fails with the **Directory lookup for the file…** error mentioned earlier.

Solution

There are two possible workarounds for the problem:

- Create the **SalesDataFile** folder at the secondary instance, DPLHA.

- Restore the transaction log manually using the **WITH MOVE** option, as specified in the error.

The second solution is the only option if the drive is not available at the secondary. Let's say that there is no **C** drive at the secondary. In that case, the file needs to be created at a different location and the transaction log is to be restored using the **WITH MOVE** option.

To fix the problem using the second solution, follow these steps:

1. Create a folder, **DPLHASales**, in the **C** drive.

2. Execute the following query to restore the transaction log using the **WITH MOVE** option:

    ```
    RESTORE LOG [Sales] FROM
    DISK = N'C:\DPLPRTlogs\Sales_20181102035401.trn'
    WITH FILE = 1,
    STANDBY = N'C:\DPLPRTlogs\rollback_undo_sales.bak',
    MOVE N'Sales_Data' TO N'C:\DPLHASales\Sales_Data.ndf'
    ```

    We changed the restore state of the secondary database to Standby in the previous problem. Therefore, we need to specify a standby file and restore the transaction log in Standby mode.

3. If the restore state of the secondary database is No Recovery, execute the following query:

    ```
    RESTORE LOG [Sales] FROM
    DISK = N'C:\DPLPRTlogs\Sales_20181102035401.trn'
    WITH FILE = 1,
    MOVE N'Sales_Data' TO N'C:\DPLHASales\Sales_Data.ndf',NORECOVERY
    ```

    The restore job, in the next run, will now restore all of the available log backups after the log backup that we restored manually.

> **Note**
>
> **Additional reading**: Refer to https://blogs.msdn.microsoft.com/sqlalwayson/2012/01/09/converting-a-logshipping-configuration-to-availability-group/ to convert a log shipping configuration to an AlwaysOn availability group.

Comparing AlwaysOn, Replication, and Log Shipping

The following table compares the three HA and DR solutions:

Feature	AlwaysOn AG	Transactional replication	Log shipping
Failover	Manual and Automatic	Manual. There is no database-level failover. The application endpoint is changed to the subscriber server.	Manual
Database-level failover	Yes	No	No
Fail over more than one database	Yes. All databases in an availability group fail over at once.	No	No
Readable secondary	Yes. Report-specific indexes or summary tables should be created on the primary replica. The reads on the synchronous secondary are not real-time; however, data replication in AlwaysOn is faster than transactional replication.	Yes. Report-specific indexes or summary tables can be created at the subscriber database.	Yes, Standby mode. The log backups can't be restored during Standby mode. Report-specific indexes or summary tables should be created on the primary replica.
High availability	Yes	Yes	No
Disaster recovery	Yes	Yes	Yes
Version supported	SQL Server 2012 + Enterprise SQL Server 2016 Standard supports the basic availability group. The secondary replica should have the same or a higher SQL Server version.	SQL Server 2000 + Standard and Enterprise. The subscriber can have either a lower or higher SQL Server version.	SQL Server 2000+ Standard and Enterprise. The secondary should have the same or a lower SQL Server version.
Data synchronization	TCP endpoint	Log reader/distributor agent	Transaction log backup and restore
Data synchronization mode	Synchronous and asynchronous	Asynchronous	Asynchronous
Configurability	Easy	Easy	Easy
Manageability	Easy	Easy	More complex than the other two as there is no GUI for monitoring and manageability is available.

Figure 6.44: Comparison table

Feature	AlwaysOn AG	Transactional replication	Log shipping
What is synced?	Schema and data with no option to choose what objects or data are to be synced.	Schema and data with option to choose which objects and data are to be replicated.	Schema and data with no option to choose what objects or data are to be synced.
Database maintenance	Index maintenance is run at primary. Backups can be run on secondary replicas. Check DB is to be run on the primary and any secondary which runs database backups.	Index rebuild is replicated. However, it may take a long time to replicate a large index rebuild. Therefore, it's suggested to rebuild indexes at both publisher and subscriber. Moreover, the subscriber may have additional indexes to support reporting. The publisher and the subscriber databases should be backed up separately. Check DB should be run at the publisher and the subscriber	Maintenance isn't supported at the secondary database.
Security	Database users can only be created at the primary replica.	Database users can be created at the subscriber database independent of the publisher database.	Database users can only be created at the primary database.

Figure 6.45: Comparison table - continued

Activity 7: Adding a New Data File to a Log Shipped Database

The **Sales** database is growing and the business has decided to add a new data file to the **Sales** database on a new hard drive. You need to add the new data file and make sure that the log shipping is not affected by this change.

To do this, follow these steps:

1. Create a new folder named **NewDataFile** in the **C** drive on both the primary and secondary instances.

2. Add the new data file to the **Sales** database on the primary instance and verify that it is created on the secondary instance as well.

> **Note**
>
> The solution for this activity can be found on page 448.

Activity 8: Troubleshooting a Problem – Could Not Find a Log Backup File that Could be Applied to Secondary Database 'Sales'

Consider the following error:

```
*** Error: Could not find a log backup file that could be applied to secondary
database 'Sales'.(Microsoft.SqlServer.Management.LogShipping) ***

*** Error: The log in this backup set begins at LSN 1136000002108000001,
which is too recent to apply to the database. An earlier log backup that
includes LSN 1078000000519200001 can be restored.
```

This error states that the log backup that is being restored as part of the log shipping configuration isn't the correct log backup based on the LSN values. The database expects the backup set with LSN **1078000000519200001**; however, the backup being restored has LSN **1136000002108000001**.

The error is mostly a result of an ad hoc transaction log backup, other than the one being done by the log shipping backup job.

Setup

To simulate the problem, follow these steps:

1. Configure log shipping as explained in *Exercise 61: Configuring Log Shipping*. Set the log shipping job schedule as follows:

    Backup job occurs every two minutes.

    Copy job occurs every two minutes.

    Restore job occurs every four minutes.

2. Once the log shipping is up and running, execute the following query at the DPLPR SQL instance to initiate an ad hoc transaction log backup:

    ```
    BACKUP LOG [Sales] TO DISK='C:\Logshipshare\Sales_adhoc_log_backup.trn'
    ```

Wait for the next restore job to run. It'll fail.

To solve this error, follow these steps:

1. Check the restore job history to find out the error details.

2. Check the **msdb** database to find out the ad hoc log database backup name.

3. Restore the missing log file on the secondary database with the **NORECOVERY** mode to fix the problem.

> **Note**
>
> The solution for this activity can be found on page 449.

Summary

In this lesson, we talked about log shipping, its pros and cons, and how to configure it as a DR solution. We learned that `sqllogship.exe`, an independent executable, is responsible for carrying out the log shipping tasks, performing transaction log backups, copying the log backup to the shared folder, and restoring the transaction log backup to the secondary server.

Each of the log ship tasks are scheduled using a SQL Server agent jobs. Log shipping is one of the old DR solutions which can also be used when migrating from one SQL Server instance to another.

This brings us to the end of this book. You can visit https://azure.microsoft.com/en-in/solutions/architecture/ to explore the different application architectures and better understand how HA and DR work with different kinds of applications.

Appendix

About

This section is included to assist the students to perform the activities in the book.
It includes detailed steps that are to be performed by the students to achieve the objectives of
the activities.

Lesson 1: Getting Started with SQL Server HA and DR

Activity 1: Troubleshooting Snapshot Replication

Solution:

To modify the publication, follow these steps:

1. Connect to the **Publisher** instance and expand **Replication | Local Publication**. Select the **WWI-Snapshot** publication and select **Properties**:

Figure 1.84: The Properties option

2. In the **Publisher Properties** window, select the pre-snapshot and post-snapshot scripts, as shown in the following screenshot:

Figure 1.85: The pre-snapshot and post-snapshot scripts

Click **OK** to continue and save the new settings. You will be asked to generate a new snapshot after saving the modifications:

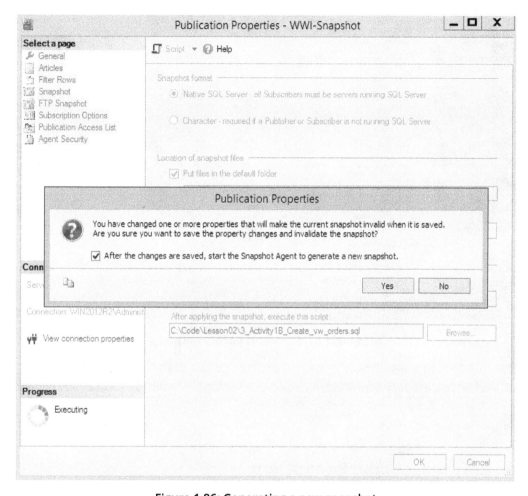

Figure 1.86: Generating a new snapshot

3. Leave the checkbox checked and click on **Yes**.

    A new snapshot will be generated. You can verify this by either checking the snapshot folder or viewing the snapshot agent history.

4. Now, apply the new snapshot and see if this fixes the issue. You can apply the snapshot (run the distribution agent) by using any one of the methods that we have discussed earlier.

Once the distribution agent runs successfully, observe the agent history output:

Figure 1.87: The agent history output

The distribution agent now runs the pre-snapshot script to drop the view. It then applies the snapshot and executes the post-snapshot script to create the view.

This completes the activity.

Lesson 2: Transactional Replication

Activity 2: Configuring Transactional Replication

Solution:

1. Navigate to **C:\Code\Lesson02\Activity** and open **RemoveReplication.sql** in SQL Server Management Studio. Modify the parameter values, as instructed in the script, and execute the script.

   This will remove the existing publication and subscription for the **AdventureWorks** database.

   This step is only to be executed if there is an existing publication and subscription for the **AdventureWorks** database.

2. Execute the following query to drop and create the **AdventureWorks** database at the subscriber:

```
DROP DATABASE AdventureWorks
GO
CREATE DATABASE AdventureWorks
```

3. Execute the **C:\Code\Lesson02\Activity\1_CreatePublication.sql** query in **SQLCMD** mode to create the **Pub-AdventureWorks** publication and add articles to the publication.

   You'll have to modify the publisher and subscriber parameter values as per your environment.

4. Execute the **C:\Code\Lesson02\Activity\2_CreateSubscription.sql** query in **SQLCMD** mode to create the **Pub-AdventureWorks** subscription.

   You'll have to modify the publisher and subscriber parameter values as per your environment.

5. Execute the **C:\Code\Lesson02\Activity\3_VerifyReplication.sql** query to verify that the replication has been configured successfully.

Lesson 3: Monitoring Transactional Replication

Activity 3: Configuring an Agent Failure Error

Solution:

1. Open the replication monitor and select the publication you wish to set the alert for. Select the **Warnings** tab in the right-hand pane:

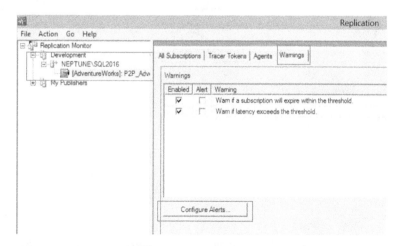

Figure 3.69: The Warnings tab

2. In the **Warnings** tab, click on the **Configure Alerts** button. In the **Configure Replication Alerts** dialog box, select the **Replication: agent failure** replication alert and click on the **Configure** button:

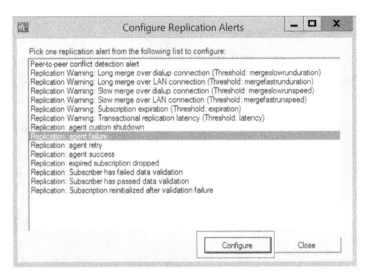

Figure 3.70: The Configure Replication Alerts dialog box

3. In the **Replication: agent failure alert properties** window, change the database name to `AdventureWorks` and check the **Enable** checkbox besides the alert name:

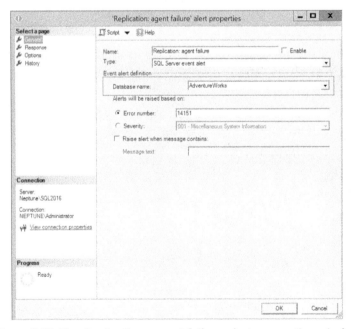

Figure 3.71: The Replication: agent failure alert properties window

4. Under **Select a page**, select the **Response** page. In the **Response** page, check **Notify operators** and then check the **E-mail** checkbox for the **Alerts** operator:

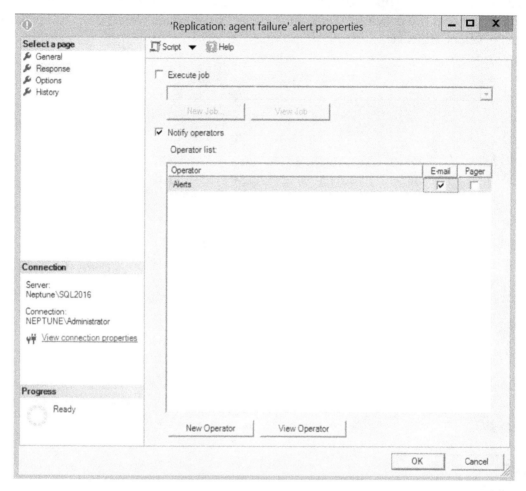

Figure 3.72: The Response page

Click on **OK** to create the alert.

5. Open SSMS, if it's not already open. Connect to the publisher SQL2016. Expand **SQL Server Agent | Alerts**. Locate and double-click on **Replication: agent failure** to open the alert properties. Observe that the alert has the same settings as configured in the previous steps. In the **alert properties** dialog box, under **Select a page**, select **History**:

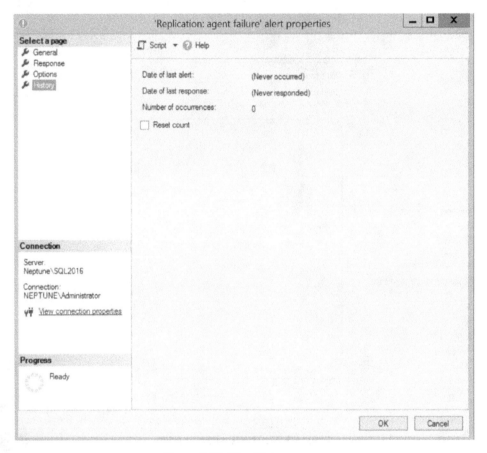

Figure 3.73: The History page

Observe that the alert history tells us how many times the alert has occurred. You can also change the alert properties from this dialog box.

Activity 4: Troubleshooting Transactional Replication

Solution:

1. Execute the following query at the publisher server to find out the error:

```
SELECT
    time,
    error_text,
```

```
   xact_seqno
FROM distribution.dbo.MSrepl_errors
ORDER BY [time] DESC
```

You should get the following error in the **error_text** column:

```
Violation of PRIMARY KEY constraint 'PK_Currency_CurrencyCode'. Cannot
insert duplicate key in object 'Sales.Currency'. The duplicate key value
is (XYZ).
```

2. As per the error, the transaction can't be applied at the subscriber database because it violates the primary key constraint. Execute the following query at the subscriber database to find out the primary key column for the **Sales.Currency** table:

```
SELECT  si.name AS PrimaryKey,
        OBJECT_NAME(sic.OBJECT_ID) AS TableName,
        COL_NAME(sic.OBJECT_ID,sic.column_id) AS ColumnName
FROM    sys.indexes AS si INNER JOIN
        sys.index_columns AS sic ON  si.OBJECT_ID = sic.OBJECT_ID
                            AND si.index_id = sic.index_id
WHERE   si.is_primary_key = 1
AND si.object_id = object_id('Sales.Currency')
```

You should get the following output:

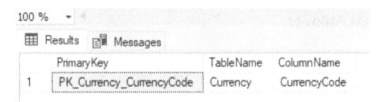

Figure 3.74: The primary key column

The primary key column is **CurrencyCode**.

3. Execute the following query to check if the currency code **XYZ** already exists at the subscriber database:

```
SELECT
   *
FROM Sales.Currency
WHERE currencycode='XYZ'
ORDER BY ModifiedDate DESC
```

You should get the following output:

	CurrencyCode	Name	ModifiedDate
1	XYZ	Test Currency 1	2018-12-20 09:52:06.727

Figure 3.75: Checking if the currency code exists at the subscriber

The currency code **XYZ** does exist at the subscriber database.

4. To fix the replication, execute the `C:\Code\Lesson03\Activity\Fix.sql` query at the subscriber. The script deletes the currency code **XYZ** at the subscriber. This allows the replication command to succeed and fixes the replication.

> **Note**
>
> You can also skip this error, as mentioned in *Exercise 24: Problem 4 – Row Not Found at the Subscriber*.

Lesson 5: Managing AlwaysOn Availability Groups

Activity 5: Manual Failover

Solution:

1. Execute the following query to failover from DPLPR to DPLHA:

   ```
   :Connect DPLHA
   ALTER AVAILABILITY GROUP [DPLAG] FAILOVER;
   ```

2. Execute the following query on DPLHA to verify that the failover is complete:

   ```
   SELECT
       ag.name AS AvailabilityGroup,
       ar.replica_server_name AS ReplicaName,
       ars.role_desc AS Role,
       ars.operational_state_desc
   FROM
   sys.availability_groups ag join sys.availability_replicas ar
   on ag.group_id=ar.group_id
   ```

```
join sys.dm_hadr_availability_replica_states ars
on ar.replica_id=ars.replica_id
```

The **Role** column for the DPLHA replica should state **Primary**.

3. To fall back to DPLPR, execute the following query:

```
:Connect DPLPR
ALTER AVAILABILITY GROUP [DPLAG] FAILOVER;
```

To verify the failover, execute the query from *step* 2 once again. The **Role** column for the DPLPR replica should state **Primary**.

Activity 6: Adding a New Database to an Existing Availability Group

Solution:

1. Execute the following query at DPLPR to add the **Customer** database to the DPLAG availability group:

```
USE Master;
ALTER AVAILABILITY GROUP DPLAG ADD DATABASE [Customer];
GO
```

2. Execute the following query to take a full backup of the **Customer** database at DPLPR:

```
BACKUP DATABASE Customer TO DISK='C:\Code\Customer_FullBackup.bak' WITH
INIT, STATS=10, COMPRESSION
```

3. Execute the following query at DPLHA and DPLDR to restore the full backup of the **Customer** database:

```
USE [master]
RESTORE DATABASE [Customer] FROM  DISK = N'C:\Code\Customer_Fullbackup.
bak' WITH  FILE = 1,  NOUNLOAD,  STATS = 5, NORECOVERY
```

4. Execute the following query to take a log backup of the **Customer** database at DPLPR:

```
BACKUP LOG Customer TO DISK='C:\Code\Customer_Logbackup.trn' WITH
COMPRESSION, INIT, STATS=10
```

5. Execute the following query to restore the log backup at DPLHA and DPLDR:

```
RESTORE LOG Customer FROM DISK='C:\Code\Customer_LogBackup.trn' WITH
NORECOVERY, STATS=10
```

6. Execute the following query at DPLHA and DPLDR to join the **Customer** database to the DPLAG availability group:

```
USE Master;
ALTER DATABASE Customer SET HADR AVAILABILITY GROUP = DPLAG;
```

You can use the AlwaysOn dashboard to verify that the database was successfully added to the availability group.

You can also use SSMS Object Explorer to add the database to the availability group. However, you'd have to perform the backup and restore manually.

Lesson 6: Configuring and Managing Log Shipping

Activity 7: Adding a New Data File to a Log Shipped Database

Solution:

1. Create a new folder named **NewDataFile** in the **C** drive on the primary instance, DPLPR, and the secondary instance, DPLHA.

2. Execute the following query at the primary instance, DPLPR, to add the new data file to the **Sales** database:

```
USE [master]
GO
ALTER DATABASE [Sales] ADD FILE
(
  NAME = N'SalesData1',
  FILENAME = N'C:\NewDataFile\SalesData1.ndf' ,
  SIZE = 8192KB ,
  FILEGROWTH = 65536KB
) TO FILEGROUP [PRIMARY]
GO
```

To verify that the file has been created, run the following query on DPLPR:

```
use [Sales]
GO
SELECT
  Name,physical_name
FROM sys.database_files
```

You should get the following output:

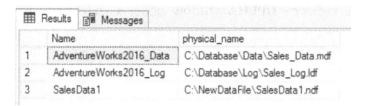

Figure 6.46: Verifying that the file has been created

Activity 8: Troubleshooting a Problem – Could Not Find a Log Backup File that Could be Applied to Secondary Database 'Sales'

Solution:

Finding the Error Details

1. Check the restore job history to find out what the error is. Connect to the DPLHA SQL instance in SSMS. In the Object Explorer, expand **SQL Server Agent | Job**. Right-click on the **LSRestore_Sales** job and select **View History** from the context menu:

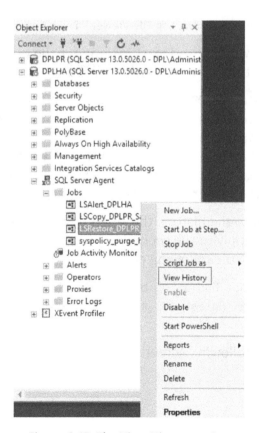

Figure 6.47: The View History option

2. In the **Log File Viewer – DPLHA** window, observe that the restore job is failing:

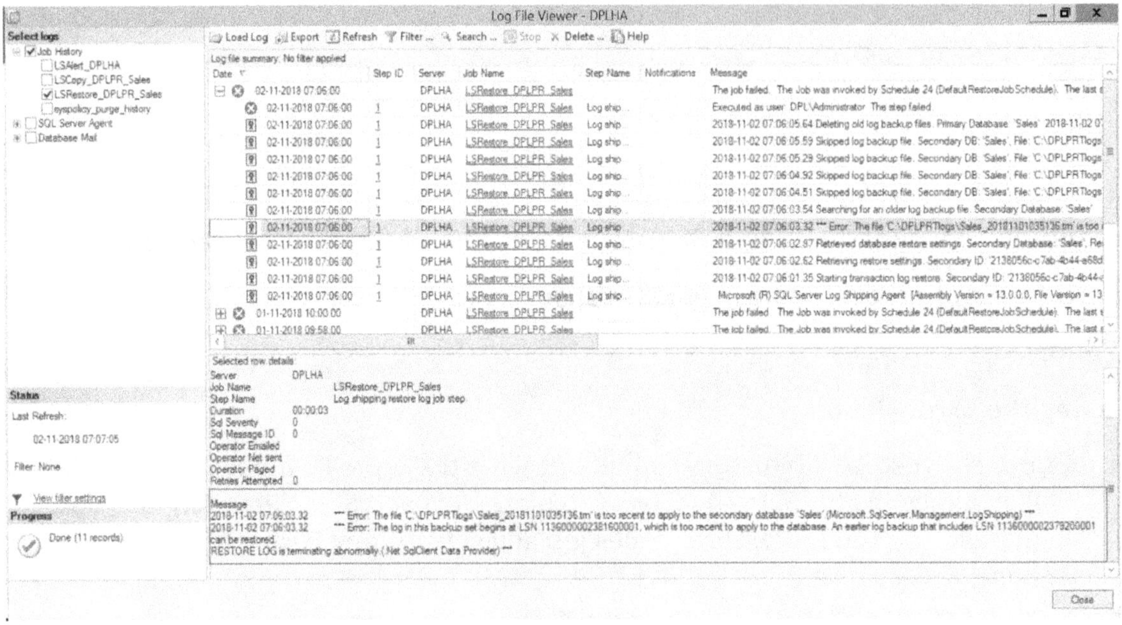

Figure 6.48: The Log File Viewer – DPLHA window

3. Expand a row in the window and start looking for the errors from the bottom row. Observe that the restore job failed with the following error:

```
*** Error: The file 'C:\DPLPRTlogs\Sales_20181101035136.trn' is too
recent to apply to the secondary database 'Sales'.(Microsoft.SqlServer.
Management.LogShipping) ***
The log in this backup set begins at LSN 1136000002381600001, which is too
recent to apply to the database. An earlier log backup that includes LSN
1136000002379200001 can be restored.
```

If you look further into the history, the restore operation starts looking for an older file that it can apply to the secondary database. However, it doesn't find any and it terminates with the following error:

```
*** Error: Could not find a log backup file that could be applied to
secondary database 'Sales'.(Microsoft.SqlServer.Management.LogShipping)
***
```

This is shown in the following screenshot:

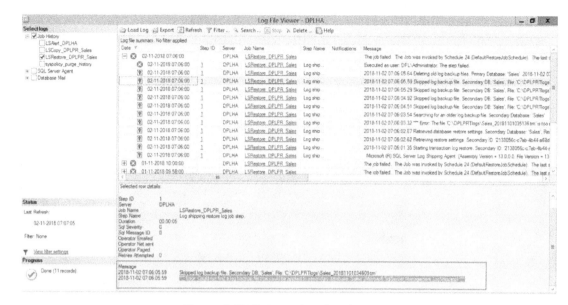

Figure 6.49: Output showing the error

Resolution

This is because of the ad hoc backup taken at *step 2* in the problem setup. Every transaction log backup contains the first and last LSN as header information. SQL Server maintains a history of all the database backups that are performed on an instance (native or using third-party tools) in the **msdb** database. We know the LSN of the log file that's missing; let's query the backup metadata tables in **msdb** and find out the missing log file:

1. Execute the following query at the DPLPR instance against the **msdb** database:

```
SELECT
    bs.database_name,
    bs.backup_start_date,
    bs.type,
    bs.first_lsn,
    bs.last_lsn,
    bmf.physical_device_name

FROM msdb.dbo.backupset bs
JOIN msdb.dbo.backupmediafamily bmf
ON bs.media_set_id = bmf.media_set_id
WHERE database_name='Sales'
AND type='L'
AND first_lsn>=1136000002379200001
ORDER BY backup_start_date
```

This query looks into the **backupset** and **backupmediaset** system tables in the **msdb** database to fetch all the log files for the **Sales** database that have LSN greater than or equal to **1136000002379200001**.

Here's the output from the query:

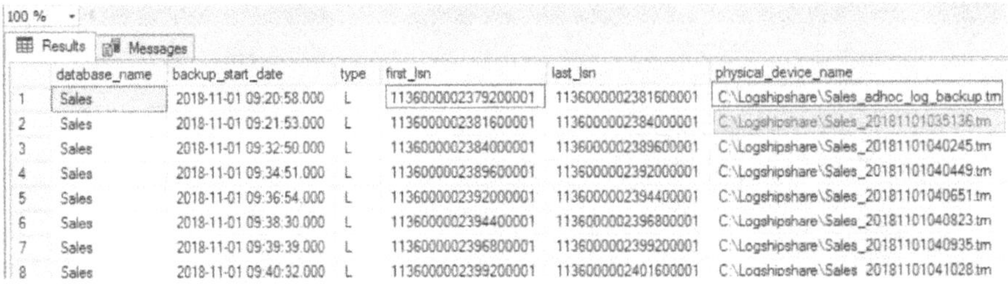

	database_name	backup_start_date	type	first_lsn	last_lsn	physical_device_name
1	Sales	2018-11-01 09:20:58.000	L	1136000002379200001	1136000002381600001	C:\Logshipshare\Sales_adhoc_log_backup.trn
2	Sales	2018-11-01 09:21:53.000	L	1136000002381600001	1136000002384000001	C:\Logshipshare\Sales_20181101035136.trn
3	Sales	2018-11-01 09:32:50.000	L	1136000002384000001	1136000002389600001	C:\Logshipshare\Sales_20181101040245.trn
4	Sales	2018-11-01 09:34:51.000	L	1136000002389600001	1136000002392000001	C:\Logshipshare\Sales_20181101040449.trn
5	Sales	2018-11-01 09:36:54.000	L	1136000002392000001	1136000002394400001	C:\Logshipshare\Sales_20181101040651.trn
6	Sales	2018-11-01 09:38:30.000	L	1136000002394400001	1136000002396800001	C:\Logshipshare\Sales_20181101040823.trn
7	Sales	2018-11-01 09:39:39.000	L	1136000002396800001	1136000002399200001	C:\Logshipshare\Sales_20181101040935.trn
8	Sales	2018-11-01 09:40:32.000	L	1136000002399200001	1136000002401600001	C:\Logshipshare\Sales_20181101041028.trn

Figure 6.50: Output of the query

> **Note**
>
> The LSN value will be different in your case.

The LSN that the restore job is expecting is in the backup file named **C:\Logshipshare\Sales_adhoc_log_backup.trn**. Observe that the backup file that the restore job is failing to apply is taken just after the ad hoc transaction log backup done in *step* 2 of the problem setup.

We have found the missing log file.

2. Now, let's restore the missing log backup manually at the secondary instance and then start the restore job to restore the remaining log file backups. To do this, execute the following query at the secondary instance DPLHA:

```
use master
GO
RESTORE LOG Sales FROM DISK='\\DPLPR\Logshipshare\Sales_adhoc_log_backup.
trn' WITH NORECOVERY
```

> **Note**
>
> The **WITH NORECOVERY** option is important as we want to restore future transaction log backups to the **Sales** database.

Once the missing log backup is restored, you can either wait for the scheduled restore job to restore the rest of the log backups or start the restore job manually.

If you look at the restore job history again, you'll see that the job resumes restoring the logs from where it failed:

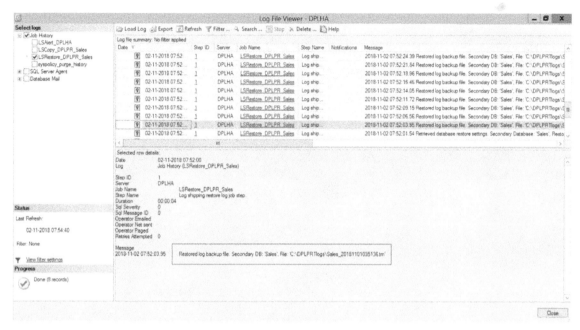

Figure 6.51: The restore job history

Index

About

All major keywords used in this book are captured alphabetically in this section. Each one is accompanied by the page number of where they appear.

www.ingramcontent.com/pod-product-compliance
Lightning Source LLC
Chambersburg PA
CBHW060637060326
40690CB00020B/4429